Refugees Welcome?

Refugees Welcome?

Difference and Diversity in a Changing Germany

Edited by
Jan-Jonathan Bock and Sharon Macdonald

berghahn
NEW YORK · OXFORD
www.berghahnbooks.com

First published in 2019 by
Berghahn Books
www.berghahnbooks.com

Library of Congress Cataloging-in-Publication Data
A C.I.P. cataloging record is available from the Library of Congress

British Library Cataloguing in Publication Data
A catalogue record for this book is available from the British Library

ISBN 978-1-78920-128-4 hardback
ISBN 978-1-78920-135-2 paperback
ISBN 978-1-78920-129-1 ebook

Contents

Figures and Tables

Figures

Table

Acknowledgements

The origin of this book project was a workshop on 'Experiencing Differences and Diversities in Contemporary Germany' at the Centre for Anthropological Research on Museums and Heritage (CARMAH), in the Institute for European Ethnology, Humboldt-Universität zu Berlin. Held in April 2016, the workshop's aim was to address questions of diversity and difference within Germany – especially in light of hundreds of thousands of refugees, asylum seekers and other migrants who had been arriving in the country since the previous summer.

The workshop was, we believe, the first substantial academic effort to bring together international scholars – from Germany, the Netherlands, the United Kingdom and the United States – to discuss the contexts, on-the-ground experiences and implications of what was widely being referred to as 'the refugee crisis'. Most of those invited had long been conducting research on migration and related topics in Germany, and all had conducted original, recent research on matters of direct relevance to the unfolding events. This thus offered a unique insight into this possibly long 'moment' of change – as does this ensuing volume.

The workshop was a collaboration between CARMAH and the Woolf Institute in Cambridge. It was initiated and mainly organized by Jan-Jonathan Bock, during his time as a guest researcher at CARMAH, where he was based while conducting research on changing attitudes to community life in Berlin for the Woolf Institute's 'Intelligent Trust' project. Sharon Macdonald and her team acted as co-organizers and hosts.

We would like to thank the Alexander von Humboldt Foundation, the Templeton World Charity Foundation and Porticus for sponsoring the workshop. At CARMAH, we are grateful to the invaluable organizational help of Christine Gerbich, Rikke Gram, Siriporn Srisinurai, Margareta von Oswald and, especially, Katherine Kaplan. At the Woolf Institute, we thank Shana Cohen and Ed Kessler for their support with the workshop. More widely, we are grateful to colleagues in the Woolf Institute, CARMAH and the Institute of European Ethnology for providing such stimulating academic environments in which to be addressing these questions.

Working on this project has been a great pleasure. Our contributors and their analyses of the 'refugee crisis' and its ramifications for perceptions of difference and diversity have allowed us to understand better a wide range of perspectives and aspirations for a plural Germany. We are grateful to them all, for their lively engagement with the theme and questions, as well as for responding to our editorial suggestions and those of the anonymous reviewers. We also thank all of those who participated in the workshop – the imprint of the depth of the discussions has, we believe, left its mark on this subsequent volume. As well as the audience, further participants included Shana Cohen, Anna Louban, Boris Nieswand, Esra Özürek and Karen Schönwälder, who all gave presentations, but who were unable, for various reasons, to contribute to the ensuing publication. Schirin Amir-Moazami and Manuela Bojadžijev made brilliant input through their roles as panel chairs and discussants.

We would like to thank two anonymous reviewers for their insightful and substantial suggestions. Sharon adds extra thanks to Jan-Jonathan for so efficiently taking the lead in keeping the show on the road and making it all happen. Finally, we are enormously grateful to Harry Eagles at Berghahn Books for his superb guidance throughout the editorial and production process.

Jan-Jonathan Bock and Sharon Macdonald
Cambridge and Berlin, May 2018

Introduction
Making, Experiencing and Managing Difference in a Changing Germany

Jan-Jonathan Bock and Sharon Macdonald

In late August and early September 2015, thousands of asylum seekers from the Middle East were stranded in Hungary's capital, Budapest. Many complained about heavy-handed mistreatment by the authorities, who also set up new 'detention centres' at the country's southeastern border (Haraszti 2015; Kallius et al. 2016). When thousands of migrants left Budapest to march on a motorway towards Austria – and Germany – the German Chancellor, Angela Merkel, and her Austrian counterpart, Werner Faymann, took a far-reaching decision. Bypassing the ordinary rules of the EU's shared asylum system, both leaders agreed to permit asylum seekers entry into their countries to process applications for protection and combat human trafficking. Only two weeks previously, the discovery of seventy-one dead bodies in a locked van on the A4 motorway in Austria – the victims of trafficking – had illustrated the fatal consequences of Europe's insufficient protection schemes for those fleeing conflict elsewhere (den Heijer et al. 2016). The pressure on European leaders to act further increased after the highly publicized death of a young boy, Alan Kurdi, who drowned on his way to Europe. Images of his lifeless body, washed up on a Turkish beach, shocked the world.[1]

According to the EU's Dublin Regulation, asylum seekers ought to apply for protection in the first EU country they reach. In most cases, these are Greece or Italy – two countries that, in the mid 2010s, struggled with unemployment and austerity, and from which asylum seekers sought to continue northwards (Lucht 2012; *Redattore Sociale* 2015; Trauner 2016).

Notes for this chapter begin on page 30.

Merkel and Faymann's decision to ease the pressure on Europe's south-eastern fringes responded to a large-scale migration movement, with dimensions most Europeans had not seen in decades. In the final months of 2015 going into 2016, a makeshift corridor opened up between Greece, at the one end, and Austria, Germany and the Scandinavian countries, at the other. State borders were opened and hundreds of thousands of people seeking refuge or migrating for other reasons reached Central and Northern Europe. State institutions struggled to manage the influx and many newcomers moved on independently to reach friends or relatives elsewhere before and after registration. According to official figures, in 2015, 890,000 asylum seekers arrived in Germany, mainly from Syria, Afghanistan and Iraq (Bundesministerium des Innern 2016: 89). At the time, pundits warned that the number of refugees entering Europe would rise to three million in 2016 and that most of them would come to Germany and Sweden (Koser 2015).

While this prediction did not come to pass – 280,000 asylum seekers entered Germany in 2016[2] – news coverage and public discourse became increasingly framed by a crisis narrative. The term *Flüchtlingskrise* – refugee crisis – flourished. The difficult experience of migration – desiring a better life away from the place of one's origin – became a focus for increasingly hysterical media commentary (Fernando and Giordano 2016). Critics denounced what they saw as Germany's descent from supposed order into chaos and emergency. Simultaneously, enthusiastic forms of civil society engagement in villages, towns and cities sprang up to provide assistance. The German government, and Chancellor Merkel in particular, surprised many with commitment to openness – showing 'a friendly face', as Merkel described the approach during a press conference in September 2015. She appeared on talk shows to explain that Germany was under an obligation to help. She couched this partly in terms of Germany's historical responsibility to protect political refugees after the experience of the Nazi dictatorship and partly in relation to her own biography, and that of millions of other Germans, who had been raised behind the Iron Curtain in authoritarian East Germany, locked in by the socialist regime. Moreover, she argued that migration into Germany was a consequence of the country's economic prosperity, political stability and commitment to the rule of law, which included protection for asylum seekers. In effect, she declared refugees to be welcome in Germany.

This volume explores the context, experiences and ramifications regarding the so-called refugee crisis in 2015–16. The term 'refugee crisis' has been criticized for contributing to a moral panic (see Kosnick, Chapter 7 in this volume), as well as for locating chaos and emergency in refugees as cultural others – rather than, say, framing the crisis as the failure of a wealthy society in managing immigration and integration. Declaring a 'crisis' can be a means by which a state legitimizes authoritarian forms of intervention and 'delegitimize(s) some forms of agency', such as those of refugees and migrants themselves (Kallius et al. 2016: 9). Nevertheless, we use it here as an object of analytical study that took on its own reality in the mid 2010s. It did so not only in Germany, but also across Europe, and indeed could be productively analysed as a 'historical and structural caving in of the European border regime' (Hess et al. 2017: 6, our translation). Indeed, the term was used globally to refer to the situation at the time. Here, we focus upon Germany, the country that took in more refugees than any other Western nation and whose role was pivotal in the developments. Moreover, while the German context was specific in various respects, such as the ways in which national memory was mobilized or the particularities of legal statuses of migrants, it also exemplifies responses to the crisis: from the emergence of a 'culture of welcome' (*Willkommenskultur*), on the one hand, to the powerful expression of rightwing anger in the rejection of ethnoreligious diversity and immigration (exemplified, for example, by the Pegida movement), on the other, as well as more complex and sometimes ambivalent reactions. The polarizing and divisive rhetoric that characterized the German discourse found its echo elsewhere in Europe. Therefore, an in-depth study of the German case can illuminate reactions across European societies and is vital for an understanding of how debates about immigrants and refugees shaped politics across the continent during the early decades of the twenty-first century.

While the book begins from a consideration of what was variously called 'the refugee crisis' or 'long summer of migration' of 2015, it has a longer and broader analytical frame. This is an important dimension of our approach in that we seek not to look at those events alone, but as part of wider and changing understandings of difference and diversity (the patterns of difference that are identified). Terms such as 'refugee' are inevitably relational and exist as part of a shifting constellation of other terms, including 'asylum seeker' and 'migrant', as well as 'citizen' or 'German'. Rather than seeking to pin down what such terms should mean, our interest in this volume is in the practical, analytical and political work that may be done through the choice of the words that are used – and by who uses them and to what effect. The insistence by some politicians on using the term 'migrants' rather than 'refugees' to refer to those arriving in Europe in 2015, for example, supported their arguments that not all of those coming deserved protection, and was part of a broader process of distinguishing between 'deserving' and 'non-deserving' people on the move (Crawley and Skleparis 2018; Holmes and Castañeda 2016; Sigona 2018). One potential German term already in circulation, *Vertriebene*, meaning those who had been expelled, was seen by some as potentially apt, but was too attached to the specific history of postwar refugees, in particular Germans expelled from what became Poland (see below and also Karakayalı, Chapter 8 in this volume).The term *Flüchtling*, which came to be most commonly used – as in *Flüchtlingskrise*, for what in English was called the 'refugee crisis' – was itself subject to debate (Fleischhauer 2015; Goebel 2016; Tinius, Chapter 10 in this volume). Putting its emphasis on the idea of 'flight', like 'refugee' it conveys the sense of a 'forced migration', though with the weight in this case on the escape rather than what is being sought at arrival. Some, however, objected that its suffix – '-ling' – implies a diminutive and even something negative, with some suggesting that the the English term *Refugee* should be used instead. It was also argued that its form acted to typologize a kind of person rather than to refer to a temporary state, as other terms, such as *Geflüchteter* – literally meaning 'one fleeing' – did. Nevertheless, it was *Flüchtling* that was prevalent in public discourse and that even became 'Word of the Year' for 2015 (Gesellschaft für deutsche Sprache 2015).

In this volume, then, we examine the changing differentiations made in practice, as well as to debates about them. To do so, we bring together analyses from anthropological, sociological and political-science perspectives. The interdisciplinary approach allows us to examine the ways in which not only government organizations but also civil society, cultural institutions, small-scale initiatives and individuals explored ways of addressing immigration and the experience of increasing diversity. Deploying this mix of perspectives, which, importantly, includes attention to legal definitions and policy-making, as well as a close ethnographic understanding of lived realities, allows us to tackle both the broader transformations and their potentials, and to grasp something of the variety and significance of experiences on the ground.

Analytically, our contributors employ a range of conceptual terms and lenses, though all give attention to how particular notions of difference – whether these be 'multiculturalism', 'cultural diversity', 'migration background' or 'post-migrant' – can be defined and mobilized in policy and practice. Using the term 'difference' allows us to incorporate a wide range of kinds of differentiations, and also identifications, that may be invoked. In other words, we do not take it as given that, say, ethnic, religious or linguistic difference will necessarily be regarded as the most significant lines of differentiation, or even as necessarily significant at all; such differences are culturally deployed in particular ways at particular times. When and how they are, and when and how they and other potential differences – such as those of class, gender, life experience, accent or skin colour – are entangled with one another is a question that our contributors explore. Equally, analysing how similarities or potentials for sharing and solidarity across differences can be developed – through, for example, notions of collective experience, empathy, community, political aspirations or historical memory – is a major focus of our approach and of the chapters brought together here. In this way, then, with the refugee crisis as our prism, we seek to make a new contribution to understanding current struggles over interpretations of identity, diversity and belonging, and to the key debates, polarizations, differentiations and directions that will shape Germany's – and Europe's – future.

The volume is divided into four parts. The first, 'Making Germans and Non-Germans', illustrates some of the political, legal and social mechanisms through which the categories of 'German' and 'foreigner' are produced, and outlines the implications that these categories had when a large number of refugees entered the country in 2015–16. Part II, 'Potential for Change', explores how emergent forms of co-existence and conviviality could challenge the concepts used to frame difference and diversity in Germany, and indicates possible avenues for innovative ways of managing a plural society. The third part, 'Refugee Encounters', investigates the spaces and activities through which engagement with new kinds of diversity became possible during Germany's 'refugee crisis', and how those who pursued involvement experienced their entanglement with the geopolitics of flight and migration. Part IV explores new avenues for connectedness in the grassroots initiatives and civil society projects that responded to the transformations of German society. This part also provides an outlook on concepts of citizenship and political behaviour that result from emergent kinds of collaboration in the face of social change. Sharon Macdonald's conclusion brings the different sections together, and speculates on the future of difference and diversity in a changing Germany, following a period of significant transformations and wide-ranging political as well as social ramifications.

Diverse Responses to the 'Refugee Crisis'

By the end of 2016, over one million asylum seekers had arrived in Germany over the course of eighteen months. The need for emergency accommodation saw school gyms, warehouses and empty administrative buildings or disused clinics converted into makeshift shelters. In Berlin, the enormous hangars of the former Tempelhof Airport, decommissioned in 2008, were turned into a camp for thousands of asylum seekers, managed by a private for-profit company on behalf of the municipal government (Muehlebach 2016). Under the German federal system, asylum seekers were distributed across the country's regions, which then continued the distribution process towards cities, towns and villages. In this way, the events of 2015–16 affected the entire country, not simply large cities, in which the effects of immigration and cultural diversity were already commonplace (Petermann and Schönwälder 2014; Schönwälder et al. 2016). Now, support groups and initiatives for asylum seekers and refugees were established all over Germany, in rural as well as urban environments, as grassroots activists responded to the apparent struggle of state institutions by putting forward their visions for coexistence and solidarity. For some, the fact that hundreds of thousands of volunteers joined new support projects amounted to a social movement (see Schiffauer, Chapter 12 in this volume). It is difficult, in this written text, to evoke the feverish and excited atmosphere that characterized Germany's 'long summer of migration' (Hamann and Karakayalı 2016; Kasparek and Speer 2015). In the autumn of 2015, media coverage incessantly updated the public on the latest figures of asylum seekers reaching Germany, mainly at the border with Austria. During the most intense weeks, the numbers often topped 10,000 arrivals per day. Politicians, social media and television talk shows discussed few other topics. The country's most-read paper, *Bild*, launched its *Wir helfen* ('We Help') campaign in September 2015. Unlike other European tabloids, which attacked politicians for supporting immigrants – and to the surprise of many German commentators – *Bild* championed the government's welcoming stance and reported daily on success stories of integration and volunteering. Faced with a similar surge in the numbers of new asylum seekers during the early 1990s, *Bild* had responded very differently and demanded a government crackdown (Gaserow 2012). Now, numerous celebrities embraced the tabloid's positive campaign and wore its *Wir helfen* badges publicly.

The need for emergency accommodation and a widespread desire to address a social challenge collectively also energized new forms of dialogue involving citizens and their democratic representatives. Across the country, MPs, mayors, city councillors, political parties, representatives from the sixteen regional governments responsible for asylum-seeker management, and other high-level officials scheduled open meetings to inform local communities, explain political decisions, and ask for grassroots and civil society support. Citizens also used such gatherings to vent frustration at a perceived lack of communication and transparency, as well as fears over a lack of state control, while support groups were established in towns and villages. Traditional civil society actors, such as the Protestant and Catholic churches, reported many phone calls from local residents who sought ways of assisting the newcomers. They turned to their local parish or diocese to ask what they could do. Picnics and welcome-refugee events were staged across the country, seeking to bring together foreigners, long-term residents and other volunteers through language classes and shared cooking sessions, women's support networks, and mosque prayers, student exchanges and much more. Social media and innovative smartphone apps connected newcomers with those offering voluntary support (see Schiffauer and Karakyalı, Chapters 12 and 8 in this volume respectively). Already before the events of 2015–16, Germany had a substantial population of residents with foreign passports, as well as German passport holders whose parents or grandparents had migrated to the country (the so-called 'migration background', or *Migrationshintergrund*) and who had brought new ways of life, religions, values, behaviours and customs to the country. Nonetheless, the refugee crisis led to intensified debates about difference and diversity, belonging and national identity.

Beyond grassroots support and activism, there were other responses. Hotels, guesthouses and other buildings earmarked to be converted into provisional emergency shelters were firebombed. In the East German region of Saxony-Anhalt, for example, the mayor of a small town, Tröglitz, resigned after rightwing groups, which included members of the neo-Nazi NPD party, had marched in front of his house to dissuade him from supporting accommodation plans for forty asylum seekers. A few weeks after his resignation, the attic of the designated shelter went up in flames before a group of Syrian asylum seekers could move in (MDR 2017). A website called *Mut gegen rechte Gewalt* (Courage against Right-Wing Violence) listed all reported acts of violence against refugees or asylum seekers, as well as attacks on shelters or other forms of accommodation. For 2016, the website detailed 595 attacks on asylum seekers, 123 arson attacks on accommodation for asylum seekers and refugees, and 3,056 further acts of violence. In that year, 434 asylum seekers were injured through arson or physical attacks.[3] In 2017, 1,938 attacks on asylum seekers or their accommodation occurred. Furthermore, out of 3,774 attacks on asylum seekers and shelters in 2016, 1,610 were committed in East Germany. The formerly socialist part has only 16 million inhabitants, compared with the regions of West Germany, where 66 million people live (in 2018). Therefore, the part of Germany with less than 20 per cent of the population witnessed 43 per cent of acts of anti-asylum seeker and xenophobic violence. Especially in East Germany, rejection, often hatred, of foreigners was expressed in brutal attacks, and through electoral support for the anti-immigration Alternative for Germany (AfD) party. Discontent and anger were also directed at the political establishment and Chancellor Merkel in particular.

On 15 January 2017, the prominent MP of a Frankfurt constituency, Erika Steinbach, published an open letter that explained her decision to leave the CDU, Germany's Christian conservative party. For decades,

Steinbach had been a vocal law-and-order politician, a key representative of the CDU's rightwing faction, opposing same-sex marriage as much as the switch to renewable energies. Angela Merkel, the CDU's leader since 2000, had modernized the party and moved it into the political centre, to the dismay of Social Democratic Party (SPD) politicians, who struggled to distinguish their party from Merkel's progressive CDU (Resing 2013; Seils 2013; Zolleis and Schmid 2014). In her letter, Steinbach attacked Merkel for radically altering the party's core objectives and accused her of hollowing out conservative values as well as the rule of law. The most disturbing development that Steinbach underlined and that ultimately led her to cancel party membership and leave the CDU's parliamentary group regarded immigration:

> All of this [Merkel's centrist policies] was eclipsed by the Chancellor's solitary decision to not simply allow over one million immigrants to enter Germany without control or checks for months, but even to transport them here on coaches and trains, despite the fact that many of them came from safe-origin countries and virtually all of them entered Germany via other third countries, and, according to EU law (Dublin Agreement), ought to have been pushed back . . . Our state authorities, nominally responsible, did and partly still today struggle with this mass immigration. Up to this day, we still do not know who exactly entered our country with this stream of people . . . With those immigrants – this is clear following terrible attacks – terrorists also came to Germany. National security and our way of life are in danger, as the two recent New Year's Eve celebrations have shown . . . The integration of this army of millions from diverse cultural backgrounds will take years, if it can be successful at all.[4]

Steinbach's letter captures the anxiety that the arrival of large numbers of foreigners induced. The idea that many were 'unknown' hints at a potentially sinister and threatening presence. Unspoken here is that many of those claiming humanitarian protection were Muslims, though other commentators were less reluctant to point this out, as we illustrate below.

Questions of integration and coexistence returned to the political agenda. They were discussed in the workplace and over the dinner table, in television shows and during election campaigns. Islam and its place in, and compatibility with, German society, as well as the presence or absence of shared values, came under scrutiny – a trend that was shared across European countries in the 2010s (Göle 2015). The well-known words by Germany's former President, Christian Wulff, made during celebrations to mark the anniversary of the country's reunification in October 2010, namely, that 'now Islam also belongs to Germany', were again openly contested. In this period of the mid 2010s, popular books on immigration-related topics appeared and were fiercely debated. Some widely read authors denounced Islam as violent, oppressive and patriarchal (Abdel-Samad 2015, 2016; Schwarzer 2016). Prior to the arrival of hundreds of thousands of Muslim asylum seekers in Germany in 2015–16, high-impact publications had criticized Germany's experiment with immigration and multicultural pluralism as flawed and detrimental to cohesion (Ateş 2007; Buschkowsky 2012; Sarrazin 2010). Other commentators, however, had criticized what they saw as a dangerous rise of Islamophobia and its threat to Germany's plural and secular democracy (Bax 2015; Benz 2010). Reactions to the refugee crisis intensified the increasingly divisive debate about the social implications of difference and diversity, and the complex manifestations of both.

In a country in which the history of the Third Reich powerfully shapes social and cultural debate (Linke 1999; Macdonald 2009; Pearce 2008), the prominent university professor and SPD politician Gesine Schwan could tell Günther Jauch, a talk-show host, in December 2014: 'what used to be Judaism in the past is Islam today. This is directed prejudice'. Her comparison drew criticism as much as support, illustrating that discussing cultural difference and diversity in Germany has particularly awkward dimensions. These derive, among other aspects, from the horrific history of the Holocaust, diverging democratic traditions following the division into a socialist east and a capitalist west, and the consequences of work immigration during the postwar economic boom years. In addition, neglect of minority communities and their aspirations for participation, a lack of engagement with German colonial history (eclipsed by the Third Reich and the Holocaust), division over the meaning of 'integration', the country's growing attraction for young Europeans, and its emergence as the leading power on the continent in the wake of the 2008 financial crisis contribute to the distinct situation of Germany. On 27 January 2016, Ruth Klüger, a Holocaust survivor and Professor Emerita of German Studies at the University of California, Irvine, addressed the German Parliament, the Bundestag, on the anniversary of the liberation of Auschwitz. At the time, thousands of asylum seekers continued to arrive in Germany every day. Very shortly before her address, acts of sexual violence committed by foreigners in Cologne during the New Year's Eve celebrations had fanned criticism regarding the challenges associated with cultural difference, eliciting what many considered xenophobic comments (see Kosnick, Chapter 7 in this volume). Klüger, born in 1931, closed her address with the following words:

> Ladies and gentlemen – I have now spoken for some time about modern slavery as forced labour in Nazi Europe, citing examples from the process of suppression that marked postwar Germany. But since then, a new generation – no,

even two or even three new generations, have grown up here. This land, which was responsible for the worst crimes of the century eighty years ago, has won the world's praise today, thanks to its open borders and the magnanimity with which you have accepted, and continue to do so, the number of Syrian and other refugees. I am one of the many people that have moved from surprise to admiration. And this was the main reason why I accepted your invitation with great pleasure, seizing the opportunity, in this event, in this capital city, to be able to speak about former wrongdoings – here, in this place in which a rival role model has emerged, following the seemingly humble and yet heroic motto: we will manage.

Her final three words – in German, *wir schaffen das* – had become a contested slogan. Uttered repeatedly by Angela Merkel as positive encouragement and reassurance, many engaged Germans put the motto into practice in pro-refugee initiatives. Those opposing the political elite's openness, however, saw the Chancellor's statement and its continuous repetition as intentionally provocative. Klügler's connection of the Nazi Holocaust with the moral implications of current political challenges, through a notion of historical responsibility (see also Karakayalı, Chapter 8 in this volume), provides the antithesis to Erika Steinbach's insistence on the rule of law and the incompatibility of different cultural traditions. These two positions represent the poles of a spectrum of responses to the refugee crisis. Whereas some commentators invoked a 'bigger picture' – or the importance of reconciliation with the Nazi past and Germany's responsibility to welcome those fleeing war and persecution – others were frustrated with the lack of a government pushback, warning of descent into chaos and cultural conflict. Within such complicated social and historical parameters, responses to the refugee crisis variously created, or bolstered, social divisions. In doing so, these responses drew upon Germany's previous experience of immigration and resulting difference.

Germany's Experiences with Immigration and Difference

Situated at the centre of the European continent, Germany has a long history of immigration and settlement, accommodating linguistic, religious, cultural, ethnic and other forms of difference. This historical fact became reflected in the country's federalist traditions, with strong regional parliaments and the principle of subsidiarity, i.e. the devolution of state power to lower levels of governance, which are more in tune with views and expectations (Ritter 2007).[5] In the late nineteenth century, when new factories and expanding industrial production offered greater economic opportunities, increasing numbers of foreigners settled in the newly-founded

German Reich. The so-called Ruhr Poles (*Ruhrpolen*), from the Polish-speaking areas of Prussia, were one of the largest groups that shaped newly industrializing urban environments. Under state control, Ruhr Poles moved from rural areas in East Prussia, Silesia and Poznan to the industrializing Ruhr Valley, in the far west of the Reich. On the eve of the First World War, in 1914, over 400,000 *Ruhrpolen* lived in this area, with their own newspapers, associations and even trade unions, testifying to 'an unprecedented extent of local political influence for a minority group' (McCook 2008: 871). Still today, surnames and customs in the Ruhr Valley reveal the legacy of otherwise indistinguishable *Ruhrpolen* descendants. Labourers from other parts of Europe followed and staffed factories and plants before 1914, particularly Italians (Del Fabbro 2008). After the First World War, during the Weimar Republic, Berlin became a centre of Russian émigrés leaving the Soviet Union (Schlögel 1994). Expellees from Alsace-Lorraine, which became French territory again, as well as other displaced persons suffering from the redrawing of state borders across Europe, settled in the country. In many cases, they experienced a hostile reception. Weimar Republic governments, which tended to be short-lived and ineffective, sought to reduce the size of migration to calm social unrest (Oltmer 2005). With the exception of cosmopolitan urban centres, such as Berlin, migration was simply regarded as a pragmatic necessity for military and industrial production. During the Third Reich, millions of forced labourers from conquered territories across the continent worked in German factories and for German companies (Spoerer 2001). Many died from malnutrition or mistreatment. Despite the humiliating experience, a large number could not return home after Nazi Germany's defeat. They were absorbed in 'displaced persons' camps and then settled or moved on to other countries, following the Soviet occupation of Eastern Europe (Bauer 2015).

Well before the postwar boom years, Germany's industrial and economic success, and its Central European location without natural borders, had turned the country into a destination for work migrants, expellees, political refugees, and young men and families searching for better lives. The Nazi dictatorship then persecuted diversion from its ideals of Germanness. There was no space for spontaneous cultural, ethnic, social or political difference in the Third Reich. Victims of Nazi persecution included ethnic minority groups – Jews and Roma most prominently – and others whose lives, views or lifestyles the Nazis considered debased, such as disabled people, homosexuals, Marxists and communists, so-called anti-social elements or Jehovah's Witnesses (Bastian 2001; Garbe 1999; Pohl 2011). Hundreds of thousands escaped into exile to avoid internment and extermination (Sherman 1994). Where flight was impossible for whole families, parents sent their children abroad (Gigliotti and Tempian 2016). The Nazi legacy shaped the new Germanies. Many countries had offered German Jews and non-Jewish German intellectuals and anti-Nazi activists protection – including the later social democratic Chancellor, Willy Brandt, who escaped to Norway, or the playwright Bertolt Brecht, who found refuge in the United States. After the Nazi regime, this history was the main reason for including Article 16 in West Germany's 1949 postwar Constitution. It simply states: 'Persons persecuted on political grounds shall have the right of asylum.'[6] The Article reflected a postwar culture of anti-nationalism and *Vergangenheitsbewältigung* – variously translated as 'mastering the past', 'coming to terms with the past' or 'overcoming the past' – which many intellectuals saw as necessary for German society (Huyssen 1994). The generous and unprecedented provision of asylum in West Germany remained in place until the early 1990s, when a surge in asylum seekers from the collapsing Eastern Bloc, political unwillingness in the conservative-led government and xenophobic street violence led to the highly contested 'asylum compromise' (*Asylkompromiss*). Under the new Article 16a, the authorities were able to deny protection when an applicant had crossed another safe country on his or her way to Germany (Angenendt 1997: Chapter 2) (for more on this, see below).

The largest migration experience in German history coincided with the end of the Second World War. Other countries in Western Europe shared Germany's experience with large-scale immigration at the end of the conflict, albeit with different characteristics.[7] Whereas Germany lost its colonies at the end of the First World War and had witnessed limited early immigration from overseas territories (Mazón and Steingröver 2005; Oguntoye 1997),[8] the end of Empire for Britain and France came with the new international order after the Second World War – and large numbers of former colonial subjects from all over the world moved to France and Britain respectively, where they were considered citizens. Germany's most significant migration movement, by contrast, consisted of people considered ethnically German, even though many of them had lived outside German lands in Central and Eastern Europe before the Second World War. Stalin's decision to move Poland westwards and expel ethnic Germans – copied by governments in other parts of Eastern Europe – meant that the now significantly smaller Germany, soon divided into East and West, had to absorb 14 million displaced persons, so-called *Vertriebene*. (Benz 1985). In 1945, these masses moved westwards with handcarts and stories of destruction, violence, killings, pillaging and mass rape at the hands of the Red Army (Kowalczuk and Wolle 2001). Many perished during the flight. With cities and towns in ruins, residents and expellees, after travelling hundreds of kilometres on foot, forcibly shared restricted living spaces, often reluctantly on part of the owners, under supervision from the occupying powers and the newly established German authorities. The millions of expellees eventually settled across the country, allocated accommodation by the authorities, and contributed to the political and cultural life of West Germany in particular. Mainly Protestants, their settlement in Germany's Catholic south and the Rhineland led to contact between different Christian denominations and their respective customs and worldviews, and thus often to conflict. Expellees set up clubs to celebrate the traditions of their former towns and villages, but they also remained an awkward presence – a constant reminder of Germany's defeat and the disproportionate suffering inflicted by the Nazi dictatorship on the country's eastern territories, whose inhabitants had forever lost their homelands (Franzen and Lemberg 2001). Residents in the villages and towns in which expellees arrived were often hostile: they feared a fight over limited resources and resented the presence of different customs, religious beliefs and lifestyles (Kittel 2007; Kossert 2008).

As expressions of longing for a return to the homeland, expellees' associations conserved culture in gatherings or festivals, which were soon considered backward or revanchist by many West Germans. Consequently, between the 1970s and 1990s, their clubs were increasingly marginalized, and the descendants of *Vertriebenen* soon blended into German society (Jakubowska 2012). During the recent refugee crisis, this experience with religious difference, flight and coexistence was instrumentalized and contested. Whereas some suggested that contemporary German society could manage the refugee situation since it had absorbed a large number of people considered culturally remote before, others claimed that the current asylum seekers' difference, and their religious identity in particular, rendered them more difficult to 'integrate' than postwar expellees (see Karakayalı, Chapter 8 in this volume).

The uneasy reception of expellees perhaps foreshadowed West Germany's complicated relationship with foreigners. West German governments sometimes attempted to attract immigrants in accordance with the needs of German companies. Between 1955 and 1973, West Germany concluded agreements with Mediterranean countries to regulate the stay of so-called guestworkers, or *Gastarbeiter*, needed in industry and agriculture. The first agreement was signed in Rome on 22 December 1955, coordinating the work migration of unskilled Italian labourers. It became a blueprint for subsequent accords with other countries (Herbert 2001: 203). The economic boom necessitated government efforts to promote what was initially considered temporary migration, and not settlement. As a result of guestworker agreements, when refugees from the socialist German Democratic Republic (GDR) are included in the figures, no region in Europe accommodated a greater number of foreign migrants in the second half of the twentieth century than West Germany (Münz et al. 1999: 17). In the 1960s, net labour migration reached the hundreds of thousands, mainly Italians, Spaniards and Greeks, but also Austrians and Dutch nationals. Two-thirds of them were male (Hubert 1998: 295). In 1961, West Germany signed an agreement with the Turkish government to coordinate the transfer of workers to West Germany. The agreement differed from previous ones with Italy, Spain, and Greece: the period of residence was limited to two years and there were no provisions to permit family members to join male labourers (Hunn 2005: 30). It was not even considered that the men who were invited to toil in factories could become German. The term *Gastarbeiter* illustrates political reasoning at the time: workers were considered guests in Germany, with a limited identity of temporary labourers, not citizens or citizens-to-be with rights comparable to those held by the native population. Their status as transient noncitizens may also account for the fact that they were accommodated in appalling conditions, as this description of a building in Düsseldorf in the 1970s reveals:

> In a room of no more than 15m², six Turkish and Greek guestworkers live together. Even though it is only half past eight in the evening, they are all lying in their beds. But what else is there to do in this hole? There aren't even enough chairs. In the middle of the room, below an awkwardly dangling light bulb, there is a small table, with 'tablecloth' made from newspapers. The floor is bare and filthy, no different from the walls. You will search in vain for a picture or curtains . . . There is no stove for these men from the south, who miss nothing more than the sun and warmth here. One struggles to find the right words to describe the toilet: the floor covered in a dirty puddle, the bare bowl without a seat. (Herbert 2001: 215)

While arrival and distribution were painstakingly planned, little consideration was given to enabling supposedly temporary migrants to live dignified lives by establishing linguistic autonomy and political or social participation. In the 1960s, the Swiss author Max Frisch famously stated with regard to Swiss and German reactions to such supposedly short-lived work-migration: 'we called for workers, but human beings came'. Frisch captured the lackadaisical attitude towards non-Germans, who were confined to their status as foreign workers and whose aspirations, plans, desires and demands later surprised German society and politics. As the critical tone in the newspaper report from Düsseldorf testifies, journalists and the public soon began to pay more attention to the presence of guestworkers and the implications for German society. In the late 1960s, social challenges became more apparent in urban quarters. With the economic crisis, guestworker agreements were stopped in 1973 (Berlinghoff 2013). A total of 14 million foreign workers had come to West Germany between 1955 and 1973, and 11 million returned home. The three million who stayed in West Germany were joined by their families and had more children, thus growing into a population of 4.8 million people by 1990.

In East Germany, the situation was different. Since many East Germans had fled the country, there existed a shortage of workers in the socialist Germany, too. In addition to Soviet troops living in barracks, without much contact to the local population (Kowalczuk and Wolle 2001), foreign labourers from fellow socialist countries were brought into the GDR to work in factories, including from Cuba, Vietnam, Mozambique and Algeria (Vogel and Wunderlich 2011; Zwengel 2011). In most cases, they were segregated from the GDR population – much more so than was the case in West Germany. Private contact was not allowed, workspaces were divided, and separate changing rooms in factories or plants were the norm (Geyer 2001). The number of these contract workers (*Vertragsarbeiter*) was small. In 1989, there were 59,000 Vietnamese contract workers in East Germany. They lived in state-sponsored and self-contained accommodation. Relationships with native Germans were not permitted: if female foreign workers became pregnant as a result of such contact, they were asked to have an abortion or leave the country (Wolle 2015). In addition to the Vietnamese, in 1989, significant groups of foreign migrants came from Poland (51,700), Mozambique (15,500) and the Soviet Union (14,900). Foreign students and socialists fleeing repressive regimes elsewhere were welcomed in the GDR – such as Greeks or Chileans. Their presence permitted some everyday interaction, even though the small numbers were often limited to urban centres, and the GDR regime emphasized national homogeneity over diversity (Behrends et al. 2003; Poutrus and Müller 2005). As a result, the total number of foreigners when the Berlin Wall fell was 191,200 – tiny compared to West Germany (Bade and Oltmer 2005). Leaving aside economic benefits, the living situation of migrants in the GDR was often difficult:

> There was much talk about the friendship among peoples in the GDR. But peoples are an ideological abstraction. People, however, are more concrete. Foreigners were only needed as a propaganda tool in the GDR. They were tolerated as labourers. As humans, however, they were unwelcome. The legacy of this situation apparently requires more than a generation to be overcome. (Wolle 2015)

In the everyday lives of many East Germans, foreigners or temporary labour migrants did not play a role. Secluded and isolated, they worked their shifts and kept to themselves. The small number of foreigners, who were in the main discouraged from mixing with the majority East German population of white industrial and agricultural workers, left a legacy of unfamiliarity with challenging types of cultural or other difference that could have undermined the GDR's ideal of homogeneity and resulting solidarity.

Finally a Country of Immigrants?

Until the 1980s, and despite the unmistakeable social reality of immigration and settlement, particularly in West German cities, there was little political recognition of, or engagement with, the lives of foreigners. The social reality had not been intended: political leaders had pursued temporary migration to fill labour shortages, and migrants themselves had not expected their stay to turn into long-term settlement with their families (Fassmann et al. 1997: 60; Hunn 2005: Chapter 3). Because of Germany's restrictive citizenship law, immigrants could not easily become 'German' and struggled for political representation (Brubaker 1998). In the late 1970s, the growing association of immigrant presence with social challenges marked a negative public discourse on *Überfremdung*, literally 'over-foreignization' or 'over-alienization' – a term suggesting that a large number of foreigners could threaten social harmony and native identity (Mandel 2008: Chapter 2). In response, in 1978, the social democratic federal government appointed a Delegate for the Promotion of Integration of Foreign Workers and Their Families (Beauftragter zur Förderung der Integration der ausländischen Arbeitnehmer und ihrer Familienangehörigen). The new office's first incumbent, Heinz Kühn, challenged assimilationist demands, which were prevalent even in his own left-wing SPD party. The use of the term 'integration' here is significant: it was part of a conscious change from assumptions that migrants would either return or should assimilate (*anpassen*) and therefore erase difference. If settlement was to be inevitable, previous political consensus had held, then immigrants should become indistinguishable from Germans. The new approach to integration supported greater degrees of difference and cultural autonomy. Heinz Kühn insisted that 'integration is also possible without assimilation (*Anpassung*) and surrender of one's own identity' (Hunn 2005: 402). Many Turkish former guestworkers in particular expected to return to Turkey and were reluctant to surrender cultural traditions, language and customs; they also had little interest in acquiring citizenship, which would have entailed giving up Turkish passports (Hunn 2005: 404). Kühn's successor, Liselotte Funcke, sought to raise the position's profile further. She published an annual report – *Statistics and Facts Regarding the Situation of Foreigners in Germany (Daten und Fakten zur Ausländersituation in Deutschland*) – and highlighted the need for immigration in an ageing society in order to maintain social and welfare standards, as well as economic competitiveness. Funcke brought together regional and local Delegates for Foreigners (*Ausländerbeauftragte*) in regular meetings (Die Bundesregierung 2017). Other politicians, however, did not match her interest in the lives of immigrants and foreigners. Frustrated, Funcke resigned in 1991, in protest over a lack of support from the federal government (*Der Spiegel* 2012).

This ambivalence with which successive West – and East – German governments, and then those of the unified Germany, addressed the presence of immigrants continued. The first eight years of the four consecutive conservative-led governments under Helmut Kohl's leadership, between 1982 and 1998, changed little, as Funcke's resignation in the early 1990s demonstrated. Instead of integration measures and proactive policies, the CDU and CSU parties sought to limit migration and immigration, and ran election campaigns with anti-immigration promises. Even in 1998, Bavaria's conservative CSU party – which, at that point, had been part of the federal coalition government for sixteen years – could state in its election manifesto that 'Germany and Bavaria are not countries of immigration' (Hell 2005: 77). This was a visibly false assertion given that, the previous year, over 7.5 million people with non-German passports had residence in Germany (Wagner et al. 2000: 66). The CSU's claim was in stark contrast with the social reality not only of the time when the claim was made in the manifesto, but indeed of previous decades. It revealed, however, the political currency that anti-immigration sentiment still had in Germany just before the turn of the millennium. Such anti-immigration rhetoric also contradicted the then valid (1990) version of Germany's *Ausländergesetz* (literally 'foreigners' legislation'). This granted those living in Germany with non-German passports a new legal status of 'immigrant' – a status that entailed guaranteed residence and limited voting rights. It also rendered the acquisition of German citizenship for the children of former guestworkers at least theoretically more straightforward. Furthermore, guestworkers could now apply for German citizenship after fifteen years in the country.

In the 1980s and early 1990s, the numbers of refugee migrants grew. In the face of this, conservative and social democratic politicians alike portrayed themselves as hard-nosed and tough on asylum seekers. Long before the summer of migration in 2015, public discourse and the media deployed a hysterical language of 'floods' and 'waves', describing Germany as a 'sinking boat' (Briest 2015; Gaserow 2012; Prantl 1993). After 1990, the collapse of the Soviet Union and Yugoslavia led to an unprecedented arrival of asylum seekers asking for protection with reference to Article 16 of Germany's Constitution. In 1992, just short of 440,000 people demanded asylum in Germany (Briest 2015). Covers of the highbrow weekly news magazine *Der Spiegel* from the time illustrate public unease shortly after the tumultuous events of reunification. Issue 15, from 1992, showed an open border gate, stormed by men with dark hair, overwhelming a handful of hapless border guards. The headline was: 'Asylum – Politicians are Failing'. Later that year, issue 31 featured the image of an elderly woman with a headscarf, surrounded by children glaring at the camera with sad eyes. The headline: 'Onslaught from the Balkans. Who Takes the Refugees?' The success of the Republikaner (Republicans) – a far-right party demanding an end to 'asylum abuse' (*Asylmissbrauch*) – led mainstream political parties to adopt harsher positions (Pagenstecher 2008). This *Asyldebatte* ('asylum debate') polarized German society shortly after the largely optimistic reception of reunification (Bade 1994a). In 1992–93, the government rallied different parliamentary parties to push through constitutional change to amend Article 16, the so-called *Asylkompromiss* ('asylum compromise').[9] The new Article 16a gave the government the power to declare certain countries 'safe places of origin' (*sicheres Herkunftsland*) and therefore to deny protection to people fleeing from there. Most importantly, it legislated that those who had crossed through a so-called safe third-party state (*sicherer Drittstaat*) on their way to Germany could no longer claim asylum, but ought to be returned to that safe country.

Coinciding with the debate about the 'asylum compromise', violent mobs attacked asylum reception centres and accommodation for foreign labourers in the East German city of Hoyerswerda (Jarausch 2004: Chapter 9; Wowtscherk 2014). Skinheads and neo-Nazis terrorized those they perceived to be 'foreign' – as well as their civil society supporters – across the territory of the former GDR, where socialist state structures had collapsed and authority was absent. Disillusioned and unanchored young people from the former GDR were attracted to aggressive youth cultures (Heinemann and Schubarth 1992). The events in Hoyerswerda and the East German city of Rostock were, however, only the most prominent examples of numerous racist attacks on people singled out as 'non-German' across East and West Germany (Panayi 1994; Partridge 2012). At the same time, protests against xenophobia and neo-Nazi violence illustrated that Germany's newly unified society was splintered along a spectrum ranging from those defending the 1949 Article 16 and anti-Nazism to violent promoters of a blood-based and exclusive nationalism (Funke 1993). For Klaus Bade – a leading scholar of integration in Germany – xenophobia was conditioned by the unwillingness of the political class to approach integration properly and finally acknowledge that Germany had long been a country of immigration (Bade 1994a: 203). In the 1990s, Bade denounced political irresponsibility with regard to immigration and integration, and rallied sixty scholars to demand more political openness and an acknowledgement of the factual reality of immigrant settlement, as well as a more honest debate about the consequences of diversity and difference for coexistence, urban and religious life, public culture, education policies and citizenship (Bade 1994b).

During that same turbulent period, other significant developments added pressure to debates around immigration and coexistence. Immediately after the war, people from Eastern European countries who could demonstrate German ancestry – many of whom were not expelled in the 1940s – were given the chance to move to Germany and be granted citizenship. These were the so-called *Aussiedler* (literally 'out-settlers'). With the opening of the Eastern Bloc under Gorbachev, their numbers increased. In the 1990s, over two million *Aussiedler* moved to Germany (BPB 2018). The *Aussiedler* were not considered immigrants, but Germans, and experienced a very different official treatment from those who asked for asylum but could not demonstrate German origin – even though their social reception was often equally frosty (Römhild 1998). Newly arrived *Aussiedler* were entitled to the kind of political inclusion through German citizenship that was still beyond the reach of many guestworkers and their descendants, many of whom had now spent decades in the country. German citizenship law, based on descent rather than place of birth, created complicated categories of inclusion and exclusion, belonging and Germanness (see Linke, Chapter 1 in this volume). Despite their ethnic identity as 'Germans', a study found that: (1) most *Aussiedler* had been brought up in Soviet society and held outdated views of Germany; (2) the main reason to leave Eastern Europe was the collapse of the Soviet Union and economic uncertainty rather than a longing to return; (3) having been labelled as 'Germans' or 'Nazis' in the Soviet Union, the *Aussiedler* were considered 'Russians' in Germany and experienced discrimination; (4) especially those who arrived around 1990 knew little to no German, and in many cases experienced a deterioration of their social situation compared with their former homeland, which, in turn, intensified social problems (Schader Stiftung 2007). The 1990s were a turbulent period for the unified country. The co-presence of different kinds of immigrants complicated debates about German identity, belonging and nationhood. While work or other migrants – i.e. foreigners who had, for some reason, come to Germany – were progressively seen by some as immigrants with a right to long-term settlement, many others, including conservative politicians, refused to acknowledge that Germany had become an *Einwanderungsland*, a country of immigration. For them, migrants remained migrants, not immigrants, and were expected to 'return' to the places they, or their parents or grandparents, had once left. Meanwhile, other facets of difference received less attention. One ramification of the presence of Muslims in the united Germany was conversions to Islam in the East, where former GDR citizens were seeking spiritual opportunities that their closed and homogeneous society had not afforded them (Hoffmann 1995; Özyürek 2015). The coexistence of religions, values, traditions and customs produced a wide-ranging diversification of ideas about what it means to live well, producing multilayered and complicated super-diversity (Vertovec 2007). At the same time, the political response remained inconclusive and tentative in the early to mid 1990s, even though the children of former guestworkers had now grown up in Germany to start their own families, alongside many other groups of foreigners, migrants, immigrants and refugees.

With the 1998 elections, the situation changed. The Social-Democrat/ Green coalition government under Chancellor Gerhard Schröder recognized the need to engage with the lives of foreigners and minorities, and initiated political change: it was accepted that immigration to Germany had occurred, would remain an important social fact, and that local, regional and national governments ought to promote integration and participation. Schröder's reform of Germany's citizenship law challenged the exclusive character of *ius sanguinis* – citizenship based only on blood or descent – through the introduction of *ius soli* – citizenship based on one's place of birth or long-term residence. The reform meant that if a parent had lived in Germany for at least eight years and had permanent residence, his or her newborn child was entitled to German citizenship. Limited options for dual citizenship were also introduced. Guestworkers and others who had lived in Germany for at least eight years could apply for a German passport. In most cases, however, applicants for German citizenship were still required to surrender their other passport. The reforms altered traditional German views on citizenship, according to which only individuals with a German parent could also be German (Storz and Wilmes 2007). Schröder established an independent expert commission to suggest changes regarding immigration and integration policy (*Unabhängige Kommission Zuwanderung*). The commission's report highlighted the positive impact of immigration and encouraged supportive political action. Even though the eventual all-party compromise watered down the commission's suggestions and disappointed many experts, the new legislation (*Gesetz zur Steuerung und Begrenzung der Zuwanderung und zur Regelung des Aufenthalts und der Integration von Unionsbürgern und Ausländern*) seemed to end decades of political denial of Germany being a country of immigration (Busch 2007: 410–12). Political recognition, even though belated and partial, and contested by some pundits and organizations, initiated new debates about belonging and coexistence. The Green Party, buoyed by government responsibility, advanced positive views on multiculturalism and diversity (Vollmer 2009: 210, 346, 375f).

Marieluise Beck, a Green Party member and the new federal government's Delegate for Foreigners – in 2002, the position was renamed Delegate for Migration, Refugees and Integration – raised awareness with the annual Migration Report (*Migrationsbericht*) and advanced progressive views on society. She highlighted the growing diversification within immigrant populations along socioeconomic and other lines, and criticized simplistic reductions to supposed ethnic community identities. Her 2005 Memorandum stated:

> Germany is a society of immigration. Immigration over the past 50 years has changed our society fundamentally. Around 14 million people with a migration background live in Germany today: they are immigrants themselves or immigrants' children, born in Germany. The official statistics on foreigners do not sufficiently mirror changing social realities. The official register tells us that currently 6.7 million people with foreign passports live in Germany. Over the past years, however, also four million *Aussiedler*, who hold German passports, moved to this country. 1.5 million children from bi-national marriages are growing up here, holding German citizenship. And since the reform of the citizenship law [in 2000], over one million foreigners have been become German ... Foreigners, naturalized citizens, *Aussiedler* or children from bi-national or foreign marriages – the population of Germany has become more diverse, ethnically, linguistically, culturally and religiously. One in five marriages is bi-national. One in four new-born children have at least one foreign parent. One in three young people in West Germany have a migration background. In some larger urban areas, 40 percent of young people come from immigrant families – and the percentage is growing. (Beck 2005)

Beck's Memorandum at the end of the Red-Green coalition government in 2005 – the autumn elections led to the first Merkel chancellorship – was an acknowledgement of a social reality that previous governments had refused, particularly the conservative CDU and CSU parties. In 1998–99, Roland Koch, who ran for premier in the state of Hesse, organized a political campaign against Red-Green's planned reform of German citizenship law, which would have permitted dual citizenship for the children of guestworkers born in Germany. Koch polarized the debate and won the elections against the SPD premier. Many voters rejected the progressive broadening of citizenship definitions and greater social inclusion (Klärner 2001). In regional elections in North-Rhine Westphalia in 2000, the CDU contender, Jürgen Rüttgers, attacked the Schröder government plans for a German Green Card, aimed at facilitating highly skilled immigration from Southeast Asia to boost the growing IT sector, with the slogan: '[German] children rather than Indians' (*Kinder statt Inder*). Thus, the changing social reality did not produce a consensus on political responses to difference around the turn of the millennium. Immigration continued to be exploited for divisive politics. Nonetheless, even the grand coalition government of the SPD and the CDU that came to power in 2005 could not turn back the clock. In 2006, the then Interior Minister, Wolfgang Schäuble, a conservative politician, established the Islam Conference (*Islamkonferenz*), seeking to construct a platform for exchange between the large number of Muslim associations and government (Busch and Goltz 2011). The Conference institutionalized a space for dialogue between politicians and Muslims, who were represented by particular Islamic organizations. The format seemed to testify to the normalizing of participation in democratic processes, but critics have shown that the Conference intensified a sense of alienation among immigrant communities that were reduced to their 'other' religious identities as Muslims, neglecting the complex and layered identities of contemporary Germans (Bayat 2016; Tezcan 2012). Discussions around the Islam Conference illustrated how the public debate on diversity and pluralism was shifting to an almost exclusive concern with those residents, some German citizens, who were increasingly reduced to their Muslim-ness, as their place in German society remained contested.

Being German and Belonging to Germany

Besides their economic importance, the contribution of immigrants and their descendants to social and cultural life in Germany can no longer be ignored. They have entered debates about living and belonging in Germany. Writers such as Navid Kermani, Rafik Schami or Wladimir Kaminer, for example, describe the challenge of living in a society in which the idea of hybrid identities or cultural difference continues to be perceived as threatening (for example, see Kaminer 2000; Kermani 2010). Fatih Akin's 2004 film *Gegen die Wand* (*Against the Wall*) problematized the clash of conservative Turkish values with the aspirations of guestworkers' children, caught in-between family constraints and the values of their younger peer groups. *Gegen die Wand* won the Golden Bear at the Berlin Film Festival and shaped debates about the negotiation of cultural customs and self-making in a heterogeneous and plural society. Scholars have suggested dropping the term 'migrant' – as in 'migrant background' – from describing the lives and identities of people who have spent decades in Germany and ought to be considered 'post-migrants', defined by their political and social attitudes, not ascribed ethnic identities (Bojadžijev and

Römhild 2014; also Foroutan and Tinius, Chapter 6 and Chapter 10 in this volume respectively).

German cities have been visibly changing as a consequence of long-term immigration and settlement (Schönwälder et al. 2016). New and grand mosques have been built across the country and Islamic cultural centres have moved into attractive buildings, rather than being hidden away in backyard rooms or disused garages (see Kuppinger, Chapter 4 in this volume for an account from the city of Stuttgart). In 2005, the Sehitlik mosque in Berlin was inaugurated, complete with proud displays of Islamic ornamental art and two large minarets, signalling the self-confidence among Berlin-based German Turks or Turkish Germans. Similar projects have been launched across the country. Cultural associations, theatres, companies, enterprises, political demands and other forms of engagement from immigrants and their descendants shape urban life across the country. At the same time, however, anti-immigration protest and often violence have accompanied pluralism. Muslims in particular, increasingly portrayed as 'other' and alien, have been on the receiving end of both physical and political attacks (Bax 2015; Benz 2010; Çakir 2016). Muslim men are popularly depicted as oppressors of wives, sisters and daughters, complicating the identities of male Muslims in a diversifying Germany while denying female agency, accompanied by accusations of an 'integration failure', usually understood as nonassimilation (Pratt Ewing 2008). At the same time, other attempts to conceptualize difference have also led to orientalizing hypersexual fantasies about the supposedly superior stamina of nonwhite men in particular (Partridge 2012). Differences also remain uneven: the Vietnamese or Chinese communities in Germany, for example, have long been considered 'good immigrants' and have popularly been viewed as hard-working and rewarded with educational success (Rüther 2010), in contrast to the more negative perceptions of Turkish or Arab groups, who are usually stereotyped indiscriminately as unsuccessful 'Muslims' (Çakir 2014; Loginov 2017). The expansion of citizenship as a project of political inclusion, launched in 2000 with Schröder's citizenship reform, did not stop debates about belonging. New divisions, categories and practices of exclusion have emerged, such as 'linguistic citizenship' and the policing of speech boundaries (see Linke, Chapter 1 in this volume).

Furthermore, as in other parts of Europe, Germany has experienced a 'multiculturalism backlash' (Vertovec and Wessendorf 2010). In 2010, Chancellor Merkel declared that multiculturalism had 'failed' as a principle of social organization, while nonetheless assuring that Islam was a part of Germany (*Spiegel Online* 2010). This led to debates about what this alleged failure of multiculturalism should entail and which policies might replace it, as well as how it could go along with the claim that 'Islam belongs to Germany' (Detjen 2015). As an alternative to *Multikulti* – the German version of multiculturalism – ideas about a *Leitkultur* were resurrected. The term is difficult to translate, but it suggests the existence of a dominant set of values, views and behaviours – a culture – that should guide or lead, and be shared by, all members of a given society. Introduced in 1996 by the Syrian-born German political scientist Bassam Tibi, *Leitkultur* was needed, he argued, as a shared set of values to provide cohesion in a diversifying society. This was especially crucial in Germany, Tibi suggested, since the country's ethnicity-focused view of identity would continue to prevent immigrants and their descendants from becoming recognized as 'German'. Values and ethics must thus act as the glue of such an otherwise unstable society (Tibi 1996). The concept was soon simplified by conservative politicians demanding assimilation and the adaptation of 'German' values. Popularly introduced in 2000 by Friedrich Merz, a CDU politician, the term still informed responses to the so-called refugee crisis when Thomas de Maizière, the then conservative Interior Minister, renewed the demand for a *Leitkultur* in 2017 (Wittrock 2017). In the wake of the 2017 general elections, which saw the anti-immigration Alternative for Germany (AfD) party surge to 12.6 per cent, various conservative politicians and pundits demanded a reorientation towards this supposed *Leitkultur* – the content of which has remained undefined and vague, but that serves to exclude certain minority values and those of Muslims in particular.

The multiculturalism backlash was also revealed in vitriolic debates about immigration and diversity following the initial discussion about *Leitkultur*. Publications by two SPD politicians incensed the public discourse. Thilo Sarrazin's (2010) *Deutschland schafft sich ab* (*Germany Does away with Itself/Germany Abolishes Itself*) suggested how immigration was undermining cohesion and weakening German society. Muslims, whom Sarrzazin considered to be generally inferior to non-Muslims in economic and educational performance, were seen as the main culprits (Geyer 2010). Sarrazin's book tour across the country attracted protests as well as large audiences; some accused him of racism, while others defended the controversial author as a voice of truth against political correctness (Fahrenholz 2011). The Sarrazin-debate polarized or highlighted existing polarization, with various experts, politicians and public commentators supporting or attacking minorities (Abadi et al. 2016). Two years later, the then Mayor of Berlin's Neukölln district, Heinz Buschkowsky, published *Neukölln ist überall* (*Neukölln is Everywhere*). Buschkowsky, who resigned in 2015, had become a prominent critical voice on integration and multiculturalism. At the time of the publication, ethnically diverse Neukölln had a negatively inflated nationwide reputation for its sizeable Turkish and Arabic minorities, high welfare dependency, poverty and crime. Buschkowsky's straight-talking and old-West-German demeanour, coupled with a grating Berlin accent, made him a talk show regular. In *Neukölln ist überall* (2012), he warned that multiculturalism forestalled integration and that too few second- or third-generation immigrants worked hard enough to escape poverty. The book was as popular and divisive as Sarrazin's (see e.g. Heine 2012).

As debates raged about the best responses to the presence of immigrants, and especially Muslim immigrants, violence against them continued. In 2011, the East German neo-Nazi National-Socialist Underground (NSU) terror organization was discovered (Gensing 2012; Schmincke and Siri 2013). The group had killed nine men considered 'foreign' between 2000 and 2006, and carried out a number of attacks on immigrants and their businesses. For years, the authorities had failed to detect a pattern and assumed that inner- or intra-ethnic conflict among minority groups was the reason for the killings. Scholars suggested that the unsatisfactory response to the murders revealed the prevalence of stereotypes and rightwing thinking inside the German state (Bade 2013b; Funke 2015). In subsequent years, as the numbers of asylum seekers arriving in Europe, and in Germany in particular, rose quickly, debates intensified. The newcomers reached a country in which ideas about what it means to live with difference, and about political and civil society responses to social pluralism, were already variously marked by contradictions, populism, fear, rejection, normalization and ambivalence. Even before the long summer of migration in 2015–16, the situation had been complex, and the corresponding debates divisive, with some drawing on notions of historical responsibility, humanitarianism and the enriching aspects of diversity to justify enthusiasm and engagement with difference, while others saw cultural coexistence in negative terms, leading to social decay and a depletion of Germany. The refugee crisis interjected more complexity and raised the question of how welcome migrants or immigrants – and especially refugees – really were.

The Chapters in This Volume

Refugees Welcome? brings together international experts to analyse this complexity. Across four parts, the volume situates the events of 2015–16 in their social and historical context. This context was shaped by a particular history of immigration, the Holocaust, defeat and occupation after 1945, ethnic visions of citizenship, and the East-West division, among other factors. Other important facets regard the long-term stabilization of supposedly temporary work migration turning into immigration and settlement, as well as belated attempts at – and debates about – integration and post-reunification struggles over creating a new Germany out of two societies (Borneman 1992). Our authors present a range of interpretations that uncover more complex realities. Some, such as Linke and Partridge, suggest a persistence of mechanisms of exclusion aimed at those considered 'foreign'. Schiffauer, Karakayalı and Heckmann, by extension, explore possibilities of new forms of solidarity and civic engagement. Many of those asylum seekers and refugees who arrived in 2015–16 will become the new Germans. Their experiences might be similar to those of the earlier generations of immigrants and their descendants, analysed by, for example, Tize and Reis, Foroutan, Tinius and Kuppinger. In some cases, what our authors describe is a persistence of 'othering' forms of differencing, as is shown to be the case even by some younger generation migrants themselves (Tize and Reis), but in others, difference itself is viewed positively as part of a vibrant diversity (Kuppinger). More than anything, what the chapters collectively show is that there is undoubtedly change underway, but that the direction of travel is not fully settled; there remain reasons for pessimism, but there are hopeful signs too.

The first half of this book – Parts I and II – covers longer-term situations and developments relating to difference and diversity in Germany, while the second – Parts III and IV – looks more directly at the refugee crisis of 2015 and 2016.

Part I, 'Making Germans and Non-Germans', begins with Uli Linke's discussion of how Germanness has been construed historically and into the present both through powerful – and often racialized and gendered – iconography, as well as through what she calls 'linguistic nationalism', in which a lack of fluency in the German language can act to reinforce exclusion and act as a proxy for other forms of non-German difference. Located in a discussion of the rise of a wider rhetoric of diversity within Europe, Linke's chapter opens up important questions about how far apparent change is belied by enduring or even revived nationalism and populism. It is followed by Friedrich Heckmann's outlining of legal developments within Germany, which formally define citizenship, and wider changing institutional responses to cultural difference and diversity. He shows that federal, regional and local levels of government have responded to the reality of an increasingly diverse society with the establishment of special offices and delegates, complemented by EU and civil society actors, including minority communities and their associations – thus importantly pointing out the range of agencies and actors involved. Gökce Yurdakul then takes us into an example of dealing with more specific difference, in

this case how religious difference has been addressed, specifically in relation to ritual male circumcision, as practised by both Jews and Muslims.
Beginning with a court case involving a botched circumcision, which dis-
figured the genitalia of a boy and was considered bodily harm by a judge,
she argues that the German state continues to stigmatize minority practices, and thus Jews and Muslims in general, placing supposedly secular values over the cultural and religious autonomy of non-Christians.
Despite moments of apparent change, then, Yurdakul argues that Jews
and Muslims tend to remain socially excluded.

Part II, 'Potential for Change', brings together chapters that suggest possible ways in which difference and diversity may be changing in Germany,
albeit not without reservations. Petra Kuppinger's chapter draws on her
long-term fieldwork with Turkish Muslims in Stuttgart to point out the
flourishing of what she calls 'vernacular creativity' in relation to cultural
practices associated with Islam. Changes in *iftar* ceremonies – ritual feasts
that are part of Ramadan – as well as certain examples of Islamic architecture and art become, she shows, further elements in diverse cities that
embrace the pluralism of multiple religious as well as secular expressions.
New practices are also the focus of Carola Tize and Ria Reis in their ethnographic research with young people inhabiting urban spaces in Berlin's
Neukölln district. While the children or grandchildren of former guestworkers, many of whom hold German passports, still struggle to refer
to themselves as 'German', the authors show that these new generations
identify strongly with their neighbourhoods. On a day-to-day basis, they
negotiate their identities, including the difficulty of bridging traditional
expectations with their own aspirations. We end this part with Naika
Foroutan's setting out of the 'post-migrant' paradigm as both an aspiration and a descriptor of a social reality in which the identities of people in
Germany should not, she claims, be limited by the migration biographies
of their ancestors. Her argument is not that those who were once labelled
'migrants' should now be called 'post-migrants', but rather that contemporary German society should be viewed through a lens in which the realities of migration experiences and histories are recognized, but not used as
fixed markers of difference to categorize and define.

Part III, 'Refugee Encounters', looks at how the events of 2015–16 challenged and transformed social realities. Kira Kosnick explores the heated
debate surrounding attacks on women during the 2015 New Year's Eve
celebrations in Cologne. She argues that what she calls the 'scandalization
of deviant behaviour', with many pundits calling for urgent intervention
to restore the social order, amounted to a 'moral panic'. Simplistic racist
and colonial representation cast perpetration as a result of ingrained cultural behaviour. Involved here were, she suggests, longstanding ways of

thinking about cultural 'others' and indeed about culture itself. Serhat Karakayalı focuses on a very different dimension of refugee encounter during 2015 and 2016, namely the culture of welcome. Based on substantial quantitative and qualitative research, he provides an in-depth analysis of civil society responses to the arrival of asylum seekers. This shows that the desire of local inhabitants to help inspired social action across the country, but that there was a wide range of motives involved. Of special interest here is the way in which political memory – though not direct intergenerational family memory – was often invoked in support of such action. In Jan-Jonathan Bock's chapter, by contrast, historical memory is deployed by the anti-Islam Pegida movement in Dresden to support a sense of victimhood and marginalization, which, he argues, is part of a more complex background to their position than is usually recognized. Looking also at volunteers involved in welcoming asylum seekers, in this case in the refugee church (*Flüchtlingskirche*) in Berlin, he draws on ethnographic fieldwork to highlight the more complex realities of encounters in practice, such as the development of more critical views on cultural difference by church volunteers through their encounter with refugees.

The final part of the book, 'New Initiatives and Directions', includes further chapters that describe in depth initiatives undertaken with refugees and that in various ways suggest possible future directions, albeit rather differently. Jonas Tinius takes a longer view, as well as looking at the more recent involvement of refugees, to examine the importance of theatre for the negotiation and performance of difference and diversity. His ethnography of two public theatre groups shows how these could act as 'interstitial agents', reflecting on civil society as well as providing participants with possibilities for trying out new forms of connectivity and transcendence of existing identities. Partly on the basis of experience of a film project with refugees or those he calls noncitizens, Damani J. Partridge examines the politics of hospitality involved in the culture of welcome. He argues that this often involved the idea of pity, claiming that this does not contribute to the development of solidarity, which he regards as a more appropriate ambition and one that might indeed transcend a focus on difference and diversity. Also examining the culture of welcome, Werner Schiffauer explores it as a social movement, offering new possibilities for political action. He shows that hundreds of thousands of Germans joined support projects and sought to shape the social response to a political challenge, creating thick local networks that could react flexibly to new expectations and demands. Schiffauer is optimistic that the enormous civil society effort was not a short-lived response to an emergency, but rather indicates a durable social trend in the face of a growing diversification of life-worlds.

Refugees and other newcomers have been both welcomed and rejected, and these two responses and the many variations in-between seem likely to continue. What the contributors here collectively show is that ways of dealing with the so-called refugee crisis were part of longer histories and memories than is usually recognized. Equally, as the volume also makes clear, they are part of more extensive and complex change. We are not only seeing accommodation or integration into existing German society, but also change in that society itself. Moreover, as we see in many of the chapters, this change is not only being formed by policy-makers, but is also being actively crafted into being on the ground. It takes place in localities and everyday encounters, and in spontaneous interactions and initiatives, as well as in more formal political processes. Attending to these and showing how deeply and thoroughly they matter is, we believe, a major contribution of this book.

Using the question of whether refugees are welcome as our springboard, then, our volume seeks to show how this question has relevance beyond the events of 2015–16. This was undoubtedly an important moment in German history, and indeed in the history of Europe, and deserves the documentation and analysis that we provide here for that reason. But it also takes us into more enduring social questions of how people can live with and across difference, and of the concepts and practices that can enable more convivial collective futures. By bringing together chapters that variously reflect directly on the refugee crisis and the wider histories and contexts of which it was part, we seek to provide new insight into both the specific context and its broader social and analytical ramifications. Looking in depth in this way is, we believe, vital to trying to grasp the implications and direction of travel of transformations that are still being worked out. Moreover, it is crucial as a contribution to ongoing debates about the kind of society that we want in the future – and about how best to achieve it.

Jan-Jonathan Bock is Programme Director at Cumberland Lodge, Windsor, United Kingdom. He received his Ph.D. in Social Anthropology from the University of Cambridge in 2015. His publications include *Austerity, Community Action and the Future of Citizenship in Europe*, coedited with Shana Cohen and Christina Fuhr.

Sharon Macdonald is Alexander von Humboldt Professor of Social Anthropology in the Institute of European Ethnology, Humboldt-Universität zu Berlin, Germany. She founded and directs the Centre for Anthropological Research on Museums and Heritage (CARMAH), and its major project *Making Differences – Transforming Museums and Heritage in the 21st Century*.

Notes

1. On the media impact of the death of Alan Kurdi, see: http://visualsocialmedialab.org/projects/the-iconic-image-on-social-media (retrieved 2 July 2018).
2. http://www.bmi.bund.de/SharedDocs/Pressemitteilungen/DE/2017/01/asylantraege-2016.html (retrieved 2 July 2018).
3. https://www.mut-gegen-rechte-gewalt.de/service/chronik-vorfaelle (retrieved 2 July 2018).
4. All translations are those of the authors, unless stated otherwise.
5. One example of historical immigration movements would be the Huguenots, French Calvinists who left predominantly Catholic France during a century-long religious war in the sixteenth and seventeenth centuries. Some 40,000–50,000 of them settled in German regions (von Thadden and Magdelaine 1985). Around 20,000 of them moved to Prussia, and first of all to Berlin, which prospered culturally as a result of Huguenot labour and creativity, developing from a rural backwater into one of Germany's leading cities (Gahrig 2000).
6. In German: 'Politisch Verfolgte genießen Asylrecht'.
7. Other colonial powers, such as France or Britain, witnessed the arrival of large numbers of African, Caribbean and South Asian migrants following the dissolution of Empire. These immigrants were granted citizenship, unlike in Germany, where legal notions of citizenship remained closely tied to descent (Brubaker 1998; Hansen 2000: Part I; Weil 1991).
8. During the Third Reich, the Nazi regime pursued the forced sterilization of the small minority of black Germans – around 20,000–25,000 people – as part of its national purification efforts (Pommerin 1979). On the uneasy legacy of colonialism in German cities, see, for example, Ulrich van der Heyden's analysis of Berlin's street names and architecture (2008)
9. The SPD, CDU/CSU and FDP parliamentary groups supported the change and provided the necessary two-thirds majority. The Greens (Bündnis 90) and PDS (post-GDR socialist party) rejected the change.

References

Abadi, D., L. d'Haenens, K. Roe and J. Koeman. 2016. '*Leitkultur* and Discourse Hegemonies: German Mainstream Media Coverage on the Integration Debate between 2009 and 2014', *Communication Gazette* 78(6): 557–84.

Abdel-Samad, H. 2015. *Mohamed – Eine Abrechnung*. Munich: Droemer Knaur.

———. 2016. *Der Koran: Botschaft der Liebe. Botschaft des Hasses*. Munich: Droemer Knaur.

Angenendt, S. 1997. *Deutsche Migrationspolitik im neuen Europa*. Wiesbaden: Springer Verlag für Sozialwissenschaften.

Ateş, S. 2007. *Der Multikulti-Irrtum: Wie wir in Deutschland besser zusammenleben Können*. Berlin: Ullstein.

Bade, K. J. 1994a. *Ausländer, Aussiedler, Asyl: Eine Bestandsaufnahme*. Munich: C.H. Beck.

_____ (ed.). 1994b. *Das Manifest der 60: Deutschland und die Einwanderung*. Munich: C.H. Beck.

_____. 2013a. 'Als Deutschland zum Einwanderungsland Wurde', *Die Zeit*, 24 November. Retrieved 2 July 2018 from http://www.zeit.de/gesellschaft/zeitgeschehen/2013-11/einwanderung-anwerbestopp/komplettansicht.

_____. 2013b. *Kritik und Gewalt: Sarrazin-Debatte, 'Islamkritik' und Terror in der Einwanderungsgesellschaft*. Schwalbach: Wochenschau-Verlag.

Bade, K.J., and J. Oltmer. 2005. 'Migration, Ausländerbeschäftigung und Asylpolitik in der DDR', *Bundeszentrale für politische Bildung*, 15 March. Retrieved 2 July 2018 from http://www.bpb.de/gesellschaft/migration/dossier-migration/56368/migrationspolitik-in-der-ddr?p=all.

Bastian, T. 2001. *Sinti und Roma im Dritten Reich: Geschichte einer Verfolgung*. Munich: C.H. Beck.

Bauer, P. 2015. 'Für immer gefangen', *Süddeutsche Zeitung Magazin*, 5 May. Retrieved 2 July 2018 from http://sz-magazin.sueddeutsche.de/texte/anzeigen/43042/1/1.

Bax, D. 2015. *Angst ums Abendland: Warum wir uns nicht vor Muslimen, sondern vor den Islamfeinden fürchten sollten*. Frankfurt: Westend.

Bayat, M. 2016. *Die politische und mediale Repräsentation in Deutschland lebender Muslime: Eine Studie am Beispiel der Deutschen Islam Konferenz*. Wiesbaden: Springer VS.

Beck, M. 2005. *Integrationspolitik als Gesellschaftspolitik in der Einwanderungsgesellschaft: Memorandum der Beauftragten der Bundesregierung für Migration, Flüchtlinge und Integration, Marieluise Beck*. Berlin: Die Beauftragte der Bundesregierung für Migration, Flüchtlinge und Integration.

Behrends, J.C., T. Lindberger and P.G. Poutrus (eds). 2003. *Fremde und Fremd-Sein in der DDR: Zu historischen Ursachen der Fremdenfeindlichkeit in Ostdeutschland*. Berlin: Metropol Verlag.

Benz, W. (ed.). 1985. *Die Vertreibung der Deutschen aus dem Osten: Ursachen, Ereignisse, Folgen*. Frankfurt am Main: Fischer Taschenbuch.

Benz, W. 2010. *Die Feinde aus dem Morgenland: Wie die Angst vor den Muslimen unsere Demokratie gefährdet*. Munich: Beck.

Berlinghoff, M. 2013. *Das Ende der 'Gastarbeit': Europäische Anwerbestopps 1970–1974*. Munich: Ferdinand Schöningh Verlag.

Bojadžijev, M., and R. Römhild. 2014. 'Was kommt nach dem "Transnational Turn"? Perspektiven für eine kritische Migrationsforschung', in Labor Migration (ed.), *Vom Rand ins Zentrum: Perspektiven einer kritischen Migrationsforschung*. Berlin: Panama Verlag, pp. 10–24.

Borneman, J. 1992. *Belonging in the Two Berlins: Kin, State, Nation*. New York: Cambridge University Press.

BPB. 2018. '(Spät-)Aussiedler', *Bundeszentrale für politische Bildung*, 21 April. Retrieved 2 July 2018 from http://www.bpb.de/61643.

Briest, R. 2015. 'Asylbewerber in Deutschland – 1992 kamen fast eine halbe Million Flüchtlinge', *Kölner Stadt-Anzeiger*, 13 May. Retrieved 2 July 2018 from http://www.ksta.de/1252196.

Brubaker, R. 1998. *Citizenship and Nationhood in France and Germany*. Cambridge, MA: Harvard University Press.

Bundesministerium des Innern. 2016. *Migrationsbericht 2015*. Berlin: Bundesministerium des Innern – Referat für Öffentlichkeitsarbeit.

Busch, A. 2007. 'Von der Reformpolitik zur Restriktionspolitik?', in C. Egle and R. Zohlnhöfer (eds), *Ende des Rot-Grünen Projektes: Eine Bilanz der Regierung Schröder 2002–2005*. Wiesbaden: VS Verlag für Sozialwissenschaften, pp. 408–430.

Busch, R., and G. Goltz. 2011. 'Die deutsche Islam Konferenz: Ein Übergangsformat für die Kommunikation zwischen Staat und Muslimen in Deutschland', in H. Meyer and K. Schubert (eds), *Politik und Islam*. Wiesbaden: VS Verlag für Sozialwissenschaften, pp. 29–46.

Buschkowsky, H. 2012. *Neukölln ist überall*. Berlin: Ullstein Verlag.

Çakir, N. 2014. *Islamfeindlichkeit: Anatomie eines Feindbildes in Deutschland*. Bielefeld: transcript.

_____. 2016. 'Pegida: Islamfeindlichkeit aus der Mitte der Gesellschaft', in A. Häusler (ed.), *Die Alternative für Deutschland: Programmatik, Entwicklung und Politische Verortung*. Wiesbaden: Springer Fachmedien, pp. 149–62.

Crawley, H., and D. Skleparis 2018 'Refugees, Migrants, Neither, Both: Categorical Fetishism and the Politics of Bounding in Europe's "Migrant Crisis"', *Journal of Ethnic and Migration Studies* 44(1): 48–64.

Del Fabbro, R. 2008. 'Italienische industrielle Arbeitskräfte in West- und Mitteleuropa im späten 19. und frühen 20. Jahrhundert', in K.J. Bade, P.C. Emmer, L. Lucassen and J. Oltmer (eds), *Enzyklopädie Migration in Europa – Vom 17: Jahrhundert bis zur Gegenwart*. Paderborn: Verlag Ferdinand Schöningh, pp. 689–96.

Den Heijer, M., J.J. Rijpma, and T. Spijkerboer. 2016. 'Coercion, Prohibition, and Great Expectations: The Continuing Failure of the Common European Asylum System', *Common Market Law Review* 53: 607–42.

Der Spiegel. 2012. 'Gestorben: Lieselotte Funcke'. 6 August. 32: 142.

Detjen, S. 2015. '"Der Islam gehört zu Deutschland": Die Geschichte eines Satzes', *Deutschlandfunk*, 13 January. Retrieved 2 July 2018 from http://www.deutschlandfunk.de/der-islam-gehoert-zu-deutschland-die-geschichte-eines-satzes.1783.de.html?dram:article_id=308619.

Die Bundesregierung. 2017. 'Liselotte Funcke'. Retrieved 11 June 2017 from https://www.integrationsbeauftragte.de/Webs/IB/DE/AmtUndPerson/BisherigeIBs/_content/liselotte-funcke.html.

Fahrenholz, P. 2011. 'Therapeut und Brandstifter', *Süddeutsche Zeitung*. Retrieved 2 July 2018 from http://www.sueddeutsche.de/muenchen/landkreismuenchen/sarrazin-wirbel-um-auftritt-in-muenchen-therapeut-und-brandstifter-1.1006734 (accessed 12 June 2017).

Fassmann, H., R. Münz and W. Seifert. 1997. 'Was wurde aus den Gastarbeitern? Türken und (Ex)Jugoslawen in Deutschland und Österreich', *Demographische Informationen* 11: 57–70.

Fernando, M., and C. Giordano. 2016. 'Introduction: Refugees and the Crisis of Europe'. *Cultural Anthropology*, 28 June. Retrieved 2 July 2018 from https://culanth.org/fieldsights/900-introduction-refugees-and-the-crisis-of-europe.

Fleischhauer, J. 2015. 'Es heißt jetzt Refugee', *Spiegel Online*, 25 August. Retrieved 2 July 2018 from http://www.spiegel.de/politik/deutschland/fluechtlinge-es-heisst-jetzt-refugee-kolumne-a-1049698.html.

Franzen, E.K., and H. Lemberg. 2001. *Die Vertriebenen: Hitlers letzte Opfer.* Munich: Propyläen Verlag.

Funke, H. 1993. *Brandstifter: Deutschland zwischen Demokratie und völkischem Nationalismus.* Göttingen: Lamuv.

_____. 2015. *Staatsaffäre NSU: Eine offene Untersuchung.* Munich: Kontur.

Gahrig, W. 2000. *Unterwegs zu den Hugenotten in Berlin: Historische Spaziergänge.* Berlin: Das Neue Berlin.

Garbe, D. 1999. *Zwischen Widerstand und Martyrium: Die Zeugen Jehovas im 'Dritten Reich'.* Munich: R. Oldenbourg Verlag.

Gaserow, V. 2012. 'Lichterketten und SDP-Asylanten', *Die Zeit*, 29 November. Retrieved 2 July 2018 from http://www.zeit.de/2012/49/Debatte-Grundrecht-Asyl-1992/komplettansicht.

Gesellschaft für deutsche Sprache. 2015. 'Wort des Jahres 2015'. 11 December. Retrieved 2 July 2018 from https://gfds.de/wort-des-jahres-2015.

Gensing, P. 2012. *Terror von Rechts: Die Nazi-Morde und das Versagen der Politik.* Berlin: Rotbuch.

Geyer, C. 2010. 'So wird Deutschland dumm', *Frankfurter Allgemeine Zeitung*, 25 August. Retrieved 2 July 2018 from http://www.faz.net/aktuell/feuilleton/buecher/rezensionen/sachbuch/thilo-sarrazin-deutschland-schafft-sich-ab-so-wird-deutschland-dumm-1999085.html.

Geyer, S. 2001. 'Die ersten Opfer der Wende', *Der Spiegel*, 23 May. Retrieved 2 July 2018 from http://www.spiegel.de/politik/deutschland/auslaender-in-der-ddr-teil-zwei-die-ersten-opfer-der-wende-a-135601.html.

Gigliotti, S., and M. Tempian (eds). 2016. *The Young Victims of the Nazi Regime: Migration, the Holocaust and Postwar Displacement.* London: Bloomsbury.

Goebel, S. 2016. 'Flüchtling, Geflüchtete, Refugee?', *Refugees Welcome Berlin*, 19 June. Retrieved 2 July 2018 from https://refugeeswelcome.berlin/2016/06/19/fluechtling-gefluechteter-refugee.

Göle, N. 2015. *Islam and Secularity: The Future of Europe's Public Sphere.* Durham, NC: Duke University Press.

Hamann, U., and S. Karakayalı. 2016. 'Practicing Willkommenskultur: Migration and Solidarity in Germany', *Intersections. East European Journal of Society and Politics* 2(4): 69–86.

Hansen, R. 2000. *Citizenship and Immigration in Post-War Britain: The Institutional Origins of a Multicultural Nation.* Oxford: Oxford University Press.

Haraszti, M. 2015. 'Behind Viktor Orbán's War on Refugees in Hungary', *New Perspectives Quarterly* 32(4): 37–40.

Heine, H. 2012. 'Was ist von Buschkowskys Buch zu halten?', *Der Tagesspiegel*, 25 September. Retrieved 2 July 2018 from http://www.tagesspiegel.de/berlin/neukoelln-ist-ueberall-was-ist-von-buschkowskys-buch-zu-halten/7174720.html.

Heinemann, K.-H., and W. Schubarth (eds). 1992. *Der antifaschistische Staat entlässt seine Kinder: Jugend und Rechtsextremismus in Ostdeutschland.* Cologne: PapyRossa.

Hell, M. 2005. *Einwanderungsland Deutschland? Die Zuwanderungsdiskussion 1998–2002.* Wiesbaden: VS Verlag für Sozialwissenschaften.

Herbert, U. 2001. *Geschichte der Ausländerpolitik in Deutschland: Saisonarbeiter, Zwangsarbeiter, Gastarbeiter, Flüchtlinge.* Munich: C.H. Beck.

Hess, S., B. Kasparek, S. Kron, M. Rodatz, M. Schwertl and S. Sontowski (eds). 2017. *Der lange Sommer der Migration.* Berlin: Assoziation A.

Hoffmann, C.H. 1995. *Zwischen allen Stühlen: Ein Deutscher wird Muslim.* Bonn: Bouvier.

Holmes, S.M., and H.Castañeda 2016. 'Representing the "European Refugee Crisis" in Germany and beyond: Deservingness and Difference, Life and Death', *American Ethnologist* 43(1): 12–24.

Hubert, Michel. 1998. *Deutschland im Wandel: Geschichte der Deutschen Bevölkerung seit 1815.* Stuttgart: Franz Steiner Verlag.

Hunn, K. 2005. *'Nächstes Jahr kehren wir Zurück . . .': Die Geschichte der türkischen 'Gastarbeiter' in der Bundesrepublik.* Göttingen: Wallstein Verlag.

Huyssen, A. 1994. 'Nation, Race, and Immigration: German Identities after Unification', *Discourse* 16(3): 6–28.

Jakubowska, A. 2012. *Der Bund der Vertriebenen in der Bundesrepublik Deutschland und Polen (1957–2004): Selbst- und Fremddarstellung eines Vertriebenenverbandes.* Marburg: Herder-Institut Verlag.

Jarausch, K. 2004. *Die Umkehr: Deutsche Wandlungen 1945–1995.* Munich: Deutsche Verlags-Anstalt.

Kallius, A., D. Monterescu and P. Kumar Rajaram. 2016. 'Immobilizing Mobility: Border Ethnography, Illiberal Democracy, and the Politics of the "Refugee Crisis" in Hungary', *American Ethnologist* 43(1): 25–37.

Kaminer, W. 2000. *Russendisko.* Munich: Goldmann.

Kasparek, B., and M. Speer. 2015. 'Of Hope: Ungarn und der lange Sommer der Migration', *Bordermonitoring,* 7 September. Retrieved 2 July 2018 from http://bordermonitoring.eu/ungarn/2015/09/of-hope.

Kermani, N. 2010. *Wer ist Wir? Deutschland und seine Muslime.* Munich: C.H. Beck.

Kittel, M. 2007. *Vertreibung der Vertriebenen? Der historische deutsche Osten in der Erinnerungskultur der Bundesrepublik (1961–1982).* Munich: R. Oldenbourg Verlag.

Klärner, A. 2001. *Aufstand der Ressentiments: Einwanderungsdiskurs, völkischer Nationalismus und die Kampagne der CDU/CSU gegen die doppelte Staatsbürgerschaft.* Cologne: PapyRossa.

Koser, K. 2015. '10 Migration Trends to Look out for in 2016', *World Economic Forum,* 18 December. Retrieved 2 July 2018 from https://www.weforum.org/agenda/2015/12/10-migration-trends-to-look-out-for-in-2016.

Kossert, A. 2008. *Kalte Heimat: Die Geschichte der deutschen Vertriebenen nach 1945.* Munich: Siedler Verlag.

Kowalczuk, I.-S., and S. Wolle. 2001. *Roter Stern über Deutschland: Sowjetische Truppen in der DDR.* Berlin: Christoph Links Verlag.

Linke, U. 1999. *German Bodies: Race and Representation after Hitler.* London: Routledge.

Loginov, M. 2017. *Muslim- und Islamfeindlichkeit in Deutschland: Begriffe und Befunde im Europäischen Vergleich.* Wiesbaden: Springer Fachmedien.

Lucht, H. 2012. *Darkness before Daybreak: Africa Migrants Living on the Margins in Southern Italy Today*. Berkeley: University of California Press.

Macdonald, S. 2009. *Difficult Heritage: Negotiating the Nazi Past in Nuremberg and Beyond*. Abingdon: Routledge.

Mandel, R. 2008. *Cosmopolitan Anxieties: Turkish Challenges to Citizenship and Belonging in Germany*. Durham, NC: Duke University Press.

Marschalck, P. 1973. *Deutsche Überseewanderung im 19. Jahrhundert: Ein Beitrag zur soziologischen Theorie der Bevölkerung*. Stuttgart: Klett.

Mazón, P., and R. Steingröver (eds). 2005. *Not So Plain as Black and White: Afro-German Culture and History, 1890–2000*. Rochester: University of Rochester Press.

McCook, B. 2008. 'Polnische industrielle Arbeitswanderer im Ruhrgebiet ("Ruhrpolen") seit dem Ende des 19. Jahrhunderts', in K.J. Bade, P.C. Emmer, L. Lucassen and J. Oltmer (eds), *Enzyklopädie Migration in Europa – Vom 17: Jahrhundert bis zur Gegenwart*. Paderborn: Verlag Ferdinand Schöningh, pp. 870–79.

MDR. 2017. 'Der Fall Tröglitz: Eine Chronik', *Mitteldeutscher Rundfunk*, last updated on 22 May 2018. Retrieved 2 July 2018 from http://www.mdr.de/sachsen-anhalt/halle/chronologie-troeglitz100.html.

Muehlebach, A. 2016. 'Camp in the City', *Cultural Anthropology*, 28 June. Retrieved 2 July 2018 from https://culanth.org/fieldsights/907-camp-in-the-city.

Münz, R., W. Seifert and R. Ulrich. 1999. *Zuwanderung nach Deutschland: Strukturen, Wirkungen, Perspektiven*. Frankfurt am Main: Campus Verlag.

Oguntoye, K. 1997. *Eine afro-deutsche Geschichte: Zur Lebenssituation von Afrikanern und Afro-Deutschen in Deutschland von 1884–1950*. Berlin: Verlag Christine Hoffmann.

Oltmer, J. 2005. *Migration und Politik in der Weimarer Republik*. Göttingen: Vandenhoeck & Ruprecht.

Özyürek, E. 2015. *Being German, Becoming Muslim: Race, Religion, and Conversion in the New Europe*. Princeton, NJ: Princeton University Press.

Pagenstecher, C. 2008. '"Das Boot ist voll": Schreckensvision Des Vereinten Deutschland', in G. Paul (ed.), *Das Jahrhundert der Bilder. Band II: 1949 bis heute*. Göttingen: Schriftenreihe der Bundeszentrale für politische Bildung, pp. 606–13.

Panayi, P. 1994. 'Racial Violence in the New Germany', *Contemporary European History* 3(3): 265–87.

Partridge, D. 2012. *Hypersexuality and Headscarves: Race, Sex, and Citizenship in the New Germany*. Bloomington: Indiana University Press.

Pearce, C. 2008. *Contemporary Germany and the Nazi Legacy: Remembrance, Politics and the Dialectic of Normality*. Basingstoke: Palgrave Macmillan.

Petermann, S., and K. Schönwälder. 2014. 'Immigration and Social Interaction', *European Societies* 16(4): 500–21.

Pohl, D. 2011. *Verfolgung und Massenmord in der NS-Zeit: 1933–1945*. Darmstadt: Wissenschaftliche Buchgesellschaft.

Pommerin, R. 1979. *Sterilisierung der Rheinlandbastarde: Das Schicksal einer farbigen deutschen Minderheit 1918–1937*. Düsseldorf: Droste.

Poutrus, P.G., and C.T. Müller (eds). 2005. *Ankunft – Alltag – Ausreise: Migration und interukulturelle Begegnung in der DDR-Gesellschaft.* Vienna: Böhlau.

Prantl, H. 1993. 'Hysterie und Hilflosigkeit: Chronik der Asyldebatte seit der Deutschen Einheit', in B. Blanke (ed.), *Zuwanderung und Asyl in der Konkurrenzgesellschaft.* Opladen: Leske + Budrich, pp. 301–37.

Pratt Ewing, K. 2008. *Stolen Honor: Stigmatizing Muslim Men in Berlin.* Stanford, CA: Stanford University Press.

Redattore Sociale. 2015. 'Quelli che se ne vogliono andare: Ecco chi sono gli immigrati "transitanti"', 12 June. Retrieved 2 July 2018 from http://www.redat toresociale.it/Notiziario/Articolo/485623/Quelli-che-se-ne-vogliono-andare-Ecco-chi-sono-gli-immigrati-transitanti.

Resing, V. 2013. *Die Kanzlermaschine: Wie die CDU funktioniert.* Freiburg im Breisgau: Herder Verlag.

Ritter, G.A. 2007. 'Der Föderalismus in Deutschland: Geschichte und Gegenwart', in T. Hertfelder and A. Rödder (eds), *Modell Deutschland: Erfolgsgeschichte oder Illusion?* Göttingen: Vandenhoeck & Ruprecht, 78–95.

Römhild, R. 1998. *Die Macht des Ethnischen: Grenzfall Russlanddeutsche.* Frankfurt am Main: Peter Lang.

Rüther, T. 2010. 'Vietnamesen in Deutschland: Aus einem unsichtbaren Land', *Frankfurter Allgemeine Zeitung*, 14 November. Retrieved 2 July 2018 from http://www.faz.net/aktuell/feuilleton/debatten/integration/ vietnamesen-in-deutschland-aus-einem-unsichtbaren-land-11071320. html?printPagedArticle=true - pageIndex_2.

Sarrazin, T. 2010. *Deutschland schafft sich ab: Wie wir unser Land aufs Spiel setzen.* Munich: Random House.

Schader Stiftung. 2007. 'Zuwanderer auf dem Land – Forschung: Integration von Aussiedlern'. Retrieved 2 July 2018 from https://www.schader-stiftung. de/themen/vielfalt-und-integration/fokus/zuwanderung-im-laendlichen-raum/artikel/zuwanderer-auf-dem-land-forschung-integration-von-aussiedlern.

Schlögel, K. (ed.). 1994. *Der große Exodus: Die russische Emigration und ihre Zentren 1917 bis 1941.* Munich: C.H. Beck.

Schmincke, I., and J. Siri (eds). 2013. *NSU Terror. Ermittlungen am rechten Abgrund. Ereignis, Kontexte, Diskurse.* Bielefeld: transcript.

Schönwälder, K., S. Petermann, J. Hüttermann, S. Vertovec, M. Hewstone, D. Stolle, K. Schmid and T. Schmitt. 2016. *Diversity and Contact: Immigration and Social Interaction in German Cities.* Basingstoke: Palgrave Macmillan.

Schwarzer, A. (ed.). 2016. *Der Schock: Die Silvesternacht von Köln.* Cologne: Kiepenheuer & Witsch.

Seils, C. 2013. 'Warum die CDU der SDP die Themen klaut', *Cicero*, 3 June. Retrieved 2 July 2018 from http://cicero.de/berliner-republik/ wahlkampf-2013-warum-die-cdu-der-spd-die-themen-klaut/54608.

Sherman, A.J. 1994. *Island Refuge: Refugees from the Third Reich 1933–1939.* Ilford: Frank Cass.

Sigona, N. 2018. 'The Contested Politics of Naming in Europe's "Refugee Crisis"', *Journal of Ethnic and Racial Studies* 41(3): 456–60.

Spiegel Online. 2010. 'Merkel erklärt Multikulti für gescheitert', 16 October. Retrieved 2 July 2018 from http://www.spiegel.de/politik/ deutschland/integration-merkel-erklaert-multikulti-fuer-gescheitert-a-723532. html.

Spoerer, M. 2001. *Zwangsarbeit unter dem Hakenkreuz: Ausländische Zivilarbeiter, Kriegsgefangene und Häftlinge im Deutschen Reich und im besetzten Europa 1939–1945*. Stuttgart: Deutsche Verlags-Anstalt.

Storz, H., and B. Wilmes. 2007. 'Die Reform des Staatsangehörigkeitsrechts und das neue Einbürgerungsrecht', *Bundeszentrale für politische Bildung*, 15 May. Retrieved 2 July 2018 from http://www.bpb.de/gesellschaft/migration/ dossier-migration/56483/einbuergerung?p=all.

Tezcan, L. 2012. *Das muslimische Subjekt: Verfangen im Dialog der Deutschen Islam Konferenz*. Konstanz: Konstanz University Press.

Tibi, B. 1996. 'Multikultureller Werte-Relativismus und Werte-Verlust: Demokratie zwischen Werte-Beliebigkeit und pluralistischem Werte-Konsens', *Aus Politik und Zeitgeschichte* 52–53: 27–36.

Trauner, F. 2016. 'Asylum Policy: The EU's "Crises" and the Looming Policy Regime Failure', *Journal of European Integration* 28(3): 311–25.

Van der Heyden, U. 2008. *Auf Afrikas Spuren in Berlin: Die Mohrenstraße und andere koloniale Erblasten*. Berlin: Tenea Verlag

Vertovec, S. 2007. 'Super-Diversity and its Implications'. *Ethnic and Racial Studies* 30(6): 1024–54.

Vertovec, S., and S. Wessendorf (eds). 2010. *The Multiculturalism Backlash*. Abingdon: Routledge.

Vogel, W.-D., and V. Wunderlich (eds). 2011. *Abenteuer DDR: Kubanerinnen und Kubaner im deutschen Sozialismus*. Berlin: Dietz.

Vollmer, L. 2009. *Die Grünen: von der Protestbewegung zur etablierten Partei: Eine Bilanz*. Munich: C. Bertelsmann.

Von Thadden, R., and M. Magdelaine. 1994. *Die Hugenotten 1685–1985*. Munich: C.H. Beck.

Wagner, U., R. van Dick and A. Zick. 2000. 'Sozialpsychologische Analysen und Erklärungen von Fremdenfeindlichkeit in Deutschland', *Zeitschrift für Sozialpsychologie* 32: 59–79.

Weil, P. 1991. *La France et ses étrangers: l'aventure d'une politique de l'immigration de 1938 à nos Jours*. Paris: Éditions Calman-Lévy.

Wittrock, P. 2017. 'Die Kirche soll im Dorf bleiben', *Spiegel Online*, 1 May. Retrieved 2 July 2018 from http://www.spiegel.de/politik/deutschland/ leitkultur-thomas-de-maiziere-und-seine-thesen-sorgen-fuer-aufregung-a-1145587.html.

Wolle, S. 2015. 'Geschlossene Gesellschaft', *Die Zeit*, 18 December. Retrieved 2 July 2018 from http://www.zeit.de/zeit-geschichte/2015/04/ ddr-propaganda-auslaender-einwanderer/komplettansicht.

Wowtscherk, C. 2014. *Was wird, wenn die Zeitbombe hochgeht? Eine sozialgeschichtliche Analyse der fremdenfeindlichen Ausschreitungen in Hoyerswerda im September 1991*. Göttingen: V&R Unipress.

Zolleis, U., and J. Schmid. 2014. 'Die CDU unter Angela Merkel: Der neue Kanzlerwahlverein?', in O. Niedermayer (ed.), *Die Parteien nach der Bundestagswahl 2013*. Wiesbaden: Springer Fachmedien, pp. 25–48.

Zwengel, A. (ed). 2011. *Die 'Gastarbeiter' der DDR: Politischer Kontext und Lebenswelt*. Berlin: LIT Verlag.

Part I

Making Germans
and Non-Germans

Chapter 1

Language as Battleground
'Speaking' the Nation, Lingual Citizenship and Diversity Management in Post-unification Germany

Uli Linke

Over the past three decades, the powerful matrix of globalization has deeply affected European nation forms and political systems. Socialist state ideologies crumbled in an era embattled by popular demands for change. Following the opening of the Berlin Wall, with the corresponding dismantling of the spatial fixity of borders and the successful push against the carceral immobility of subjects, German unification became a plausible reality (Stone 2014). By the end of the Cold War, new possibilities for envisioning society had energized public discourse, impelling major transformations in the fabric of Europe's ethno-national landscape (Linke 1999, 2010; Partridge 2012; Smith 2006). The formation of the European Union further promoted the creation of open borders and 'market liquidity' (Gotham 2009). The subsequent entanglement of state and corporate interests not only changed the political contours of Europe but also altered the conditions under which imaginaries of national belonging were brought to public visibility (Fenner and Linke 2014). How have conceptions of nationality and citizenship been affected in this globally transformed political space?

In the European Union, the realities of ethnic diversity, cultural pluralism and multilingualism have unravelled the idea of *nationals* as a homogeneous or undifferentiated group (Geraghty and Conacher 2016; Gogolin 2002; Rindler Schjerve and Vetter 2012; Studer and Werlen 2012). Yet as Europe struggles to retain political and economic unity by coming to terms with secessionist challenges and exit strategies pursued by some

---

Notes for this chapter begin on page 61.

Member States, we see a concurrent push towards inequality, cultural exclusion and linguistic marginalization (Linke 2002, 2010). The legacies of colonialism and fascist nationalism not only continue to imprint the privilege of whiteness onto the new map of Europe, but also sustain the fortification of Europe as a hegemonic 'white' space (Gilroy 2004; Hall 2000; Linke 2011, 2014). From this perspective, the focus on belonging in Europe requires a critical reassessment. In efforts to both accommodate and repel the tension-fraught effects of a globalizing Europe, local reassertions of national distinction have given rise to new measures of exclusion, framed by anti-immigrant sentiments and ethnoracial solidarities.

In this chapter, I examine how such commitments to nationhood have regained prominence in EU countries. My analysis of the shifting parameters of national belonging proceeds by a focus on post-unification Germany. While specific concerns about border security or nationalist history might not be applicable to all EU Member States, there has been a coordinated push towards national distinction and forms of lingual citizenship across all sovereignties (Barát et al. 2013; Kamusella 2012). Since the late 1990s, the projected frontiers of European nation states are increasingly mapped through the medium of language. In Germany, as in France or Denmark, national identity politics have become language politics, a terrain marked by fears of linguistic estrangement and a public preoccupation with preserving an authentic national interior (Barbour and Carmichael 2000). The German nation is configured as a speech community of ethnic Germans. Such a performative vision of nationhood draws on quasi-mythic notions of the German political community as a language-body, a closed linguistic corpus, which is sustained by a phantasmatic landscape of intensely charged concepts: nation, nature and race.

Building on these insights, my reflections on language politics in contemporary Germany rely on a montage of data from multiple sources. Informed by earlier studies of ethnoracial machinations in Europe (Carter 2010; Goldberg 2006; Hine et al. 2009; Hintjens 2007; Linke 1999, 2014; Wacquant 2008), my project draws on long-term fieldwork in Germany. During a four-year residence as a faculty member at the University of Tübingen from 1997 to 2001, I had the opportunity to become an observing participant of the problematic formation of the European Union, the shared currency of the eurozone and the subsequent implementation of Europeanizing initiatives, such as language reform and the rearticulation of immigration policies. Living and working in Germany provided me with access to diverse forms of community and modalities of research. In addition to follow-up study trips, my insights about German nationalism and ethnic diversity were further enhanced by an extensive scrutiny of media images, news reports and political discourse, as well as EU documents.

Guided by the expansive scholarship on global racial formations in the twenty-first century (Appadurai 2003; Gilroy 2003; Goldberg 2009; Thomas and Clarke 2006; Winant 2001), the presentation of my research findings follows a critical approach to contemporary forms of national belonging. My chapter begins with a brief sketch of the broader context of transborder politics in Europe. I draw on Germany's visual self-presentation to the world, central to which is the trope of the nation as a white female icon, whose promotional allure propagates open borders for global investors. This gendered fantasy of nationhood coexists with national discourses about the entry of immigrants and Muslim refugees into Europe, which is perceived by some segments of the German population as a threat to sovereignty and culture. It is noteworthy that in 2015–16, a multitude of responses crystallized in public discourse. When Angela Merkel's government showed its willingness to accommodate around one million refugees from the war-torn Middle East, this decision was conveyed to voters by an appeal to Germany's historical obligation to atone for its past and by suggesting that to offer protection to the victims of war was both a Christian ideal as well as a humanitarian act (Gauck 2015). When thousands of refugees from Iraq and Syria entered Europe to seek asylum in Germany, the news media observed a nationwide compliance with these state directives. By promoting a 'culture of welcome' (*Willkommenskultur*), a display of hospitality and integration assistance, Germans initially participated in a government policy of 'diversity management', a policy put in place several years earlier to support the short-term recruitment of high-tech professionals from Asia (Amrute 2016; BAMF 2011; *The Economist* 2015; Merx et al. 2013). In 2014, this national action plan was expanded to include refugees (Ulrich 2015). According to one observer, 'thousands of Germans have pitched in; they take food and clothes to the camps, take refugees to meetings with the authorities in their own cars, pay their fares, foot their medical bills, teach German, translate forms, share couches and bikes, act as nannies, open up soccer clubs, schools and kindergartens for refugee kids, and go on demonstrations against rightwing attacks across the country' (Akrap 2015). This affective participation in Germany's 'culture of welcome' turned into fear in 2016, when the national media began to report mass sexual assaults of women by North African and Middle Eastern men in Cologne, Hamburg and other metropolitan centres (Noack 2016). As rumours of the attacks circulated on social media, the public resentment against border-crossers intensified. When government officials linked the sexual assaults to the influx of refugees, the welcoming sentiments towards asylum seekers diminished. Muslim men were depicted as sexual predators, whose uncontrolled presence posed a danger to

German society (see also Kosnick, Chapter 7 in this volume). This was the context for the formation of anti-immigrant movements and a growing resistance to ethnic diversity.

In aligning these shifting approaches to German experiences of national and cultural insecurity, my aim is first to offer an overview of European racializing practices before analysing the emergent phenomenon of linguistic nationalism. In subsequent sections of this chapter, my discussion turns to German citizenship debates and the push for border fortification via the instrument of a national language. My evidence derives from a diversity of intersecting sociopolitical fields that render visible the phantasms of language purity and fears of linguistic difference. In this chapter, I interrogate the role of language as a battleground for contested notions of immigrant presence and national belonging in post-unification Germany. Central to my analysis is the German experience of cultural difference and its implications for immigration and refugee policies.

Whiteness as a National Emblem: Branding Distinctions

What resources are mobilized by European nation states to reclaim their sovereignty under globalization? In the twenty-first century, the manufacture of European national distinction has increasingly shifted to the marketplace, the terrain of advertising, fashion and media. Culture industries manufacture nationalist longing by means of commodity desire and consumption. When circulated across political borders to attract foreign investment and international consumer attention, such promotional discourses rely on familiar motifs: gender, sex and race. Consider the following example, a worldwide marketing campaign co-sponsored by the German government, which provides a glimpse of the nationality project that has buttressed the lingual citizenship debates in Germany: in London, New York and Tokyo, gigantic billboards in subway stations and airports promote financial investment opportunities in Germany by featuring supermodel Claudia Schiffer (Land of Ideas 2018; see Figure 1.1). Seductively posed, her pale white body is stretched horizontally across the visual frame: an endless space of whiteness. She is casually positioned, reclined on her side. The silky fabric of the German national flag, which is tenderly draped across her torso, accentuates her body's nudity, revealing the immaculate smoothness of her legs and arms. She is facing the camera, her head slightly propped up, framed by her arms and cascading blond hair. Posed against a white screen, she extends an invitation as part of the global marketing campaign. This advocacy of German business ventures is further articulated by a series of suggestive slogans: 'Discover the

Figure 1.1 Invest-in-Germany campaign poster in New York 2008. Photo credit: Timothy A. Clary/AFP/Getty Images, used with permission.

beauty of the deal'; 'Invest in Germany, boys'; 'Interested in a serious relationship?'; 'Want to get down to business?'; 'Come on over to my place'; 'Follow your instincts'.

In these spaces of transborder capitalism, the German marketing initiative is infused with erotic messages. The campaign toys with the seductive image of the goddess Europa and her political counterpart Germania, a female personification of the German nation, thereby not only calling upon myth, history and ancestry, but also shifting attention to the lure of the 'white woman' to evoke gendered fantasies of sexual conquest and erotic capture. The campaign designers envision international investors as male, as business-*men*, whose economic desires can be fulfilled by intimacy with the German nation as a female plaything. In this promotional fantasy, transnational financial endeavours are staged as intimate erotic encounters. Capital investment in Germany is presented as a sexual adventure. The white female body/nation is offered up as a consumable commodity in global capitalist space. Although the white female figure inhabits this imaginary terrain, she is branded as a political subject: the German flag envelops her body; she is marked as a national icon. Like a ventriloquist's doll, she gives corporal form and voice to the nation's desires.

Yet the work of neoliberal economies, with their seductive promise of unlimited possibilities, is simultaneously defended as a state-protected privilege, a concession of citizenship reserved for German nationals. The political spaces of capitalism are closely guarded. Law-makers, politicians and media industries call upon imaginaries of language, gender and race to authorize or deny participation in the dreamworlds of prosperity. The formation of the security state after 9/11 has intensified this process, giving rise to new border regimes that have fundamentally altered the possibilities of negotiating matters of national belonging (Linke 2010, 2014). My research across Europe's multinational spaces reveals that the collusion of global economic restructuring and entrenched local commitments propagates old as well as new disparities.

This trajectory is evident in various domains of social experience, including gender politics. The European Union takes a protective stance to women, such as codifying their reproductive/maternal agency, while at the same time conjuring foreign masculinities as a security risk. In turn, as I suggest in the subsequent sections, national discourses of diversity normalize white womanhood while ignoring differences in sexual or ethnic subjectivities.

Modalities of Difference: Gender, Race and Immigration

As a reformist entity, the European Union has positioned itself as a legal order against the unprecedented fluidity and instability of global power relations: the judicial system, according to Clare McGlynn (2006), has become the 'Union's genetic code'. Although founded on a political order sensitive to difference and inequality, the quest for unity and uniformity has tended to erode the acceptance of otherness. In other words, Europe's preoccupation with judicial matters, which seeks to neutralize legal pluralism and minimize the incoherence of rights in local political practice, produces unforeseen results. Following McGlynn (2006: 9), '[t]here is a tendency for the presence of rights to somehow construct the ideal rights-bearing citizen. This assertion of "ideal citizen" models, with its consequent marginalization and exclusion of the non-ideal, carries a particular resonance for feminists', and for civil rights advocates.

European family policy reforms provide an instructive example: by a focus on protecting women's reproductive capacity, the figure of the single, childless or lesbian woman is rendered invisible (Griffin and Braidotti 2002). While granting generous provision for maternity leave and maternal healthcare, such policy measures confirm prevailing gender expectations. In the family reform documents, 'women are presented as a homogeneous category without race, sexual orientation, ethnic origin, ability or any other life dimension' (Lombardo and Meier 2002: 157–8). Women's distinguishing feature is defined as the ability to produce children. Europe's legal intervention in the family aims to protect female procreativity as a matter of equal opportunity, thereby reifying women's traditional roles as mothers and caregivers. Although focused on enabling women's participation in the marketplace without infringing upon maternal responsibilities, Europe's legal rights discourse does not prioritize gender equality. The reforms and provisions speak to political concerns about a demographic crisis, a shrinking European and German population, which is attributed to decreasing fertility rates among white women (Linke 2011: 132–34, 2014). If white women, as in Germany, are both idealized as alluring national icons and as vulnerable subjects in need of state protection, then white womanhood can be culturally reimagined as a critical issue in the terrain of national security. According to this logic, white motherhood and female reproduction require defensive measures against racialized minorities.

Negotiating Europeanness: The Muslim-Arab-Other

Seen through the affective resonance of a global security lockdown, transborder migration in Europe is linked to an intrusive, negative presence that needs to be diminished or controlled. Under such conditions, marked by a politics of fear and fluctuating demands for border fortification, divergent images of dangerous alterities are assembled to create a unitary figure: the Muslim-Arab-Other (see also Kosnick, Chapter 7 in this volume). This iconic template presents a montage of diverse tropes: the immigrant, the terrorist, the refugee and the enemy-outsider. Criminalized as agents of global instability, disorder and terror, Muslims are stripped of their right to belong. In the European Union, however, this imaginative turn against Muslim minorities has not yet garnered uniform support. Global anxieties are variously galvanized in different EU countries.

In Germany, the figure of the Islamic Other is given life by anti-Turkish sentiments, a racial formation energized by memories of postwar economic reconstruction, the 1950s 'guestworker' recruitment programme, and the desired impermanence of a mobile ethnic labour force (Amrute 2016: 7, 27–28, 38–39; Mandel 2008). Anti-Islamic politics in France are nourished by resentments against Muslim immigrants from North Africa, whose precarious status as a racial minority in the centre of Europe is an effect of the aftermath of French colonial violence. In the Netherlands, the figure of the Muslim is populated by Indonesian immigrants, whose citizenship rights are entangled with their status as descendants of slave labourers in Dutch plantation colonies. In each of these cases, the ethnographic life of Europe's Muslim communities has been variously shaped by political histories, societal memories and demographic realities. But such local complexities are globally unremembered, replaced by a singular, ahistorical, spatially mobile figure: the Muslim Other. The negated icon can thereby subsume salient ethnicities, 'drawing together West Indians, Africans, South Asians into a blackening singularity as uninvited immigrant presence' (Goldberg 2009: 179). Reified by global ideologies, the construct of the Islamic Other furnishes a distorted lens for assessing difference and alterity.

Embedded in political fantasies about national security, as Achille Mbembe (2003: 23) observed, Europeanness 'is imagined as an identity against the Other'. Tangible alterities or figures of difference (the Muslim male, the Arab terrorist, the black immigrant) occupy a strategic place in the determination of Europeanness and in the articulation of the corresponding national fields of whiteness. These 'largely unspoken racial connotations' of national belonging in Europe, as Stuart Hall (2000) suggested, are encoded by a cultural logic of difference that promotes either assimilation or exclusion. National distinction is manufactured along a narrow register that 'accords differing groups cultural normativity or deviance' (Ong 1996: 759). In this volatile terrain, following Leora Bilsky (2009: 306), the European nation state is 'caught between the need to enforce sameness and the fear of absolute difference'. What modalities of gender or race, and what machinations of national belonging, are deployed by Europe's border regimes when assessing residence or citizenship privileges for immigrants?

Europeanness is both confirmed by appearance and corroborated by performance. Practices of 'cultural citizenship' or 'social processes of whitening', as Aihwa Ong (1996: 745) points out, are monitored by public officials to ascertain whether a person's 'embodiment of culturally correct citizenship and privilege' has been successful. The Europeanization of Muslim minorities not only prohibits the public assertion of ethnic difference but also demands a refashioning of a gender-specific demeanour (Linke 2014). The forcible unveiling of the Muslim woman's body in European nation states, as in France or Germany, suggests that integration or assimilation requires compliance with the representational regimes of capitalist consumer culture (Breeden and Blaise 2016; Linke 2014). Minorities and immigrants are rendered white or socially acceptable when they exhibit the performative habitus of national privilege. Such a performance of citizenship, as I discuss below, not only includes appearance and dress codes but also 'speaking the nation', the acquisition of language proficiency.

Shifting Signposts of National Belonging

Since the cultural politics of national belonging in Europe continue to be haunted by the legacies of empire and colony, how have German nationals 'fashioned their distinction' (Cooper and Stoler 1997: 16) in attempts to reconstitute themselves as global citizens in a multiethnic, plurilingual and post-imperial Europe? As defined by Germany's historical self-imagination, publicly validated signs of belonging are bound to physical appearance (relative degrees of 'whiteness') as much as performative expressions of cultural citizenship. Expressive affirmations of nationality, as I argue here, have shifted from visual to auditory signposts. National language competence and speech habits have become political instruments for measuring degrees of assimilation and, in turn, suitability for immigrant status or citizenship. EU Member States have begun to fiercely defend their sovereign borders by mandating language proficiency for immigrants. While forged by a unique political history, Germany is a case in point. In the attempt to create a single nation state and transform subjects into nationals, a unified Germany needed alternative ways of *thinking* and *feeling* the nation.

By what means could such a sense of participation in a unified political community be produced? According to Etienne Balibar (1995: 94), there are two complementary routes to this: by *language* and by *race*. These principles of national belonging, as my research reveals, often operate together. Although the opening of the Berlin Wall in 1989 and the subsequent end of the socialist regime were supported internationally, segments of the German population wanted to 'reaffirm ethnocultural homogeneity – as expressed in the slogan "Germany for Germans" and the often-repeated mantra "Germany is not an immigration society"' (Kurthen and Minkenberg 1997: 5–6). Such sentiments re-emerged in 2014, energized by the Pegida movement (Patriotic Europeans against the Islamization of the West; see Bock, Chapter 9 in this volume) and its slogan: 'We are the people/nation' (*'Wir sind das Volk'*). This very slogan was first coined in 1989, during the popular uprising against the socialist East German state. At this time, the term *Volk* carried a semantic field that was defined by a Marxist political ideology, whereby the 'people' – the proletarian workforce – was clearly in the centre of attention: as potential revolutionaries with a collective voice who would overthrow or render unnecessary the institution of the socialist state. When protesters recovered this identical slogan twenty-five years later, the meaning of 'the *Volk*' had radically changed. In 2014, in a neoliberal democracy, as in the case of post-unification Germany, subjects had become nationals, that is, voting citizens in a democratic system. In the German nation state, the connotations of 'we are the *Volk*' shifted from the previously liberative potential of 'the people' to the constituents of 'the nation'. The term had come to refer to national subjects who demanded a directional change in immigration policies by protesting against the influx of foreign border-crossers into Germany. The Pegida movement tapped into this sense of national discontent by rallying supporters around a common destiny of *ethnos*, a German national community, which accentuated unity and sameness by defining boundaries of difference through race, religion and language (Rehberg 2016: 17). Founded in Dresden in 2014, this populist response to the 'migrant crisis' in Europe has been variously described as a nationalist, anti-Muslim, anti-immigrant and far-right political movement (Heim 2017; Rehberg et al. 2016; Vorländer et al. 2016). The uncertainties of German unification, the influx of immigrants, Muslim refugees and European anti-terror measures to achieve border security, combined with existential economic concerns, became trigger points for excavating cultural sentiments and memories of a national community of ethnic Germans. By instrumentalizing existential fears, Pegida activists demanded either the reduction of minorities by expulsion or the cultural assimilation and linguistic integration of foreign residents in Germany. Diversity without difference emerged as a new political vision for a united Germany.

What were the political responses to the national identity formation of a unified Germany since the 1990s? Preoccupied with gatekeeping and national armament, the German government was persistent in its refusal to 'improve the protection of minorities through detailed anti-discrimination legislation' (Erb 1997: 215). The political answer to the challenges of inclusion at first took form through government campaigns 'against the perceived abuse of the liberal right of asylum by so-called economic refugees' (Erb 1997: 215). Applicants for political refugee status were criminalized (Linke 1999). Portrayed as parasites, freeloaders and welfare spongers, ethnic minorities were treated as a threat to the German nation. The political instrumentalization of anti-foreign sentiments by mainstream democratic parties promoted an ethnic fortress mentality: the closing of national borders and the reduction of the resident alien population, in particular that of refugees (Linke 2010, 2014). A political climate that encouraged a renaissance of ethnoracial nationalism effectively impeded the implementation of policies designed to safeguard the legal status of foreign nationals. In fact, despite EU legislative pressure since 2000, it would take another six years before anti-discrimination and equal opportunity laws came into effect in Germany (BGBl 2006; BMJV 2006; Bundestag 2006).

Nurtured by an understanding of nationhood as a homogeneous community based on common descent (*Abstammungsgemeinschaft*), the formation of a united Germany was complicated by an organic notion of belonging (Linke 1999). The citizenship law of the Federal Republic of Germany determines national membership through the idiom of descent, as expressed by the Latin term *ius sanguinis*, 'right/law of blood' (Basic Law, art. 116a). Enacted in 1913 – and still in effect today – the German citizenship law permits, and even encourages, the 'nation's racial closure' (Frankenberg 1999: 11). In other words, migrant children born in Germany do not automatically acquire citizenship status.

Making Nationals: Blood, Space and Language

How can migrants become German citizens when nationality is rooted in descent by blood? This question became a much-contested issue in 1998, when the centre-left coalition government made a concerted effort to reform the country's naturalization practices. The German Chancellor wanted 'to create an open society, with flexible borders, to make Germans capable of joining the European Union' (Darnstädt 1999: 30). Yet attempts to reform the citizenship law by eliminating the blood-principle of national belonging proved unsuccessful (Böhm 1999). A subsequent proposal, introduced by the independent democrats (FDP) under the heading 'dual citizenship for children' seemed more palatable. Dual citizenship or binationality was to create a hyphenated identity for second-generation immigrants by appending German citizenship to that of national origin.

The proposed changes to citizenship, which became law in 2000 (Worbs 2008: 5), affirmed the privileged status of native-born Germans. As citizens by hereditary sanguinity, German nationals retained their membership in an ethnoracial community of descent. But immigrants, perceived as transient bodies in geopolitical space, merely gained an identity supplement. Dual citizenship, acquired by *ius soli* (territory/residence), was read as a signifier of otherness, marking a life course of displacement and uprootedness. The legal reform, I argue, instituted a two-tiered, caste-like system of national belonging: by blood (descent) and by space (residence); one native-German, based on consanguinity, which is legally presumed to be natural, authentic and permanent; the other foreign-German, based on territorial affinity, which is culturally deemed artificial, inauthentic, contractual and impermanent. This distinction is encoded in the dual citizenship status of immigrant children. Given the underlying ethnoracial paradigm, it seemed only logical that the citizenship status of immigrant children in Germany be temporary: German nationality can be abrogated upon a child's entry into adulthood, when the option of dual citizenship expires and the forcible choice of a singular citizenship must be declared (Bischoff 1999: 2; Böhmer 2008, 2012). The hyphenated citizen is thereby treated as a flexible commodity. German nationality is issued on loan; the German passport is granted to immigrant children as a revocable entitlement.

This mandate of a single nationality 'option' was modified in 2014 with a Eurocentric provision: immigrant children born or raised in Germany were now able to retain their dual citizenship status if their parents were nationals of a European Union country (BMI 2014), thereby again privileging ancestry or descent. This legislative change also articulates Germany's longing for affinity with Europeanness, for in a united Germany, natural or inherited citizenship enshrines claims of allegiance to a national community of blood. By contrast, 'flexible' citizenship (Ong 1999) is treated as a counterfeit form. But the altered citizenship legislation attests to German assumptions of a common ancestry and kinship with white European nationals.

The nationality debates had a decisive impact on border matters, resulting in ever more drastic restrictions on third-country nationals' access to citizenship. In response to the mandates of unification and in seeking to reconcile the uneven recruitment of subjects by regimes of blood and space, German politicians began to redefine the frontiers of the nation state in terms of linguistic practices. By the late 1990s, issues of sovereignty and nationhood were recast by visions of the German body politic as a discrete community of native-language speakers. This premise of linguistic unity was transferred to the threshold of nationality. Germanness was to be expressed through the idiom of language. The transformation of political subjects into nationals should now require an act of linguistic performance: speaking German. Such a formation of linguistic nationality, although intended to promote inclusion, became simultaneously a mechanism of segregation and exclusion.

In the accompanying public debates, the criteria of eligibility for naturalization and citizenship (*Einbürgerung*) were linked to language: the immigrants' knowledge of German. Christian Democrats insisted that applicants for citizenship status needed to document their 'integration into German society' by having achieved an 'attestable level of language fluency' (FAZ 1999: 6). Prospective immigrants, according to this proposal, were expected to enrol in mandatory German language courses, preferably in their home countries; the applicants' linguistic competence was to be certified by means of a final exam (Ruf 2000). The working draft of the dual-citizenship proposal likewise insisted on 'sufficient familiarity with the German language' as a prerequisite for naturalization (Finke 1999: 1). The primary aim was to 'promote the integration of foreigners by offering German language courses. Foreigners completing such courses could obtain "integration certificates" that entitled them to receive unlimited work permits' (Martin 1998: 36–37). Representatives from liberal and conservative political parties regarded a formal evaluation of the applicants' knowledge of the German language as indispensable. The Bavarian Christian Union Party (CSU) demanded a standardized 'spelling test' for citizenship applicants (Guyton 1999). Likewise, the Social Democrats wanted to determine whether resident aliens had acquired 'sufficient mastery of German' (Tagblatt 1999). Otto Schilly, then Federal Interior Minister, suggested in his original draft proposal that foreigners should be denied German citizenship if 'communication with them proved impossible' and 'they were unable to make themselves understood in German' (John 1999). As ratified by Germany's parliament in 2002, the legal provisions of the national integration legislation determine 'German language competence' as a prerequisite for residence permits and naturalization (BMI 2004). Yet this attempt to create a unified nation by manufacturing a national community of assimilated German-language speakers should eventually encounter resistance. In 2011, the German Supreme Court and the EU High Court successfully contested the rigid implementation of the language policy as incompatible with anti-discrimination legislation (Alscher and Grote 2013; BGBl 2006; BMJV 2006; Bundeszentrale für politische Bildung 2011; Wöhrle et al. 2013). By recourse to due process, individual actors could now obtain a compliance exemption. Under exceptional circumstances, spouses or children of immigrants were thus rendered eligible for residency without attestable proficiency in German.

The politics of linguistic nationalism might explain why German lawmakers agreed to extend the right of citizenship to children: second-generation immigrants, who were born or raised in Germany, are expected to 'inhabit the national language and through it the nation itself' (Balibar 1995: 99). The linguistic construction of national membership 'possesses plasticity', for a language community 'is by definition *open*': ideally, it 'assimilates anyone, but holds no one', and although it continuously absorbs new members, it 'produces the feeling that it has always existed' (Balibar 1995: 98–99). Linguistic nationality fabricates 'a collective memory which perpetuates itself at the cost of an individual forgetting of "origins"' (Balibar 1995: 99). This formative power of linguistic systems, which provides nation states with the capacity to absorb and assimilate a diversity of subjects, seems to exhibit a democratic propensity. But such a making of nationals, I argue, is also inherently coercive. Through the medium of language, and its strategic deployment in citizenship and immigration, the nation state seeks to engraft a linguistic memory of national belonging, creating an 'affective citizenship' (Casey 2009) that offers an experience of collective solidarity with the shifting imaginaries of state.

Nationalizing Immigrants: Language Proficiency and Racial Hierarchies

Language politics in a united Germany sought to reinvigorate a fic-
tive ethnicity of Germanness: the national community – that is, the
population – included and governed within the political territory of the
state would be ethnicized through language. By imagining the German
nation-form as a linguistic entity, social or political disparities could be
'expressed and relativized as different ways of speaking the national
language' (Balibar 1995: 97). This has obvious political consequences.
While the unity of a language community appears naturally predestined,
German unification shows that linguistic uniformity is not sufficient
to produce or to sustain ethnonational solidarities among millions of
people. A given language may be used as the official medium of communication by a multitude of countries (Ammon 1996: 243–49; Reiher
and Läzer 1996). For language 'to be tied down to the frontiers of a particular' nation, it requires 'an extra degree of particularity', a 'principle
of closure, of exclusion' (Balibar 1995: 99). This principle is evident in the
racialization of language.

The ability of foreign-born individuals to increase the range of their linguistic competence, and to thereby become German nationals, is guarded
by an ethnoracial imaginary of segregation and prohibition. Until the
end of 2004, access to language learning was severely restricted. Public
language programmes for immigrants were offered, but the eligibility for
enrolment was determined by their origin and legal status. Former labour
migrants with their families and offspring, refugees, immigrants and
ethnic German resettlers from the former Soviet republics were treated
differentially (Bundestag 2007: 5–7). The categories of foreignness and
ethnic difference were reified by variable degrees of permissible language
learning. For instance, applicants for asylum were officially forbidden to
participate in state-funded German classes: 'No public efforts must be
made to promote the assimilation or integration of individuals, whose
long-term presence in Germany has not been confirmed' (Kabis-Alamba
1999: 18). Certain foreign populations were to remain culturally excluded
and linguistically isolated. This policy of the linguistic segregation of refugees stood in stark contrast to the nation state's treatment of other foreign-
born individuals. Ethnic German resettlers from Russia or Eastern Europe
were granted unconditional access to language courses: legally defined as
nationals, based on the principles of filiation and *ius sanguinis*, the blood-
right of extended kinship, their linguistic integration was supported by
a multitude of separate government budgets. Resident aliens or immigrants, however, could enrol in subsidized German language courses
only if they met certain conditions. The decisive factor was their national

origin: citizens of EU Member States were permitted to enhance their competence in German (Kabis-Alamba 1999). However, even in such cases, learning was restricted (Bundestag 2007: 8): the duration and intensity of language programmes (by hours, vocabulary and grammar) varied with each category of the ethnic register.

Therefore, the 'openness of the linguistic community is an ideal openness' (Balibar 1995: 103); its permeability is in reality controlled by the official German phantasm of hereditary ethnic substance. And the greater the state's intervention in the foreigners' access to German, 'the more do differences in linguistic competence function as "caste" differences, assigning different "social destinies" to individuals' (Balibar 1995: 103–4). Under these conditions, strategies of linguistic exclusion come to be associated with 'forms of a corporal habitus' (Bourdieu 1984), which 'confer on the act of speaking', in its particular, idiosyncratic traits, 'the function of a racial or quasi-racial mark' (Balibar 1995: 104): 'foreign accents', degrees of language competence (broken German), unaccustomed and nonstandard 'styles of speech, language "errors" or, conversely, ostentatious "correctness"' instantly designate a non-native speaker as 'belonging to a particular population and are spontaneously interpreted as reflecting a specific origin' and judicial or 'hereditary' status (Balibar 1995: 104). The production of Germanness thus also entails, following Balibar, a 'racialization of language' and a 'verbalization of race'.

During the past decade, legislative changes have introduced reforms intended to mitigate inequality and discrimination. Taking effect in 2005, the German immigration and residence laws have altered the structurally diffuse treatment of migrants (BMJV 2008; Bundestag 2007; Worbs 2008). Focused on 'protection and integration' (BAMF 2015, 2016), German law-makers created a centralized educational programme for foreign nationals that promised greater transparency and standardization in the delivery of language courses (Bundestag 2007). By prioritizing cultural integration, German parliamentarians devised a uniform need- and skill-based lingual training system for all immigrants (BMI 2006, 2007; BAMF 2010). Encoded in Germany's integration legislation of 2016, the national action plan for teaching German as a second language has dismantled the discriminatory architecture of access, opportunity and participation for immigrants, including the grouping of foreign residents by categories of ethnolegal status (BMI 2015, 2016). The precise impact of these newly implemented policies on the racialization of language cannot yet be assessed. It does point to a hopeful development for migrants' rights in Germany. At the same time, opponents to diversity have forged alliances that seek to deglobalize the national idiom by censoring ways of speaking German.

Linguistic Nationalism: The Rise of Language Purists

In post-unification Germany, the sense of belonging to a linguistic community re-emerged as a sign of Germanness, invigorated by the desire for national unity through language purity. Since the 1990s, a range of literary societies has come into existence to reclaim and protect the nation's linguistic heritage. EU building set into motion a transnational hypermobility that should give rise to plurilingual countries, hybrid forms of multilingual communication, and the saturation of everyday life with foreign phrases. Under such conditions, the survival of Germanness, as suggested by the supposed permeability or 'thinning' of the national idiom, was deemed to be threatened (Ammon 1997; Janich 1997). The rapid formation of literary societies attests to this reinvigoration of a populist (white) nationalism committed to the closure of linguistic frontiers and a desire to purge the national idiom, the 'beloved mother tongue', of contaminating foreign influences.

Most prominent is the German Language Society (Verein Deutsche Sprache). Founded in 1997, it recruited over 16,000 fee-paying members in less than four years. The Society more than doubled its membership by 2013 (VDS 2018). The members, drawn from a broad social spectrum, stand united as 'citizens for the preservation and cultivation of German' (VDS 2018: *Startseite* [homepage]). According to the Society's official charter, the members are bound 'to defend the self-esteem and dignity of all human beings whose native tongue is German', 'to combat the amalgamation of German' and its 'excessive inundation' by foreign words, and to protect the 'cultural distinction' and 'survival of the German language' (VDS 2018: *Startseite* [homepage], *Satzung* [charter]). The movement's publicity campaigns, via the internet, newspapers and television, seek to implant in public consciousness a sense of linguistic ruin: the adulteration and corruption of the 'national character' of German by the infiltration of foreign idioms (VDS 1999, 2018). Media headlines in both local and national papers articulate the movement's concerns: 'battling against word heretics'; 'safeguarding the German language'; 'language purification'; 'the shambles of language'; 'against language trash'; 'the corruption of the German language'; 'protection against language dirt'; 'the purging of language'; 'fighters for the purity of German'; 'the foreign subversion of language is shameful'; 'against language colonization'; 'the murder of language'; 'pro German' (VDS 2018: *Artikel* [news articles], *Pressespiegel* [press coverage]).

In an effort to sustain media coverage and public support, the German Language Society has launched a series of initiatives: the establishment of local and regional chapters; the creation of a nationwide language forum;

the production of Germanized glossaries and dictionaries; literary prizes and awards; and the administration of language tests. Moreover, in trying to gain recognition as a public service advocate, the German Language Society has inaugurated a 'linguistic consumer protection' programme. Under this rubric, the language practices of major service sectors are scrutinized for potential assaults on the national idiom: the use of foreign words, especially Anglicisms, is rendered a public offence. The targets of inspection include the postal service, hospitals, funeral homes, airlines, train companies and 'German health insurance providers, German TV guides, German political parties, German travel agencies, German utilities, and German mail order companies' (VDS 2018: *Sprachtest* [language test]). The furore of public scandal provoked by such language tests and linguistic consumer protection surveys has effectively placed an entire society of German speakers on language probation: national allegiance is enforced by linguistic censorship; nationalization proceeds by the erasure of non-German vocabularies (*Fremdwörter*), which is also a turn against Europeanization. Although the German Language Society is not officially part of the government bureaucracy, it is an agency of the ideological state apparatus (Althusser) by fusing national belonging to language practices. The association exerts influence over public opinion by the collusion of media and culture industries in pushing the nationalist language agenda into the domain of popular spectacle and political discourse.

Language patriotism is promoted by various other publicity campaigns. Since 1997, this movement of 'language warriors' or linguistic purists regularly conducts nationwide media contests in search of 'the most un-German word [*Unwort*] of the year', the 'language heretic [*Sprachhunzer*] of the month' and the 'language adulterator [*Sprachpanscher*] of the year' (VDS 2018). The finalists, typically businesses, institutions or public figures, are chosen on the basis of nationwide opinion polls; the protagonists are then put at the pillory to be publicly ridiculed or shamed on charges of language defilement (Nölkensmeier 1999; Steinhoff 1999: 56–69; VDS 2018: *Pressespiegel* [press coverage], *Sprachpanscher* [language adulterator]). Since the selected targets are typically high-profile companies or individuals whose membership in the German community is uncontested, this public critique of speech patterns suggests that Germanness requires, as I have argued, an expressive performance: the speaking of the national language (Adorno 1969). The mandate of linguistic purity is modelled on the political management of German bodies: a historically racist body politic that 'criminalized interbreeding' and 'the mixing of populations' (Balibar 1995: 103), a notion transferred to national language practices. Although some segments of the population might interpret the Society's linguistic theatrics as a funny or tongue-in-cheek undertaking, such matters do carry nationwide cultural resonance. The mediated interventions and spectacles staged by language nationalists are integral to a political discourse of 'cultural hegemony' (Crehan 2002: 165–205), which continuously attempt to expunge alternative practices of creative language use and linguistic hybridity. The German media contests, ushered in by a Frankfurt-based linguist, attempt to censure 'the irresponsible use of public language' (Janich 1997: 82). These annual campaigns produce a form of ethnonational purging by a focus on the 'misuse' of words: language practices are monitored for 'un-German' transgressions and forms of miscegenation. Such a public censorship of speech acts seeks to normalize nationalist practices and nativist values through the policing of language. The results of the contests are circulated in print, televised by news outlets and disseminated electronically by social media platforms such as Facebook and Twitter, thereby broadening the public reach of verbal shaming. Linguistic nationalists present themselves as soldiers or vigilantes, who act in defence of Germany, a political community made vulnerable by open borders, immigrants and refugees, and the incursions of global cultural dynamics.

Linguistic Justice: German Language Politics in a United Europe

The importance of language in diversity politics is not a novel phenomenon. German nationhood 'accorded a privileged place to the symbol of language in its own initial process of formation: it bound political unity closely to linguistic uniformity' (Balibar 1995: 104). Movements of language reform, language cultivation and language purging have been an integral part of German national history (Straßner 1995). But in the twentieth century, with the constitution of the phantasm of race, the symbolic coding of linguistic nativism was radically transposed. Linguistic nationalism, a language ideology encoded by tropes of blood and nature, was remade and refurbished by racialist regimes. German national distinction reified the ethnicization of language.

The ethnonational fabrication of language has profoundly altered the conditions under which issues of immigration, citizenship and national sovereignty are brought to light in public debates in Germany. According to Claudia Breger (2014: 2):

> Inclusivity with respect to race, national origin and/or religion has perhaps proven to be more challenging in the German context. To be sure, the new century brought belated – and internally fraught – processes of opening up hegemonic German conceptions and practices of national distinction. These

hopeful developments have been counteracted by the confluence of local legacies of exclusion with transnational Islamophobia trends.

In this sociopolitical climate, questions of immigration and national identity have been variously thematized in terms of language practices. In addition to legal and popular machinations of linguistic uniformity, ordinary Germans monitor public space for language transgressions. In everyday social encounters, black subjects cannot escape the optical mask of difference: 'People think I am a foreigner'; 'I am not viewed as a German'; 'As soon as they see me, they think I can't speak German' (in Baum et al. 1992: 151, 145, 154). In this panoptic theatre of race, difference is conjured on sight. Yet in post-unification Germany, becoming national also requires language conformity. In a 2015 video recording (Olsen and Eddy 2015), a young migrant Muslim woman living in Dresden reports being consumed by fears of public taunting:

> Germany, it's not something where I am welcome. Home is where you must be welcome, where you can be safe. But here, I am scared to go outside on most days. I am scared to go outside when it's dark. When I speak another language, then they scream at me, in the supermarket, very loud: 'don't speak another language! You are in Germany!' It's not so good for us here, for us young people, I think'.

Linguistic nationalism has become commonplace, implanted into the security habitus of the mundane.

Language has become an ethnoracial formation within the broader European concerns about national identity. Germany is not an isolated case. France has declared French the official national language by a constitutional mandate: government offices and public education, including universities, are bound to the exclusive use of French. Despite the European Union's advocacy of multilingualism and the push for 'languages without borders', recent surveys suggest that less than 42 per cent of the European student population achieve rudimentary competence in a second language (Eurydice/Eurostat 2012; Krzyzanowski and Wodak 2011). There are notable national differences in multilingual proficiencies. In the United Kingdom, second-language competence drops to 14 per cent and in France to nine per cent. These statistics, however, are misleading. The 2011 and 2012 surveys focus exclusively on formal language education in schools, where English, French, German, Spanish or Russian remain privileged. These studies thereby ignore immigrant students' native language skills and multilingual competence in Arabic and Turkish or other Asian or African languages, which are not perceived on equal terms with Europe's national speech communities. The political and educational institutions of the European Union not only negate non-hegemonic forms of multilingualism, but also treat native speakers of non-national languages as foreign. Language nationalism is articulated in terms of race in the United Kingdom, where the members of the white British working class fear becoming 'invisible' or 'ethnically erased' by immigrant speech communities, a process imagined as a blackening of the white phenotype by non-European language speakers (BBC Two 2008). In discussing BBC's *White Season* production, Vron Ware (2008) observed that 'five specially commissioned documentaries' 'were accompanied by news items, national opinion polls and archival resources drawn from across the BBC and coordinated on an interactive website'. In these media productions, members of the white working class see themselves as an endangered ethnic group and, as confirmed by ethnographic studies (Evans 2006; Smith 2012), with feelings of resentment against a system of unfairness and muted voices.

The presence of diverse populations in the European Union, whether immigrants, refugees or citizens, has complicated matters of national distinction by the signs of colour: the racializing codes of 'whiteness' or 'blackness' are no longer reliable visual tools for ascertaining national membership. In turn, language practices have become new signposts of belonging. Such a notion of linguistic nationality is operative in practices of European border security. Refugees and asylum seekers are linguistically screened at border transit points and assigned nationalities based on native-language competence (Maniar 2016). This system operates without sufficiently trained interpreters, and ignores local language variations and histories of displacement. Regardless of national origin, refugees might have acquired different language proficiencies by living in exile or in detention camps in countries across the world. The ascription of lingual citizenship, just as in the case of race, classifies newcomers by Eurocentric assumptions of nationality and corresponding future rights. Although a globalizing Europe can serve as a catalyst for linguistic pluralism, such currents of change are always culturally mediated, resisted and politically negotiated. While the future of a plurilingual Europe remains uncertain, the push for national sovereignty and the ethnoracialization of language has had a decisive impact on restrictive access to German citizenship.

Uli Linke is Professor of Anthropology at Rochester Institute of Technology (Rochester, New York), United States. She received her B.A. in anthropology and sociology from Macalester College, and her Ph.D. in anthropology from UC Berkeley. Her research specialities include the cultural politics of memory, visual culture, the political anthropology of the body, and trauma and genocide.

Note

An earlier, different version of this chapter was published as Uli Linke. 2016. 'Speaking in Tongues: Language and National Belonging in Globalizing Europe', *disClosure: A Journal of Social Theory* 25(9). DOI: https://doi.org/10.13023/disclosure.25.8.

References

Adorno, T.W. 1969. 'Auf die Frage: Was ist deutsch', in *Stichworte: Kritische Modelle 2*. Frankfurt am Main: Suhrkamp, pp. 102–12.

Akrap, D. 2015. 'Germany's Response to the Refugee Crisis is Admirable. But I Fear it Cannot Last', *The Guardian*, 6 September. Retrieved 4 July 2018 from https://www.theguardian.com/commentisfree/2015/sep/06/germany-refugee-crisis-syrian.

Alscher, S. and J. Grote. 2013. 'Kurzmeldungen – Deutschland: Vertragsverletzungverfahren wegen Sprachtests', *Migration & Bevölkerung 6*, 11 August (Bonn: Bundeszentrale für politische Bildung). Retrieved 4 August 2018 from http://www.bpb.de/gesellschaft/migration/newsletter/166674/kurzmeldungen-deutschland.

Ammon, U. 1996. 'Die nationalen Varietäten des Deutschen im Spannungsfeld von Dialekt und gesamtsprachlichem Standard', *Muttersprache* 106(3): 243–49.

_____. 1997. 'Schwierigkeiten bei der Verbreitung der deutschen Sprache heute', *Muttersprache* 107(1): 17–34.

Amrute, S. 2016. *Encoding Race, Encoding Class: Indian IT Workers in Berlin*. Durham, NC: Duke University Press.

Appadurai, A. 2003. 'Sovereignty without Territoriality', in Setha M. Low and D. Lawrence-Zúñiga (eds), *The Anthropology of Place and Space*. Oxford: Blackwell, pp. 337–49.

Balibar, E. 1995. 'The Nation Form', in Etienne Balibar and Immanuel Wallerstein (eds), *Race, Nation, Class*. London: Verso, pp. 86–106.

BAMF. 2010. *Bundesweites Integrationsprogramm*. Berlin: Bundesamt für Migration und Flüchtlinge.

_____. 2011. 'Willkommenskultur und Annerkennungskultur', *Aktuelle Meldungen des Bundesamts für Migration und Flüchtlinge*, 19 May. Retrieved 4 July 2018 from http://www.bamf.de/SharedDocs/Meldungen/DE/2011/20110519-nuernberger-tage-integration-willkommenskultur.html.

_____. 2015. *Einbürgerung in Deutschland*. Berlin: Bundesamt für Migration und Flüchtlinge.

_____. 2016. *Ausländische Staatsangehörige*. Berlin: Bundesamt für Migration und Flüchtlinge.

Barát, E., P. Studer and J. Nekvapil (eds). 2013. *Ideological Conceptualizations of Language*. Frankfurt am Main: Peter Lang.

Barbour, S. and C. Carmichael (eds). 2000. *Language and Nationalism in Europe*. Oxford: Oxford University Press.

Baum, L., K. Oguntoye and M. Opitz. 1992. 'Three Afro-German Women in Conversation with Dagmar Schultz', in M. Opitz, K. Oguntoye and D. Schultz (eds), *Showing Our Colors*. Amherst: The University of Massachusetts Press, pp. 145–164.

BBC Two. 2008. *Is White Working Class Britain Becoming Invisible?* Video Performance for BBC Two's The White Season, 7 March. Retrieved 10 August 2018 from http://www.dailymotion.com/video/x4n8oc_bbc-two-the-white-season_news.

BGBl. 2006. 'Gesetz zur Umsetzung europäischer Richtlinien zur Verwirklichung des Grundsatzes der Gleichbehandlung', *Bundesgesetzblatt* I 39(17 August): 1897–1910.

Bilsky, L. 2009. 'Muslim Headscarves in France and Army Uniforms in Israel', *Patterns of Prejudice* 43(3–4): 287–311.

Bischoff, J. 1999. 'Staatsbürgerschaft', *Schwäbisches Tagblatt*, 12 February, 2.

BMI. 2004. *Gesetz zur Steuerung und Begrenzung der Zuwanderung und zur Regelung des Aufenthalts und der Integration von Ausländern*. Berlin: Bundesministerium des Innern.

———. 2006. *Evaluation der Integrationskurse nach dem Zuwanderungsgesetz*. Berlin: Bundesministerium des Innern.

———. 2007. *Nationaler Integrationsplan*. Berlin: Bundesministerium des Innern.

———. 2014. *Optionspflicht*. Berlin: Bundesministerium des Innern. Retrieved 4 July 2018 from http://www.bmi.bund.de/DE/Themen/Migration-Integration/Optionspflicht/optionspflicht_node.html.

———. 2015. *Integrationskurse*, 30 June. Berlin: Bundesministerium des Innern.

———. 2016. *Integrationsgesetz vom Bundestag verabschiedet*, press release 7 July. Berlin: Bundesministerium des Innern.

BMJV. 2006. 'Allgemeines Gleichbehandlungsgesetz' (BGBL I. 39. 1897), *Bundesministerium der Justiz und für Verbraucherschutz*. Retrieved 4 July 2018 from https://www.gesetze-im-internet.de/agg/BJNR189710006.html.

———. 2008. Gesetz über den Aufenthalt, die Erwerbstätigkeit und die Integration von Ausländern im Bundesgebiet (Aufenthaltsgesetz). *Bundesministerium der Justiz und für Verbraucherschutz*.

Böhm, A. 1999. 'Die Mischung macht's', *Die Zeit* 8, 13–16.

Böhmer, M. 2008. *Wege zur Einbürgerung*. Berlin: Besscom.

———. 2012. *Das staatsangehörigkeitsrechtliche Optionsverfahren*. Berlin: Besscom.

Bourdieu, P. 1984. *Distinctions*. London: Routledge & Kegan Paul.

Breeden, A., and L. Blaise. 2016. 'French Town's Ban of "Burkini" Violates Rights', New York Times, 27 August, A1.

Breger, C. 2014. 'Hardboiled Performance and Affective Intimacy', in Angelica Fenner and Uli Linke (eds), *Contemporary Remediations of Race and Ethnicity in German Visual Cultures* (Special issue, Transit 9). Berkeley: University of California Press, http://transit.berkeley.edu/2014/breger/.

Bundestag. 2006. *Allgemeines Gleichbehandlungsgesetz (AAG)*. Berlin: Juris Gmbh.

_____. 2007. *Erfahrungsbericht der Bundesregierung zu Durchführung und Finanzierung der Integrationskurse nach § 43 Abs. 5 des Aufenthaltsgesetzes (Drucksache 16/6043)*. Cologne: Bundesanzeiger Verlagsgesellschaft.

Bundeszentrale für politische Bildung. 2011. 'EU/Deutschland: Sprachtests auf dem Prüfstand', *Migration & Bevölkerung* 7, 6 September. Retrieved 10 August 2018 from http://www.bpb.de/gesellschaft/migration/newsletter/56856/ sprachtests.

Carter, D.M. 2010. *Navigating the African Diaspora*. Minneapolis: University of Minnesota Press.

Casey, C. 2009. 'Mediated Hostility: Media, "Affective Citizenship", and Genocide in Northern Nigeria', in A.L. Hinton and K.L. O'Neill (eds), *Genocide: Truth, Memory and Representation*. Durham, NC: Duke University Press, pp. 247–78.

Cooper, F., and L.A. Stoler (eds). 1997. *Tensions of Empire*. Berkeley: University of California Press.

Crehan, K. 2002. *Gramsci, Culture and Anthropology*. Berkeley: University of California Press.

Darnstädt, T. 1999. 'Staatsbürgerschaft', *Der Spiegel* 7, 15 February, 30–32.

The Economist. 2015. 'The Syrian Exodus: "Germany! Germany!"', 12 September. Retrieved 4 July 2018 from https://www.economist.com/briefing/2015/09/12/ germany-germany.

Erb, R. 1997. 'Public Responses to Anti-Semitism and Right-Wing Extremism', in Hermann Kurthen, Werner Bergmann and Rainer Erb (eds), *Antisemitism and Xenophobia in Germany after Unification*. New York: Oxford University Press, pp. 211–23.

Eurydice/Eurostat. 2012. *Key Data on Teaching Language at School in Europe*. Brussels: Education, Audiovisual and Culture Executive Agency.

Evans, Gillian. 2006. *Educational Failure and Working Class White Children in Britain*. Basingstoke: Palgrave Macmillan.

FAZ. 1999. 'Vorschläge zur Reform des Staatsangehörigkeitsrechts', *Frankfurter Allgemeine Zeitung* 24, 29 January, 6.

Fenner, A., and U. Linke (eds). 2014. *Contemporary Remediations of Race and Ethnicity in German Visual Cultures* (Special issue, *Transit* 9). Berkeley: University of California Press.

Finke, H.-P. 1999. 'Kommentar: Doppelter Ärger', *Schwäbisches Tagblatt* 54, 6 March, 1.

Frankenberg, G. 1999. 'Eine Rolle rückwärts: Streit um den Doppelpaß', *Die Zeit* 8, 18 February, 11.

Gauck, J. 2015. *Rede des Bundespräsidenten anlässlich des ersten Gedenktages für die Opfer von Flucht und Vertreibung am 20. Juni 2015 in Berlin*. Berlin: Bundespräsidialamt. Retrieved on 10 August 2018 from https://www.bundespräsident.de.

Geraghty, B., and J.E. Conacher (eds). 2016. *Intercultural Contact, Language Learning and Migration*. London: Bloomsbury.

Gilroy, P. 2003. 'Where Ignorant Armies Clash by Night', *International Journal of Cultural Studies* 6: 261–76.

_____. 'Migrancy, Culture and a New Map of Europe', in Heike Raphael-Hernandez (ed), *Blackening Europe*. New York: Routledge, pp. xi–xxii.

Gogolin, I. 2002. *Linguistic Diversity and New Minorities in Europe*. Strasbourg: Council of Europe.

Goldberg, D.T. 2006. 'Racial Europeanization', *Ethnic and Racial Studies* 29(2): 331–64.

_____. 2009. *The Threat of Race*. Malden, MA: Blackwell.

Gotham, K.F. 2009. 'Creating Liquidity out of Spatial Fixity', *International Journal or Urban and Regional Research* 33(2): 355–72.

Griffin, G., and R. Braidotti (eds). 2002. *Thinking Differently*. London: Zed Books.

Guyton, P. 1999. 'Staatsangehörigkeit', *Schwäbisches Tagblatt* 55, 13 October, 2.

Hall, S. 2000. 'A Question of Identity (II)', *The Observer*, 15 October. Retrieved 4 July 2018 from http://www.guardian.co.uk/uk/2000/oct/15/britishidentity. comment1.

Heim, T. (ed). 2017. *Pegida als Spiegel und Projektionsfläche*. Berlin: Springer-Verlag.

Hine, D.C., T.D. Keaton and S. Small (eds). 2009. *Black Europe and the African Diaspora*. Urbana: University of Illinois Press.

Hintjens, H.M. 2007. 'Citizenship under Siege in the Brave New Europe', *European Journal of Cultural Studies* 10(3): 409–14.

Janich, N. 1997. 'Sprachkultivierung', *Muttersprache* 107(1): 76–84.

John, B. 1999. *Who is German*? Washington DC: American Institute for Contemporary German Studies.

Kabis-Alamba, V. 1999. 'Deutsch für alle – nein Danke?' *Die Tageszeitung*, 1 November, 18.

Kamusella, T. 2012. *The Politics of Language and Nationalism in Modern Central Europe*. Basingstoke: Palgrave Macmillan.

Krzyzanowski, M., and R. Wodak. 2011. 'Political Strategies and Language Policies', *Language Policy* 10: 115–36.

Kurthen, H., and M. Minkenberg. 1995. 'Germany in Transition', *Nations and Nationalism* 1(2): 175–96.

Land of Ideas. 2018. 'Laptop and Lederhosen: How Should Germany Present Itself in the Future?'. Berlin: Innovationskraftwerk. Retrieved 4 August 2018 from http://m.innovationskraftwerk.de/Wettbewerb/landderideen/Laptop-und-Lederhosen/Details/24.

Linke, U. 1999. *German Bodies*. New York: Routledge.

_____. 2002. 'Die Sprache als Körper', in Thomas Hauschild and Bernd Jürgen Warneken (eds), *Inspecting Germany*. Münster: LIT Verlag, pp. 290–317.

_____. 2010. 'Fortress Europe', in Jody Berland and Blake Fitzpatrick (eds), *Cultures of Militarization*. Sydney: Cape Breton University Press, pp. 100–20.

_____. 2011. 'Technologies of Othering', in Manuela Ribeiro Sanches et al. (eds), *Europe in Black and White*. Chicago: Intellect/ University of Chicago Press, pp. 123–42.

_____. 2014. 'Gendering Europe, Europeanizing Gender', in Dan Stone (ed.), *Postwar European History*. Oxford: Oxford University Press, pp. 420–42.

Lombardo, E., and P. Meier. 2002. 'Gender Mainstreaming in the EU', *European Journal of Women's Studies* 13(2): 151–66.

Mandel, R. 2008. *Cosmopolitan Anxieties: Turkish Challenges to Citizenship and Belonging in Germany*. Durham, NC: Duke University Press.

Maniar, A. 2016. '(Language) Policing at Europe's Borders', Institute of Race Relations, 23 June. Retrieved 4 July 2018 from http://www.irr.org.uk/news/language-policing-at-europes-borders.

Martin, P.L. 1998. *Germany: Reluctant Land of Immigration*. Baltimore, MD: Johns Hopkins University Press.

Mbembe, A. 2003. 'Necropolitics', *Public Culture* 15(1): 11–40.

McGlynn, C. 2006. *Families and the European Union*. Cambridge: Cambridge University Press.

Merx, A., J. Ruster and Y. Szukitsch. 2013. *Willkommenskultur (und Annerkennungskultur)*. IQ Fachstelle 'Diversity Management', Working Paper 02/2013. Munich: Verband für Interkulturelle Arbeit, Bayern.

Noack, R. 2016. 'Leaked Document Says 2,000 Men Allegedly Assaulted 1,200 German Women on New Year's Eve', *Washington Post*, 11 July. Retrieved 4 July 2018 from https://www.washingtonpost.com/news/worldviews/wp/2016/07/10/leaked-document-says-2000-men-allegedly-assaulted-1200-german-women-on-new-years-eve/?utm_term=.a5e6cbfc573c.

Nölkensmeier, P. 1999. 'Sprachpflege'. *Spiegel Online*, 21 April. Retrieved 4 July 2018 from http://www.spiegel.dc/kultur/gesellschaft/0,1518,18793,00.html.

Olsen, E., and M. Eddy. 2015. 'Europe: Pegida Movement Divides Germany', *New York Times*, 11 February: Retrieved 4 July 2018 from http://www.nytimes.com/2015/02/12/world/europe/pegida-movement-divides-germany.html?_r=0.

Ong, A. 1996. 'Cultural Citizenship as Subject-Making', *Current Anthropology* 37(5): 737–62.

———. 1999. *Flexible Citizenship*. Durham, NC: Duke University Press.

Partridge, D.J. 2012. *Hypersexuality and Headscarves*. Bloomington: Indiana University Press.

Rehberg, K.-S., F. Kunz and T. Schlinzig (eds). 2016. *PEGIDA: Rechtspopulismus zwischen Fremdenangst und 'Wende' – Enttäuschung?* Bielefeld: transcript Verlag.

Rehberg, K.-S. 2016. 'Dresden-Szenen', in K.-S. Rehberg, F. Kunz and T. Schlinzig (eds), *PEGIDA*. Bielefeld: transcript Verlag, pp. 15–33.

Reiher, R., and R. Läzer (eds). 1996. *Von 'Buschzulage' bis 'Ossinachweis'*. Berlin: Taschenbuch Verlag.

Rindler Schjerve R., and E. Vetter (eds). 2012. *European Multilingualism*. Bristol: Multilingual Matters.

Ruf, R. 2000. 'Ausländer: Umstrittenes Integrationsgesetz', *Schwäbisches Tagblatt* 56, 21 July, cover page.

Smith, A.L. 2006. *Colonial Memory and Postcolonial Europe*. Bloomington: Indiana University Press.

Smith, K. 2012. *Fairness, Class and Belonging in Contemporary England*. Basingstoke: Palgrave Macmillan.

Steinhoff, J. 1999. 'Sprach-Störung', *Stern* 36, 2 September, 56–60.

Stone, D. (ed.). 2014. *Postwar European History*. Oxford: Oxford University Press.

Straßner, E. 1995. *Deutsche Sprachkultur*. Tübingen: Niemeyer.

Studer, P., and I. Werlen (eds). 2012. *Linguistic Diversity in Europe*. Berlin: Mouton de Gruyter.

Tagblatt. 1999. 'Staatsbürgerschaftsreform', *Schwäbisches Tagblatt* 55, 18 January, 2.

Thomas, D.H., and K.M. Clarke (eds). 2006. *Globalization and Race*. Durham, NC: Duke University Press.

Ulrich, B. 2015. 'Muslims: The End of Arrogance', *Zeit online*, 24 November, 1–11. Retrieved 4 July 2018 from http://www.zeit.de/2015/47/muslims-islam-west-terrorism.

VDS. 1999. Verein zur Wahrung der deutschen Sprache. Dortmund: Technische Universität Dortmund.

_____. 2018. Verein Deutsche Sprache (German Language Association). Dortmund. Retrieved 10 August 2018 from http://www.vds-ev.de/.

Vorländer, H., M. Herold and S. Schäller. 2016. *PEGIDA: Entwicklung, Zusammensetzung und Deutung einer Empörungsbewegung*. Berlin: Springer-Verlag.

Wacquant, L. 2008. *Urban Outcasts*. Cambridge: Polity Press.

Ware, V. 2008. 'Towards a Sociology of Resentment: A Debate on Class and Whiteness', *Sociological Research Online* 13(5). Retrieved 4 July 2018 from http://www.socresonline.org.uk/13/5/9.html.

Ware, V., and L. Back. 2001. *Out of Whiteness: Color, Politics, and Culture*. Chicago: University of Chicago Press.

Winant, H. 2001. *The World is a Ghetto*. New York: Basic Books.

Wöhrle, C., U. Pape and S. Alscher. 2013. 'Kurzmeldungen – Deutschland: Türkin wird nicht zum Integrationskurs verpflichtet', *Migration & Bevölkerung* 7, 16 September. Retrieved 10 August 2018 from http://www.bpb.de/gesellschaft/migration/newsletter/169178/kurzmeldungen-deutschland.

Worbs, S. 2008. *Die Einbürgerung von Ausländern in Deutschland*. Nuremberg: Bundesamt für Migration und Flüchtlinge.

Chapter 2

Diversity and Unity
Political and Conceptual Answers to Experiences
of Differences and Diversities in Germany

Friedrich Heckmann

> A Catholic priest and a rabbi were attending a banquet. Roast pork was the
> main dish. The priest asked the rabbi: 'when, my dear friend, will you finally
> start enjoying this wonderful dish?' And the rabbi answered: 'at your wedding,
> my dear colleague'.

While teasing one another may be a practical way of dealing with cultural
differences and diversities in private and concerning interpersonal relations, there is a need for political concepts and practices at the higher level
of society. Such political answers to the challenges of diversity in Germany
are the focus of this chapter. The topic of diversity itself is embedded
in a broader discourse on integration and participation of migrants and
minorities. Integration is understood here as the acquisition of full membership of society and the reduction of differences between natives and
migrants regarding life chances and lifestyles.

I work with the hypothesis that integration and participation of
migrants and minorities in the major general institutions of society are
macrosocietal prerequisites for peaceful relations between culturally
diverse groups. Thus, in order to understand intercultural or interethnic
relations, we have to look first at integration policies for inclusion in general institutions, such as the labour market, self-employment possibilities,
welfare and political systems. These have been referred to as 'general integration policies' (Hammar 1985: 9). General integration policies are major
conditions and the background for intercultural or diversity policies that

---

Notes for this chapter begin on page 80.

aim at improving relations between culturally diverse groups by addressing attitudinal, behavioural and institutional changes. While acknowl-
edging the importance of general social integration policies, this chapter
focuses on special policies, i.e. intercultural and diversity policies for relations among groups. Special integration policies, if successful, strengthen
mutual respect among ethnic groups, and contribute to peaceful intergroup relations and the stability of a democratic system.

Supposing and observing that integration and intercultural policies are
successful, the question then arises as to what kind of concepts we might
use to describe this new reality. An attempt to answer this question will be
a second focus of this chapter, where I discuss such concepts, particularly
regarding processes of new nation building. New nation building refers
to a process of systemic integration of constituent groups of nations, in
which new principles of membership acquisition and collective identity
are introduced and practised.

For a more systematic overview that entangles the complex web of diversity policies and its various actors, it is useful to distinguish among different
levels of policies. It is certainly not enough to look at the national level alone.
We have to investigate a range of different authorities and decision-making
bodies from: (1) the EU level; (2) the national level; (3) the regional or Länder
level; (4) and the municipal or local level, as key actors implementing diversity policies. In the first part of this chapter, I describe major developments
regarding each level, focusing on relevant actors and their influence. The
second part discusses conceptual responses to the challenges of new diversity.

Political Responses to Challenges of Diversity

The EU as an Actor in Intercultural Policies

Since the conference of Tampere in 1999, the EU has been taking a stronger
role in the intercultural and integration policies of its Member States.
Directives that have to be transposed into national law are the strong-
est policy instrument that the EU has at its disposal. Directives 2000/43
and 2000/78 have obliged Member States to enact legislation against discrimination, and racial discrimination in particular. To give extra weight
and support to its anti-discrimination policy, the EU established the
Fundamental Rights Agency in 2008, based in Vienna, which monitors
the situation with regard to discrimination in Member States and advises
the European Parliament. Directive 2003/109 guaranteed the right for a
safe-residence status of third-country nationals after five years of legal
residence. A safe-residence status is a prerequisite for integration, since it
enables migrants to plan and organize their future life in the new country.

In 2004, the EU Council of Ministers of Justice and the Interior pro-claimed eleven Basic Principles for the Integration of Immigrants in the European Union. Principle Seven concerns the value of intercultural exchange and dialogue; Principle Eight regards the value of cultural diversity; and Principle Nine supports political participation of migrants. In the following years, among other policies, the EU founded the so-called EU Integration Fund for the fiscal period 2007–13, which supported integration measures and projects in EU countries, many of which have had much relevance for intercultural relations. A part of the funding is distributed by the EU directly and another part by agencies for migration and integration in Member States. The Integration Fund was succeeded by the Asylum, Migration and Integration Fund (AMIF) with even more means. In addition, and starting a long time before the Integration Fund was established, the EU Social Fund supported projects for disadvantaged groups, including migrants. Bendel (2010: 43) estimates that, through a combination of binding directives and various methods of political coor-dination, a process of convergence of integration policies in different Member States has been set in motion. The core influence on this policy field, however, as well as the power to shape particular integration poli-cies, remains in the hands of the EU Member States.

The National Level

In 2001, Germany's federal government set up an independent expert commission to review the state of migration and integration. The so-called Zuwanderungskommission included representatives from the most important groups in German society – business, unions, churches, fed-eration of cities, etc. – and declared in its final document: 'there has been progress regarding the integration of immigrants . . . but there has been no systematic overall strategic approach to the issue, and this has hindered the integration of immigrants. Reflecting today on the necessities of a future integration policy, we should design an overall national concept for integration that serves the needs of the host society as much as the needs of the migrants' (Unabhängige Kommission Zuwanderung 2001: 199). In Germany, the following legal acts and other developments have been important milestones for a new approach to integration and diversity policy affecting intercultural relations: (1) the 2000 Citizenship Law; (2) the 2005 Immigration Law; (3) the 2007 National Integration Plan; (4) the institutionalization of an anti-discrimination policy; (5) the new German Islam Conference; (6) the first chairs for Islamic theology at German uni-versities; and (7) initiatives for the monitoring and evaluation of these political measures.

The Citizenship Law, which was passed in 2000, established the principle of *ius soli* (the right to citizenship based on being born in a certain country) in addition to *ius sanguinis* (the right to citizenship based on descent). The implication of *ius soli* for diversity is that it permits the emergence of new kinds of individual and collective identity: you can now be German without having German parents or grandparents. The introduction of *ius soli* into official definitions of citizenship also affected, and broadened, imaginations of what it means to be German. In combination with the simultaneous reduction of prejudice and racism across society, introducing *ius soli* as a novel way of defining political belonging to the country made possible a more inclusive sense of togetherness and collective identity. In addition, the 2005 Immigration Law not only institutionalized a new kind of systematic integration policy, but also acknowledged once more officially that Germany was a country of immigration (*Einwanderungsland*), whose population has been shaped in significant ways through the experience of migration (see also Foroutan, Chapter 6 in this volume). The law thus also established a new kind of definition of society, framing the immigration process differently. Recognizing migrant organizations as partners and relevant players in intercultural policies has been an important aspect of the so-called national integration plan. Its 2007 version was a coordinated plan for measures of integration by the federal government, sixteen different regional administrations, and representatives of local government and civil society organizations. The partners committed themselves to a certain number of integration measures in their respective fields of competence.

The institutionalization of an anti-discrimination policy was not a national initiative, but started at the EU level. This set of policies included anti-discrimination legislation as well as the creation of a federal anti-discrimination office. Anti-discrimination policy is important for integration, since discrimination hinders the participation of migrants in institutions and social life of the receiving society. Anti-discrimination legislation is not only a signal against discrimination, but opens up legal possibilities for sanctions and compensations. The German Islam Conference, initiated by the Ministry of the Interior in 2006, has sought to define and improve the relations between the state and Islamic organizations. At the same time, the desire to establish a regular format that permits exchanges between politicians, institutions and Muslim civil society actors was an important act of recognizing Islam as a relevant religion in Germany, not only with relevance for Germany's Islamic believers, but also highlighting the important role of Islam for many non-Muslim Germans. Five chairs for Islamic theology have been funded by the federal government at universities in Tübingen, Frankfurt/Gießen, Münster, Osnabrück and

Erlangen-Nürnberg. These acts send out important signals: Islam has become part of Germany.

The Role of Germany's Regions

Germany is a country with a federal system of government, giving much power to the sixteen regions (called *Länder* in German) that constitute it. Regions collect a substantial part of tax revenues and control their own police forces – a reminder of the authority different kingdoms and duchies wielded before the foundation of the modern German nation state in 1871. Another legacy of Germany's origin as a nation state forged out of autonomous states is the regions' almost exclusive competence in matters of education, regarding preschool, school and higher education levels. Since education is also a principal strategy to enhance the participation and social mobility of migrants' descendants, Germany's *Länder* have a major responsibility in integration processes. There has been a range of different schemes to support the children of immigrants in school – such as transition classes for newly arrived children to learn the language, preschool language training and the installation of mentoring systems – but, on the whole, the *Länder* have failed to develop thorough and effective measures to support education and mobility for second-generation immigrants (writing in 2018). Germany's regions have only become more interested in, and committed to, education for migrants and their responsibility to turning schooling into a success in the wake of the Programme for International Student Assessment (PISA), which showed that German educational institutions were particularly ill-equipped to deal with diversity and offer support.

With regard to intercultural policies in a narrower sense, the *Länder* are developing programmes for Islamic religious education in the public school system. Faculties or departments of Islamic theology are educating teachers for religious studies classes in schools. Furthermore, attempts have been made, involving civil society actors, to recruit and train more schoolteachers who also have a migration background. At a lower level, many schools have acted faster than the regional ministries responsible for them: head teachers and others have been willing to recognize and celebrate the cultural diversity of their school population, for instance, by staging the relevant cultural festivals of different groups.

Intercultural relations also feature in the education of police officers, for which regional Interior Ministries are responsible. Within the police, there have been proactive and successful attempts to recruit more staff with migration backgrounds, usually second- or third-generation immigrants. The *Länder* also support local integration projects with public funding.

Some have even appointed regional integration ministers and have passed relevant integrations laws.

The Role of Cities

'Integration happens at the local level.' This has become a frequently heard claim in the wake of the so-called refugee crisis and subsequent political debates in Germany. Many larger cities in Germany, as well as some small- or medium-sized ones, have populations that include up to 40 per cent of people with diverse migration histories.[1] The region of Bavaria in southern Germany serves as a good example: in 2015 in Munich, the regional capital and largest city, 41.4 per cent had a migration background, up from 34 per cent in 2005. In Nuremberg, the second city of Bavaria, the figure for 2015 was even higher, 42.2 per cent, up from 37 per cent in 2005. These figures are similar to Augsburg, the third-largest Bavarian city: in 2005, 35.9 per cent of Augsburgers had a nontraditional German background, but by 2015, the percentage had risen to 43.4. All of these examples share one particular characteristic: the younger the demographic group, the higher the percentage of people with a migration background is. In the future, this number is thus set to increase.

There are numerous municipal or local policies that address intercultural and interethnic relations directly. These include (and are outlined in detail below): (1) the development of local integration concepts; (2) the establishment of relations between cities and migrant organizations; (3) adapting the administration to the needs of migrants and minorities; (4) policies for improving intergroup relations; and (5) policies for improving relations between the police force and minorities.

Most cities in Germany have developed local integration concepts, a so-called *Leitbild*. This framework describes the goals, needs, resources and measures to improve integration. In most cases, an integration concept is not simply devised by the city administration, a research institute or a thinktank, but is collaboratively developed through wide-ranging participation, permitting interested citizens, migrants and non-migrants, civil society organizations including migrant organizations, and the city administration to work together and design a public policy concept that respects expectations and aspirations. The city council serves as a kind of local parliament in German towns and cities. It discusses and votes on intercultural policies and integration measures. With the power to regulate the use of local public funds, the council can decide whether or not a particular department or office should be created to design and execute intercultural policies or whether intercultural policies should be organized as a cross-departmental task – or demand a combination of the two approaches. Funding decisions also have to be taken by the council on larger projects of immigrant integration and support for migrant and minority organizations. This means that the municipal level has enormous political leverage in designing approaches to integration and intercultural activities in a given city or town.

A large majority of cities and towns in Germany have created a special administrative diversity unit, or a department for intercultural affairs within the administration, and have organized these issues as cross-departmental tasks. Relations between city councils and migrant groups can be promoted by extending special membership to migrant representatives in the council or by the creation of a consultative body of migrant organizations. In most town and city councils in Germany, however, the share of people with a migration background in elected positions is rather low and does not in a single case reflect the demographic reality of the local population, even though there has also been a positive trend towards increasing participation. This means that the prime articulation and representation of migrants' interests at the local level still occurs through consultative bodies for migrants and their organizations (and/or organizations that represent only particular ethnic or religious groups). In most towns and cities, relations between local diversity departments and ethnic organizations representing only specific groups are not institutionalized and often informal. The intensity of contacts usually depends on concrete issues that both sides seek to address together. Contacts can be initiated from either the minority organization or the official position. Most municipal authorities in Germany have conducted a mapping process to create lists of migrant and minority organizations to enhance collaboration; they also support them financially, either through direct funding or the provision of resources, such as rooms for meetings or material for their organization. Mayors have considerable political and administrative authority in German towns and cities rather than performing merely representative functions, and are therefore also key players regarding intercultural policies. They control the local administration and can turn intercultural projects and activities into a central priority for its work and outlook. The mayors also have a significant influence on the city, town or municipal councils. Their views and comments are widely debated and recognized as relevant in the local public sphere and media discourses. Through their relative autonomy and ability to prioritize independently, mayors can also design a close link between their offices, on the one hand, and migrant ethnic and religious organizations and their needs and aspirations, on the other.

A further important local power concerns the adaptation of administrations to fit the needs of migrant populations. This process is usually referred to as *interkulturelle Öffnung*, or intercultural opening, and the ensuing focus on a welcoming and open bureaucratic structure. This involves the availability of translation services, the active recruitment of personnel with different migration backgrounds, and adapting regulations for public institutions that affect housing and construction, food, dress codes, sports, slaughtering, burials and others. The development and constant expansion of intercultural competence on the part of administrative staff through special training courses is also part of these policies. Additionally, the improvement of intergroup relations often features importantly on local political agendas. Such policies are often practised in close cooperation with, and following the initiative of, civil society organizations. The following types of policies fall into this category: (1) institutionalized intercultural and interreligious dialogue; (2) intercultural contact schemes; (3) encouragement of migrants' participation in established organizations or voluntary associations; (4) intercultural events; (5) anti-prejudice and anti-discrimination measures and campaigns; and (6) intercultural mediation and public space management. These policies can be summarized as 'policies of recognition' (*Politik der Anerkennung*).

With regard to dialogue and contact schemes, research has shown that they can improve intercultural relations.[2] Intercultural events, such as *Interkulturelle Wochen* (Intercultural Weeks), have a long tradition in Germany; they encompass many kinds of common activities that bring together people from diverse backgrounds, such as sports competitions, music performances, creative arts and political discussions. Cities often engage in anti-discrimination work and organize campaigns against prejudice. The Bavarian city of Nuremberg, for example, is in the midst of organizing such a campaign, inspired by a similar initiative in Barcelona.[3] Urban neighbourhoods and other public spaces, such as markets, parks, institutions – libraries, swimming pools and community centres – and street corners are important locations for encounters and interactions across ethnic and religious groups. Different groups possess different concepts of how such spaces ought to be used and engaged, which can become a source of conflict. A useful method of managing such tensions regards the establishment of mediation services for specific urban neighbourhoods. Conflicts over the use of public spaces often revolve around noise issues, litter and cleanliness, or the permissibility of certain public activities – such as barbeques – in areas that might not, in the eyes of some, be suitable. In many cases, the city administration and migrant organizations can create joint partnership schemes to manage public space more successfully and permit a range of activities to foster understanding and encounter, and reduce conflict.

Regarding urban public policies to improve relations between police and minorities, there are generally three different types that can be distinguished: (1) intercultural training for the police; (2) information for migrants regarding police activity; and (3) institutionalized dialogue between the police and migrant organizations. Gaining intercultural competence helps the police to understand conflict within migrant communities, involving different migrant groups, and among migrant groups and the self-defined 'native' population. Policies aimed at increasing mutual knowledge for both sides have been established and have proven very effective. The work of migrant organizations and civil society actors is also very important in the development of intercultural policies at a local level. Migrant organizations are mostly structured on the basis of a combination of ethnic-national, regional and cultural-religious characteristics, on the one hand, with activities in specific areas, such as education, culture, religion, politics, sports, labour or self-employment, on the other. Examples might include a Spanish parents' organization, an Italian football club, a Turkish Sunni mosque or a Greek cultural association. Depending on their size and level of activity, migrant organizations can play a significant role in the development and shaping of local policies. Activity in migrant organizations also helps to develop communicative and social skills necessary for taking part in democratic processes in society.

Conceptual Responses to Challenges of Diversity

The second part of this chapter examines the role that ethnicity may play in different forms of incorporation of immigrants.[4] We start with the assumption that there is a process of minority formation in the early phases of an incorporation process and we use the term 'immigrant minorities' to describe the sociostructural position of such groups. The concept of minority refers to forms of only partial incorporation. It also stands for a position of disadvantage in society, possibly even subject to discrimination. In addition, 'minority' implies the retention of a particular ethnic identity by the members of a group within the context of immigration. Ethnicity or ethnic identity refers to the shared belief in common descent (Weber 1972: 237) and is characterized by common cultural features and norms of solidarity, and by a definition of membership criteria that delineate boundaries between one's own and other groups (Barth 1969: 15). For groups, ethnicity and ethnic identity are not static, but are shaped by the continuous influence of different forces in the integration process and are therefore subject to change. During the incorporation process, ethnic

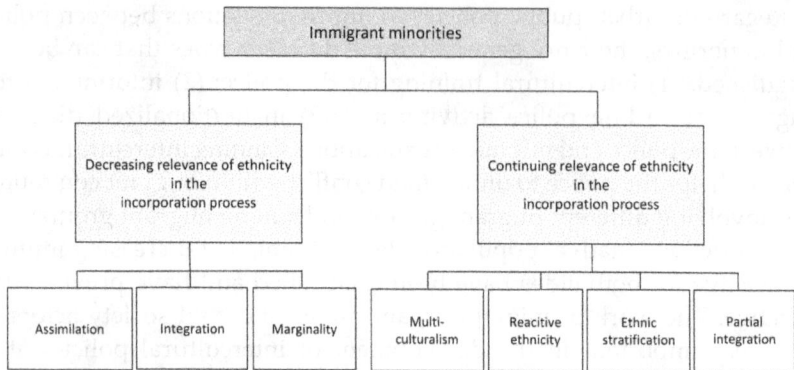

Figure 2.1 Typology of possible outcomes of incorporation of migrants.
© Europäisches Forum für Migrationsstudien (efms), used with permission.

identity may evolve in different ways and with different outcomes. We
have developed a typology for such possible outcomes (Figure 2.1).

The right-hand side in Figure 2.1 symbolizes outcomes in which ethnicity continues to play an important role regarding the incorporation of
migrants. 'Multiculturalism' refers to a political view that sees ethnicity as
a structuring principle for the macro-organization of society, desiring and
describing a reality in which ethnicity continues to play an important role
for the social positioning of the descendants of migrants generations after
the initial arrival. Some political forces in Germany – most notably the
Green Party – have advocated multiculturalism as an ordering concept
for society; others, such as the conservative CDU party, have expressed
strong views against multiculturalism as an organizing principle for
society, while nonetheless supporting cultural and religious diversity.
Multikulti funktioniert nicht – or 'multiculturalism does not work' – became
a popular slogan of conservative groups in the 2010s. In this context,
and among groups that are sceptical of multiculturalist views, one commonly finds references to what are supposed to be unanimously negative experiences of multiculturalism in the Netherlands (Entzinger 2003).
'Reactive ethnicity' is a concept that describes a reaction to discrimination,
a conscious effort to keep one's ethnic identity, while 'ethnic stratification'
refers to ethnicity as a major systematic factor in the process of positioning individuals with regard to unequal societal structures. While there is
only partial evidence for the existence of reactive ethnicity in Germany
(Diehl and Schnell 2006: 811), it seems that paying attention to other factors – length of stay, professional qualification levels and cultural capital –
can more successfully illuminate the positioning of migrants in Germany
than the narrow focus on ethnicity (Esser 2001). The concept of 'partial

integration' – sometimes referred to as 'segmented assimilation' in the American literature (see Portes and Zhou 1993) – describes a process of incorporation and participation for groups in major institutions of society, while they simultaneously manage to retain a strong cultural identity and pattern of ethnic group reproduction. Vietnamese migrants in particular correspond to this pattern in Germany.

The left-hand side of Figure 2.1 illustrates types of incorporation in which ethnicity loses its relevance for the positioning and identity of immigrant groups over time. Assimilation – referring to the complete loss of a specific group identity and characteristics by fully adopting the characteristics and identity of the majority society – is probably a merely theoretical scenario, while 'integration' invokes a mutual adaptation process, during the course of which the so-called receiving society retains its dominant influence, but is reciprocally changed by the process of incorporation of novel cultural views and behaviours. The term 'integration' implies a decrease of perceived differences between migrants and the native population. Assimilation has become a predominantly negatively received counter-concept to integration in German public debate, often associated with the suppression of, and violence against, minorities. However, one school of integration research, led by Hartmut Esser, employs a different scientific concept of assimilation, which is understood as a mutual process in the tradition of Alba and Nee (1999): immigrants also shape the culture of the country in which they settle. This use of the concept often leads to confusing debates in scientific and public discourse whenever its meaning is not clarified. One group of arguments understands assimilation as a one-directional process, while another understands it as a mutual process.

The term 'marginality' is used to describe the situation of a group that has cut relations with its social and cultural descent, but has not managed to acquire membership status of the new society to which it aspires to belong. Until today (2018), however, there does not seem to exist a body of systemic empirical research that uses the concept in Germany. Nonetheless, one notable study used the concept of marginality to examine and analyse the radicalization process of Islamist terrorists from Germany who attacked the World Trade Center in New York on 11 September 2001 (Heckmann 2004).

Integration and New Nation Building in Present-Day Germany

In 2015–16, Germany experienced a significant influx of asylum seekers of over one million people. Some of these will ultimately return to the countries from which they escaped, but a majority are likely to stay.

It can be expected that these groups will form minority structures on the basis of ethnicity. From the point of view of sociostructural analysis, one particular important question remains: how will migrant groups that have been in the country for several generations react? Will they retain a minority status? Are they now in a transition period to something different that is still unknown? Indicators show that, over time, the main trend in the incorporation process of migrants in Germany is integration. Studies have found that there is a positive correlation between length of stay in a country, on the one hand, and the degree and kind of integration individuals experience, on the other (Diehl und Schnell 2006). Diehl and Schnell have also shown that the second generation is generally more successfully integrated than the first. Furthermore, in relation to indicators of structural, cultural, social and identity integration, differences are decreasing between native population groups and those with a migration background (Berliner Institut für Bevölkerung und Migration 2014; Lutz and Heckmann 2010).

The model represents three levels of explanation (macro, meso and micro) and identifies major influences on integration and their interrelationships. Arrow 1 illustrates that openness and support are necessary conditions for successful integration at the macrolevel. This indicates that, for a growing number of people from a range of migration backgrounds, social and economic positions, as well as levels of participation, are decreasingly determined by their origin. The arrow is also interrupted because influence does not happen in a direct, but an indirect way. Structures cannot act; only individuals can do so. The explanation of successful integration

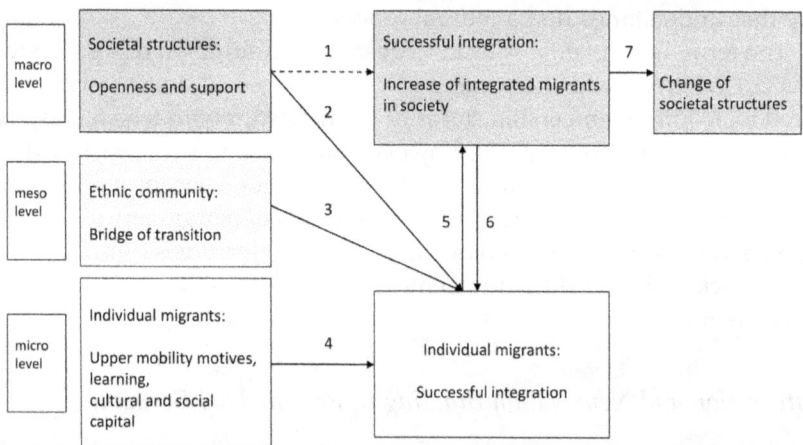

Figure 2.2 The explanation of successful integration. © Europäisches Forum für Migrationsstudien (efms), used with permission.

on a macrosocietal level can only exist as the combined result of many individual integration processes. Therefore, individual integration has to be explained first of all. Arrow 2 shows that openness and support enable individuals to develop and apply their competences for participation in the major institutions of society. Arrow 3 indicates that ethnic community structures support integration when they promote an early adaptation process, but that they hinder integration when they block the development of relations beyond the ethnic community. Arrow 4 illustrates the individual motivations, learning abilities and skills that support integration. An aggregation process is represented by arrow 5, whereas arrow 6 reflects how an increase in individual integration stories develops into a self-perpetuating trend, since these experiences encourage other individuals to follow such examples.

On the macrolevel, these processes result in a change of population structures. A range of individuals and groups, incorporated into a new collective, constitute the emergent society type. Individual backgrounds, however, do not simply disappear, but merge with the existing social groups and identities and structures into an emergent reality of society (arrow 7). I suggest calling this a process of new nation building. Yet, this process happens within the larger context of globalization and in interaction with Europeanization. Nation is a concept for a large-scale institution, a legal body organized as a state, with membership criteria and a collective sense of identity, what Germans call *Wirgefühl*, or 'we-feeling'. This *Wirgefühl* is of an 'imagined community' (Anderson 1991), and not of a real one, since nations are usually too large in scale to make it possible for all members to know one another.

New nation building implies that novel membership criteria develop and that the definition of collective identity changes. The 2000 German Citizenship Law involved a change: from a more strictly ethnonational concept to that of a republican vision of collective belonging. One can be a German without being of German descent. This republican nation is still also a nation defined by descent, but shared values have been added as a major constitutive principle for nation building. This process of new nation building is not evolving without opposition from nationalist ideologies and movements. These have been mobilized and gained support in 2015–16, during the so-called refugee crisis, expressed through hate speech against immigrants in the social media as well as through actual physical attacks on shelters or reception centres. The populist Alternative for Germany (AfD), which made significant gains in the 2017 national parliamentary elections, is a product of this development. However, support for the new concept of collective identity is also growing across society. While – in somewhat simplified terms – nationalist and racist ideologies find support among people who suffer from downward mobility and/or have little experience with intercultural contact, society's elites and the educated middle classes generally are open for developing a new definition of collective belonging. The hesitation among many authors and parts of the public to identify these processes as nation building results from the long period of 'denationalization' in Germany after the Second World War, which has for some time delegitimized the concept of the 'nation'. In terms of a social scientific analysis, however, support for the idea of the nation and for processes of nation building are societal realities. While, in many parts of the world, nation building is concerned with efforts aimed at overcoming the loyalties of tribe and clan, and with the aftereffects of artificial colonial boundary drawing, immigration and integration set the agenda for nation building in Germany and other new immigration countries in Europe. Integration and nation building take time, often generations. The new republican concept of the nation, and the many efforts regarding integration and diversity policies in Germany described above help to create a conflictual, yet productive, symbiosis of unity and diversity in the process of nation building.

Friedrich Heckmann is Emeritus Professor of Sociology and Director of the European Forum for Migration Studies at the University of Bamberg, Germany. His research interests include migration, interethnic relations, integration, socialization, Germany's social structure and sociological theory. He is the founder of the research committee 'Migration and Ethnic Minorities' in the German Sociological Society. He has served as a policy adviser and expert consultant on migration and integration for the EU, the German Parliament, the German federal government, regional governments, cities and nongovernmental organizations. He heads the Expert Forum at the Federal Office for Migration and Refugees.

Notes

1. See for the following Lüken-Klaßen and Heckmann (2010).
2. See, for example, Wagner and van Dick (2001).
3. The city of Barcelona has initiated an 'anti-gossip programme'. Volunteers participate in a course that explores the roots of prejudice as well as anti-prejudice measures to enable them to interfere in everyday life situations and argue against stereotypical statements and feelings.
4. 'Incorporation' is used here as a concept that is more general than 'integration', which refers to a form of incorporation according to the typology in Figure 2.1. For an extensive discussion of the concept of integration, cf. Heckmann (2015: 69–84).

References

Alba, Richard D., and Victor Nee. 1999. 'Rethinking Assimilation Theory', in Charles Hirschman, Phillip Kasinitz and Joshua DeWind (eds), *The Handbook of International Migration: The American Experience*. New York: Russell Sage Foundation, pp. 137–67.

Anderson, Benedict. 1991. *Imagined Communities: Reflections on the Origin and Spread of Nationalism*. London: Verso.

Barth, Fredrik. 1969. *Ethnic Groups and Boundaries: The Social Organisation of Culture Difference*. Oslo: Universitetforlaget.

Bendel, Petra. 2010. *Integrationspolitik der Europäischen Union. Gutachten im Auftrag des Gesprächskreises Migration und Integration der Friedrich-Ebert-Stiftung*. WISO Diskurs Bonn, October.

Berliner Institut für Bevölkerung und Migration. 2014. 'Neue Potenziale. Zur Lage der Integration in Deutschland'. Retrieved 8 July 2018 from http://www.berlin-institut.org/fileadmin/user_upload/Neue_Potenziale.

Diehl, Claudia, and Rainer Schnell. 2006. '"Reactive Ethnicity" or "Assimilation"? Statements, Arguments, and First Empirical Evidence for Labour Migrants in Germany', *International Migration Review* 40(4): 786–816.

Esser, Hartmut. 2001. *Integration und ethnische Schichtung*. Mannheimer Zentrum für Europäische Sozialforschung, Working Papers (40).

Entzinger, Han. 2003. 'The Rise and Fall of Dutch Multiculturalism'. Presentation at the *Migration – Citizenship – Ethnos. Incorporation Regimes in Germany, Western Europe and North America Conference*, Toronto, 2–4 October.

Hammar, Thomas. 1985. *European Immigration Policy: A Comparative Study*. Cambridge: Cambridge University Press.

Heckmann, Friedrich. 2004. 'Islamische Milieus: Rekrutierungsfeld für islamistische Organisationen?', in Bundesministerium des Inneren (eds), *Extremismus in Deutschland: Erscheinungsformen und aktuelle Bestandsaufnahme*. Berlin: BMI, pp. 273–90.

_____. 2015. *Integration von Migranten: Einwanderung und neue Nationenbildung*. Wiesbaden: Springer.

Kommunaler Qualitätszirkel. 2014. *Einblicke – Rückblicke – Ausblicke*. Stuttgart.

Lüken-Klaßen, Doris, and Friedrich Heckmann. 2010. *Intercultural Policies in European Cities*. Dublin: European Foundation for the Improvement of Living and Working Conditions.

Portes, Alejandro, and Min Zhou. 1993. 'Segmented Assimilation and its Variants', *Annals of the American Academy of Political and Social Science* 530: 74–96.

Unabhängige Kommission Zuwanderung. 2001. *Zuwanderung gestalten, Integration fördern*. Berlin.

Wagner, Ulrich, and Rolf van Dick. 2001. 'Fremdenfeindlichkeit "in der Mitte der Gesellschaft": Phänomenbeschreibung, Ursachen, Gegenmaßnahmen', *Zeitschrift für Politische Psychologie* 9: 41–54.

Weber, Max. 1972. *Wirtschaft und Gesellschaft. Grundriss der verstehenden Soziologie*. Tübingen: Mohr, Studienausgabe.

Chapter 3

Jews, Muslims and the Ritual Male Circumcision Debate

Religious Diversity and Social Inclusion in Germany

Gökce Yurdakul

On 7 May 2012, a German regional court in Cologne ruled that the specific case of a male circumcision that had gone wrong was a form of bodily harm (*Körperverletzung*). Although both Muslim and Jewish families circumcise infant boys as a religious practice, the Cologne court found that a child's 'fundamental right to bodily integrity' superseded the religious rights of parents. This potentially placed Muslim and Jewish parents under suspicion of causing bodily harm to their children. After a heated public debate, international political pressure and a speedy legal process, a new national law permitting the ritual circumcision of male children addressed the regional court's ruling. Despite this piece of legislation, male circumcision continues to be a highly contested issue in Germany. On 7 May 2015, thirty-five civil society organizations held a rally in Cologne for 'genital autonomy', calling for a ban on ritual male circumcision. The practice continues to be an integral part of Jewish and Muslim lives in Germany, existing in the shadow of political and legal challenges.

In this chapter, I examine the role of the German debate on ritual male circumcision in shaping perceptions and practices of religious diversity. Although religious diversity has been defined in multiple ways, ranging from demographic description of a society to institutional recognition of religious minority groups, I focus on the aspect of social inclusion of religiously diverse groups in institutional settings (Bouma et al. 2010; Vertovec and Wessendorf 2006). I highlight emerging relations between two religious minority groups who make claims to the German state

---

Notes for this chapter begin on page 96.

authorities in order to practise ritual male circumcision – an act that challenges the norms of German society.

As a key aspect of social inclusion, religious diversity is undergoing contested changes through minority and immigrant claims for religious accommodation (Koopmans 2013; Vertovec and Wessendorf 2006). The impact of religious diversity with regard to the social cohesion of Western European nations has been widely debated in politics and the media, without any conclusion concerning the question of whether or not religious diversity causes the disintegration of societies. What is clear is that Muslim and Jewish practices challenged European legal orders. This chapter explores a specific challenge, encapsulated by the male circumcision debate in Germany. I argue that the changes introduced by diversity are best understood through an analysis of Muslim and Jewish claims to practise their respective religions, exploring how these claims get taken up in public debate. Jews and Muslims in Germany have previously collaborated in putting forward claims regarding religious practices, such as highlighting the parallel dynamics of anti-Semitism and anti-Muslim racism in Germany. This does not mean, however, that both communities collaborate on religious diversity claims. Jews and Muslims in Germany also have important faultlines, which divide both groups, as I have elaborated elsewhere (Yurdakul 2010).

Through a discourse analysis of political debates, newspaper reports, focus group interviews with Muslim men and meetings[1] with key actors in public discussions, I show that religious diversity debates are a litmus test for social inclusion: how can societies include minority groups if their religious practices come into conflict with the norms of the majority? The decisive point here is whether or not minority groups are considered to be 'full members' or 'foreigners' in a given society. In this context, I suggest that Muslim and Jewish groups are both objects of social inclusion policies and active participants in negotiating religious diversity, thereby playing both passive and active roles in the shaping of a socially inclusive German society.

These passive and active roles of minorities in shaping German society inform each other. Minorities fulfil specific roles, which Michal Bodemann calls 'ideological labour' (1991). Bodemann shows that Jews who returned to Germany fulfilled specific ideological labour after the Second World War in the construction of minority identities. Following Bodemann, I argue that while legal challenges remain with regard to the religious practices of Jews and Muslims, these groups also fulfil the ideological labour of marking a multicultural way of life, a cosmopolitan and socially inclusive German society. This is their active role. However, Jews and Muslims also have a passive role as subjects of legal cases and negative media attention, which I illustrate in the case of circumcision. These passive and active roles are important to demonstrate how minorities can simultaneously belong and not belong to Germany. They belong as the cosmopolitan face of Germany, while they do not belong since their practices can still be contested in court and public life. In this context, being circumcised – or not – becomes a marker of belonging or nonbelonging.

Who Has the Right to Decide on the Limits of Religious Diversity?

Political and legal authorities establish institutional arrangements in order to accommodate religious diversity (Bramadat and Koenig 2009; Giordan 2014). The regulation of religious diversity often occurs in a top-down manner, such as through government policies. Furthermore, legal institutions – for example, national and European courts – play an important role in establishing what kinds of practices of religious diversity are permissible in the European public sphere (Greenfield 2013; Koenig 2007). However, religious groups, in this case Jews and Muslims in Germany, also challenge legal interpretations or regulations in their everyday lives (Kastoryano 2002; Laurence 2001; Peck 1998). Despite the top-down legal decision-making process, many Jewish and Muslim groups may continue practising their religion and, as a result, they may be excluded from certain social institutions and areas of the labour market. For Muslims, this includes women who choose to wear the headscarf being excluded from jobs in many educational institutions, for example (Korteweg and Yurdakul 2014).

Stigmatization of Jews and Muslims

Ritual male circumcision is the practice of removing the foreskin of a newborn or prepubescent male child (Gollaher 2000), and is a practice mainly associated with Jewish and Muslim religious traditions. The political significance of the ritual stems in part from the fact that it is irreversible. As some legal, political and medical authorities and scholars argue, it therefore ought to be considered a major infringement on a child's rights to bodily integrity (Schüklenk 2012). While circumcision is a practice that affects minority religious groups in many European countries, social service agencies, legal institutions and other state-related institutions, such as hospitals, have a limited understanding of the practice itself. For many such social actors, circumcision is often understood as a sign of cultural backwardness – and in some cases even as an act of violence against children. Such views of circumcision as evidence of violence and backwardness – rather than as a contested faith-based practice, for example – are produced by reifying minority cultures as monolithic traditions marked by their inherent ignorance of a child's wellbeing (Benatar 2013; Lang 2013).

Scholars have examined the body politics of Jewish histories across Europe. Sander Gilman discusses the stigmatization of the Jewish body through medical constructions in *The Jew's Body* (1991). He explains how the rhetoric of modern science marks the Jewish body as different. He also shows how modern medicine, as a discursive agent of the secular authorities, stigmatizes the Jewish body by reducing it to its parts (such as the infamous Jewish nose) and describing it as deviant from 'the norm'. Law and medical sciences distil and embody non-Muslim and non-Jewish values, i.e. those of Christian or, at least, liberal Christian values. Similarly, the Muslim body politics in Western Europe, for example in France, Germany or the Netherlands, concerns how Muslim bodies are marked as different and are excluded from the Western European public sphere (Korteweg and Yurdakul 2014; Lettinga and Saharso 2014). Drawing on analyses of Jewish and Muslim bodies, I aim to show how discursive agents, such as legal authorities, news-makers and key political stakeholders, try to shape minority bodies in Europe. I will focus on two major areas where secular discourse prevails, namely, science and law. These are highly influential in setting limits to religious diversity and social inclusion into German society.

This chapter draws on an ongoing research project on male circumcision in Germany and contributes to scholarly discussions about ritual male circumcision among legal scholars, bioethicists and sociologists. I argue that many legal scholars fail to appreciate the perspectives of minorities, and instead simplify debates about rights and obligations (Merkel and Putzke 2013). Criminalizing religious practices through law enables governing authorities to gain greater control over minority religious practices. This focus on legal aspects prevents us from understanding the performative effects of religious diversity. In other words, I suggest that we look at how the law affects people rather than just consider law in books. In this chapter, then, while I examine the German court decision of 2012, I also delve into how social actors have discussed the outcomes of the legal case. In addition, my analysis of the circumcision debate considers factors such as Jewish history in Germany as a potentially important contextual factor that affected the decision-making process in 2012.[2]

In drawing on this contextual framework as a sociologist, I focus on the majority–minority power relations and on the interrelations between the two minority religious groups in this debate. I do this by reconstructing how key stakeholders talk to each other in the public sphere by referring to their own political positions. Exploring these two groups permits an examination of how they interact with each other in terms of making claims to the German state. This analysis offers us a new perspective that would not be reflected in the state–minority relational analysis. In the following, I discuss the historical context of the circumcision debates and link them to current media and political controversies. My fieldwork in public discussions, focus group interviews and meetings with key stakeholders shows how religious diversity is discussed within minority groups and how various discourses frame the topic.

Historical Context

The 2012 circumcision debate in Germany was not the first debate on religious diversity within the German context. There have been many such throughout history in relation to the particular traditions of Jews in Germany (Judd 2007; Kokin 2014; Lavi 2009). With the incoming flux of immigrants from Muslim countries (most notably Turkish immigrants) and their eventual settlement in postwar Germany, debates on religious practices, such as that concerning ritual slaughtering (Lavi 2009)[3] as well as that on ritual male circumcision (Yurdakul 2013),[4] were re-ignited. As we shall see, the stigmatization of minorities remains a constant in these discussions, regardless of the specific outcome of the discussions.

The history of debates around circumcision prior to the 2012 law has been detailed in *Contested Rituals* by the historian Robin Judd (2007). Judd describes the political and social circumstances of Jewish life in Germany, and illuminates exclusionary approaches found in the writings of German scholars since the turn of the nineteenth to the twentieth century. These writings have stigmatized Jewish ritual behaviour for centuries, from defaming their masculinities to denouncing ritual practices as barbarism (Judd 2007; see also Heil and Kramer 2013). Although this debate on circumcision took place in another sociopolitical period (in the nineteenth century) it is interesting to see that some of the political actors (medical doctors, state attorneys and Jewish community leaders) and the theme (circumcision ban) similarly took centre stage. In terms of stigmatization, Judd quotes the example of a ritual male circumcision case in Baden in 1881. The state medical examiner, E. Sausheim, argued that the *mohel* (circumciser) should be suspended and oral suction (*metistsah be'peh*) outlawed (Judd 2007: 1–2).

The use of science and law to exclude Jewish religious practices has been pointed out in Sander Gilman's essay in *Haut Ab!*, the Jewish Museum's temporary exhibition catalogue on ritual male circumcision (2014–15). Gilman states that '[n]o medical circumcision discussion had been independent from an ideological perspective' (2014: 123, my translation) and points to the variety of unproven allegations about positive and negative effects of circumcision, ranging from it being a cure for syphilis, cervical cancer or even HIV, or it leading to sexual impotence (see also Stehr 2012). Gilman concludes that what is decisive in these debates are questions of cultural acceptance (Gilman 2014). This, it is perhaps not surprising that arguments for the abandoning of ritual male circumcision have sometimes been part of assimilatory efforts by Jews themselves, such as in 1843 in Frankfurt, when a liberal group of Jews, including Rabbi Abraham Geiger, who was the leading figure of Reform Judaism in Germany, argued that it was barbaric and should therefore cease (Gollaher 2000; see also Dobbernack (2016) on the civilization debate).

Muslim immigrant integration and the criminalization of Muslims mark a shift in the current debates. Sander Gilman asks why ritual circumcision returned to the political agenda in recent years in Germany and even beyond, including in Scandinavian countries or in Britain. He argues that a major reason is 'fear of Islamization' (Gilman 2014: 125), circumcision becoming a renewed focus as Muslims struggle to be included into German life and as some journalists and politicians argue that Islam is not compatible with German society.

Methodology

The data for this chapter have been collected from various media resources, legal documents, participant observations, meetings with key stakeholders and focus groups. The legal data were collected from court decisions and press releases of the Cologne local and regional courts (Amtsgericht and Landgericht), and from the website of the German Ethics Council.

The media data are from three German newspapers that spanned the political spectrum, from the beginning of the legal circumcision debate on 26 June 2012 to 31 December 2014, when the circumcision debate continued on a smaller scale. I collected all articles that discussed 'circumcision' from online archives, excluding those regarding female circumcision or circumcision debates in non-Western countries to refine the sample.[5] The German newspaper data were collected from three major sources: *Süddeutsche Zeitung* (SZ), *Tageszeitung* (taz) and *Frankfurter Allgemeine Zeitung* (FAZ). I chose these three newspapers in order to cover the political spectrum in the German media. *SZ* appeals to a left-liberal readership, *FAZ* is a conservative newspaper and *taz* is a left-leaning newspaper, which captures the perspectives of the Green party.[6] For all these newspapers, I created a chronology of events, which documented what was discussed in each newspaper on a weekly basis. In addition to the systematic data collection from these German daily newspapers, I also used newspaper articles from *Jüdische Allgemeine*,[7] a weekly newspaper of the Jewish Central Council; *Der Spiegel*, a popular weekly magazine; *Die Zeit*, a highbrow weekly newspaper; and the European edition of the Turkish national newspaper *Hürriyet*.

In addition to media data, the study also includes data from a focus group and four meetings with key stakeholders. The focus group participants were four Turkish Sunnite Muslim men, all of whom reside in Germany.[8] All of these men were circumcised as children either in Turkey or in Germany, and they discussed how they had been affected by the circumcision debate. I also met with key informants who were active in the circumcision debate: Ilhan Ilkilic, a medical doctor and member of the German Ethics Council that drafted the circumcision law; Mustafa Yeneroğlu, a lawyer and the former head of the Islamic Community of Milli Görüş, who politically supported the legal case of male circumcision in Germany; and Zulfükar Çetin, the coauthor of the controversial book on circumcision, *Interventionen gegen die deutsche 'Beschneidungsdebatte'* (*Interventions against the German 'Circumcision Debate'*). This book was cited frequently in the German circumcision debate in order to illuminate the perspective of the minority men concerned. A further informant for this research was Felicitas Heimann-Jelinek, the curator of the Jewish Museum exhibition on circumcision, whom I interviewed in December 2014.

Social Inclusion, Exclusion and Religious Diversity

The centre point of the circumcision debate was the Cologne regional court's decision on 7 May 2012, which criminalized Jewish and Muslim parents for causing bodily harm to their children. The German public was divided into two polarized groups. Those who were in favour of the ban on circumcision argued their case on the grounds that circumcision is irreversible and irreparable, that it entails a child losing a healthy part of his body, that surgery is inherently risky and dangerous, and that acting upon the body of a child violates his self-determination. As such, it should only be permitted in those cases in which it is medically necessary. Those against the ban argued that the exercise of parental care of § 1627 I BGB (German Civil Code) covers the parents' decisions as long as they benefit the wellbeing of the child. They also maintained that preventing circumcision would mean that parents could not pass on their values and beliefs to their children, that an uncircumcised child would be excluded from his religious group and thus that his wellbeing would be at risk. As my discourse analysis showed, the idea of the 'child's wellbeing' was used by both sides, with both using it in only vaguely defined ways, sometimes phrased as a 'child's right to bodily integrity' or 'a child's right to self-determination'. For example, in its legal decision, the Cologne Regional Court concluded that:

> Neither is the request of the parents capable of justifying the act, since the right of the parents to raise their child in their religious faith does not take precedence over the right of the child to bodily integrity and self-determination. Consequently, the parental consent to the circumcision is considered to be inconsistent with the wellbeing of the child. (Landgericht Köln, 151 Ns 169/11)[9]

In this legal statement, 'children's wellbeing' is constructed through an individualistic understanding of the child, isolated from the parental social context, which is shaped by the status of minorities.[10] In a similar logic, the medical doctor Matthias Franz, an opponent of circumcision, argued that 'in this context, religious freedom cannot be a justification for (sexual) violence against young boys, who are unable to consent' (*FAZ*, 21 July 2012). In this case, the German legal and medical authorities, rather than Jewish and Muslim parents, decide on behalf of a child who cannot give consent. In other words, the child's wellbeing is regarded as best decided by the state authorities. One such argument along these lines is that circumcision is a form of stigmatization of children, since they cannot reverse the operation. The Cologne court's judgement elaborated:

> Moreover, the circumcision changes the child's body permanently and irreparably. This change runs contrary to the interests of the child in deciding his religious affiliation independently later in life. On the other hand, the parental right of education is not unacceptably diminished by requiring them to wait until their son is able to make the decision himself of whether or not to have a circumcision as a visible sign of his affiliation to Islam. (Court decision from 7 May 2012; Landgericht Köln, 151 Ns. 169/11)

The marking of the body in a way that indicates belonging to Islam or Judaism is further interpreted as stigmatization: 'This is also a way of preventing a threatening stigmatization of the child' (court decision from 21 September 2011; Amstgericht Köln, 528 Ds 30/11). The argument of criminal law scholar Holm Putzke in a paragraph in which he discussed the importance of context in deciding in the child's best interest, stated that: 'For the more frequently boys are not circumcised, the less this condition will give reason for stigmatization' (2008: 21). In other words, as fewer parents circumcise, their children being uncircumcised will face less stigma. This ignores the problem that it positions Muslim and Jewish parents as responsible for the stigmatization of their children and their exclusion from German society.

Even before 2012, however, there had been anti-circumcision arguments, even made by immigrant political actors. The Turkish-German sociologist and Islam-critic Necla Kelek, for example, brought up the issue during a German Islam Conference – a gathering organized by the Ministry for the Interior, bringing together leaders of Muslim civil society organizations and politicians – and also highlighted what she regards as the potential harm of ritual male circumcision in her book *Die verlorenen Söhne* (Kelek 2006, translated as *Lost Sons*). She was, however, only in favour of banning Muslim circumcision. The Jewish practice, according to her, is based on religion and therefore should be permitted, whereas the Muslim is 'a tradition' (*fard*) rather than a religious obligation and therefore could be done away with. In this way, Kelek argued that only religious practices should be legally permitted in Germany, disregarding other arguments that might be made, including that of a child's wellbeing.

The German media were divided in the debate. German newspapers, such as *FAZ* and *Die Welt*, or weeklies, such as *Der Spiegel*, were quick to publish photos of rabbis practising circumcision ceremonies. They used provocative headlines, such as 'Ritual, Trauma, Kindeswohl' ('Ritual, Trauma and Child Wellbeing'), 'Auch die Seele leidet' ('The Soul Also Suffers') and 'Freiheit ist wichtiger als Tradition' ('Freedom is More Important than Tradition'). Anti-ban viewpoints also featured mostly in editorial pieces for minority newspapers, such as *Jüdische Allgemeine*, which published a piece on the necessity of having a national law, 'Together for Circumcision: Jews and Muslims Demand Legal Security' (Neumann 2012). *Hürriyet* used the headline 'We Will Not Circumcise' (Tosun 2012), addressing speculation that many Turks in Germany may take their sons to Turkey in order to be circumcised. The Central Council of Jews in Germany, and the Islamic Council of Germany, reacted immediately, basing their arguments in different social and historical interpretations. Ali Kizilkaya, the then Chairman (*Vorsitzender*) of the Islamic Council, drew on integration debates and argued that Cologne court's pro-ban decision undermined Muslims efforts to integrate into German society. Dieter Graumann, the then Chairman of the Central Council of Jews in Germany, argued that this decision made Jewish life in Germany impossible. Although the court's decision was about the specific case of a Muslim boy, politicians and pundits soon focused on the implications for Jewish circumcision in Germany, with central figures of the Jewish community in Germany, as well as the Chief Rabbi from Israel, commenting on the case. News-makers in the European edition of *Hürriyet* were not as concerned about the decision, perhaps because Turkish communities in Germany had faced similar bans in the past, such as calls for a prohibition of the headscarf among public employees. The circumcision issue carried second- or third-rate importance in their reporting. Some reporters mentioned that families might travel outside Germany, such as to Turkey, to carry out circumcisions if the practice were to be banned in Germany.

At the same time, there were opponents of the ban who were not represented in the media. In particular, social workers supporting Muslim communities in Berlin lamented their exclusion from the debate. Although they came from migrant families and had face-to-face contact with many Muslim families as part of their job, their views were not sought out by journalists and so went unheard. In my meeting with Zülfukar Çetin, a social scientist in Berlin, he reported that no one had asked the youth in Berlin's multicultural Kreuzberg district about their thoughts, even though they were the subjects of this debate. In an article coauthored with Alexander Salih Wolter, he pointed out that the debate polarized men into two groups: circumcised and uncircumcised. This created two masculinities in competition with each other. Furthermore, they argued that the so-called 'Judaeo-Christian tradition of the West' was in effect referring to Jewish traditions as crimes and therefore was being anti-Semitic (Çetin and Wolter 2013). Çetin and Wolter argued that, as the circumcision debate most dramatically showed, both Jews and Muslims were excluded from being full members of German society due to their religious practices.

Another key actor in the debates was the German Ethics Council (*Ethikrat*), a government agency responsible for making recommendations for drafting the 2012 circumcision law. The Ethics Council adopted an anti-ban position and made suggestions to the legal authorities on how to draft new circumcision legislation. In a meeting with Ilhan Ilkilic, a medical doctor and member of the German Ethics Council, for him, religious freedom is a more important liberal value than the bodily integrity of children (see also Ilkilic 2014).[11] According to the Ethics Council's suggestions for regulating male circumcision, religious circumcisers should only be allowed to practise circumcision up until the eighth day after birth, after which medical personnel would be responsible. The German Parliament approved the Ethics Council's draft legislation. With this law, Muslim and Jewish practices became lawful. As such, it seemed that Muslims and Jews were being religiously and socially included in Germany. One member of the Ethics Council, however, Reinhard Merkel, opposed the law. He argued that it resulted in a situation in which there was no obligation to take the child's consent and no obligation for anaesthesia (*Die Zeit*, 1 October 2012). Merkel had previously pointed out the ethical, legal and historical problems of the decision, claiming that 'no right to freedom permits an interference with a human body. This is also true for circumcision in boys. And yet the case is difficult' (*SZ*, 30 August 12, my translation).

As he highlighted, Jewish history in Germany played an important role in passing the decision:

> If an unknown religious group were to come to Germany today with the ritual of male circumcision, common in no other place of the world, it would be prohibited on the spot. And if it were solely Muslim religious practice, the Bundestag certainly would not have responded to the Cologne judgment with a resolution as on 19 July. But circumcision is an ancient custom and constitutive of Judaism. And that's the real problem of legal policy. Hiding this fact is useless, because only this origin illuminates the real significance. The most terrible mass murder in history shapes German politics and established a prominent and unique duty to show particular sensitivity to all Jewish matters. This cannot be changed. Circumcision is obviously a matter of particular importance. (*SZ*, 30 August 2012, my translation)

Merkel's argument that it is German awareness of historical responsibility towards the Jewish minority that allowed the law to pass demonstrates that Jews and Muslim are still not considered part of German society, but are seen as outsiders on account of their religious practices. He implies that such practices could not belong to German society under ordinary circumstances. As Sander Gilman has shown, cultural acceptance of religious practices is the decisive factor in social inclusion (2014). In this case, the Jewish and Muslim ritual of male circumcision remains a practice contested by the legal and political authorities, despite the fact that it can be legally practised in Germany.

The debate spread to the international media, with the importance given to the debate, especially in Israel and Turkey, varying markedly. In the Israeli daily newspaper *Haaretz*, the circumcision debate was a daily discussion. The Chief Rabbi of Israel, Yona Metzger, came to Germany to discuss the issue with politicians and to hold an official press conference. He addressed the national and international media to warn against anti-Semitism in Germany (*taz*, 21 August 2012). Similarly, Israel's President, Shimon Peres, sent a letter to his German counterpart, Joachim Gauck, and asked him to intervene to safeguard the religious rights of Jews in Germany (*SZ*, 25 August 2012). In Turkey, by contrast, the possible ban on circumcision did not find much political resonance, with little more being reported than the fact that Turkish citizens carried out some independent campaigns to protest against the legal ruling (Tosun in *Hürriyet*, 29 June 2012).

Germany's Chancellor Angela Merkel personally followed the circumcision debate, infamously commenting: 'I do not want Germany to be the only country in the world where Jews cannot practise their rituals. Otherwise, we turn into a laughing stock [*Komikernation*].'[12] The statement showed her support for passing the circumcision law without causing more damage to Germany's international reputation (*FAZ*, 17 July 2012). Just before the law was passed, Merkel paid a political visit to the Central Council of Jews in Frankfurt, where she highlighted that Germany would defend religious tolerance (*FAZ*, 25 November 2012). On 12 December 2012, approximately six months after the debate had started in Cologne, Germany's federal parliament adopted the proposed law explicitly permitting male circumcision to be performed under certain conditions (§ 1631(d) as part of the German Civil Code (BGB)), making ritual male circumcision a lawful religious practice in Germany.

A One-Way Street: Inclusion into a Minority, but Exclusion from a Majority

As the political scientist Kerem Öktem mentions in his study 'Signals from the Majority Society' – for which he interviewed Jews, Muslims and Germans on the circumcision debate – both Jewish and Muslim interviewees clearly stated that they felt excluded from European societies as their religious practice and male bodies are criminalized and stigmatized (2013). In fact, in a focus group interview that we conducted with four religious Turkish and Sunnite Muslim men, we also heard many times that their circumcised male body was an integral part of their minority identity (see also Kokin 2014). For example, in the group interview, Ali (pseudonym) told us that 'being circumcised is a form of belonging. It is a part of being a man'. Similarly, Tarik (another psuedonym) mentioned that he would find it shameful if a man were not circumcised. Our focus group participants discussed how being circumcised is an in-group identity marker for a minority group in Germany that is striving to belong. This finding was also evident in other public testimonials by Turkish men, such as the coleader of the Green Party and a prominent politician of Turkish background, Cem Özdemir, who has likewise explained that his relationship with his body gives him in-group recognition and a sense of belonging (2008: 235–38).

A key finding in our focus group was that circumcision practices were part of shared identity markers among Muslim and Jewish groups, and that this could bring the groups together. One participant, Hasan, said: 'in Judaism, in the Torah, it is definitely in it [in their religion]. I mean . . . when we are all circumcised, then "hey! You are also circumcised!" I find it positive. Normal. You are also one of us'.[13] He thus cast circumcision as a shared identity marker for Jews and Muslims in Germany, a constitutive marker of their minority belonging. Although some men considered circumcision to express belonging to a minority group in Germany, it was also regarded as a marker of social exclusion at the hands of the German legal, medical and political authorities. These groups expressed concern over whether or not granting freedom of religious practice to immigrants and minorities would cause social disintegration. Reflecting on minority perspectives from the debate, the Jewish Museum in Berlin organized an exhibition and a series of events. Focusing on the inclusion/exclusion dichotomy in a playful way, the exhibition *Haut Ab!* (October 2014–March 2015) played with German words meaning both 'skin off!' and 'get out!'. Felicitas Heimann-Jelinek, the curator of the exhibition, explained that her aim was to contextualize the controversial circumcision debate historically. At the same time, the exhibition showed the diversity of male circumcision practices, ranging from photos of crying boys from Turkish immigrant families, in order to reflect the contemporary history of ritual male circumcision in Germany, to videos on Jewish life in Germany. A panel of scholars discussed Jewish–Muslim relations as an event connected with the exhibition in December 2014. The panel included the historian Alexander Hasgall, the political scientists Mounir Azzaoui and Kerem Öktem, as well as Hannah Tzuberi, a scholar of Judaism and Islam. It was emphasized that the circumcision debate in Germany brought Jews and Muslims together as minorities who have been struggling for their religious practices to be acknowledged as part of a diverse Germany. Referring to a public poll, the academic director of the Jewish Academy, Yasemin Shooman, stated that 70 per cent of German respondents were against allowing circumcision (see also Heimann-Jelinek and Kugelmann 2014). She questioned whether there was sufficient legal protection for minorities, since their religiously diverse practices had been challenged in court.

With the introduction of the circumcision law – which protected the practice legally – the debate on legal recognition and regulation of male circumcision in Germany seemed to be over. But German criminal lawyers have argued that § 1631d BGB is in breach of Germany's constitution and are preparing to continue the debate, with the support of some medical doctors.[14] On 3 June 2015, the Elisabeth Hospital in the West German city of Essen organized a conference on medical and legal perspectives on the circumcision debate. The conference included medical doctors who spoke out publicly against circumcision. They argued that 'surgery in the genital area of a little boy means a painful and traumatic experience, which therefore should be considered independent of its [religious] implications' (Liedgens and Eckert 2015). In short, the male circumcision debate continued to produce legalizing and medicalizing discourses that served to criminalize and pathologize Jewish and Muslim religious practices, leaving little opportunity to discuss other dimensions of religious diversity in a socially inclusive society.

Conclusion

Ritual male circumcision has returned to the Western secular political agenda with new vigour (for a historical debate, see Judd (2007)). Debate about it is not exclusive to Germany, but is also ongoing in other Western countries, such as in France and the Netherlands, where many Jews and Muslims are still socially constructed outsiders by some legal and political authorities (for France, see Mandel (2014); for Germany, see Shooman (2014); and for a general analysis of Jews and multiculturalism, see Gilman (2006)). An exploration of how social inclusion is determined by legal authorities and through court decisions, political actors and scholars, as well as in media discussions, reveals that Jewish and Muslim religious practices are still discussed in the contexts of public threat and stigmatization. As shown above, the language employed in legal decisions by specific juridical, medical and political authorities, and used in specific media outlets in Germany featured stigmatizing terms such as 'barbaric', 'archaic' or 'threat to children's wellbeing', and portrayed Jewish and Muslim families as putting their children at risk.

The purpose of this chapter is not to endorse ritual male circumcision, but rather to show how the social inclusion and exclusion of minorities is shaped in public debate through courts, the media and scholarly publications. Ritual male circumcision is but one significant case of a wider dynamics in which religious difference plays a role in the inclusion and exclusion of minorities. Future research might take the analysis further by looking critically at how minority group social actors challenge existing sociolegal discourses through their religious practices and bodily performances. My suggestion is that a systematic research agenda, which focuses on how legal decisions are interpreted and debated by minority groups, will enable us to reflect differently on how claims of belonging to Germany and Europe are made and thus on who will shape German and European futures.

Gökce Yurdakul (PhD University of Toronto) is Professor of Sociology and the head of the Department of Diversity and Social Conflict in the Institute of Social Sciences at the Humboldt-Universität zu Berlin, Germany. She is also the Chair of a research cluster at the Berlin Institute for Integration and Migration Research. Her most recent book is *The Headscarf Debates: Conflicts of Belonging in National Narratives* (2014, Stanford University Press, co-authored with Anna Korteweg). Currently she is working on a book manuscript on borders, boundaries and bodies in Europe.

Notes

An earlier version of this chapter was published as Yurdakul, G. 2016. 'Jews, Muslims and the Ritual Male Circumcision Debates: Religious Diversity and Social Inclusion in Germany', *Social Inclusion* 4(2): 77–86. The funds to publish the original open-access article were provided by the German-Israeli Foundation Regular Faculty Grant (co-investigator with Shai Lavi, Van Leer Institute Jerusalem).

1. These are meetings rather than interviews because our conversations did not have a traditional interview structure in a sociological sense. In addition, I had the chance to ask questions to some of them in public meetings.
2. This contextual analysis of the circumcision debate, which brings social factors into the debate, is present in some recent legal scholarship (Fateh-Moghadam 2012).
3. The Turkish butcher Rüstem Altinküpe brought the case of ritual slaughter to the court and won his case in 2006 (*Jüdische Allgemeine*, 1 October 2009). *Halal* slaughtering of meat is permitted in Germany under restricted conditions. For Jewish and Muslim ritual slaughtering in Germany, see Lavi (2009).
4. As I will discuss in the following pages, ritual male circumcision is permitted in Germany after a court case in 2012, but it is practised under restricted conditions.
5. In this time period, hundreds of newspaper articles appeared in the newspapers; for example, in the *FAZ*, there are 352 mentions of the words 'Jewish' and 'circumcision' compared to 181 mentions of the words 'Muslim' and 'circumcision'. In the *SZ*, such words appeared 370 and 186 times respectively, and in the *taz* 248 and 160 times respectively. The articles consider only male circumcision.
6. *SZ* has the highest circulation at 1.1 million per day. *FAZ* has an estimated circulation of almost 400,000, while *taz* has the lowest circulation (about 60,000).
7. I thank Zülfukar Çetin for opening his newspaper archive for the missing resources.
8. Due to the gender sensitivity of the subject, this focus group interview was conducted by my assistant, Özgür Özvatan, at the Humboldt-Universität zu Berlin.
9. This English translation is available at https://www.dur.ac.uk/resources/ilm/CircumcisionJudgmentLGCologne7May20121.pdf (retrieved 2 July 2018).
10. 'Children's wellbeing' appears as a nebulous concept in policy-making and legal discussions. According to the UN Convention on the Rights of the Child: 'In all actions concerning children, whether undertaken by public or private social welfare institutions, courts of law, administrative authorities or legislative bodies, the best interests of the child shall be a primary consideration' (1990, Article 3). This statement may involve excessive statism (state authorities deciding on behalf of parents), but also discrimination against certain minorities (state authorities prohibiting Islamic rituals). It should be noted, however, that circumcision is irreversible and the child must decide later himself if he belongs to Islam. This statement of the Landgericht Köln brings Islamic practices under spotlight.
11. Ilkilic thus elaborated in another interview: 'In my view religious freedom is more important than the violation of physical integrity, because the practice does not alter the function of the organ, if the operation is carried out safely and correctly. And in addition, a ban puts huge pressure on Muslims because circumcision represents an important ritual for them' (Ilkilic 2013).
12. The German original: 'ich will nicht, dass Deutschland das einzige Land auf der Welt ist, in dem Juden nicht ihre Riten ausüben können. Wir machen uns ja sonst zur Komikernation' (Jones 2012).
13. Regarding forms of minority belonging, in our book on the headscarf debates, we focus on the ways in which Muslim women use the headscarf as a method of protest and asserting national belonging (Korteweg and Yurdakul 2014).

14. Bürgerliches Gesetzbuch (BGB) § 1631d Beschneidung des männlichen Kindes (German Civil Code, Circumcision of Male Children), http://www.gesetze-im-internet.de/bgb/__1631d.html (retrieved 8 July 2018).

References

Benatar, D. 2013. 'Evaluations of Circumcision Should Be Circumscribed by the Evidence', *Journal of Medical Ethics* 39(7): 431–32.

Bouma, G.D., Ling, R. and Pratt, R. 2010. *Religious Diversity in Southeast Asia and the Pacific*. Dordrecht: Springer.

Bodemann, Y.M. 1991. 'The State in the Construction of Ethnicity, and Ideological Labour: The Case of German Jewry', *Critical Sociology* 17(3): 35–46.

Bramadat, P., and Koenig, M. (eds). 2009. *International Migration and the Governance of Religious Diversity*. Ontario: Metropolis.

Çetin, Z., and S.A. Wolter. 2013. 'Fortsetzung einer Zivilisierungsmission: Zur deutschen Beschneidungsdebatte' in F. Hafez (ed.), *Jahrbuch für Islamophobieforschung*. Vienna: New Academic Press, pp. 19–37.

Dobbernack. J. 2016. 'Zivilisation und Politik. Positionen in der Beschneidungsdebatte', *Forschungsjournal Soziale Bewegungen* 29(2): 34–43.

Fateh-Moghadam, B. 2012. 'Criminalizing Male Circumcision – Case Note: Landgericht Cologne Judgment of 7 May 2012 – No. 151 Ns 169/11', *German Law Journal* 13: 1131–45.

Franz, M. 2012. 'Ritual, trauma, Kindeswohl', *Frankfurter Allgemeine Zeitung* (*FAZ*), 21 July. Retrieved 8 July 2018 from http://www.faz.net/aktuell/politik/die-gegenwart/beschneidung-ritual-trauma-kindeswohl-11813995.html.

Gilman, S. 1991. *The Jew's Body*. New York: Routledge.

_____. 2006. *Multiculturalism and the Jews*. London: Routledge.

_____. 2014. 'Gesundheit, Krankheit und Glaube: Der Streit um die Beschneidung', in F. Heimann-Jelinek and C. Kugelmann (eds), *Haut ab!: Haltungen zur rituellen Beschneidung, Jüdisches Museum Berlin*. Berlin: Wallstein, pp. 119–29.

Giordan, G. 2014. 'Introduction', in G. Giordan and E. Pace (eds), *Religious Pluralism: Framing Religious Diversity in the Contemporary World*. Dordrecht: Springer, pp. 1–12.

Gollaher, L.D. 2000. *Circumcision: A History of the World's Most Controversial Surgery*. New York: Basic Books.

Greenfield, A.K. 20132. 'Cutting away Religious Freedom: The Global and National Debate Surrounding Male Circumcision', *Rutgers Journal of Law and Religion* 15(353): 361–63.

Heil, J., and Kramer, J.S. (eds). 2013. *Beschneidung: Das Zeichen des Bundes in der Kritik*. Berlin: Metropol Verlag.

Heimann-Jelinek, F., and Kugelmann, C. 2014. 'Haut ab!: Haltungen zur rituellen Beschneidung', in F. Heimann-Jelinek and C. Kugelmann (eds), *Haut ab!: Haltungen zur rituellen Beschneidung, Jüdisches Museum Berlin*. Berlin: Wallstein, pp. 19–26.

Ilkilic, I. 2013. 'Inter-religious Dialogue on Matters of Health', *Qantara*, 4 July. Retrieved 8 July 2018 from https://en.qantara.de/content/interview-with-medical-ethicist-ilhan-ilkilic-inter-religious-dialogue-on-matters-of-health.

_____. 2014. 'Islamische Aspekte der Beschneidung von minderjährigen Jungen', *Zeitschrift für medizinische Ethik* 60: 63–72.

Jones, G. 2012. 'German Circumcision Ban Makes Nation a "Laughing Stock", Angela Merkel Says', *National Post*, 17 July. Retrieved 8 July 2018 from http://news.national post.com/news/german-circumcision-ban-makes-nation-a-laughing-stock-angela-merkel-says.

Judd, R. 2007. *Contested Rituals: Circumcision, Kosher Butchering, and Jewish Political Life in Germany*. Ithaca, NY: Cornell University Press.

Kastoryano, R. 2002. *Negotiating Identities: States and Immigrants in France and Germany*. Princeton, NJ: Princeton University Press.

Kelek, N. 2006. *Die verlorenen Söhne: Plädoyer für die Befreiung des türkisch-muslimischen Mannes*. Cologne: Kiepenheuer & Witsch.

Koenig, M. 2007. 'Europeanising the Governance of Religious Diversity? An Institutionalist Account of Muslim Struggles for Public Recognition', *Journal of Ethnic and Migration Studies* 33(6): 911–32.

Kokin, D.S. 2014. '"Der Bund, den Du an unserem Fleisch besiegelt hast": Beschneidung in jüdischem Denken und jüdischer Praxis', in M. Langanke, A. Ruwe and H. Theißen (eds), *Rituelle Beschneidung von Jungen: Interdisciplinäre Perspektiven*. Leipzig: Evangelische Verlagsanstalt, pp. 99–112.

Koopmans, R. 2013. 'Multiculturalism and Immigration: A Contested Field in Cross-national Comparison', *Annual Review of Sociology* 39: 147–69.

Korteweg, A.C., and Yurdakul, G. 2014. *The Headscarf Debate: Conflict of Belonging in National Narratives*. Stanford, CA: Stanford University Press.

Lang, D.P. 2013. 'Circumcision, Sexual Dysfunction and the Child's Best Interests: Why the Anatomical Details Matter', *Journal of Medical Ethics* 39(7): 429–31.

Laurence, J. 2001. '(Re)constructing Community in Berlin: Turks, Jews, and German Responsibility', *German Politics & Society* 19(2): 22–61.

Lavi, S. 2009. 'Unequal Rites: Jews, Muslims and the History of Ritual Slaughter in Germany', in J. Brunner and S. Lavi (eds), *Juden und Muslime in Deutschland*. Göttingen: Wallstein, pp. 164–184.

Lettinga, D., and Saharso, S. 2014. 'Outsiders within: Framing and Regulation of Headscarves in France, Germany and the Netherlands', *Social Inclusion* 2(3): 29–39.

Liedgens, P., and Eckert, K. 2015. 'Symposium Brochure for the Male Circumcision'. Symposium zur Jungenbeschneidung, Hörsaalzentrum im Elisabeth-Krankenhaus Essen, 3 June.

Mandel, M.S. 2014. *Muslims and Jews in France: History of a Conflict*. Princeton, NJ: Princeton University Press.

Merkel, A. 2012a. 'Umstrittene Rechtslage: Kanzlerin warnt vor Beschneidung sverbot', *Spiegel Online Politik*, 12 July. Retrieved 8 July 2018 from http://www.spiegel.de/politik/deutschland/umfrage-beschneidungsverbot-entzweit-deut sche-a-845208.html.

_____. 2012b. 'Gesetzentwurf bis zum Herbst', *Frankfurter Allgemeine Zeitung (FAZ)*, 17 July. Retrieved 8 July 2018 from http://www.faz.net/aktuell/ politik/inland/beschneidung-gesetzentwurf-bis-zum-herbst-11823355/ juedische-11823604.html.

_____. 2012c. 'Merkel kritisiert Antisemitismus', *Frankfurter Allgemeine Zeitung (FAZ)*, 25 November. Retrieved 8 July 2018 from http://www.faz.net/aktuell/ politik/inland/toleranz-merkel-kritisiert-antisemitismus-11971611.html.

Merkel, R. 2012. 'Die Haut eines Andere', *Süddeutsche Zeitung (SZ)*, 30 August. Retrieved 8 July 2018 from https://www.sueddeutsche.de/wissen/ beschneidungs-debatte-die-haut-eines-anderen-1.1454055.

Merkel, R., and Putzke, H. 2013. 'After Cologne: Male Circumcision and the Law. Parental Right, Religious Liberty or Criminal Assault?', *Journal of Medical Ethics* 39(7): 444–49.

Münch, P. 2012. 'Streit um ein göttliches Gebot', *Süddeutsche Zeitung*, 25 November. Retrieved 8 July 2018 from https://www.sueddeutsche.de/ politik/beschneidungsdebatte-in-israel-streit-um-ein-goettliches-gebot-1.1449976.

Neumann, L. 2012. 'Gemeinsam für Beschneidung: Muslime und Juden fordern Rechtssicherheit' *Jüdische Allgemeine*, 12 July. Retrieved 8 July 2018 from https://www.juedische-allgemeine.de/article/view/id/13465.

Öktem, K. 2013. 'Signale aus der Mehrheitsgesellschaft: Auswirkungen der Beschneidungsdebatte und staatlicher Überwachung islamischer Organisa-tionen auf Identitätsbildung und Integration in Deutschland', Oxford: European Studies Centre, St Antony's College. Retrieved 8 July 2018 from https://tezhamburg.files.wordpress.com/2013/09/signale-aus-der-mehrheitsge sellschaft.pdf.

Özdemir, C. 2008. 'Kulturelle Unterschiede – Kleine Hindernisse', in C. Özdemir (ed.), *Die Türkei: Politik, Religion, Kultur*. Weinheim: Beltz & Gelberg, pp. 235–39.

Peck, J. 1998. 'Turks and Jews: Comparing Minorities in Germany after the Holocaust', in J. Peck (ed.), *German Cultures, Foreign Cultures: The Politics of Belonging*. Washington DC: AICGS, pp. 1–16.

Putzke, H. 2008. *Criminal Relevance of Circumcising Boys: A Contribution to the Limitation of Consent in Cases of Care for the Person of the Child* (K. McLarren, Trans.). Retrieved 8 July 2018 from http://www.holmputzke.de/images/stories/ pdf/2008_putzke%20fs%20herzberg%20essay%20on%20circumcision.pdf.

Schüklenk, U. 2012. 'Europe Debates Circumcision . . . But What about the Child's Best Interests?', *Bioethics* 26(8): ii–iii.

Schwarze, T. 2012. 'Interview with R. Merkel: Ein kläglicher Gesetzentwurf', *Die Zeit*, 1 October. Retrieved 8 July 2018 from https://www.zeit.de/gesellschaft/ zeitgeschehen/2012-10/beschneidung-ethikrat-reinhard-merkel.

Shooman, Y. 2014. '. . . *weil ihre Kultur so ist*': *Narrative des antimuslimischen Rassismus*. Bielefeld: Transcript Verlag.

Stehr, M. 2012. 'Unzumutbare Schmerzen', *Der Spiegel*, 27 July. Retrieved 8 July 2018 from http://www.spiegel.de/spiegel/print/d-87482746.html.

SZ. 2012. 'Schwerster Angriff auf jüdisches Leben seit dem Holocaust', 16 July. Retrieved 8 July 2018 from http://www.sueddeutsche.de.

taz. 2012. 'Rabbiner will Medizinkurse'. 21 August. Retrieved 8 July 2018 from http://www.taz.de/!5085935/.

Tosun, M. 2012. 'Sünnet Yapmayiz', *Hürriyet*, 9 June. Retrieved 8 July 2018 from http://www.hurriyet.com.tr/planet/20870182.asp.

Vertovec, S., and Wessendorf, S. 2006. 'Cultural, Religious and Linguistic Diversity in Europe: An Overview of Issues and Trends', in R. Penninx (ed.), *The Dynamics of International Migration and Settlement in Europe*. Amsterdam: Amsterdam University Press, pp. 171–99.

Yurdakul, G. 2010. 'Juden und Türken in Deutschland: Integration von Immigranten, Politische Repräsentation und Minderheitenrechte', in G. Yurdakul and M. Bodemann (eds), *Staatsbürgerschaft, Migration und Minderheiten: Inklusion und Ausgrenzungstragien im Vergleich*. Wiesbaden: Verlag Sozialwissenschaften, pp. 127–60.

_____. 2013. 'After the Ritual Male Circumcision Debate: Jews, Turks, and the Accommodation of Minorities in Germany' Paper presented at the *Council for European Studies Conference*. Amsterdam, 25–27 June.

Part II

Potential for Change

Chapter 4

Islam, Vernacular Culture and Creativity in Stuttgart

Petra Kuppinger

On a Ramadan evening in June 2015, my friends Emine, Feride and I, after getting off a city train, hurried along a suburban street to reach Stuttgart's (predominantly Turkish) Garden Mosque in time for the breaking of the daily fast, or *iftar*.[1] When we arrived at the back gate of the mosque's garden, a mosque official was already delivering his opening remarks. He stood in the centre of the large lot of this former industrial complex and faced about 300 guests, who were seated in two huge rectangular tents set up in an L-shape along the compound's southwestern perimeter. The tents were open at their entire length towards the centre of the tree-shaded garden. Facing the setting sun, Emine, Feride and I quickly passed behind the speaker towards the western tent, where we tried to find the friends who were keeping seats for us. While we were still looking, a Social Democratic Regional Parliament MP took the microphone and greeted the audience. He elaborated on the close cooperation between the mosque and the local community, and explained how much he enjoyed attending the annual public fast-breaking event at the Garden Mosque. As we settled into our seats, he mentioned that he had been invited to attend the official festivities for the 350th anniversary of the founding of Karlsruhe (the second city in the state) on the same night, but emphasized that he preferred spending his time at the mosque with his constituency, much like he had done in recent years. Next, a representative of the Turkish consulate added his greetings. Following him, the local Protestant minister talked about the

---

Notes for this chapter begin on page 118.

close cooperation between the Protestant community and the Garden Mosque, and ended her remarks with a prayer asking for protection for those present and the continued success of the close cooperation between the two communities.

As sunset was rapidly approaching, some guests were getting impatient, ready to break their fast. After the minister, the mosque's imam recited the call to prayer for people to start eating and drinking. Once he had finished, guests reached for the dates that were neatly placed in small dishes on the tables and drank water or juices. Immediately afterwards, a long line of mostly younger women and teenage girls appeared from the space where the two tents met, where the kitchen tent was located. They carried huge trays loaded with soup bowls, which they passed out, starting from the tables furthest away from the kitchen. Some guests went to the mosque (in the northern part of the compound) to pray before eating. Soon everybody enjoyed the meals that were served with speed, grace and efficiency by the long procession of tray-carrying women. Conversations in German and Turkish could be heard. Laughter came from tables. Children soon played and ran in the yard. Sharing a table with friends and acquaintances, we stayed almost until midnight on this warm summer night. Intermittently, individuals from our table left to visit friends at other tables, and guests also joined our table for a chat. Emine and I talked to Ms Demirel, whom we knew from an interfaith event and who had invited us two years ago for the first time to this celebration. The by now traditional annual open-invitation *iftar* at the Garden Mosque was once more a huge success, as members mingled with officials, political and religious representatives, friends, neighbours and diverse other guests.

Public and scholarly debates about Islam in Germany often focus on questions regarding the 'integration' of Muslims and their communities (Mannitz 2006; Öztürk 2007). Yet the lifeworlds of most pious Muslims and their communities in Germany cannot adequately be analysed using a concept that implies recent arrival and newness. The Garden Mosque's vibrant *iftar* illustrates that this event is an ordinary element of urban life and hence is in no need of 'integration'.[2] It is an event or activity of an established and civically engaged urban institution. The Garden Mosque is an integral part and respected member of civil society, as the presence of the local politician, the Protestant minister and numerous Muslim and non-Muslim guests illustrates. The mosque is solidly 'integrated' and participates in the city's public sphere alongside other urban groups and constituencies. This popular *iftar* thus requires a different analytical approach. The breaking of the fast and similar events demonstrate the active civic engagement and, very importantly, the creative contributions of Muslims and their communities in German cities. Pious Muslims and their communities are firmly established constituencies who participate in the urban public and creatively contribute to the articulation of present and future urban cultures. The Garden Mosque's public *iftar* is an established element of the local cultural landscape, deeply rooted and invested in this context and, very significantly, its existence has remade this landscape. Communities such as the Garden Mosque produce culture and creatively change their urban environments.

In this chapter, I examine questions of pious Muslims' urban vernacular cultural creativity. I engage theoretical debates about such creativity and the role of urban religions in innovative cultural processes. I explore concrete contexts in Stuttgart, where pious Muslims and their communities insert creative forms and expressions of belonging and civic participation into the cityscape. Central to my discussion are questions about how pious Muslims creatively contribute to and remake urban cultures. How, often in the face of resentment and exclusion, do pious Muslims and their communities insert ideas, practices, crafts or arts into German cityscapes? How do they make their creative voices heard or works seen despite dominant notions about Muslims' supposed cultural rigidity or blind traditionalism? Most pious Muslims have long transcended the status of recent arrivals and have established themselves as creative cultural producers, who negotiate their roles and contributions in innovative manners. In doing so, they remake the urban cultural fabric even if many of their fellow urbanites do not see or recognize these faith-inspired contributions. Based on ethnographic fieldwork in Stuttgart, which I began in 2006, I examine creative cultural contributions of Muslim individuals and groups. I situate Islam in the realm of dynamic urban cultures and describe instances of Muslim vernacular creativity that are integral parts and relevant dynamics of the cityscape. I also demonstrate how pious Muslims insert new forms, practices, celebrations and artefacts into urban cultures and transform urban civic life.

Urban Religion

For much of the twentieth century, religion did not figure large in the analysis of cities and urban cultures. Scholars and commentators assumed that religion would eventually fade out of most urbanites' lives and would rapidly diminish in increasingly complex (secular) cities. Early debates about migrants focused largely on ethnic issues while religious questions took a back seat (e.g. Borris 1973). Some questions emerge here: did religion indeed no longer play a role in the cities of the 1960s and 1970s? Were religious voices, faith-inspired creativity and cultural production ignored or even actively pushed aside in the analysis of, especially, liberal European cities? In recent decades, earlier notions of the 'secular' city were challenged, which resulted in a surge of studies of urban religions and especially also immigrant religions and an insistence on the continued relevance of religion and religious diversity in cities (e.g. Livezey 2000; Peach and Gale 2003). Robert Orsi's (1985) pioneering study of the religious lives and practices, or 'lived religion', of Italian immigrants in Harlem, New York City, chronicles the rise (and later decline) of Italian American religious and cultural creativity in East Harlem as it moulded unique neighbourhood symbols, practices and events that eventually transcended the area, and much later even its ethnic context. Orsi's book helped to (re) situate religion, religiosities and lived religions in cities and urban studies, and pointed to religion's continued importance; very significantly, he also insisted on the creative culture-producing role of religion and faith-inspired actors in urban streets and spaces. Orsi's collaborators in the edited volume *Gods in the City* (1999) take his argument further and examine diverse and complex experiences of individuals, groups and communities in the context of (established and new) urban religions, religiosities and faith-based activities. They illustrate how religion and hugely diverse religiosities are interwoven with the urban fabrics in different contexts and settings. They neatly illustrate the continued relevance of religion, religiosities and diverse faith-inspired cultures and cultural practices in contemporary cities, and here especially also in migrant quarters.

Other works map the localization of immigrant religions in European and US cities (Ceylan 2006; David 2012; Garbin 2013; Keaton 2006; Stepick et al. 2009; Tamimi Arab 2013; Warner and Wittner 1998). They explore changing urban spiritual landscapes in which diverse immigrant communities articulate their positions, and analyse how established communities can change in the process of these broader transformations. They produce nuanced understandings of religious urban dynamics and transformations, and underline that religion is not waning in global cities. These texts highlight that increasingly diverse faith-based or faith-inspired activities are integral urban features and that, in order to understand the role of urban lived religion, it is important to explore moments, spaces and constituencies beyond the established spaces of mainstream religious worship. This is not to say that mainstream places of worship are not important, but new groups and trends often emerge among smaller groups in less conspicuous places. Two points are central in such recent studies of urban religious cultures. First, scholars attribute agency to faith-based urban actors and institutions in general, as they analyse contexts of change and innovations that are initiated or carried by the pious individuals and groups. And, second, scholars point to the significance of diverse immigrant religious forms and practices in global cities, and more concretely they point to the important culture producing activities and role of religiously inspired immigrants and their communities.

Urban lived religion and its multitude of newer spiritual experiences are frequently located in small, invisible, obscure or unlikely spaces, where new or minority faith groups, as well as immigrant religious communities, meet and articulate local practices and agendas. Once rudimentarily established, some faith-inspired activities move to other urban spaces. In the process of localization, their respective spatial and cultural environments influence new congregations or religious movements, as much as their spatiality and sociality eventually radiate into the surrounding cityscape (Deeb and Harb 2013; Tweed 1997). Forms and practices once limited to the confines of small communal spaces or contexts over time can become part of larger urban contexts (e.g. the well-established Muslim fast-breaking events in German cities). More recently, the analysis of creative faith-based urban interventions has gained momentum, as scholars examine different material manifestations (houses of worship), events (processions, feast days) or creative contributions, such as food, music and fashions (e.g. Bowman and Valk 2014; Dwyer et al. 2013; Dwyer et al. 2016; Saint-Blancat and Cancellieri 2014; Tarlo 2010). These works highlight the creative nature of pious individuals and communities' contributions and cultural interventions, and illustrate how diverse faith-based groups are vibrant, visible and creative urban constituencies whose often hidden and sometimes even resented contributions are relevant urban cultural dynamics. For immigrants, faith-based activities are often their first engagement with host societies. Such activities make diverse religions and religious practices visible to other urban dwellers (Garbin 2012; Saint-Blancat and Cancellieri 2014). Religion and faith-inspired activities can thus constitute a 'path to civic engagement' (Levitt 2008).

Vernacular Creativity

Debates about urban religions are paralleled by those about creative cities, creativity in the city, public art and the transforming role of arts and creativity in globalized cities (Florida 2002; Ivey 2008; Landry 2000; Tepper and Ivey 2008), yet the two rarely intersect. Richard Florida (2002) argues that the future belongs to the urban creative class and that cities are well advised to cater to the wishes of this class to attract and retain its members. He suggests that this class (visual artists, musicians, media professionals, professors, etc.) produces much-needed products, innovations and urban dynamics that will boost a city's reputation, commercial potentials and quality of life. He attributes little or no cultural creativity to the lower classes or immigrants. Simultaneously, he praises vibrant neighbourhoods, in which culture 'grows organically' (Florida 2002: 182), but fails to mention that this urban cool was painstakingly created by working-class and immigrant communities, as many of today's (gentrified) hip quarters were yesterday's working-class and immigrant neighbourhoods (Abu-Lughod 1994; Bernt and Holm 2009; Lloyd 2006; Zukin 2010). Florida invests this predominantly white, upper-middle-class crowd with a quasi-monopoly of creativity. Yet, there is more to urban aesthetics, social, cultural and spatial creativity or, as Bill Ivey calls it, 'expressive life' (2008: 23). In addition to dominant and commercialized elite creative spheres, there exists a vast and vibrant urban vernacular landscape of hugely diverse aesthetic, symbolic and cultural creativity, whose plentiful manifestations are less visible, spectacular and profitable (Hallam and Ingold 2007; Lippard 1997; Zukin 2010). Edensor and his collaborators (2010) describe vernacular creativity as manifestations of popular and often unplanned expressive activities that are unmediated by dominant artistic tastes and movements. They have little use for or even oppose such tastes and fashions. Most such expressions remain local; some might even be ridiculed by outsiders as 'cheap' or 'trashy'. Often such creativity exists despite, or even in opposition to, dominant aesthetics, the current cool and profitable cultural ideas and ideals. It emerges in hidden and unlikely places. This creativity of the lower classes, immigrants or religious minorities is frequently resented or viewed with considerable distrust and suspicion.

Seeking out such hidden or even criminalized creativity, Ben Chappell (2010, 2012) explores the creative work of lower-class Mexican-American men in Austin, Texas, who customize lowriders as a 'form of automotive aesthetics' (2010: 25). Associated with marginalized working class and immigrant constituencies, this automotive creativity and its cultural practices (cruising, exhibiting their cars, meeting fellow enthusiasts) are neither considered relevant to urban aesthetic production, nor are they welcome in the city (police frequently chase lowriders from parking lots). Despite the lack of recognition, and in the face of resentment, men who customize vehicles create their own and unique vernacular aesthetics. They take pride and receive recognition from their peers (when none is forthcoming from dominant society). They produce elaborate artefacts, articulate aesthetic forms, propose venues of display for their creations, remake spaces and assert their creative participation as a marginalized and occasionally even criminalized group. They are not recognized as creative cultural producers and their creative work is even labelled an urban nuisance. Similarly, Tim Edensor and Steve Millington (Edensor 2009;

Edensor and Millington 2010) examine the display of Christmas lights in English working-class neighbourhoods. These lights are frequently discredited as tacky, yet the authors argue they 'are a form of creativity that has emerged in communities that largely ignore orthodoxies about fashion and design to produce economies of generosity and a sense of conviviality' (Edensor and Millington 2010: 170f). They highlight the creative contributions of those 'who are deemed to lack the necessary creative skills, cultural tastes and competencies to enter a circumscribed definition of the cultural or knowledge economy' (Edensor and Millington 2010: 172) and describe Christmas lights as an 'example of embedded practice' (Chappell's 'poetic wisdom' or Ivey's 'expressive life') that unfolds at a distance to bourgeois aesthetics, when families embellish their homes to please their neighbours. Edensor and Millington emphasize the value of unacknowledged working-class cultural creativities and insist on the cultural relevance of diverse hidden or disenfranchised creative practices. They do not regard Christmas lights as an overtly religious practice, but hint at their religious background (2010: 177). The question emerges as to whether religious sentiments do play a role for Christmas lights enthusiasts. Similarly, it is interesting to note that Chappell's book cover image is a car with a huge Madonna depiction on its hood. As scholars examine diverse neglected or resented working-class, immigrant and rural creativities, spirituality is often woven into their texts, yet it remains surprisingly undertheorized.

Muslim Life in Stuttgart

Stuttgart is the sixth-largest city in Germany (600,000 inhabitants). The larger metropolitan region (Region Stuttgart) includes the city and five additional counties (Böblingen, Esslingen, Ludwigsburg, Rems-Murr and Göppingen), and is home to more than 2.5 million residents. Stuttgart cannot boast the concentration of political power and innovative cultural production of Berlin, the financial power and centrality of Frankfurt, powerful fashion and film industries located in Munich, or a major port and dominant media companies that have chosen Hamburg. Stuttgart is a high-tech, car and banking city that struggles with a reputation of being somewhat provincial and boring (*bieder*). In the early twenty-first century, Stuttgart – in the competition of German cities – scores with its global industries (e.g. Mercedes, Porsche and Bosch) and growing banking sector (second after Frankfurt). Unemployment rates are among the lowest in Germany, and social programmes and projects receive substantial funding. While Stuttgarters experience considerable differences in terms of wealth, income and size and quality of housing, the differences are less pronounced than in other Germany cities and seem benign when compared with many global cities. Stuttgart, like all large German cities, is a contender in the race of (secondary) global cities, as the city seeks to attract investments, tourists, and globalized events and spectacles. At the dawn of the twenty-first century, the city added the new Mercedes Benz Museum, the Porsche Museum and a vast fair or exhibition centre to its list of attractions. Similarly, the city has attempted to remain associated with European and global events (e.g. Stuttgart was one venue of the FIFA World Cup in 2006 and hosted the 1993 World Athletics Championship); it also maintains its stake in the global art scene, through, among other institutions, the Stuttgart Ballet and a famed art gallery, the Staatsgalerie.

Stuttgart is the German city with the largest share of residents who are either immigrants themselves or trace their descent from postwar migrants to the city (what Germans call migration background, or *Migrationshintergrund*).[3] In 2012, 39.9 per cent of all residents in Stuttgart had such a *Migrationshintergrund*. For those under the age of three, the figure was even higher (57.5 per cent); about a fifth of the urban population are foreign nationals (Landeshauptstadt Stuttgart 2013: 12). With regard to the experiences of Muslims and their communities in Stuttgart, economic aspects without doubt play a role, but everyday lifeworlds are not centrally marked by fierce struggles over economic resources. Tensions are much more of a cultural and political nature, often over issues of recognition, participation, civic rights and access to space. Controversies over the construction of mosques, for example, are not so much about whether or not a community owns the funds to buy adequate real estate, but about whether this real estate is indeed made available to them (Kuppinger 2014b). The position of Islam and Muslims in Stuttgart is characterized by neither ghettoization and substandard housing conditions nor dramatically high rates of unemployment. While some Muslims do occupy the lower end of Stuttgart's rental market and experience higher rates of unemployment, Stuttgart does not share the social problems of some Parisian housing projects or British cities (e.g. Keaton 2006).

Despite its considerable Muslim population – almost 10 per cent of the population, which equates to about 60,000 people (Baden-Württemberg 2005: 10) – Stuttgart, unlike other regional hubs (e.g. Sindelfingen and Mannheim), nationally important centres (e.g. Cologne and Duisburg) or European cities (e.g. Dublin and Rotterdam), does not have a purpose-built mosque. Nonetheless, over the years, Stuttgart's Muslim spiritual geography has consolidated (Kuppinger 2014a). Starting from the late 1980s and gaining momentum in the 1990s, many Muslim associations bought buildings, but Stuttgart's mosques remain predominantly located in defunct industrial facilities in marginal, distant and largely nonresidential areas. Many have to make do with less than perfect spaces (Kuppinger 2010). The search for better facilities continues to create a certain movement among communities. For instance, in 2007, a Moroccan community moved from rented to owned premises; in 2008, a Bosnian association moved from a smaller owned to a larger owned location. At present there are about twenty-five mosque associations in Stuttgart, which are organized as registered legal associations (*Verein*). This status conveys advantages, since German law favours this format of public organization, which gives the respective associations certain privileges (e.g. access to facilities and funding possibilities).

Creative Celebrations

The *iftar* at the Garden Mosque I described at the outset is not an isolated instance that reveals how a mosque can become a creative cultural agent. Since the 1990s, pious Muslims and their communities have played an increasingly active and creative role in German cities. They participate in established public events, join discussions or panels, found and engage in interfaith activities, and introduce new events, activities and celebrations, like *iftar* and *kermes* events (Kuppinger 2015: 156).

It is hard to miss Ramadan in German cities. Mosques, (secular) community centres, cultural centres, clubs, political parties, public institutions and individual families organize numerous *iftars*, to which they invite family, friends, neighbours and sometimes the public. In a city like Stuttgart, one could easily spend every Ramadan night at a public *iftar*. The Garden Mosque, which has an *iftar* for members every night, has for years had one specially designated night when the community invites friends, neighbours, officials from other mosques, politicians and others. As the local politician noted, the Garden Mosque *iftar* has long been a regular item in his calendar. Like other celebrations, the *iftar* is a fixture in the local cultural scenery.

A few days after I had attended the Garden Mosque event, I read an announcement in a local newspaper that an interfaith group (Haus Abraham) was organizing a public *iftar*. Everybody was welcome as long as they registered in advance. Once more, the wonderful weather turned this into an outdoor event, which took place in the yard of the Hospitalhof, a 500-year-old monastery and church, renovated and expanded into an educational and conference centre of the Protestant Church. When I arrived about forty-five minutes before sunset, the yard was filled with tables and benches set for the meal. About forty people were already seated. After surveying the tables, I chose a table where a woman sat by herself. She turned out to be a retired teacher from a regional town, who had participated in other activities at the centre. As we talked, the yard filled with a diverse crowd of about 150 guests. Protestant, Jewish and Muslim representatives greeted the visitors and emphasized how important it was to sit, eat and celebrate together, and how this was the best way to create peace and a better world. They spoke prayers and words of blessing. The Muslim representative spoke last and ended with the call to prayer. Some of the Muslim guests went inside to pray. Outside, a buffet was offered. Non-Muslims and nonfasting guests were asked to let those who had fasted fill their plates first. I observed the crowd and recognized some local pioneers and veterans of Christian–Muslim interfaith dialogue. I saw Mr Mamdouh and his wife, who for years have been my fellow travellers at *iftar* and other events. I noticed Professor Al-Mudarris, who is active in interfaith dialogue and other political and cultural debates (Kuppinger 2015: 115). As I talked to Mr and Mrs Mamdouh and Professor Al-Mudarris, they invited me to the next celebration: a barbeque of their interfaith association after Ramadan ('that way we can barbeque on a Sunday afternoon'). I gratefully accepted. As everybody was busy eating, a group of young women played traditional Turkish music. Much like at other *iftar* events, taking advantage of the summer weather, the diverse company and the beautiful music, people stayed well into the night on this weekday evening.

On the following Friday, the Takva Mosque organized a large invitation-only *iftar* for friends, other mosque representatives, and an impressive assortment of local politicians and representatives of churches and other organizations. The guests were received in a large conference room, lined with huge, comfortable upholstered chairs around the perimeters of the room. About forty-five minutes before sunset, guests began to arrive. When about twenty-five people had found their seats, a mosque official greeted the guests and explained what had changed with the completion of a recent renovation project of the mosque complex. More guests arrived and we moved down the hall to visit the men's prayer room. The guide pointed out architectural and design features of this vast former industrial production hall. The room was painted in calm tones of beige and grey, which created an unusually serene atmosphere, setting this space apart from its peers in the city. The guide said a few words about the custom-made features, such as the elaborate square chandeliers, the marble *mihrab* (niche to indicate the direction of prayer) and the choice of colours.

After visiting meeting rooms and administrative spaces, the group moved upstairs to a sizeable dining room, where large square tables were neatly set up, resembling a wedding (including name cards and menu information). Guests were seated in gender-segregated arrange-ments, which caused initial confusion among some of the ethnic German dignitaries, who had come as couples and found themselves separated from their spouses. There were two all-female tables surrounded by six or seven all-male tables. I ended up seated between a suburban dentist, who was a member of the community, and a lecturer at a local teachers' college (not a community member); both were of Turkish descent. Before and during the *iftar*, representatives of the local and regional mosque associa-tions gave speeches and addressed issues regarding Islam and political concerns about immigration, clearly aware of the presence of political representatives among the audience.

The setting, guest list, speeches and menu for this evening had been meticulously planned. The mosque community and its board carefully used this occasion to present their fabulous facilities, showcase and strengthen their network of friends and connections, teach outsiders about Ramadan and convey political messages to various representatives. They neatly mixed different guests by way of the assigned seats, which made for interesting encounters and conversations. The community pre-sented itself as a gracious and generous host. At the same time, the com-munity illustrated elements of cultural difference, for example, by way of the gender-segregated tables. Weaving together the familiar (with regard to the ethnic German or non-Muslim guests), like menu cards or speak-ers, with the unfamiliar (symbolic gender segregation, as all guests were accommodated in one larger room), the community made a clear state-ment of belonging and simultaneously illustrated its cultural particulari-ties. Neither one precluded the other.

Over the years, I attended numerous *iftars* organized by mosques, inter-faith associations, civic centres, political groups or private individuals. They took different shapes, used varying venues and addressed diverse constituencies. The interfaith dialogue association of which Mr and Mrs Mamdouh and Professor Al-Mudarris are core members has for many years been organizing an *iftar* series for which a different mosque hosts the meal each week. This *iftar* has travelled through Turkish, Bosnian and Arab mosques, allowing guests a view of the ethnic, cultural and religious diversity across local Muslim faith groups. Notes in newspapers announce the events and invite the public.

Iftar evenings or celebrations are not the only creative events that mosque communities and other Muslim groups and associations have added to the urban event schedule. Equally important and prominent are mosque *kermes* events, which are a mix of community get-together, open-house and fundraising occasions. Marked by the availability of lavish amounts of food for sale, the exhibition of homemade crafts, book tables, occasional commercial exhibits of merchandise and sometimes small exhibits of arts, these events address community members and non-members alike. They offer outsiders the possibility to get to know mosque communities in the relaxed atmosphere of homemade food and good company as people sit – often on long, shared wooden benches – and talk with, or at least observe, each other. A third creative contribution by Muslim communities to the urban events' calendar are open houses, or open days, scheduled in many mosques on the German national holiday of 3 October. Announced in the press or on websites, different mosques offer different activities, ranging from tours through mosques to elaborate events with speakers that inform visitors about Islam.

Communal activities, such as *iftar* or *kermes* events, are important cultural additions and mediating occasions. Since they address and include larger constituencies, they can and have clearly made a mark in the city. This does not mean, however, that individual activities or creative work are irrelevant. In fact, the many small steps and activities of individuals are yet another significant realm of urban vernacular cultures and their transformations. I will turn to one such example next.

Emine and *Ebru*

A few years ago, Emine Yıldız signed up for a course in *ebru* in a mosque in a regional town not far from Stuttgart.[4] The course was taught by a Turkish artist, who came to Germany to teach and spread *ebru* art. Emine, who was in her forties, was excited to learn a new craft, since she was active and creative, possessing a large repertoire of practical creative skills, ranging from sowing and knitting to upholstery and decorative and renovation expertise. In the course, Emine learned about the historical origins of *ebru* in the Ottoman era. Her teacher stressed that *ebru* was first and foremost about patience because, without time and patience, the long process of creating *ebru* art could not be successful. Emine was quickly pulled into the universe of *ebru*, with its careful preparation and detailed procedures. Already within ten days of her first course, Emine developed considerable expertise and a growing love for this art form. She learned how to prepare the water, using specific plant-based pigments and oily materials for the colours to float and later stick to the paper. A few weeks after her first course, she signed up for a second ten-day course of advanced techniques. She eventually gained expertise in about forty techniques of how to create forms and especially floral patterns, such as roses and tulips. She understood that calm and patience were central to the success of *ebru*; one hasty move could ruin a pattern and thus hours of preparation. Upon completion of the second course (and receipt of a second certificate), Emine continued to work and experiment with her art at home. Minute elements – temperature or dust – or stress levels and lack of concentration influence artistic results. Emine explained to me that it takes a lot of patience to refine one's skills and that one has to 'wake up the angels that sleep in one's fingers'.

After two to three years of additional practice at home, Emine felt that she had gained enough expertise to show her work not only to family and friends, but also to outsiders. She was also ready to teach *ebru* to others. Upon finishing her two courses, she had exhibited some work in the same mosque where the courses had taken place. She showed her work to family and friends, and gave some pieces away as gifts. People appreciated her work; she was proud that her accountant and physician both displayed her work in their offices. A mosque community in Stuttgart asked her not only to exhibit her images at their *kermes*, but to set up a table for the event to demonstrate her skills. Other mosques, groups and associations followed. Emine was thrilled by this unexpected public interest in her work. She also found a calligrapher who superimposed words or Quran verses on her work. She continuously seeks to improve her work by practice and watching *ebru* clips online. 'You have to watch them and immediately copy what you see', she explained. Since *ebru* needs considerable time and space, Emine converted an unused attic room into a studio, where she could leave her water pan for days at a time. As more people heard about Emine's artwork, she received more invitations to exhibit at mosque events and showcase her artistic process: 'at this point, however, I cannot always accept these invitations as it takes time, effort and money to set up a demonstration table'.

Since Emine continued her regular job, her engagement was limited to occasional weekend events. A highlight for Emine was the Salam Mosque *kermes* in the summer of 2015. Stuttgart's Mayor, Fritz Kuhn, came to her table and asked her questions about her artwork. Emine built up a reputation. One day when Emine, her daughter and I walked into a *kermes*, a man approached us and wanted to talk to her. Her daughter and I were surprised, since we did not know him. When Emine joined us again, we asked about him. 'Oh', she said with a smile, 'he is from another mosque, he knew about my work, and asked me whether I could do a table at their mosque.' We laughed, realizing how much of a celebrity Emine had become. Her work transcends mosque circles. At her daytime job with a large social agency, she also occasionally exhibits her artwork and receives much positive feedback.

Within six years, Emine learned and mastered a new art form that she greatly enjoys and constantly refines. Without advertising, only by way of her exhibited pieces, word of mouth and demonstration tables at events, she built a reputation in mosques and beyond. Her creative work helped to establish *ebru* as a new art form in the city. She demonstrates her art, has a few pieces on exhibit in public spaces and, whenever time permits, participates in public events. Clearly, art has become a venue for civic participation for her. While she is by no means a well-known artist, Emine has created a small space for herself in the urban public sphere and Stuttgart's cultural landscape.

Concluding Remarks: Creative Contributions

If observers limit their search for urban arts and creativity to the pre-dictable and privileged venues of celebrated galleries or downtown spaces, they miss many unique, and in Sharon Zukin's (2010) sense 'authentic', contributions of other, often less visible or marginalized, city dwellers. In order to understand the diverse, fascinating and multifac-eted forms of urban creativity and instances of everyday 'poetic wisdom' and 'expressive life', it is paramount to explore small and often seem-ingly irrelevant spaces. Creativity and urban innovation also flourish in invisible, unlikely or even shunned urban practices and areas (Bain 2013; Gibson 2012; Lippard 1997). We need to explore spaces that are written off by cultural elites and spaces that seem to disregard or chal-lenge dominant aesthetic conventions and expressions, and question notions of the secular nature of art, creativity and cultural innovation (Wuthnow 2001, 2003, 2008). Creative cultural seeds take root and blos-som in unlikely, hidden and also contested spaces (Potts 2010). They are often independent of cultural policies and mainstream creative agendas (Edensor and Millington 2010; Milbourne 2010). Culture, as Raymond Williams noted over half a century ago, 'is ordinary' (2011 [1958]). In this chapter, I showed that a more inclusive view of urban cultural creativ-ity allows for a more nuanced understanding of urban cultural inno-vation and cultural beginnings (Zukin 2010). For example, individuals like Emine are part of larger cultural transformations as they experi-ment with, introduce and strengthen new creative forms. Communities like the Garden Mosque similarly create and maintain new social prac-tices. Examples like these of individual art productions or communal cultural creativities illustrate the often initially invisible nature of ver-nacular cultural innovation. A look at new forms and activities discloses a broader field of increasingly diverse cultural production that is often neglected at the expense of more profitable contexts of cultural consump-tion (Hall 2004). This approach brings to light a vast and diverse urban vernacular creative scene in general and faith-based cultural creativity in particular.

I illustrated aspects of the creative vernacular urban cultural contributions and production of pious Muslims and their communities. At first sight, celebrations or paintings might seem trivial or could be quickly brushed off as inconsequential in the urban cultural landscape. However, understanding the latter as a vast and vibrant woven tapestry, it becomes clear that it is the endless number of small threads that hold this tapestry together. Even minute threads produce intriguing aesthetics, vibrancy and effects. Once woven in, even the smallest thread becomes vital to the overall appearance and thickness of the tapestry. These threads add to the tapestry's vibrancy and, if removed, leave visible voids. In addition to more visible pious Muslims' creative contributions, such as mosque design or modest Islamic fashion, smaller creative interventions have in recent decades remade cityscapes. With the introduction of new art forms or public events and celebrations, Muslims of diverse religiosities have infused considerable creative energy into German cities. They added noticeable elements: sizeable *iftars*; cultural work, such as the music played by a mosque-based women's group at the public fast-breaking; or artefacts, such as Emine's *ebru* paintings. The cultural contributions and innovations discussed in this chapter represent a more comprehensive field of faith-based or faith-inspired Muslim professional and lay artists and creative workers (e.g. musicians, photographers, DJs and architects), whose work radiates into the city. They insert their creativity into diverse cultural circuits and remake urban spaces, lifeworlds and cultures.

Communities such as the Garden Mosque and individuals such as Emine are not in need of simplistic political tools to achieve integration. They arrived at the heart of local society a long time ago. They are established cultural actors and producers, who use their creative events or art as vehicles for civic participation. By way of her art, Emine became more visible in the city. Her faith-based art is not only a 'path to civic engagement' (Levitt 2008), but also a solid venue of permanent civic participation. Similarly, the Garden Mosque uses public events to showcase its work, vibrant community life, and local roots and commitments to the urban population. The Garden Mosque and Emine are solid and committed participants in the urban civil society and cultural landscape. By way of their contributions, they express themselves, articulate their positions in the city and creatively participate in the shaping of diverse future urban cultures. As faith-inspired creative agents, they transform a predominantly secular cityscape and as pious Muslims, they insert their contributions into a largely Christian spiritual landscape. In order to understand such faith-based cultural production, it is paramount to seek out hidden, excluded and controversial spaces, since cultural innovation often unfolds in small and unlikely places, such as the attic of a pious woman.

Petra Kuppinger is Professor of Anthropology at Monmouth College in Monmouth, IL, United States. She has conducted research on space, globalization and consumerism in Cairo, and on space, culture and Islam in Stuttgart. She authored *Faithfully Urban: Pious Muslims in a German City* and co-edited *Urban Life: Readings in the Anthropology of the City*. Her work has been published, among other journals, in *City and Society*, *Anthropological Quarterly*, *Social and Cultural Geography*, *Journal of Urban Affairs* and *Culture and Religion*. She has served as President of the Society for Urban National and Transnational Anthropology (SUNTA) and as editor of *City & Society*.

Notes

My special thanks go to friends and interlocutors in Stuttgart and to my parents Gudrun and Helmut Kuppinger for their help and support. My greatest debt is to my daughters, Tamima and Tala. I am grateful to Jan-Jonathan Bock and Sharon Macdonald for inviting me to the very inspiring conference 'Experiencing Differences and Diversities in Contemporary Germany' in Berlin in April 2016 and for making this volume possible. I greatly benefited from their careful remarks on this chapter.

1. All personal and place names are pseudonyms.
2. Integration refers to becoming part of something. The Garden Mosque is already an established actor in its urban environment. To talk about integration disregards the fundamentally local nature of individuals and communities. Debates about integration situate individuals and groups as outsider in the city, which they are not. The question is not how this mosque becomes local, but how it participates in the city.
3. While this category *mit Migrationshintergrund* remains problematic, it is frequently used in public debates.
4. *Ebru* is a Turkish marbling art whereby powdered colour pigments are dispersed on the surface of oily water in a large rectangular and flat container. *Ebru* art uses patterns and often flowers, but in accordance with Islamic teaching does not depict human shapes. Emine buys all her supplies in Turkey.

References

Abu-Lughod, J. 1994. *From Urban Village to East Village*. Cambridge: Blackwell.
Baden-Württemberg, Staatsministerium. 2005. *Muslime in Baden-Wuerttemberg*. Stuttgart: Bericht für den Ministerrat.
Bain, A. 2013. *Creative Margins*. Toronto: University of Toronto Press.
Bernt, M., and A. Holm. 2009. 'Is it, or is Not? The Conceptualisation of Gentrification and Displacement and its Political Implications in the Case of Berlin-Prenzlauer Berg', *City* 13(2–3): 312–24.

Borris, M. 1973. *Ausländische Arbeiter in einer Grossstadt*. Frankfurt am Main: Europäische Verlagsanstalt.

Bowman, M., and Ü. Valk (eds). 2014. *Vernacular Religion in Everyday Life*. London: Routledge.

Ceylan, R. 2006. *Ethnische Kolonien*. Wiesbaden: VS Verlag für Sozialwissenschaften.

Chappell, B. 2010. 'Custom Contestations: Lowriders and Urban Space', *City & Society* 22(1): 25–47.

_____. 2012. *Lowrider Space*. Austin: University of Texas Press.

David, A. 2012. 'Sacralising the City: Sound, Space and Performance in Hindu Ritual Practice in London', *Culture and Religion* 13(4): 449–67.

Deeb, L., and M. Harb. 2013. *Leisurely Islam*. Princeton, NJ: Princeton University Press.

Dwyer, C., D. Gilbert and B. Shah. 2013. 'Faith and Suburbia: Secularisation, Modernity and the Changing Geographies of Religion in London's Suburbs', *Transactions of the Institute of British Geographers* 38(3): 403–19.

Dwyer, C., J. Tse and D. Ley. 2016. '"Highway to Heaven": The Creation of a Multicultural, Religious Landscape in Suburban Richmond, British Columbia', *Social and Cultural Geography* 17(5): 667–93.

Edensor, T. 2009. 'Illuminations, Class Identities and the Contested Landscapes of Christmas', *Sociology* 43(1): 103–21.

Edensor, T., D. Leslie, S. Millington and N. Rantisi (eds). 2010. *Spaces of Vernacular Creativity*. London: Routledge.

Edensor, T., and S. Millington. 2010. 'Christmas Light Displays and the Creative Production of Spaces of Generosity', in T. Edensor, D. Leslie, S. Millington and N. Rantisi (eds), *Spaces of Vernacular Creativity*. London: Routledge, pp. 170–82.

Florida, R. 2002. *The Rise of the Creative Class*. New York: Basic Books.

Garbin, D. 2012. 'Marching for God in the Global City: Public Space, Religion and Diasporic Identities in a Transnational African Church', *Culture and Religion* 13(4): 425–47.

Garbin, D. 2013. 'The Visibility and Invisibility of Migrant Faith in the City: Diaspora Religion and the Politics of Emplacement of Afro-Christian Churches', *Journal of Ethnic and Migration Studies* 39(5): 677–96.

Gibson, Chris (ed.). 2012. *Creativity in Peripheral Places*. London: Routledge.

Hall, P. 2004. 'Creativity, Knowledge and the City', *Built Environment* 30(3): 256–58.

Hallam, E., and T. Ingold (eds). 2007. *Creativity and Cultural Improvisation*. Oxford: Berg.

Ivey, B. 2008. *Arts, Inc.: How Greed and Neglect Have Destroyed our Cultural Rights*. Berkeley: University of California Press.

Keaton, T.D. 2006. *Muslim Girls and the Other France*. Bloomington: Indiana University Press.

Kuppinger, P. 2010. 'Factories, Office Suites, Defunct and Marginal Spaces: Mosques in Stuttgart, Germany', in M. Guggenheim and O. Söderström (eds), *Reshaping Cities*. New York: Routledge, pp. 83–99.

_____. 2014a. 'The Stuttgart Crescent: Muslim Material and Spiritual Geographies in Germany', in A Fábos and R Isotalo (eds), *Managing Muslim Migration in the 21st Century*. Basingstoke: Palgrave Macmillan, pp. 153–70.

_____. 2014b. 'Mosques and Minarets: Conflict, Participation and Visibility in German Cities', *Anthropological Quarterly* 87(3): 793–818.
_____. 2015. *Faithfully Urban*. New York: Berghahn Books.
Landeshauptstadt Stuttgart (ed). 2013. *Datenkompass Stadtbezirke Stuttgart*. Statistik und Informationmanagement.
Landry, C. 2000. *The Creative City*. London: Earthscan.
Levitt, P. 2008. 'Religion as a Path to Civic Engagement', *Ethnic and Racial Studies* 31(4): 766–91.
Lippard, L. 1997. *The Lure of the Local*. New York: New Press.
Livezey, L. (ed). 2000. *Public Religion and Urban Transformation*. New York: New York University Press.
Lloyd, R. 2006. *Neo-Bohemians: Art and Commerce in the Postindustrial City*. New York: Routledge.
Mannitz, Sabine. 2006. *Die verkannte Integration*. Bielefeld: transcript.
Milbourne, Paul. 2010. 'Growing Places: Community Gardening, Ordinary Creativities and Place-Based Regeneration in a Northern English City', in T. Edensor, D. Leslie, S. Millington and N. Rantisi (eds) *Spaces of Vernacular Creativity*. London: Routledge, pp. 141–54.
Öztürk, H. 2007. *Wege zur Integration: Lebenswelten muslimischer Jugendlicher in Deutschland*. Bielefeld: transcript.
Orsi, R. 1985. *The Madonna of 115th Street*. New Haven, CT: Yale University Press.
_____. (ed.). 1999. *Gods in the City*. Bloomington: Indiana University Press.
Peach, C., and R. Gale 2003. 'Muslims, Hindus, and Sikhs in the New Religious Landscape of England', *Geographical Review* 93(4): 469–90.
Potts, T. 2010. 'Creative Destruction and Critical Creativity: Recent Episodes in the Social Life of Gnomes', in T. Edensor, D. Leslie, S. Millington and N. Rantisi (eds), *Spaces of Vernacular Creativity*. London: Routledge, pp. 155–69.
Saint-Blancat, C., and A. Cancellieri. 2014. 'From Invisibility to Visibility? The Appropriation of Public Space through Religious Ritual: The Filipino Procession of Santacruzan in Padua, Italy', *Social and Cultural Geography* 15(6): 645–63.
Stepick, A., R. Rey and S. Mahler (eds). 2009. *Churches and Charity in the Immigrant City*. New Brunswick, NJ: Rutgers University Press.
Tamimi Arab, P. 2013. 'Mosques in the Netherlands: Transforming the Meaning of Marginal Spaces', *Journal of Muslim Minority Affairs* 33(4): 477–94.
Tarlo, E. 2010. *Visibly Muslim*. Oxford: Berg.
Tepper, S. and B. Ivey (eds). 2008. *Engaging Art*. New York: Routledge.
Tweed, T. 1997. *Our Lady of the Exile*. New York: Oxford University Press.
Warner, R.S., and J. Wittner (eds). 1998. *Gatherings in Diaspora*. Philadelphia, PA: Temple University Press.
Williams, R. 2011 [1958]. 'Culture is Ordinary', in I. Szeman and T. Kaplan (eds), *Cultural Theory*. Malden, MA: Wiley Blackwell, pp. 53–59.
Wuthnow, R. 2008. 'Faithful Audiences: The Intersection of Art and Religion', in S. Tepper and B. Ivey (eds), *Engaging Art*. New York: Routledge, pp. 127–46.
Wuthnow, R. 2001. *Creative Spirituality*. Berkeley: University of California Press.
_____. 2003. *All in Sync*. Berkeley: University of California Press.
Zukin, S. 2010. *Naked City*. Oxford: Oxford University Press.

Chapter 5

'Neukölln Is Where I Live, It's Not Where I'm From'

Children of Migrants Navigating Belonging in a
Rapidly Changing Urban Space in Berlin

Carola Tize and Ria Reis

> To me, Germany means: 'A normal country like Iraq'; 'Where I live'; 'Not my homeland, because my family is from Palestine'; 'My place of birth, where I live'; 'Germany is nothing for me, I hate Germany'; 'Where I spent my childhood'; 'Germany is nothing for me, only Berlin-Neukölln is where I was born – my home is Lebanon'; 'Where I live; my home is Bulgaria'; 'Neukölln is where I live, but it's not where I'm from'.
> —Quotes from students, Berlin-Neukölln, January 2015[1]

When eighth-grade students at a comprehensive secondary school in Berlin were given a writing assignment to describe 'what Germany means to me', a remarkably coherent picture emerged: although Germany was where they were born and/or where they lived, it certainly was not what they described as their home – the place 'that I'm from'. Their school is situated in northern Neukölln, an area shaped by three inner-city boroughs that gained the German media's attention as Berlin's 'end of the line' (*Endstation*) neighbourhoods (Wensierski 1997). The students' parents, all labelled in German statistics as possessing a 'history of migration', came as refugees or guestworkers from countries such as Bangladesh, Romania, Turkey and Iraq, as well as from Palestinian refugee camps in Lebanon, forming part of Neukölln's highly diverse and vibrant multi-ethnic communities. Since the 1950s, people of foreign descent in Germany have faced challenges posed by the expectation to adapt to what some conservative German politicians have called 'guiding culture' (*Leitkultur*), a concept, critics argue, used to demand assimilation.

Notes for this chapter begin on page 137.

Research by Ehrkamp (2006), Çelik (2015) and Mannitz (2012) highlights how, in reaction to such exclusionary discourses, young Turkish men and women have become unable, even unwilling, to take on a German identity. Furthermore, the tendency of immigrant populations to cluster in certain neighbourhoods has been framed as 'problematic' (Münch 2009). Neukölln, with its high percentage of families with a migrant background, its prevalence of dependence on social support, low levels of education and social problems, was considered an example of failed integration (Bezirksamt Berlin-Neukölln 2009). Since the mid 2000s, however, Neukölln's image has changed: contributing effects, such as rising housing prices across Berlin and policy initiatives to improve the local quality of life and infrastructure, resulted in the district's increased popularity with young expats and German families and students. Previously, the diverse multi-ethnic population residing in the northern district had infrequently interacted with the majority German population, apart from some neighbours, teachers, social workers and the police. Now, however, such interactions in public spaces – with increasing numbers of neighbours and classmates and encounters representing the mainstream German culture – are increasingly common.

Despite educational reforms, Neukölln's secondary schools continue to have a 'ghetto' reputation and suffer from what Eksner (2013) has identified as a devaluation of local educational capital.[2] Young people growing up in Neukölln are confronted with stark contrasts between the highly diverse multi-ethnic school environment and the newly up-and-coming gentrified neighbourhoods. These changes in the neighbourhoods were taking place during an insecure time of political turmoil in the Middle East and rising xenophobia across Europe. In combination, for young people from migrant families in Germany, these developments were making an already tenuous sense of belonging even more ambiguous.

By focusing on how young people socially navigate their environment (Vigh 2006, 2009), this chapter examines how everyday uncertainties, such as social marginalization, actual and perceived discrimination, and social control, influence perceptions and actions that impact on an ambiguous sense of belonging to Germany. Simultaneously, we show how for young people, whose (grand)parents immigrated to Germany, belonging is more strongly rooted in Neukölln as a multi-ethnic space rather than in the city of Berlin or in Germany as a nation state. Amid ambivalent public spaces, we explore how the school can become a particularly important space, where students contemplate and confront what it means to be considered, as well as self-identify, as a 'foreigner' in Germany.

This chapter builds on the work of others (Berckmoes 2014; de Martini Ugolotti and Moyer 2016; Rosenkrantz-Lindegaard 2009;

Vigh 2006, 2009) to further our understanding of how young people in rapidly changing environments interpret, negotiate and seize opportunities in order to improve their lives and reach goals (Vigh 2009). Vigh elaborates on de Certeau's (1984) theory of tactics, and thereby allows a perspective on how young people as agents manoeuver amid social situations intrinsically shaped by power dynamics. Tactics are the short-term responses in a social environment – the actions of those without power to change their immediate environment. Tactical agency stands in contrast to strategic agency, which is the ability to anticipate the future and take advantage of those who use tactical agency (see also Utas 2005). Using the lens of social navigation allows us to focus on both spatial and social dimensions in how 'agents act in difficult situations, move under the influence of multiple forces or seek to escape confining structures' (Vigh 2009: 419). In this chapter, the focus is on how social change impacts on young people's potential to move in different social environments, and their opportunities to make choices and affectively employ their creative tactics. This approach also helps us to identify gender differences in how these rapidly changing environments affect young people's navigational potential and how everyday social processes, such as actual or perceived discrimination and social control, impact on their sense of belonging to German society.

Following Antonsich (2010: 646), we see belonging as multidimensional and intrinsically linked with identity and citizenship. As a result, 'where do I belong?' and 'who am I?' cannot be answered in isolation from one another. We also draw on Antonsich, as well as on Yuval-Davis (2006), in conceptualizing belonging as having two major analytical dimensions: the first is situated in 'place-belongingness' and relates to feeling 'at home' and safe in a particular place. Feeling 'at home' can be analysed on multiple scales, such as the apartment, the neighbourhood, a community or a nation. Within these multilayered contexts, 'home stands for a symbolic space of familiarity, security and emotional attachment' (Hooks, quoted in Antonsich 2010: 646). The second dimension, the 'politics of belonging', reflects on the social dimensions that separate 'us' and 'them' (Yuval-Davis 2006: 204). Since belonging tends to become naturalized, the social dimension of belonging only comes to attention when it is threatened in some way (Yuval-Davis 2006: 197). If someone experiences being rejected by a group or host culture, this can undermine a sense of belonging, both to a place and to the social groups complicit in the rejection. In other words, the 'politics of belonging' highlights forms of sociospatial inclusion and exclusion, thereby providing a lens for analysing the creative tactics (grand)children of migrants employ as they navigate the sociospatial divides in their environment.

The data presented here are based on nineteen months of ethnographic fieldwork[3] by the first author, conducted between 2013 and 2015 at a local primary school and a comprehensive secondary school, in northern Berlin-Neukölln, including participant observation and interviews with school students' families. The writing assignment 'what Germany means to me' was part of the research. The focus was on the children, as well as grandchildren, of immigrants and on their use of tactical agency with regard to positioning themselves between the school, home and neighbourhood spaces.

In order to show how forms of belonging are shaped as well as challenged, we start with introducing Neukölln's migration history and an overview of the impact of rapid urban change in that district. We then focus on how young people navigate Berlin and beyond, followed by a look at how their navigational potential is influenced by the social forces in Neukölln. Finally, the school as a navigational space is explored and the focus is on students of diverse ethnic backgrounds. Despite a large majority following the Islamic religion, we also included non-Muslim students who identified as 'foreigners', as their experiences and navigational tactics reflected similarities. In our conclusion, we argue that the effects of actual and perceived discrimination, communal gossip and social control restrict these young people in their navigational potential and attempts to shape belonging outside of the home and in the migrant-dominated school environment.

Neukölln

Migration History

The area that is today known as Neukölln, and prior to 1912 as Rixdorf, has a longstanding history of migration. Already in the eighteenth century, Protestant refugees from the area that is now the Czech Republic established a historical neighbourhood known as the Böhmische Dorf ('Bohemian Village'). In the nineteenth century, migration flows from the countryside continued, from as far as Silesia and Poland, and later, in the 1940s, from the former East Prussia. Following the Second World War, Neukölln became part of the American-controlled sector. The looming presence of the Berlin Wall along the southern and eastern district periphery between 1961 and 1989 caused economic decline – particularly in the already low-income and densely populated northern parts. Many of the better-to-do families moved further south, into comfortable postwar condominiums. As a result of vacant property and affordable rents, Neukölln's north attracted so-called guestworkers (*Gastarbeiter*), who were recruited to fill the labour shortage in Germany's booming postwar economy. They came from a range of countries, including Yugoslavia, Italy, Spain, Greece, Tunisia, Morocco and Turkey, and settled in Neukölln as well as other so-called 'foreigner districts' *(Ausländerbezirke)* of West Berlin. In the 1970s and 1980s, as a result of the introduction of permanent residence permits and family reunification, immigrant numbers rose further. Diversity increased with the influx of refugees from the Balkans, Africa and the Middle East. In 2011, between 50 and 60 per cent of north Neukölln residents were guestworkers or postwar immigrants and their descendants – in the district's southern parts, the corresponding figure was between 20 and 30 per cent (Bezirksamt Neukölln 2012: 14).[4] Also significant is the share of young people in the north: in the late 2000s, 80 per cent of residents below the age of eighteen were from families that had migrated after the Second World War (Bezirksamt Berlin-Neukölln 2009).

These multi-ethnic communities have often been described negatively as 'parallel societies' *(Parallelgesellschaften)*, for whom the lack of assimilation is assumed to be the result of free choice – supposedly a cohesive community resisting integration (Gestring 2011). In particular, Germany's largest minority group, the Turks, has been labelled as inassimilable because of cultural and religious differences (Adam 2015). On closer examination, however, it becomes apparent that what is often represented as 'Turkish' is in fact a highly diverse population of Turks, Arabs and Kurds, who have little in common apart from sharing regional origins and the highly diverse Islamic faith. As research by Schönwälder and Sohn (2009), Drever (2004) and Stolle et al. (2013) has shown, Germany's multi-ethnic boroughs are marked by significant cultural and religious internal differences, as well as by a lack of social cohesion among these diverse communities. In other words, they do not constitute coherent parallel societies.

In Neukölln, the diverse communities do exhibit some common features: low education attainments and high levels of poverty (Bezirksamt Berlin-Neukölln 2012). As a result, northern Neukölln has been considered 'in need of special development' and received extra funding because of its concentrated social problems (Gude 2011). Growing up in such an environment exposes young people to the intergenerational transmission of social vulnerabilities, such as low levels of education, economic marginalization and social isolation (Berkemeyer et al. 2013). In view of these interconnected characteristics, Neukölln came to be seen as one of Germany's prime examples of failed integration, as Berlin's most dangerous district (Behrendt et al. 2008) or even as an unsafe and unpleasant ghetto (see Eksner 2013).

Gentrification

Gentrification is the process of upgrading urban neighbourhoods through renovation and initiatives to attract new and higher-income residents into run-down and low-income areas (Bernt and Holm 2009). By highlighting the process of gentrification in the popular Berlin district of Prenzlauer Berg, Bernt and Holm point out how, for many politicians, policy-makers and real estate agents, as well as for the middle and upper classes, the urbanization process is seen as a means of battling dilapidation and decay. For the urban poor, however, the results are rising costs of living, the destruction of social networks and the risk of having to move to more peripheral and cheaper housing.

While much of Berlin had already undergone massive upgrading, as well as population changes, since the fall of the Berlin Wall – low-income districts such as Kreuzberg have undergone gentrification since the early 2000s – the trend only caught noticeable attention in Neukölln in the wake of the closure of Tempelhof Airport in 2008. Instead of planes flying low above houses in the neighbourhood, the airfield became an attractive urban park. Berlin was also gaining in international popularity for its hip-and-happening vibe and was drawing new crowds of middle- and upper-class residents, resulting in rising housing prices particularly in popular areas, displacing students, artists and young families to districts like Neukölln, where housing was still affordable. The move to Neukölln was promoted by the local administration's initiative Social City[5] (*Soziale Stadt*), which aimed at reoccupying vacant shop fronts and housing.

The effects of the demographic shift through gentrification became particularly evident in local schools. School administrations, as well as many of the teachers, described the increasing mix of students as a first step towards the necessary mixing of social classes and ethnicities, and provided greater opportunities for those who were once marginalized. At the same time, for some students, gentrification led to them changing schools or commuting long distances, as their families were forced to relocate to cheaper peripheral areas. Additionally, research has shown that social contacts between groups can become fleeting despite living in the same neighbourhoods (Drever 2004; Stolle et al. 2013; Veldboer et al. 2002). In Neukölln, divisions between 'old' and 'new' residents found expression in social and spatial segregation through separate areas for commercial activities and educational spaces.

Whereas well-educated parents are prepared to register their children in local primary schools, for the career-determining subsequent phase they usually choose private schools or secondary schools in other districts.

As a result, at the secondary level, many local schools were still character-ized by a high percentage of students from low-income families with a migration background (from 80 to over 90 per cent).

How young people, coming of age in these secondary schools, confront the contrast between their low-income and migrant-dominated schooling environment, on the one hand, and their increasingly hip-urban-middle-class neighbourhood, on the other, will be explored in the next section. We now turn to the voices and experiences of the students themselves – how did they perceive their positions as 'foreigners' first beyond, and later within, the fast-changing urban space of northern Neukölln?

Students' Perspectives: Being a Foreigner in Germany

For many of the students, it was uncommon to leave Neukölln. Small shops and markets, as well as service providers catering to local com-munities, were accessible within walking distance – as were friends and extended family. Plus, being singled out as a foreigner was something many avoided. 'Looking' and 'being' foreign influenced where students felt they belonged and where they went, and hindered them from self-identifying as German (on such identity, see also Çelik (2015)). For Akil, a seventh-grader, being German was rooted in what it means to 'look German', as he compared his appearance to that of Bastian Schweinsteiger, the blond and blue-eyed football player: 'I'm not German! Germans are white like Schweinsteiger, he's, like, *really* German!' Akil referenced an ideal type or even classical stereotypical Germanness with which he strug-gled to identify because of his appearance: dark skin, dark hair and dark eyes. Despite having been born in Germany – his parents possess perma-nent residence – Akil, like many of his peers, reasoned that his appearance and Islam were the main reasons for him not being willing or able to take on German identity.

For students like Akil, the term 'foreigner' (*Ausländer*) marked identity – used with pride and sometimes distain. An example of the latter was Alyas, who described himself as having a 'migration background' (*Migrationshintergrund*), the official denominator of difference, to identify himself as a foreigner and to explain why in some places he 'does not feel good':

They [the Germans] look at you differently. Here, in Neukölln and Kreuzberg, everything is fine, but in Charlottenburg, Marzahn, Mitte, and such places, I don't feel good. When I'm in those kinds of places, where I'm the only one with a migration background, they look at me with their blue eyes as if they're saying 'eh, foreigners are not needed here!' I mean places like the district administration. When someone does that, I look back at them without looking away, so that they think I can defend myself. (Alyas, fifteen)

Alyas distinguished several districts of Berlin in which he 'does not feel good', containing neighbourhoods or areas that are either middle class and have smaller migrant populations (i.e. Charlottenburg and Mitte) or have a reputation for xenophobia (i.e. Marzahn).[6] Marzahn in particular, in former East Berlin, was almost unanimously named as a district to be avoided. Where Alyas went, and where he felt good, was largely defined by being amongst other 'foreigners' like himself, who similarly had a dark complexion; in his own words 'black-head' (*Schwarzkopf*).

Zara, a shy girl of thirteen, described herself as 'not feeling good' in Germany because of feelings of discrimination. She drew on others' stories to express her fears as a young Muslim woman:

I don't feel good in Germany at all, because almost all Germans have something against Islam. When you wear a headscarf, they look at you weirdly. A while back, my mother had a similar experience: she went to the bus and they all stared at her because of her *hijab*. My mother feared a man sitting behind her could do something. This happened recently to another woman. She was wearing only black clothes, and two German men tried to pull off her headscarf!

Accounts such as Zara's, based on fears and stories of attacks on other people, frequently circulated amongst young women as well as their mothers and made them feel unsafe outside of Neukölln. However, despite the frequency of such stories, we did not come across any first-hand experience of physical aggression against either male or female informants during the research period. Accounts remained vague and referenced anonymous women who were alleged to have endured an attack. Other experiences of first-hand discrimination, by contrast, were more common among young men, women and their families. An example of such an encounter was witnessed by the first author while on a field trip with a grade-six class. Several of the girls were wearing headscarves and, as they were leaving the train, an elderly man stopped with a look of disapproval and said to the girls 'have you looked at yourselves? Despicable! Despicable!', and he turned with disgust and entered the metro.

Feelings of being uncomfortable were countered by enacting postures suggesting strength. Alyas, a leader within his class and a good student who was interested in playing classical music, aimed to look threatening when he felt vulnerable in social situations by virtue of his apparent migration background. He explained he would 'stare back' to make others think he could defend himself. Likewise, when he uses public transport, he makes sure not to travel alone in order to avoid feeling vulnerable:

> I feel restricted and observed when I'm not around other migrants. When I'm sitting on the metro, I always make sure that there is another migrant on there with me. A black, an Arab, I don't care! But when there is no other migrant, I don't feel good.

The importance of not being the only foreigner in public spaces was emphasized repeatedly by Alyas and his peers. Being alone triggers feelings of being at risk. In order to counter such feelings, especially outside the foreigner spaces, they seek the company of other people they assume to be equal and move in groups. They are alert with regard to the urban and social environment as they tactically move across the city: they cautiously observe their surroundings, their stance characterized by an alertness towards change in the form of possible acts of power and shifting social forces (Vigh 2009).

Interactions, positioning and turning oneself into a particular persona in a particular place shaped how these young men were perceived (Rosenkrantz-Lindegaard 2009). Fiercely staring back or moving across urban spaces in groups paradoxically reinforces negative encounters, as young people may be perceived as hostile or threatening. In public places, they were approached as a population in need of being controlled and contained (Lipsitz 2005). The young men we spoke to reported frequent police checks, especially on public transport, and harassment by adults as they socialized and hung out in public spaces.

Such negative encounters increased after leaving high school, as young people had to venture beyond the familiarity of their immediate environment in search of employment or higher education. At a community event, the first author met a group of four young men who were enrolled at a university in the nearby region of Brandenburg, which has a reputation for xenophobia and neo-Nazi groups. They had graduated from the same *Gymnasium*, the equivalent of a state grammar school, not far from the integrated secondary school where our research took place. The four young men were in their first year of university. Their experience of living outside of Neukölln gave them a new perspective on the relative 'safety' that the multi-ethnic district provided. Hamza, a young nineteen-year-old Arabic man, explained what consistently brought them back to Neukölln:

> We come back every weekend. This is where our families and friends are. It's like Nazi-land out there in Brandenburg. We only hang out together, and we don't really talk to anyone else [the other three shake their heads in agreement].

Here is where the action is! As soon as I'm done, I'm back here [Neukölln]. We have no racism here.

Despite the rapid urban change and unsettled communities, Neukölln continued to draw young people back, seemingly providing a greater sense of belonging than other districts or cities. For these young men, the importance of routine returns was explained by reference to anti-migrant sentiments in Brandenburg – 'Nazi-land out there'. Compared with their experiences in Brandenburg, they appreciated Neukölln as a safe space marked by the relative absence of racism – a place where they felt a sense of belonging alongside others with a migration background.

Salim (nineteen), who was about to graduate from high school and attend university, preferred to stay close to home and not move his social life outside of Neukölln: 'I love the Arab community here, and when I'm not here I miss it. I want to study in Berlin or Potsdam so that I can still be here. In other cities I don't feel so good.' Listed as a model student at the comprehensive secondary school, Salim did not have a group of friends sharing the same goals, and he felt more secure being close to the Arabic community and his family on a daily basis. The assumed tolerance towards being a *Schwarzkopf* (black-head) or a Muslim in Neukölln prevented many young people from leaving the district for other parts of Berlin, let alone other cities in Germany.

Being a Foreigner 'at Home'

In a joint interview with his classmate, Antwan (thirteen) beamed while exclaiming: 'Neukölln is the bomb! It's the foreigner district!' His friend immediately agreed, with equal enthusiasm. As Antwan pointed out, Neukölln was at times viewed as a space that signified pride and foreigner ownership. While Antwan's view was shared particularly amongst younger students (eleven to fourteen years old), those who were older became increasingly aware of social and spatial challenges, as they faced the stark reality of a changing neighbourhood, dirty streets and social divides.

Young men between twenty and thirty years of age recounted how, during their time in secondary school, they used to meet in groups on the streets of Neukölln to socialize. They identified specific areas or street corners that had been 'theirs', and yet respected others who passed. With the rapid changes towards a more diverse public in the neighbourhoods of northern Neukölln, the young men were irritated that gathering in public aroused surveillance by neighbours and the police. Likewise, a local youth centre was surprised at the request to make sure its guests would disappear quickly at closing time, rather than linger outside, to avoid intimidating new residents. Instead of feeling that they were able to roam freely in Neukölln and shape a sense of 'place belongingness' (Antonsich 2010) in public space, these young men felt increasingly restricted in terms of where and how they moved around their own neighbourhoods.

With increasing diversity came unpredictability, both on the streets and within residential buildings. Several mothers lamented how they did not let their children play in the courtyard any longer, since they were scared of being evicted as a result of complaints from neighbours. As a consequence of such concerns, boys and girls were forced to spend much free time in the small, crowded apartments, limiting interactions and movement across the neighbourhood.

Limited movement in public spaces was furthermore restricted by the fear of gossip within the communities and large family networks, resulting in social control through behaviour monitoring. This social control of the young people's movements, especially the movements of girls, was enacted in line with what parents or relatives deemed 'correct' interactions in and between communities, as well as with newer residents. These forms of social control had a significant impact on the ways in which girls and young women structured daily lives and social encounters. The case of Aleah provides an appropriate example of how girls negotiated this tension created by communal social control:

> I came home and my mom was like, 'you had fun, didn't you?' I just asked, 'how did you know that?' She said that someone had phoned and said that I was having fun and laughing with classmates on the metro, just to let my mom know what I was doing, and also with boys! Thankfully I'd phoned her earlier and she knew what I was up to.

Aleah's open communication with her mother protected her from the family risks of gossip and social control. Girls who did not communicate with their parents as openly faced greater risks of being reported and scolded, as well as being increasingly restricted in their movements, and thus experienced more caution moving around even supposedly safe community spaces. Young women in particular had to be wary in terms of whether their actions could be 'exposed' by relatives or gossip.

For young girls, the influence of fear and gossip reduced their freedom to move about and restricted social interaction. Aleah spent hours talking to her mother in order to convince her that it was safe and appropriate for her to go out with her classmates and to participate in school trips. Unlike her elder sisters, Aleah employed unusual tactics: she took her mother to school to meet her teachers, which helped her develop trust in, and understanding of, her daughter's social environment. Aleah was able to provide her parents, who had fled Palestinian camps in Lebanon shortly before her birth, with new perspectives and thus reduce their fears:

> It was hard for my mother, because I was the first one in my family to go out and do things on my own. Following my final exams, we did a lot together with classmates, both boys and girls. We went out for dinner, for example: the whole class! For other parents, it took a lot of convincing, and some girls weren't allowed to join. Other girlfriends of mine, who were a grade or two lower, could not believe it. They were like, 'really? You guys can go out together? Together as a class?' For my mother, it was always important that I was not out too long: get back before it is dark. I'm not really the type who wants to go out all the time. I think I would have difficulties if I were that type. I like being out occasionally. I like to go shopping, which I often do, but it is not my thing to do something every day. That's why I didn't have too much difficulty and I could join my classmates for outings, like dinner or bowling.

Aleah was proud that she was often the only girl who was allowed to go out with others. Her close relationship with her mother reduced intergenerational conflict. Many girls asserted that at home especially, they were not 'the type who always likes to go out' anyway. As we will see in the next section, however, their statements were often contradicted by their actions. In fact, many young women often pushed boundaries when they were outside the family environment.

Navigating School

The social space provided by the school interlinked friendships that crossed ethnic and gender boundaries. However, contact with new residents was still limited; of the high school students interviewed, few had German friends. In most primary school classes, German students were a minority, and in the secondary levels there were often none; those of European descent were often the children of migrants or refugees from Eastern European countries, especially Poland, Romania and the former Yugoslavian states, such as Bosnia and Serbia. Many pupils at the school were Muslim, and wearing a headscarf or looking like a 'foreigner' was common. Young people would frequently describe this as 'normal'.

For Madu, a thirteen-year-old girl whose parents were planning to move to another district with a noticeably less diverse population, the transition was tinged with the fear of not being liked, as she described it, for having 'brown skin':

> I'm afraid of going to the secondary school: it's in a different district, and they are different there. In our class in Neukölln, everyone is either foreign or partly

foreign; I'm worried that in my new school there are fewer foreigners – that there will be a majority of white students. And I'm worried they might not like me because I'm not white. I'm just different from them. I'm just used to this here, yeah?

For Madu, the appeal of the integrated secondary school where the research took place lay in its high proportion of students with foreigner status – people that she saw as being similar to herself, despite the high ethnic variability amongst her classmates. Her parents migrated from South Asia and her dark brown skin made her stand out next to most of her peers. She recounted how her peers used to call her 'chocolate' and how hard that was for her when she first started at the school. As they got to know her and they became friends, these comments rarely came up and she felt increasingly excited about school.

Madu's hesitancy in switching districts and schools lay in her fear of not being accepted for looking and being different from the German students. Interestingly, Mannitz observed a similar trend in her research at Berlin's schools: pupils expressed a wish for continued segregation because of feeling 'under pressure' and 'under observation' around Germans (2012: 187). An important element observed in our research was the fear of being misunderstood, of 'not being liked' by the majority population, and curbed desires for intermingling.

Madu further provided a contrast to the middle-class neighbourhood to which her parents had decided to move with the school space in Neukölln:

> In Zehlendorf there are way fewer foreigners, yes? I don't feel as good there. In Neukölln, there are a lot of dodgy people, but the school is a place in which I can feel good.

At school, young people knew each other and the wider student population, and could develop a sense of familiarity with teachers and varying class dynamics.[7] Particularly for the girls, the migrant-dominated school environment was a place of relative security in comparison to the district's unpredictable and socially patrolled streets. The girls considered the school an important place for socializing, interacting and friendship building. However, bullying, fights and confrontations often involved insults and reflections of difference along ethnic and religious grounds. The social control prevalent in communities also affected school interactions. While rumours and gossip spread through different grades, classes and networks, there was generally a strong effort to keep what happened at the school separate from what happened at home. Some cousins and siblings formed pacts to prevent transgressing this home–school divide.

Naima (thirteen) did not wish for her parents to be involved in her school experience. She considered the school 'her space', where she could interact relatively freely without family interference. A few days prior to the first day of school after the summer holidays, Naima explained her excitement for regaining the freedom of school as a space where she could interact freely with her peers:

> The summer was shit! Totally shit. I didn't do anything and we had so much family visiting, and they were so loud! There was no space and I was going crazy! I'm so excited for school to start again. That's where the fun and action is!

For the young Naima, online chatting via popular smartphone apps such as Snapchat and WhatsApp comprised much of her social interaction when she was not at school. With five male siblings and a large family network in Neukölln, she described the school holidays as stressful, with limited personal space and largely confined to a small, overcrowded apartment. The school was an enjoyable social space she could not access otherwise.

This wish to separate home and school was especially actively pursued by young men, who did not want to trouble their parents and feared reprimand by the family. Instead, the young men hoped to solve problems themselves. When teachers called parents at home to report misbehaviour or transgressions, students considered this an act of betrayal and ultimate punishment. The students' desire to keep the home and the school separate creates distinctive social spaces between the two, which young people have to navigate carefully, adjusting and adapting to the distinct cultures, bridged by ambivalent public spaces.

Discussion and Conclusion

The ways in which students talk about 'home', as detailed in excerpts from the eighth-grade class in the introduction, show that they do not associate feeling 'safe' or being 'at home' with life in Germany, albeit there is more ambivalence about the situation in Neukölln. We maintain that young people's navigational potential – that is, their capacity to feel at ease, interact and socialize with others in different social spaces – impacts on their ability to form a sense of 'place belongingness' (Antonsich 2010) in the public realm. We have argued that feelings of discrimination reduce mobility outside of migrant-dominated areas. Furthermore, the reshaping of the social environment through gentrification within Neukölln has, instead of positively contributing to opportunities to interact with others, reduced young people's movements and their sense of belonging and safety regarding their social environment. Through the arrival of members of mainstream German society, such as young families and international students, feelings of being discriminated against or misunderstood are now associated with everyday interaction in the neighbourhood. Navigational potential is furthermore reduced by gossip, rumours and social control within communities. Given this limitation of public spaces to navigate within and beyond Neukölln, the space of the school is gaining greater significance in the development of a sense of belonging. The high proportion of migrant children among school students creates a relative shield from the insecurity of urban public spaces in which being visible for cultural difference continues to attract comments or looks.

Public spaces are the arena for constructions of similarities and differences (Ehrkamp 2008), and it is there that feelings of alienation are produced.[8] Research by the German Antidiscrimination Union (Uslucan and Yalcin 2012) revealed that the more frequent and severe someone's experience of discrimination, the more resistance he or she develops towards integration. Furthermore, this research emphasized how repeated exposure to discrimination can lead to low self-esteem and deteriorating health, and can contribute to the probability of becoming a victim of, or even committing, violent acts. Repeated discrimination hinders integration into the work environment and prevents migrants from becoming active participants in society. These findings were based on indicators relating to experiences of individual migrants who were faced with discrimination in Germany. Such discrimination is embedded both in structures (e.g. insufficient access to services, housing or employment, due to cultural and language barriers) and in person-to-person interactions (e.g. rejection and racist or discriminatory encounters, based on religion or ethnicity). Being a foreigner – and therefore not part of Germany – then emerges as a powerful and shared identity marker. In response, the clustering of migrant communities in specific neighbourhoods is, at least in part, a protective measure against discrimination.

While gentrification has its benefits and disadvantages, for the low-income or multi-ethnic residents, rapid changes have exacerbated feelings of alienation in their immediate environment.[9] Ehrkamp's (2008, 2013) research among young Turkish and Kurdish men and women provides particularly relevant insights regarding how gendered practices shape these spaces. Young women's lives are influenced in particular by social control, seen as 'out of place' in public migrant spaces; the ways in which they negotiate resistance with, as well as compliance to patriarchal practices, reveals paradoxes and tensions. At the same time, men's spatial practices of gathering or moving in groups are seen as 'outside of the normal function of cities' (Ehrkamp 2008: 118) and, as we show, their tactics create a racialization of space and a division into 'us' and 'them'. Ehrkamp illustrates how the use and appropriation of public space is important for Turkish and Kurdish men to form their political identities, and we have argued that it is also the public spaces that are vital to shaping a sense of belonging beyond the home, including access to public space as a requirement for full citizenship and civic participation (Brodie 2000).

The need to belong is a fundamental human motivator (Baumeister and Leary 1995) and is situated in both 'place belongingness' and the 'politics of belonging'. The young people we worked with illustrated and emphasized their search for belonging, which they expressed through their desire to feel 'at home' in Neukölln, while they also confronted experiences of sociospatial exclusion. As a result, for the participants, this sense of being at ease and comfortable with one's surroundings was primarily situated in the private, or semi-private, spaces of the home and their ethnic or religious communities.[10] As authors such as Çelik (2015) have shown, tendencies to encapsulate and distance through oppositional or 'reactive' ethnicities are rather increasing among more migrant generations in Germany. It is also in the private (or semi-private) spaces and encounters that gossip and rumours contribute to preventing young people from feeling part of the larger society. Gossip and rumours play their part in them wishing to remain amongst others 'like them' in their educational environment, and in schools in particular. These influential dynamics in their everyday lives limit the seizing of opportunities and thus also prevent the social transition towards an increasingly diverse neighbourhood, as well as further integration into German society.

With the introduction of full-day schooling, students' educational environments form an important space to contemplate and situate – and make comparisons between – each other.[11] Schools shape a particular form of belonging (see Osterman 2000), and the school climate, influenced by social dynamics and environmental and spatial dimensions, plays a vital role (Cemalcilar 2010). In recent years, Germany's education system has been facing many challenges in providing opportunities for children in families with a history of migration and for low-income students (Alba and Foner 2015). Contributing to these challenges are findings of discrimination within the school environment, which continue to play a vital role in how mainstream German society is perceived by the young people portrayed in this chapter (Hirseland and Lüter 2014). As Wellgraf (2013) observed among Neukölln students, schools are the places in which issues of recognition are addressed and feelings of contempt are contemplated and produced. Despite its controlled as well as contested character, particularly for girls, the school environment is an important resource to socialize and breach ethnic and gender divisions, as well as to contemplate forms of belonging outside of the private spaces of the home. The wish to separate the school from the home environment expresses young people's desire for forms of autonomy.

Members of the generations that succeed those who moved to Germany many decades ago seek recognition and belonging in Germany. Belonging is an active process and we have shown how infringements on the ability of young people to navigate socially can prevent the development of a sense of belonging and being 'at home' beyond strictly private and semi-private spaces. As a result of the processes that limit navigational potential, young people may experience a lack of acknowledgement as being an important part of the country in which they were born and raised, and where they desire to shape their futures.

Carola Tize is a Ph.D. candidate in medical anthropology at the University of Amsterdam, the Netherlands, within the Amsterdam Institute of Social Science Research (AISSR). Her Ph.D. research focuses on the processes influencing the intergenerational transmission of inequity in Berlin-Neukölln, and the role of youth agency in either reiterating or resisting the trends through the generations.

Ria Reis is full Professor of Medical Anthropology at Leiden University Medical Center and Associate Professor in the Department of Anthropology at the University of Amsterdam, the Netherlands, as well as Honorary Professor at the Children's Institute, University of Cape Town, South Africa. Whereas her earlier research centred on culture, epilepsy and disability in different cultural settings, in particular in Africa, her current research focus is on young people's health perceptions and strategies, and the transgenerational transmission of vulnerabilities in the context of inequality. Most of her research is qualitative and applied, contributing to multidisciplinary health research and interventions.

Notes

1. All translations are our own unless otherwise specified.
2. In 2001, Germany received what is today called the 'PISA shock', which was the revelation that, of all the member states of the Organisation for Economic Co-operation and Development (OECD), Germany has the lowest level of social mobility (Quenzel and Hurrelmann 2010). This confirmed that poverty and low educational achievement are

transmitted across generations among lower social classes. This was attributed predominantly to the three-tiered school system and has had a particularly significant impact on young people whose (grand)parents migrated to Germany, who continue to have low chances of social mobility even years after school reforms and attempts to bridge the divide (Statistisches Bundesamt 2016). The regional city government of Berlin abolished the three-tier school system to allow greater social mobility for those in the lower classes, especially those with a migrant background. Instead, the city administration introduced a two-tier school system, composed of integrated secondary schools and grammar schools (*Gymnasium*). Nevertheless, the German education system continues to face criticism for failing to maximize the potential of children from lower classes, and children's performance has been said to be influenced by factors (such as discrimination) unrelated to capability (Geissler 2008).

3. Ethnographic fieldwork consisted of participant observation and over ninety semi-structured and informal interviews with students, as well as young people no longer in school, parents, teachers and other professionals. The first author participated in everyday schooling activities, such as classes and field trips, and was present during breaks and in the counselling office. Outside of school hours, she went with the students to eat or explore the neighbourhood and beyond. During a photo project with four students, she documented their navigational paths through Neukölln, as well as places they liked, feared and avoided. The interviews included young men and women aged eleven to twenty-seven from sixteen nationalities, as well as mothers and key neighbourhood figures. The focus on mothers was chosen because they were more accessible and open to the first author, who is also a woman. Although interviews with fathers were possible, the choice to not interview them fostered trust within the circles of the mothers. The main research focus was on school students aged twelve to sixteen, in grades five to eight.

4. This separation between northern and southern Neukölln does not include Gropiusstadt, with a share of 40 per cent of people with a migration background (Bezirksamt Berlin-Neukölln 2012: 14).

5. Social City (*Soziale Stadt*) has been promoted as a key mechanism to battle social and economic exclusion. Its effects, however, are contested. For an analysis of this initiative, see Bockmeyer (2006) or Silver (2006).

6. In 2012, Neukölln, Charlottenburg and Mitte were among the districts with the highest numbers of people classified as migrants or migrant descendants, above Berlin's average of 27 percent. Mitte contained the highest, at 46 percent; Neukölln was at 40 percent; and Charlottenburg at 35 percent. However, neither Mitte nor Charlottenburg are popularly perceived as problematic migrant districts. Marzahn, in East Berlin, by contrast, only has a migration history population of around 12 percent (Bezirksamt Berlin-Neukölln 2012).

7. While some have noted that youth centres (*Jugendclubs*) are an important place for young people in Berlin (den Besten 2010), for the participants of this research, these spaces were rarely mentioned as a place to spend time.

References

Adam, H. 2015. 'Xenophobia, Asylum Seekers, and Immigration Policies in Germany', *Nationalism and Ethnic Politics* 21(4): 446–64.

Alba, R., and N. Foner. 2015. *Strangers No More: Immigration and the Challenges of Integration in North America and Europe*. Princeton, NJ: Princeton University Press.

Antonsich, M. 2010. 'Searching for Belonging: An Analytical Framework', *Geography Compass* 4(6): 644–59.
Baumeister, R.F., and M.R. Leary. 1995. 'The Need to Belong: Desire for Interpersonal Attachments as a Fundamental Human Motivation', *Psychological Bulletin* 117(3): 497–529.
Behrendt, M., A. Lier and S. Pletl. 2008. 'Nachtstreife durch Berlins gefährlichsten Bezirk', *Welt N24*. Retrieved 8 July 2018 from https://www.welt.de/regionales/berlin/article1539168/Nachtstreife-durch-Berlins-gefaehrlichsten- html.Bezirk.
Berckmoes, L.H. 2014. 'Elusive Tactics: Urban Youth Navigating the Aftermath of War in Burundi', Ph.D. dissertation. Amsterdam: Vrije Universiteit.
Berkemeyer, N., W. Bos, V. Manitius, B. Hermstein and J. Khalatbari. 2013. *Chancenspiegel 2013: Zur Chancengerechtigkeit und Leistungsfähigkeit der Deutschen Schulsysteme mit einer Vertiefung zum Schulischen Ganztag*, Bertelsmann Stiftung. Retrieved June 7 2013 from https://www.chancenspiegel.de/typo3conf/ext/jp_downloadslm/pi1/download.php?datei=fileadmin/contents/downloads/Chancenspiegel_2013_Langfassung.pdf&ftype=pdf.
Bernt, M., and A. Holm. 2009. 'Is it, or is Not? The Conceptualization of Gentrification and Displacement and its Political Implications in the Case of Berlin-Prenzlauer Berg', *City* 13(2–3): 312–24.
Bezirksamt Berlin-Neukölln. 2009. 'Integrationspolitik in Neukölln', Berlin. Retrieved 8 July 2018 from https://www.berlin.de/ba-neukoelln/_assets/dokumente/beauftragte/pdf-datei_in_deutscher_sprache___integrationspolitik_.pdf.
———. 2012. 'Gesundheitsbericht: Neukölln- Daten zur sozialen Lage', Berlin. Retrieved January 1 2016 from https://digital.zlb.de/viewer/rest/image/15589954_2012_1/sozialdaten_bericht_final_august2012_1.pdf/full/max/0/sozialdaten_bericht_final_august2012_1.pdf.
Bockmeyer, J. 2006. 'Social Cities and Social Inclusion: Assessing the Role of Turkish Residents in Building the New Berlin', *German Politics & Society* 81(24): 49–76.
Brodie, J. 2000. 'Imagining Democratic Urban Citizenship', in E.F. Isin (ed), *Democracy, Citizenship and the Global City*. London: Routledge, pp. 110–28.
Çelik, Ç. 2015. '"Having a German Passport Will Not Make Me German": Reactive Ethnicity and Oppositional Identity among Disadvantaged Male Turkish Second-Generation Youth in Germany', *Ethnic and Racial Studies* 38(9): 1646–62.
Cemalcilar, Z. 2010. 'Schools as Socialisation Contexts: Understanding the Impact of School Climate Factors on Students' Sense of School Belonging', *Applied Psychology* 59(2): 243–72.
De Certeau, M. 1984. *The Practice of Everyday Life*. Berkeley: University of California Press.
De Martini Ugolotti, N. and E. Moyer. 2016. '"If I Climb a Wall of Ten Meters": Capoeira, Parkour and the Politics of Public Space among (Post)Migrant Youth in Turin, Italy', *Patterns of Prejudice* 50(2): 188–206.
Den Besten, O. 2010. 'Local Belonging and "Geographies of Emotions": Immigrant Children's Experience of Their Neighbourhoods in Paris and Berlin', *Childhood* 17(2): 181–95.

Drever, A. 2004. 'Separate Spaces, Separate Outcomes? Neighbourhood Impacts on Minorities in Germany', *Urban Studies* 41(8): 1423–39.

Ehrkamp, P. 2006. '"We Turks are No Germans": Assimilation Discourses and the Dialectical Construction of Identities in Germany', *Environment and Planning* A38:1673–93.

_____. 2008. 'Risking Publicity: Masculinities and the Racialization of Public Neighborhood Space', *Social and Cultural Geography* 9(2): 117–33.

_____. 2013. '"I've Had it with Them!" Younger Migrant Women's Spatial Practices of Conformity and Resistance', *Gender, Place & Culture* 20(1): 19–36.

Eksner, H.J. 2013. 'Revisiting the "Ghetto" in the New Berlin Republic: Immigrant Youths, Territorial Stigmatisation and the Devaluation of Local Educational Capital, 1999–2010', *Social Anthropology* 21(3): 336–55.

Geissler, R. 2008. 'Die Metamorphose der Arbeitstochter zum Migrantensohn: Zum Wandel der Chancenstruktur im Bildungssystem nach Schicht, Geschlecht, Ethnie, und deren Verknüpfungen', in P.A. Berger and H. Kahlert (eds), *Institutionalisierte Ungleichheiten: Wie das Bildungswesen Chancen Blockiert.* Weinheim: Juventa, pp. 71–100.

Gestring, N. 2011. 'Parallelgesellschaft, Ghettorisierung und Segregation- Muslime in Deutschen Städten', in H.Meyer and K.Schubert (eds), *Politik und Islam.* Wiesbaden: VS Verlag, pp. 168–90.

Gude, S. 2011. 'Sozialstrukturentwicklung in Nord-Neukölln', Berlin. Retrieved 13 July 2013 from http://schillerpromenade-quartier.de/uploads/media/NNK_TOPOS_End.pdf.

Hirseland, A.S., and A. Lüter. 2014. 'Zusammenleben in Nord-Neukölln: Eine Bestandsaufnahme', Berlin. Retrieved 13 July 2016 from https://camino-werkstatt.de/downloads/Zusammenleben_in_Nord-Neukoelln.pdf.

Hooks, B. 2009. *Belonging: A Culture of Place.* New York: Routledge.

Lipsitz, G. 2005. 'Midnight Children: Youth Culture in the Age of Globalization', in S. Maira and E. Soep (eds), *Youthscapes: The Popular, the National, the Global.* Philadelphia: University of Pennsylvania Press, pp. vii–xiv.

Mannitz, S. 2005. 'Coming of Age as "the Third Generation": Children of Immigrants in Berlin', in J. Knörr (ed.), *Childhood and Migration: From Experience to Agency.* Bielefeld: transcript, pp. 23–50.

_____. 2012. 'Integration Norms and Realities in Diverse Urban Neighbourhoods in Germany', *Nordic Journal of Migration Research* 2(2): 182–91.

Münch, S. 2009. '"It's All in the Mix": Constructing Ethnic Segregation as a Social Problem in Germany', *Journal of Housing and the Built Environment* 24(4): 441–55.

Osterman, K. 2000. 'Students' Need for Belongingness in the School Community', *Review of Educational Research* 70(3): 323–67.

Quenzel, G., and K. Hurrelmann. 2010. 'Bildungsverliehrer: Neue Soziale Ungleichheiten in der Wissensgesellschaft', in G. Quenzel and K. Hurrelmann (eds), *Bildungsverliehrer: Neue Ungleichheiten.* Wiesbaden: VS Verlag, pp. 11–33.

Rosenkrantz-Lindegaard, M. 2009. 'Navigating Terrains of Violence: How South African Male Youngsters Negotiate Social Change', *Social Dynamics* 35(1): 19–35.

Schönwälder, K., and J. Sohn. 2009. 'Immigrant Settlement Structures in Germany: General Patterns and Urban Levels of Concentration of Major Groups', *Urban Studies* 46(7): 1439–60.

Silver, H. 2006. 'Introduction: Social Integration in the "New" Berlin', *German Politics & Society* 24(4): 1–48.

Statistisches Bundesamt. 2016. 'Bevölkerung und Erwerbstätigkeit: Bevölkerung mit Migrationshintergrund- Ergebnisse des Mikrozensus 2015-', Wiesbaden. Retrieved 8 July 2018 from https://www.destatis.de/DE/Publikationen/Thema tisch/Bevoelkerung/MigrationIntegration/Migrationshintergrund.html.

Stolle, D. et al. 2013. 'Immigration-Related Diversity and Trust in German Cities: The Role of Intergroup Contact', *Journal of Elections, Public Opinion & Parties* 23(3): 279–98.

Uslucan, H.H., and C.S. Yalcin. 2012. 'Wechselwirkung zwischen Diskriminierung und Integration – Analyse bestehender Forschungsstände', Antidiskrimnie rungsstelle des Bundes, Essen. Retrieved 8 July 2018 from http://www.antidis kriminierungsstelle.de/SharedDocs/Downloads/DE/publikationen/Expertisen/ Expertise_Wechselwirkung_zw_Diskr_u_Integration.pdf?__blob=publication File.

Utas, M. 2005. 'Victimcy, Girlfriending, Soldiering: Tactic Agency in a Young Woman's Social Navigation of the Liberian War Zone', *Anthropological Quarterly* 78(2): 403–30.

Veldboer, L., R. Kleinhans and J.W. Duyvendak. 2002. 'The Diversified Neigh-bourhood in Western Europe and the United States: How Do Countries Deal with the Spatial Distribution of Economic and Cultural Differences?', *Jimi/Rimi* 3(1): 41–64.

Vigh, H. 2006. *Navigating Terrains of War: Youth Soldiering in Guinea-Bissau.* New York: Berghahn Books.

———. 2009. 'Motion Squared: A Second Look at the Concept of Social Navigation', *Anthropological Theory* 9(4): 419–38.

Wellgraf, S. 2013. 'Facing Contempt: Dealing with Exclusion among Berlin Hauptschüler', *Ethnography* 15(2): 160–83.

Wensierski, P. 1997. 'Endstation Neukölln', *Spiegel Online*, 20 October. Retrieved 8 July 2018 from http://www.spiegel.de/spiegel/print/d-8805068.html.

Yuval-Davis, N. 2006. 'Belonging and the Politics of Belonging', *Patterns of Prejudice* 40(3): 197–214.

Chapter 6

The Post-migrant Paradigm

Naika Foroutan

Germany attracted major international attention for its role in the so-called European refugee crisis in 2015–16. The country's experience with migration featured prominently in debates about social cohesion, pluralism and heterogeneity. Whereas migration to Germany has a long history, migrants and their descendants used to be viewed as short-term residents and did not play an important role in discourses on Germany's national identity. However, their struggles for political and social recognition, equality and participation, as well as demographic changes, pushed the political establishment to accept officially Germany's status as a country of immigration (*Einwanderungsland*). In 2001, a German parliamentary commission suggested legal recognition of this fact and thus initiated processes to grant greater minority rights and promote participation. This shift required a national narrative to incorporate migrants and their descendants as part of a 'New Germany'. This emancipatory approach, which seeks to go beyond established migrant–native divides, became contested and led to a polarization between nativist ideologies and pluralist concepts of belonging. The more migrants and their descendants demand equal access to forms of belonging, which is the promise of a pluralist democracy, the more visible they become, with increasingly harsh responses in debates on national identity. This is the main challenge of the 'post-migrant' paradigm, which dismantles this artificial migrant–native binary. The paradigm instead emphasizes the complex dynamics of plural democracies, in which migration becomes a dominant code for any kind of plurality and a key social division splits pluralists from nativists: those who embrace growing diversity, hybridity and ambiguity, on the one hand, and those who reject such concepts, on the other.

Data on Migration

The International Organization for Migration (IOM) defines 'migrant' as:

> any person who is moving or has moved across an international border or within a state away from his/her habitual place of residence, regardless of (1) the person's legal status; (2) whether the movement is voluntary or involuntary; (3) what the causes for the movement are; or (4) what the length of the stay is.[1]

By contrast, 'immigration' is defined as 'a process by which non-nationals move into a country for the purpose of settlement' (IOM 2017) while the term 'migration' points to the ongoing dynamics of a process that does not end after settlement. In addition, the United Nations High Commissioner for Refugees (UNHCR) supports a terminological distinction between migrants and refugees:

> Migrants choose to move not because of a direct threat of persecution or death, but mainly to improve their lives by finding work, or in some cases for education, family reunion, or other reasons. Unlike refugees who cannot safely return home, migrants face no such impediment to return. If they choose to return home, they will continue to receive the protection of their government.[2]

In this chapter, the term 'migrant' is used according to the definition of the Council of Europe: 'to refer, depending on the context, to emigrants, returning migrants, immigrants, refugees, displaced persons and persons of immigrant background and/or members of ethnic minority populations that have been created through immigration'.[3]

In Germany, it is common to use the term 'migration background' (*Migrationshintergrund*) when talking about immigrants and their descendants. The German Federal Statistical Office coined the term in its 2005 annual micro-census to describe individuals who themselves, or whose parents or grandparents, moved to Germany after 1949. It is similar to the term 'migrant' as it is used by the Council on Europe and refers to first-generation immigrants as well as to second- and third-generation citizens. In the public debate, the term 'migrant' is used loosely to describe any person who does look like a 'real German' – white – or whose family has non-German roots. The term 'migrant' in German – and even European – public discourse is not a straightforward technical term, but a category of distinction that is used not only for the denial of belonging to a collective identity, but also to justify structural inequalities and social distance (Sidanius and Pratto 2001). Although decades have passed, the ascription of 'originally being from somewhere else', intended to mean 'remaining an outsider', is still prevalent. Migrants are not considered a 'natural' part of society, but rather are addressed as transitive aliens. This outgrouping concerns a denial of belonging and symbolic rights, but also discrimination and lower structural integration. Being a migrant signifies being treated differently and being negated of inclusive concepts of a collective identity. The tem 'post-migrant' thus seeks to expose the exclusionary power of 'migration' as a dominant category of distinction when used to describe a lack of social inclusion. The post-migrant paradigm deconstructs 'migration' as a dominant marker of social difference by stressing the normality of migration and mobility in a globalized world. When, according to the German Federal Bureau of Statistics, nearly one in three young families in Germany include members with a migration background, the category loses its relevance as a marker of exceptionality.[4]

Of course, 'migration' remains a relevant category to conduct research or describe social composition, but it cannot be seen any longer as an aberrant or transitory social situation that creates anxiety or chaos. The post-migrant paradigm pushes migration and ethnicity as markers of social division into the background and seeks to describe the hybridization of societies beyond the migrant–native binary. Instead, it foregrounds political attitudes as more significant markers that create different in-and out-groups, reshuffle belonging and lead to the emergence and acceptance, on the one hand, as well as the rejection, on the other hand, of an ambiguity grounded in plurality. In post-migrant societies, in-groups and out-groups are no longer defined predominantly by ethnicity, but rather by attitudes and ideologies towards migration, plurality, heterogeneity and diversity – groups are distinguished by their positions towards plural(ist) democracies.

According to Dahl, the main conflict in pluralist democracies regards autonomy or control. It centres on the question of 'how much autonomy ought to be permitted to what actors, with respect to what actions, and in relation to what other actors, including the government of the state? Plus, the complementary question: how much control ought to be exercised by what actors' (Dahl 1982: 2). At the same time, Dahl and Shapiro describe democracies as being centred on citizens' direct or representative rule, with control mechanisms and checks and balances among executive, legislative and judicative powers, and referring to a constitutional state of law that guarantees the equality of citizens (Dahl and Shapiro 2015). Sniderman describes pluralism as a multiplicity of ideas, of institutions and of values, while putting the conflict on the plurality of values in the centre: 'our argument, put in the broader terms, is that conflicts over democratic rights are inescapable, not simply because many citizens do not understand what the values of a democratic politics require in practice, but because many of these values clash with one another, and some of them even clash with themselves' (Sniderman 1996: 235). Isaiah Berlin and Bernard Williams argue that pluralism and liberalism equally contradict monism in questions of values (Berlin and Williams 1994). In this chapter, plural democracy is used to describe societies that rely on the understanding of equality of all, regardless of one's gender, origin, ethnicity, language, nationality, belief or religious and political orientation. The promise of equality in plural democracies also exists despite migration and is only enhanced through the increasing heterogeneity and pluralisation that migration produces. The existence of religious, cultural, ethnic and national diversity introduces a new complexity of different value systems that may clash against each other or with already established value systems. This adds hybridity, antagonisms and ambiguities, and leads to the idea of a new disorder.

As democracies rely on the promise of granting all citizens the same political, juridical and symbolical rights, claims for recognition keep multicultural societies occupied and trigger negotiation processes and conflicts on distribution of social and symbolic resources and privileges (Taylor 1997). The main thesis of this chapter is that the dominant conflict line in post-migrant societies regards this promise of equality, which becomes politically manifest and enforceable by migrants and their descendants when societies change their narrative into being a country of immigration. This narrative regards the division along the migrant/non-migrant or migrant/native binary as politically problematic and morally wrong.

In 2015, 17.1 million migrants or people with a so-called migration background lived in Germany, or 21 per cent of the country's population of 82 million. The majority of immigrants (9.3 million people) held German citizenship; 7.8 million were citizens of other countries. Every third child under eighteen had a so-called migration background (Statistisches Bundesamt 2016). These numbers illustrate that cultural, ethnic, religious and national diversity shapes German society. Plurality and heterogeneity form the everyday experience of many residents in Germany, although not all of them manage this new reality in the same way (Foroutan et al. 2014: 38). This is due to the uneven distribution of immigrants and their descendants: approximately 95 per cent of them live in West Germany, and approximately 5 per cent in the East (Statistisches Bundesamt 2014). Cultural, ethnic, religious and national plurality differ significantly between regions.

Pluralization, Growing Heterogeneity and Hybridization Cause Uncertainty

Over time, many migrants become part of established groups and challenge boundaries and classifications into insiders and outsiders. According
to the late sociologist Zygmunt Bauman, immigrants' descendants in particular can be seen as a 'third element': they are hybrids that cannot be
classified. These hybrids are not simply opposed to the opposition, 'but
question the principle of the opposition, the plausibility of a dichotomy'
(Bauman 2005: 100). This raises an important question: is it the hybridization of society or the act of migration itself that creates uncertainty?
While the first generation of immigrants, who came to Germany as guestworkers after the Second World War, seemed to be more 'controllable'
through resettlement and return policies, the second and third generations claim equal belonging in political, legal and symbolical ways. Their
in-betweenness confronts binary social orders built on ideas of national
identity that identify between natives and non-natives (Hall 2004). This
poses a challenge, especially in the determination of what is and is not
'German' in an ever more hybridized society (Foroutan et al. 2014: 26–27).
Debates on national identity and on the definition of 'who we are' and
a 'guiding German culture' (*deutsche Leitkultur*) gained weight in parallel to the reform of German citizenship law in 2000–1, when descent
based exclusively on blood (*ius sanguinis*) was joined by descent based on
birth and upbringing (*ius soli*), allowing migrants and their descendants
to acquire German citizenship. Being German thus became an achiev-
able attribute rather than an inherited privilege. The consequences have
been ambivalences and dynamics that see migrants and their descendants
'othered' and excluded from a national collective identity, even if they
are naturalized Germans or German-born citizens. Simultaneously and
empirically, society is becoming more diverse and hybrid – a pool of culturally, ethnically, religiously and nationally heterogeneous individuals.

The insecurity caused by growing hybridity and diversity particularly
affects East German regions, which have remained more homogeneous
and lack opportunities for interpersonal contact involving migrants and
natives. The intergroup contact hypothesis (Allport 1954; Dovidio et al.
2005) explains that interpersonal encounter reduces prejudice, which could
be a reason for stronger antipathy towards diversity and migration in East
Germany. In parallel to demographic, cultural and narrative changes of
German society, neoliberal economic developments caused greater social
inequality and unearthed questions about democracy's capacity to provide equality (Crouch 2009; Nachtwey 2010). Insecurities around visible
demographic changes, growing hybridity and heterogenization merge

with rather invisible, but powerful, fears regarding one's economic and symbolic status in a society in which migrants are consciously or unconsciously held responsible for unwanted change.

Migration, it seems, has become a ubiquitous topic, covering major security and inequality debates in Germany and Europe. It has become a trigger for increasingly outspoken racism and growing nationalism. 'Migration' as a topic is connected with economic, political, social or gender insecurities. It has turned into a metanarrative to explain generic failures and challenges. The Dresden-based Pegida movement (Patriotic Europeans against the Islamisation of the Occident) became one such actor appropriating interconnected discourses through claims that disease, delinquency and despair would arrive in Germany with refugees and migrants, who are regarded as the bearers of violent and confrontational cultural behaviour. Pegida members fear Islam as a power that seeks to infiltrate Germany and undermine, or even destroy, the character of European culture and society (see also Bock's analysis of Pegida in Chapter 9 of this volume). Behind such arguments, framed in culturalist terms, there are different causes: general dissatisfaction with the political situation, a sense of being neglected by political and economic elites, the polarizing media and the impact of dominant racist discourses, shaped by ignorance and lack of antiracist education. The migration narrative frames these emotions connected to the fear of losing national identity, merging topics of social injustice, insecurity, anti-elite criticism, cultural supremacy and structural racism, on the one hand, with a utopian ideal of a Germany that returns to its good old past, on the other hand– the period before it became a country of immigration.

All kinds of discomfort and uneasiness that are felt towards an increasingly complex global world are subsumed under the topic of migration, which manifests, for many, the loss of borders, control, the past and identity. Even criticism towards elites or the European Union (EU) is intertwined with 'migration': elites supposedly betrayed citizens because they opened borders for migrants, Islam, refugees. The EU is accused of manipulating ordinary people with their ideologies of diversity and plurality. We need to analyse the mass murder conducted by Anders Breivik in Norway 2011 in this context. Breivik killed members of a social democrat youth group as part of his fight against multiculturalism. The *New York Times* quoted a manifesto written by Breivik, in which he argued that multiculturalism destroyed European Christian civilization: 'The manifesto, entitled "2083: A European Declaration of Independence," equates liberalism and multiculturalism with "cultural Marxism," which the document says is destroying European Christian civilization' (*New York Times*, 24 July 2011). The political allies of those who favour multiculturalism hence equally become victims in anti-diversity and anti-migration attacks. Those who argue that the rise of rightwing populism in Europe is simply a result of class conflict and not of attitudes to race and ethnicity (subsumed by the migration topic) ignore the fact that populist parties also garnered support from the middle classes, as well as from economic and academic elites who usually act as their leaders. Such parties do not represent the underprivileged, white working classes, at least in the case of the populist Alternative for Germany (AfD) party (Bergmann et al. 2016).

Post-migrant: The Term, Notion and Approaches

The term 'post-migrant' (*postmigrantisch*) was initially introduced in 2008 by the German artist Shermin Langhoff, director of Berlin's Maxim Gorki Theater. Langhoff envisioned and experimented with a new type of performance: post-migrant theatre – a theatre performing traditional German plays while adding the perspectives of migrants and their descendants, thus giving their stories a part in German narratives. Her approach aimed at reflecting contemporary German social reality, which is shaped by migration, by portraying hybridity and second-generation migrant culture in the art scene. Post-migrant theatre initially focused on the individual hybrid-migrant-descendant as a performative artist of social change. It used the actors' perspective to demonstrate that individuals labelled as migrants, despite the absence of their own personal migration experience (i.e. second-generation migrants, who constitute one-third of the people in Germany with a migration background), have different family histories, experiences, perspectives and stories from first-generation immigrants or those who do not have a migration background. 'It makes sense that their stories need to be told differently and apart from those that have actually migrated, hence post-migrant' (Langhoff 2009: 27).[5] In this context, the post-migrant concept referred to a chronological, descriptive and actor-centred perspective: it started with the moment of migration and continued with the shifting self-perception of the migrant as a hybrid identity from the first to the second to the third generation. These stories, according to Yildiz (2013: 144f), need to be included in hegemonic narratives and the country's collective memory.

Parallel to these initial actor-focused perspectives, a new one was added by German academia. This focused on the critical meta-analysis and interpretation of society and its transformation processes after migration. The post-migrant term hence slowly moved away from the actor-centred neolabelling of second-generation migrants as post-migrants. Riem Spielhaus, an Islamic Studies scholar, wrote: 'the term explicitly does not pertain to a person's situation or history as a new word for difference in physiognomy, accent or family history' (Spielhaus 2013: 329). Manuela Bojadžijev and Regina Römhild have also cautioned against labelling future generations of immigrants as post-migrants, which they consider a way of rehashing the migration aspect as central to ascribed identity categories (Bojadžijev and Römhild 2014: 18).

The prefix 'post' in post-migrant contains a twofold objective, as it tries to reflect the ambivalent simultaneity of migration in society: while migration is ongoing and a global phenomenon of mobility, the arrival of migrants remains contested on the basis of ethnic, cultural, religious or national backgrounds. On the one hand, migration is a demographic normality, but on the other, this demographic normality is turned into an anomaly by 'migrantizing' one part of society, which entails exclusion from a country's shared identity. The 'post' thus reflects a period and situation that follows after migration has occurred, but during which migration-based exclusion remains a common experience. The concept exposes the dominant continuity of the migration narrative as a basis for social division, while at the same time seeking to challenge and go beyond this divide. At the same time, however, the 'post' prefix creates a semantic conflict (Mecheril 2014); the term suggests that migration needs to be transcended. Mecheril criticizes the idea that if migration constitutes a particular set of circumstances – such as colonialism, nationalism or racism – the addition of 'post' would describe a process of overcoming this set's limiting conditions. This raises a question: does 'post' indicate the end of a particular situation or signal that something needs to be overcome? Both interpretations would not be fruitful, Mecheril concludes, and a terminological challenge. The term demands a rupture of migration-based division. Instead, he suggests, the focus should be shifted towards the regulation of migration-related phenomena (Mecheril 2014: 107f).

The post-migrant paradigm shares in that sense the political dimensions of other 'posts' – describing a transitional situation and analysing trajectories of the past and the present rather than knowing the directions in which society is heading. Theoretical approaches such as postcolonial (Bhabha 1994; Said 1978; Spivak 1988), postnational (Habermas 1998), postdemocracy (Crouch 2009), post-black (Touré 2011) or postgender (Haraway 1991) have sought to question, deconstruct or rethink powerful categories (such as nation, gender, race or blackness), highlighting their empirical as well as analytical and normative limitations. 'Post-migrant' aspires to transcend 'migration' as a disguised marker for racist exclusion, on the one hand, while embracing migration as social normality, on the other. Hence, post-migrant does not seek to depict – as falsely assumed and even criticized – a state in which migration has ended (Mecheril 2014). Rather, it provides a framework of analysis for conflicts, identity discourses and social and political transformations that occur after migration has taken place, while migrants struggle to be recognized as legal stakeholders in society. However, similarly to 'postcolonial', 'post-migrant' could be understood as a strategy for empowerment, surpassing old structures of authority and creating awareness regarding emancipation. Society as whole has experienced migration – not only those who have actually migrated. As implied by the term 'post-colonial', the colonial epoch might have ended, but this does not mean that all structures of exploitation, economic suppression, domination and political power have disappeared. On the contrary, divisions and imbalances, which existed during colonialism, continue to shape life in post-colonial settings. Nevertheless, some post-isms imply a different kind of discontinuity: the concept of post-nationalism does not suggest that nationalism has ended, but rather urges us to think beyond nationalism. Hence, the conceptual aspiration behind the term 'post-migrant' seeks to surpass divisions and rigid categories that have been constructed around the fact and history of migration. Taking inspiration from this analysis, the term 'post-migrant' seeks to change the dominant discourses on migration by (1) embracing migration as an experience and a form of cultural capital. and (2) deconstructing the migrant–native divide, while considering the importance of migration for identity-building processes. In doing so, we need to be aware that discrimination and hegemonic differences among classes and other collective bodies continue to exist – even without migration. 'Post-migrant' does not imply forgetting about migration or disregarding it as a historical phenomenon, but rather calls for a different analytical angle to describe migration.

The term post-migrant has therefore been developed and operationalized across the social sciences (Tsianos and Karakayalı 2014). The term has to feature both as an analytical description and an aspiration for social development. 'Post-migrant' thus describes a chronological and empirical-analytical 'after', a critical-dialectical 'behind', and an aspirational and normative 'beyond' at the same time. The concepts works in an empirical-analytical way by looking at the social effects *after* migration has occurred and *after* it has been politically considered as an irreversible fact of society; it works in a critical-dialectical way by depicting underlying conflicts of migration and looking *behind* constructed dominant conflict lines that have turned migration into a metanarrative and turn other conflict lines related to class, race and gender invisible; and, additionally, this research paradigm seeks to develop a new aspirational mission statement that gives recognition to migrants and other marginalized groups that enter the public sphere and claim rights on representation, participation and equality. The normative approach of this research paradigm is therefore based on the democratic promise of equality and aims to overcome established inequalities and get *beyond* the dominant migrant–native divide in order to approximate the norm of equality to the empirical reality.

The empirical-analytical approach examines and focuses on the empirically existent and observable inequalities, transformations and developments, and analyses their consolidation on institutional, structural, sociopolitical and legal levels. It analyses attitudes and reactions within and towards a pluralizing society with regard to migration policy issues on symbolic and material belongings.

The critical-dialectical approach further embeds the empirical-analytical findings in prevailing social conditions and already established power structures. Empirical findings and observations further examine social inequalities in post-migrant societies and pose the following question: to what extent is it about securing privileges, maintaining positions of power and a socially established status? In addition, the critical-dialectical approach allows a (de)constructivist perspective on the very substance of the migrant–native conflict line: is it really about migration and does the overwhelming dominance of the migration discourse stand in proportion to the empirical reality, or is it rather a constructed hyper-reality that goes hand in hand with a fiction of formerly constructed storylines on homogeneity and the supposed purity of distinctive societies?

The normative-ontological approach introduces new hypotheses into empirical-analytical and critical-dialectical migration research by factoring normative aspirations into the question on what additional elements next to sociostructural dimensions block social cohesions. The 'post-migrant' perspective therefore has a clear stance with regard to the negotiation of equal rights, where it finds validation through the democratic principle of equality. The perceivable gap between norm and reality makes it clear that existential changes would be necessary in order to dissolve the dissonance.

The post-migrant paradigm thus has a threefold approach: (1) an empirical-analytical approach seeking to describe how societies change after migrants have entered society (acknowledgement procedures, population attitudes, narratives, knowledge, contact and more); (2) a critical-dialectical approach deconstructing the anatomy of a public discourse on migration by depicting underlying stereotypes and conflicts; and (3) a normative approach that calls for overcoming the migrant–native divide at a time when migration and mobility constitute everyday normality.

The Post-migrant (PMG) Framework

The post-migrant framework enables the deconstruction of migration as a scapegoat for social insecurities and threats by offering a counter-response to debates on migration and security that are framed around identity and cultural conflict. The new paradigm seeks to understand ambivalences and antagonism in societies by zooming out of narrow identity-politics and depicting the structural and political context of society as a whole, and by deconstructing reported fears and anxieties that are placed in the migration-security nexus. Rightwing populist parties are quick to embrace that nexus and load it with xenophobic and particularly anti-Muslim rhetoric (Decker et al. 2014; Zick et al. 2016). The combination of anti-elite, anti-immigrant and anti-Muslim rhetoric occupying public discourse occurred across European societies affected by migration and pluralization, as well as by growing economic inequality. Through the emancipation of unprivileged groups, such as migrants and their descendants, who are now demanding social and political power, society experiences further resource allocation conflicts (Caselli and Coleman 2013) that lead to antagonistic opposition towards a new claim for unconditional belonging. Contested resources are not only structural and economic but also social, cultural and symbolic.

The claim for equality relies on the promise that a country of immigration and plural democracies carries a social contract to treat all citizens equally, regardless of their social, ethnic or religious origin and sexual orientation. Through the political acknowledgement of being a country of immigration, established hegemonic positions are challenged by formerly marginalized groups, demanding participation, equality and access to rights and privileges. Such demands cause conflict and fear within established social groups, which in turn deny belonging (as symbolic equality) as the denial of political and legal equality becomes increasingly difficult. The post-migrant paradigm dismantles the narrow binary of natives versus migrants as a constructed and reductive description that is empirically inconsistent, and points to deeper-rooted conflicts over power and resource allocation, which explode when subalterns finally start to speak and enter the distributive arena (Spivak 1988). While the pro-plurality-allies demand equal opportunities, the antagonists highlight the importance of ancestry and ethnic belonging. The distributive struggle is symbolically fought on the back of migration, which becomes shorthand for 'diversity'. Other marginalized groups are equally affected: women, LGBTQI+, Jews and blacks. Their claims for representation have long caused ambivalent reactions, under the guise of anti-immigration rhetoric, anti-Semitic and anti-gender discourses emerge as well.

Post-migrant societies are hence characterized by a new bipolar conflict that can be described as the growing polarization between those who can (or sometimes even desire to) live with plurality and form moral majorities (Hall 1997), on the one hand, and antagonists, on the other. Pluralists craft powerful alliances to realize the structural, social, cultural and symbolic distribution of resources across society. At the other end of the spectrum, antagonists claim that equality ought to be reserved for those who belong to a narrow group. Their imagined circle of inclusion is not consistent at all; it features nativist ideas of belonging, authoritarianism, conservative ideas of family and anti-LGBTQI+ positions while defending Jews, homosexuals, gender equality and women's rights against Muslims (on the notion of postliberal, see Pieper et al. (2011)). The glue that binds these fuzzy and contradicting ideas is a deeply rooted aversive racism (Gaertner and Dovidio 1986), combined with a patronizing self-image that demarcates clearly who ought and who ought not to enter the distributive arena. While such antagonists unite against 'genderism' and same-sex marriages and reclaim masculinity, their entitled position as gatekeepers of the nation, the *Volk*, partially allows homosexuals, women and even migrants into the circle – as long as they behave in a certain manner and as long as the gatekeepers remain in their position to decide on inclusion and exclusion.

For the 'post-migrant society' framework, this means the following: migration is a twofold trigger. It is a metanarrative loaded with accusations of social conflict and insecurity, against which social antagonisms are constructed, while also serving as a currency (Clifford 1994) for identity formation that trades in the normality of diversity, hybridity and plurality as new markers of alliances and changing post-migrant peer group identities. The tension of these two positions within the contested arena of plural democracies creates ambivalences and turns the migration narrative into a symbolic battlefield for social self-description. The gap between the normative goal of equality and the empirical reality seems to reveal an instance of cognitive dissonance. Such dissonance entails openly expressed anti-migration sentiment or disguised hostility, accusing immigrants of not being able to follow local norms. Such dissonance, however, can also create new alliances to mobilize resources and adjust norms and actions. The 'post-migrant societies' paradigm has two objectives: (1) it demands a shift away from social constructions on the basis of a migrant-native divide, since this binary glosses over disparities based on class, race and gender; and (2) it produces a different framework of analysis to grasp transformations within a society that has been shaped by migration and its consequences concerning deepening pluralization.

Five Key Findings to Operationalize the PMG Framework

Operationalizing the PMG framework for social science, we can derive five key processes that describe the conflictive dynamic of migration-impacted societies. The process fields interact subsequently and simultaneously:

1) We observe strong ambivalences around the acceptance of ambiguity, diversity and hybridity, which are introduced as concomitant dynamics through the presence, interaction and incorporation permeation (Spivak 1988) of migrants in society. These dynamics are becoming key elements of plural democracies, and dealing with them becomes the core challenge of post-migrant societies.
2) The discursive reworking of plural democracies connects to questions of migration, equality and participation, and leads to new pro-plurality positions and post-migrant alliances that pursue a moral majority and seek to transcend the conservative–liberal binary.
3) Social ambivalences reinforce antagonistic anti-plurality positions, which centre specifically on negative attitudes towards immigrants, Muslims or other ethnic, religious or national minorities. Homogeneous and nationalist groups aim to re-install a less ambiguous order as well as re-invoke equality claims of immigrants.

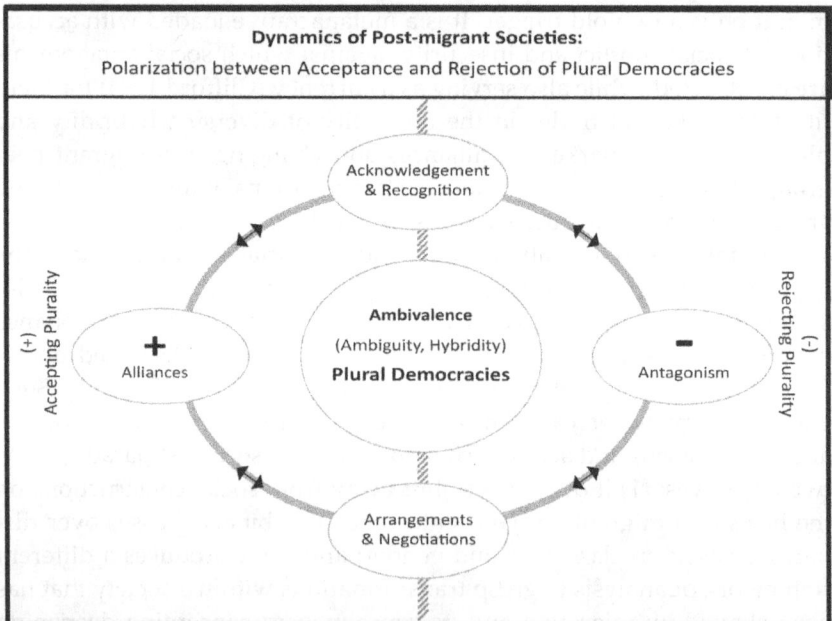

Figure 6.1 Dynamics of post-migrant societies. Figure by the author.

4) The result is polarization, which stems from a dynamic process of arrangements and negotiations involving structural, social, cultural and emotional belonging of migrants and their descendants. These claims are drivers of social change and conflict, since they lead to cultural and resource allocation conflicts among socially established and socially marginalized groups.

5) The idea of equal political, legal and symbolic rights is a promise rooted in the acknowledgement and recognition of being a country of immigration. It has legitimized immigrants' claims for more participation, anti-discrimination policies, equality and visibility.

Five Key Processes of Interaction

As outlined above, post-migrant societies contain five main key processes of interaction that can be analysed by social scientists: (1) political or legal acceptance, and recognition of being a country of immigration; (2) negotiations of rights, positions and representations for minority groups; (3) ambivalences and ambiguities on national identity concepts and concepts of belonging; (4) alliances based on ideological positioning on diversity and migration; (5) antagonism and radicalization against those that embrace diversity.

In the following, these five key processes will be discussed briefly.

Acknowledgement and Recognition

Post-migrant societies emerge when the dominant narrative acknowledges the reality of being a country of immigration rooted in diversity and heterogeneity. This acknowledgement can be articulated through official statements. This happened in Germany in 2001 (Süssmuth 2001: 1), Canada in the 1970s and the United States in the 1960s. Such political shifts led to legal changes and adaptations, as well as to symbolic transformations regarding definitions of belonging that granted immigrants and their descendants equality and viewing them as legitimate stakeholders in society. This shift paves the way for plural democracies based on the idea of equal rights, and breaks ground for legal negotiations on positions, visibilities and privileges.

Migration is a concomitant of globalization, which needs to be considered in political, social and economic debates (Peters 2015). Migratory movements transform society in multiple directions, and it is the responsibility of politicians to adapt legal and political frameworks to reflect such changes. Accepting migrants as political and legal stakeholders in a given state means that they are legitimized to claim rights and achieve representation. This emancipation often involves struggles. It is important to note that these struggles also exist prior to the establishment of an immigration country discourse – and they have, in fact, most likely contributed to official acknowledgement. The difference is that the political and legal acknowledgement of being a country of immigration legitimizes minorities' rights beyond moral and ethical concerns, instead establishing a political reality that allows them to challenge existing inequalities. These struggles for rights are therefore both a precursory and a constitutive element of a post-migrant society. The political recognition of being a country of immigration provides a key platform for the negotiation of positions, representation and equality. It also enables a politically and legally legitimate battle for social justice and the passing of comprehensive immigration legislation.

Arrangements and Negotiations

Once the political establishment acknowledges the status of being a country of immigration, migrants and minorities are able to put forward demands for rights and representations in the political realm, and are now in a position to start a negotiation process with the established authorities and other actors. This process is usually accompanied by arrangements and conflicts at the same time: migrants and their descendants demand more representative, visible positions in politics, culture, sports, public spaces and so on. The privileges of established native groups are questioned in claims to equality, representation and participation. This triggers the emergence of pro- and anti-diversity identities that blame migration for social changes or the dissolution of national identity. Existing values and norms of previously hierarchically constructed concepts of society are challenged, and demands for anti-discrimination action and positive discrimination legislation become more vocal. As demands for minority rights and representations increase, hegemonic actors that fear the loss of their status resist. This conflict-inducing dynamic is part of post-migrant societies. Minority groups seize the opportunity to shape a new, rival discursive hegemony that assembles a moral majority, motivated by the demand for equality as relevant elements in social discourse. Granting migrants and natives the same civil rights creates harsh battles without any guarantee of success, in which minorities confront established structures that are hard to permeate (Spivak 1988).

Ambivalences and Ambiguities

The obsession with migration as a ubiquitous, dominant debate topic creates two kinds of reaction: on the one hand, migration seems to be a 'natural' aspect of contemporary societies, and an empirical and demographic reality for many people going about their everyday lives. On the other hand, the lack of anti-racist political education allows imaginations of hegemonic privileges for established groups (Elias and Scotson 2002: 7) and produces fears of infiltration, population exchange by stealth and the loss of one's own – supposedly homogeneous and easily demarcated – culture through immigration. This reveals a schism between the rational recognition of migration as normality and the emotional rejection of migrants and minorities. Cognitive acceptance and an emotional distance exist at the same time (Foroutan and Canan 2016).

In Germany, for example, this normative paradox becomes apparent in attitudes towards Muslim minorities (Foroutan and Canan 2016: 164): politically legitimized fundamental rights are attacked and questioned on the basis of emotional experience. A study conducted by the Berlin Institute for Integration and Migration Research (Foroutan and Canan 2016) showed that almost 70 per cent of Germans agreed that Muslims in the country should be legally entitled to put forward cultural, religious and social demands. At the same time, however, 60 per cent of survey respondents did not want Muslims to be able to circumcise young men, 50 per cent want to ban female Muslim teachers from wearing a headscarf and 40 per cent supported restricting permission to build mosques in Germany (see Foroutan et al. 2014: 35ff). Although all these rights are guaranteed by Germany's protection of religious freedom, Muslim insistence on making use of their rights causes scepticism, animosity and rejection. Ambivalences also exist within minority groups: on the one hand, there exist demands for greater representation, identity politics, successful spokespersons, and the introduction of quota and anti-discrimination laws. On the other hand, there exists longing for the disappearance of categories that emphasize ethnic backgrounds (see Supik 2014). The first aspiration requires the production of official empirical data on ethnic, national and religious identities of minority groups, whereas the second aspiration implies greater anonymity and the downplaying of different identities. So, whereas plurality and heterogeneity are cognitively accepted – based on constitutional values of equality – even fundamental rights are emotionally rejected when claimed by minorities. This dissonance between cognitive acceptance and emotional distance creates conflictive ambivalences and ambiguities in societies (Foroutan and Canan 2016).

Alliances
Societal structures show that personal relations between people of different origins and trajectories have become increasingly entangled through

personal, professional and social ties. Connections through family, friends, school, clubs, unions, political engagement or the workplace have produced new kinds of knowledge, empathy and attitudes, which construct post-migrant alliances that go beyond the abstractly defined subject and instead give rise to novel relationships based on attitudes, neighbourhood and opportunities rather than on ethnicity or colour (Foroutan 2016: 228). Immigrants and their descendants are not alone in their struggle for representation and participation. They have supporters for their cause who do not necessarily have a migration background, but share views on democracy and equality. This shapes a new moral majority embracing the values of plural democracy, which grants security, fundamental rights, mobility and participation to all its citizens irrespective of ethnic background. Post-migrant alliances are a powerful tool to challenge structures of discrimination: they enable a shared fight against racist attitudes and the isolating othering of migrants, transcending socially constructed divisions and concepts. The post-migrant perspective enables the formation of new equal relationships in the form of rising heterogeneous peer groups that are no longer paternalistically structured (Broden and Mecheril, 2014: 15; Foroutan, 2015: 18).

Ethnicity, colour or nationality do not have dominant roles in these groups. They are replaced by a focus on shared agendas, common values and solidarity (Parsons 1967: 704; Sabatier 1993: 21). Cultural alliances appreciate diversity and the hybridization or exchange of cultural codes; political alliances create a shared fight for democracy and against discrimination and residues of racism; emotional alliances empathize against the 'othering' of citizens and their exclusion from collective identity. Empathy serves as a glue for social relationships, fosters pro-diversity behaviour and emotional alliances, and is needed for the foundation for democracy and social change (Nussbaum 1997: 90). 'Post-migrant alliances' emerge from friendships, family relationships, social interactions and professional relationships or other forms of contact. However, they are also possible without contact or interaction, on the basis of empathy and proximity. Alliances can also be more than just empathetic; they can be political or strategic, sharing have the same objective, vision or reasoning on plural democracies, heterogeneity or diversity.

These post-migrant alliances are reshuffled peer groups, in which members are no longer connected along ethnic, religious, national markers, but are forged together through similar attitudes on diversity, heterogeneity and plurality (Foroutan et al. 2015). These alliances thereby reshuffle concepts of identity and belonging that are centred on ethnicity, ancestry or homogeneity (Bauman 1992) and create new hybrid peer-group identities (Brah and Coombes 2005).

Antagonism

Post-migrant societies have a significant potential for conflict. The idea of a 'new nation' (new Germany, new Canada, new France) formed by historical and contemporary migration is contested by antagonistic groups, such as nationalistic and ethnic homogeneity group, who challenge state authorities, migrant communities and their allies in a political battle for dominance and supremacy (see, for example, the famous slogan of the French extreme-right wing party Le Front National: 'les Francais d'abord' (Laurence and Goodliffe 2013: 36)). Conflicts between groups that favour plurality and those that oppose it intensify noticeably. Minorities' claims to greater access to power and resources lead to visible polarizations around the questions of belonging and national identity or hegemonic power. The dualism of plurality advocates and plurality opponents dominates the political agenda and creates a new binary conflict.

These are opposed developments in post-migrant societies: the emergence of a moral majority that accepts the reality of diversity, raised with a positive or pragmatic outlook on difference and transcending ethnic, religious and colour lines when conceptualizing belonging. This moral majority faces a vocal, antagonistic and growing minority, which opposes hybrid identities and narratives that normalize migration, instead calling for a reversed social order based on exclusive nationalism and ethnic homogeneity. As mentioned above, minority rights in post-migrant societies are more openly contested than in societies that are not officially recognized as countries of immigration. In the latter, national identity is not questioned in the same way as in post-migrant societies, where political conviction, belonging, privileges and representation are constantly negotiated and hegemonic privileges are challenged (Foroutan 2016: 241). The fight over resources and the negotiation of national identity intensify debates about the arrival of newcomers and their social position as outsiders towards established actors (Elias and Scotson 2002: 7). Migration becomes a metaphor for this resource-allocation conflict: pro- and anti-immigration groups develop polarizing positions with reference to migration, confronting one another in the political arena.

In-between these diametrically opposed groups, there is a large and undecided middle ground, shifting from side to the other side. Mobilization efforts of either camp make use of economic and demographic contexts to gain support. In France, Denmark, Hungary, Poland and the United Kingdom, where rightwing populist parties gained between 25 and 50 per cent in elections during the 2010s, the large middle ground was swayed by arguments regarding the economy, demographics and the labour market, which both groups connect with discourses on migration. However, the popularity of rightwing parties cannot simplistically be justified by arguments about the fear of economic decline. Even prosperous European economies, such as Austria, Switzerland or the Scandinavian countries, witnessed the rise of anti-immigrant parties since the 1990s or 2000s. There seems to exist much fertile ground for extremist, anti-migration mobilization, which pushes governments further towards hard-rightwing positions (Mudde 2007).

Conclusion

In the mid 2010s, Europe experienced a rightwing shift (Greven 2016) and social antagonism towards minorities (and Muslims in particular). The increase of anti-migrant attitudes in Europe was accompanied by post-migrant alliances fighting for a different Europe that recognizes diversity and hybridity as a new kind of normality and desirable social reality. The refugee crisis of 2015 and 2016 rekindled debates not only on migration, border security, increasing diversity, and anti-immigrant and anti-Muslim attitudes, but also on questions of asylum and resource allocation for humanitarian causes. The polarization of pro- and anti-refugee positions, rooted in pro- and anti-diversity attitudes, was accompanied by questions regarding economic benefits or disadvantage, the allocation of housing and public space, and other related concerns about resources. The German economy benefited not only from incoming labour power, but also through investments in sectors related to refugee care and aid (such as urban development, vocational training and educational services; Fratzscher and Junker 2005: 615). Nonetheless, the reality that Muslim refugees might stay in Germany intensified debates on immigrant participation and equality, creating a new bipolar conflict around 'migration'. Previously established differences, based on notions of race, class and gender, were increasingly woven into this new conflict line, dividing Europe into countries in favour of strong protectionism, making use of the rhetoric of individual national interests and rigid patriotism, on the one hand, and those in favour of European solidarity, cooperation and openness, on the other. Once again, harsh debates and parliamentary decisions to tighten asylum and immigration laws entered the political mainstream, evaluating critically realities of multiculturalism and plural forms of belonging. European policies became progressively ambivalent in response to this impasse.

These dynamics are inherent to the post-migrant society paradigm: post-migrant societies are marked by the political acknowledgement of being a country of immigration. They recognize migration as a foundational element of their societies and therefore permit legal and political negotiations to create equality. This does not mean that society as a whole embraces migration; on the contrary, many people can perceive it as threatening. However, the political act of recognition is like a social contract that enables the legitimation of demands on equality and participation. While equality is cognitively accepted, emotional and affective responses can block policies aimed at guaranteeing it. Ambiguities and ambivalences are the consequences of this cognitive–emotional divide. This ambivalence complicates political processes. Politically, post-migrant societies are a battlefield of negotiation procedures of marginalized groups seeking to become part of the hegemonic structures. Those who endorse migration and plurality challenge their opponents in a fight over regulatory policies, as migration turns into a metaphor for social disorder that hybridity and plurality supposedly entail. Rightwing populist parties emerged alongside a political narrative of 'cleaning up' in Europe. In the mid 2010s, such parties entered many European parliaments. They led a discourse on 'order' to blame social problems on migration, while promising the return to a nationalist social harmony by curbing or rigidly steering migration.

These challenges of post-migrant societies can be observed in the following five main dynamics, processes and constitutive elements: (1) political acknowledgement; (2) negotiations and arrangements concerning minority rights; (3) post-migrant alliances formed beyond ethnic, religious and national markers; (4) antagonisms against the pro-diversity camp; (5) ambivalences and ambiguities that are the result of these. Post-migrant societies thus witness a polarization that can be described as a new bipolar conflict. The two opposite poles form two camps: those who demand equal rights for each citizen and those who seek to maintain the hegemonic power of their own group. Post-migrant societies are societies in transition. One group's aim is to abolish hegemonic markers, structures and processes – such as dichotomizations, culturalization, ethnicization, racism, stereotyping and other perceptions – to dissolve the dogma of 'otherness' ascribed exclusively to those whose ancestors migrated to Germany. This clashes with revisionist imaginations of the nation as composed of those who have always been there.

The theoretical framework of post-migrant societies seeks an alternative rationale behind antagonism and polarization that goes beyond social and economic explanations. It asks for new perspectives to describe and understand anti-immigrant attitudes, noticing that they are not only linked to economic wealth or social status. Research shows that

Islamophobic attitudes also exist among elite and middle-class groups that are not affected by insecurity (see Gross et al. 2010; Heitmeyer 2012: 33). Anchored hostility towards the upward mobility of minorities became apparent, fostered by the growing support minority groups have received from the establishment through anti-discrimination laws and diversity concepts (see Sutterlüty 2010).

Furthermore, anti-plurality reactions can be seen as an effort to fight ambiguity. For many people, ambiguity causes insecurity because, like hybridity, it questions established borders that are social-psychologically needed to grasp abstract concepts, such as nation, identity, ethnicity or gender. Counter-ambiguity responses offer concepts that are rooted in the idea of purity, exclusivity and clear borders – whether national, religious or ethnic. As a consequence, more people feel attracted to simple responses to complex problems that rightwing populist parties or Islamic extremists offer. The idea of reversing the social order back to homogeneity is rooted in the promise to resolve 'disorder' or 'chaos'. The result of such polarization can be growing violence directed not simply towards minority groups, but also against those who support them. The terror attacks carried out by Anders Breivik revealed how accusations that 'cultural Marxism' enables foreign infiltration can be directed towards those who support migrants politically – in this case, liberal social democrats with their history of pro-migration attitudes. These 'migration allies' are likewise, and perhaps even to a greater extent, held responsible for the loss of cultural identity because of their influential positions and policies on immigration. The term 'post-migrant alliances' captures such novel political forms, since sharing a migration background does not necessarily determine that different individuals would fight for the same cause. Similarly, not having a migration background does not mean that one is necessarily anti-immigrant – and self-identifying as a democrat or a liberal also does not automatically guarantee that someone cannot also harbour racist views.

Naika Foroutan is a political scientist, Professor at the Department of Social Sciences at Humboldt-Universität zu Berlin, Germany, Director of the Berlin Institute for Integration and Migration Research (BIM), as well as Head of the German Center for Integration and Migration (DeZIM). Her research focuses on nation states transforming into countries of immigration and its implications for migration and integration politics. She analyses norm and value debates, collective identities and hybridizations, as well as conflict parameters in plural democracies, with a particular focus on Islam and Muslims.

Notes

1. http://www.iom.int/key-migration-terms#Immigration (retrieved 8 July 2018).
2. Edwards 2016.
3. Council of Europe 2017.
4. https://www.destatis.de/DE/Publikationen/STATmagazin/Bevoelkerung/2012_03/2012_03Migrationshintergrund.html (retrieved 8 July 2018).
5. In German: 'Es scheint mir einleuchtend, dass wir die Geschichten der zweiten und dritten Generation anders bezeichnen. Die stehen im Kontext der Migration, werden aber von denen erzählt, die selber gar nicht mehr gewandert sind. Eben postmigrantisch.'

References

Allport, G.W. 1954. *The Nature of Prejudice*. Oxford: Addison-Wesley.
Bauman, Z. 1992. 'Soil, Blood and Identity', *Sociological Review* 40(4): 675–701.
_____. 2005. *Moderne und Ambivalenz: Das Ende der Eindeutigkeit*. Hamburg: Hamburger Edition.
Berlin, I., and B. Williams. 1994. 'Pluralism and Liberalism. A Reply', *Political Studies* 42: 141–51.
Bergmann, K., M. Diermeier and J. Niehues. 2016. *Parteipräferenz und Einkommen: Die AfD, eine Partei der Besserverdiener?* Cologne: Institut der Deutschen Wirtschaft Köln, IW-Kurzberichte 19-2016.
Bhabha, H.K. 1994. *The Location of Culture*. London: Routledge.
Bojadžijev, M., and R. Römhild. 2014. 'Was kommt nach dem "transnational turn"? Perspektiven für eine kritische Migrationsforschung', in Labor Migration (eds), *Berliner Blätter. Ethnographische und ethnologische Beiträge 65, Vom Rand ins Zentrum. Perspektiven einer kritischen Migrationsforschung*. Berlin: Panama Verlag, pp. 10–24.
Brah, A., and A. Coombes (eds). 2005. *Hybridity and its Discontents: Politics, Science, Culture*. London: Routledge.
Broden, A., and P. Mecheril. 2014. 'Solidarität in der Migrationsgesellschaft: Einleitende Bemerkungen', in Anne Broden and Paul Mecheril (eds), *Solidarität in der Migrationsgesellschaft: Befragung einer normativen Grundlage*. Bielefeld: transcript Verlag, pp. 7–20.
Bundesamt für Migration und Flüchtlinge. 2014. *Migrationsbericht des Bundesamtes für Migration und Flüchtlinge im Auftrag der Bundesregierung: Migrationsbericht 2014*. Nuremburg: BAMF.
Caselli, F., and J. Coleman II. 2013. 'On the Theory of Ethnic Conflict', *Journal of the European Economic Association* 11(1): 161–92.
Clifford, J. 1994. '"Diasporas", Further Inflections: Towards Ethnographies of the Future', *Cultural Anthropology* 9(3): 302–38.
Council of Europe. 2017. 'Glossary', Retrieved 8 July 2018 from https://www.coe.int/en/web/compass/glossary.
Crouch, C. 2009. *Post-democracy*. Cambridge: Polity Press.
Dahl, R.A. 1982. *Dilemmas of Pluralist Democracy: Autonomy vs. Control*. New Haven, CT: Yale University Press.

Dahl, R.A., and I. Shapiro. 2015. *On Democracy*. New Haven: Yale University Press.

Decker, O., J. Kiess and E. Brähler. 2014. *Die stabilisierte Mitte. Rechtsextreme Einstellungen in Deutschland 2014*. Leipzig: Kompetenzzentrum für Rechtsextremismus- und Demokratieforschung. Universität Leipzig.

Dovidio, J.F., P. Glick and L.A. Rudman. 2005. *On the Nature of Prejudice: Fifty Years after Allport*. Malden, MA: Blackwell Publishing.

Elias, N., and Scotson, J.L. 2002. *Etablierte und Außenseiter*. Frankfurt am Main: Suhrkamp.

Edwards, A. 2016. 'UNHCR Viewpoint: "Refugee" or "Migrant" – Which is Right?' Retrieved 8 July 2018 from http://www.unhcr.org/news/latest/2016/7/55df0e556/unhcr-viewpoint-refugee-migrant-right.html.

Foroutan, N., et al. 2014. *Deutschland postmigrantisch I: Gesellschaft, Religion, Identität*. Berlin: Humboldt-Universität zu Berlin.

_____. 2015. *Deutschland postmigrantisch II: Gesellschaft, Religion, Identität*. Berlin: Humboldt-Universität zu Berlin.

Foroutan, N. 2015. 'Konviviale Integration in postmigrantischen Gesellschaften', in Frank Adloff and Volker M. Heins (eds): *Konvivialismus. Eine Debatte*, Bielefeld: transcript Verlag, pp. 205–16.

_____. 2016. 'Postmigrantische Gesellschaften', in Heinz Ulrich Brinkmann and Martina Sauer (eds), *Einwanderungsgesellschaft Deutschland: Entwicklung und Stand der Integration*. Wiesbaden: Springer VS, pp. 227–54.

Foroutan, N., and C. Canan. 2016. 'The Paradox of Equal Belonging of Muslims', *Islamophobia Studies Journal* 3(2): 159–76.

Fratzscher, M., and S. Junker. 2015. 'Integrating Refugees: A Longterm, Worthwhile Investment', *DIW Economic Bulletin* 5(45/46): 612–16.

Frontino, A. 2012. 'Postmigrantische Gesellschaft behaupten, eine neue Perspektive auf die Szene Europa', *Andere Europas*. Retrieved 17 March 2017 from https://www.euroethno.hu-berlin.de/de/archiv/studienprojekte/other_europes/forschung/Postmigrantische%20Gesellschaft%20im%20Ballhaus%20Naunynstrasse.

Gaertner, S.L., and J.F. Dovidio. 1986. 'The Aversive Form of Racism', in J.F. Dovidio and S.L. Gaertner (eds), *Prejudice, Discrimination, and Racism*. Orlando, FL: Academic Press, pp. 61–89.

Greven, T. 2016. 'The Rise of Right-Wing Populism in Europe and the United States: A Comparative Perspective'. Retrieved 8 July 2018 from http://www.fesdc.org/fileadmin/user_upload/publications/RightwingPopulism.pdf.

Gross, E., J. Gundlach and W. Heitmeyer. 2010. 'Die Ökonomisierung der Gesellschaft. Ein Nährboden für Menschenfeindlichkeit in oberen Status- und Einkommensgruppen', in W. Heitmeyer (ed.), *Deutsche Zustände Folge 9*. Berlin: Suhrkamp, pp. 138–57.

Habermas, J. 1998. *Die postnationale Konstellation. Politische Essays*. Frankfurt am Main: Suhrkamp.

Hall, S. 1997. 'The Local and the Global: Globalization and Ethnicity', in A. McClintock, A. Mufti and E. Shohat (eds), *Dangerous Liaisons: Gender, Nation, and Postcolonial Perspectives*. Minneapolis: University of Minnesota Press, pp. 173–87.

_____. 2004. 'Das Spektakel des Anderen', in Stuart Hall (ed.), *Ideologie. Identität. Repräsentation.* Hamburg: Argument Verlag, pp. 108–67.

Haraway, D. 1991. 'A Cyborg Manifesto: Science, Technology, and Socialist-Feminism in the Late Twentieth Century', in D. Haraway (ed.), *Simians, Cyborgs and Women: The Reinvention of Nature.* New York: Routledge, pp. 149–81.

Heitmeyer, W. 2012. 'Gruppenbezogene Menschenfeindlichkeit (GMF) in einem entsicherten Jahrzehnt', in W. Heitmeyer (ed.), *Deutsche Zustände 10.* Berlin: Suhrkamp, pp. 15–41.

Hyman, I., N. Vu and B. Beiser. 2000. 'Post-migration Stresses among Southeast Asian Refugee Youth in Canada: A Research Note', *Journal of Comparative Family Studies* 31: 281–93.

International Organization for Migration. 2017. 'Key Migration Terms'. Retrieved 8 July 2018 from http://www.iom.int/key-migration-terms.

Jenkins, R. 2010. 'Rethinking Ethnicity: Identity, Categorization and Power', *Ethnic and Racial Studies* 17(2): 197–223.

Langhoff, S. 2009. 'Wir inszenieren kein Getto-Theater'. *taz*, 18 April. Retrieved 8 July 2018 from http://www.taz.de/taz/nf/etc/2009_04_18_S27-29-kultur-08. pdf.

Laurence, J., and G. Goodliffe. 2013. 'The French Debate on National Identity and the Sarkozy Presidency: A Retrospective', *International Spectator* 48(1): 34–47.

Mecheril, P. 2014. 'Was ist das X im Postmigrantischen?', *sub\urban. Zeitschrift für kritische Stadtforschung* 2(3): 107–22.

Modood, T. 1999. 'New Forms of Britishness: Post-immigration Ethnicity and Hybridity in Britain', in L. von Ronit (ed.), *The Expanding Nation: Towards a Multi-ethnic Ireland.* Dublin: Trinity College, pp. 34–40.

Mudde, C. 2007. *Populist Radical Right Parties in Europe.* Cambridge: Cambridge University Press.

Nachtwey, O. 2010. 'Legitimationsprobleme im Spätkapitalismus revisited', in K. Becker, L. Gertenbach, H. Laux and T. Reitz (eds), *Grenzverschiebungen des Kapitalismus. Umkämpfte Räume und Orte des Widerstands.* Frankfurt: Campus Verlag, pp. 359–79.

New York Times. 2017. 'Oslo Suspect Wrote of Fear of Islam and Plan for War', 23 July, Retrieved 8 July 2018 from http://www.nytimes.com/2011/07/24/world/europe/24oslo.html.

Nussbaum, M.C. 1997. *Cultivating Humanity: A Classical Defense of Reform in Liberal Education.* Cambridge, MA: Harvard University Press.

Parsons, T. 1967. *The Structure of Social Action.* New York: Free Press.

Peters, M. 2015. 'Migration and Globalization', in R.A. Scott and S.M. Kosslyn (eds), *Emerging Trends in the Social and Behavioral Sciences: An Interdisciplinary, Searchable, and Linkable Resource.* Hoboken, NJ: John Wiley & Sons, pp. 1–10.

Pieper, M., E. Panagiotidis and V. Tsianos. 2011. 'Konjunkturen der egalitären Exklusion: Postliberaler Rassismus und verkörperte Erfahrung in der Prekarität', in M. Pieper, T. Atzert, S. Karakayali and V. Tsianos (eds), *Biopolitik in der Debatte.* Wiesbaden: VS-Verlag für Sozialwissenschaften, pp. 193–226.

Sabatier, P.A. 1993. 'Policy Change over a Decade or More', in Paul A.Sabatier and Hank C. Jenkins-Smith (eds), *Policy Change and Learning: An Advocacy Coalition Approach*. Boulder, CO: Westview Press, pp. 13–39.

Said, E.W. 1978. *Orientalism*. New York: Pantheon.

Sharifi, A. 2011. 'Postmigrantisches Theater: Eine Agenda für die deutschen Bühnen', in W. Schneider (ed.), *Theater und Migration: Herausforderung und Auftrag für die Kulturgesellschaft*. Bielefeld: transcript Verlag, pp. 35–46.

Shirpak, K.R., E. Maticka-Tyndale and M. Chinichian. 2011. 'Post-migration Changes in Iranian Immigrants' Couple Relationships in Canada', *Journal of Comparative Family Studies* 42(6): 751–70.

Sidanius J., and F. Pratto. 2001. *Social Dominance: An Intergroup Theory of Social Hierarchy and Oppression*. Cambridge: Cambridge University Press.

Sniderman, P.M. 1996. *The Clash of Rights: Liberty, Equality, and Legitimacy in Pluralist Democracy*. New Haven, CT: Yale University Press

Spielhaus, R. 2013. 'Clichés are Funny as Long as They Happen on Stage: Comedy as Political Criticism', in Joran Nielsen (eds), *Muslim Political Participation in Europe*. Edinburgh: Edinburgh University Press, pp. 322–38.

Spivak, G.C. 1988. 'Can the Subaltern Speak?', in C. Nelson and L. Grossberg (eds), *Marxism and the Interpretation of Culture*. Chicago: University of Chicago Press, pp. 271–313.

Statistisches Bundesamt. 2009. *Bevölkerung und Erwerbstätigkeit: Bevölkerung mit Migrationshintergrund. Ergebnisse des Mikrozensus 2005*. Fachserie 1, Reihe 2.2, Wiesbaden: Statistisches Bundesamt.

_____. 2012. 'Familien mit Migrationshintergrund: Traditionelle Werte zählen', *Destatis*, 13 March. Retrieved 8 July 2018 from https://www.destatis.de/DE/Publikationen/STATmagazin/Bevoelkerung/2012_03/2012_03Migrationshinterrgrund.html.

_____. 2014. 'Mikrozensus 2013: 16,5 Millionen Menschen mit Migrationshintergrund'.

Press release No. 402, 14 November. Retrieved 8 July 2018 from https://www.destatis.de/DE/PresseService/Presse/Pressemitteilungen/2014/11/PD14_402_122.html.

_____. 2016. 'Bevölkerung mit Migrationshintergrund auf Rekordniveau'. Press release No. 327, 16 September.

Supik, L. 2014. *Statistik und Rassismus: Das Dilemma der Erfassung von Ethnizität*. Frankfurtam Main: Campus Verlag.

Sutterlüty, F. 2010. *In Sippenhaft: Negative Klassifikationen in ethnischen Konflikten*. Frankfurtam Main: Campus Verlag.

Süssmuth, R. 2001. 'Zuwanderung gestalten, Integration fördern: Bericht der unabhängigen Kommission ‚Zuwanderung''. Berlin: Bundesminister des Innern.

Taylor, C. 1997. 'The Politics of Recognition', in A. Heble, D.P. Pennee, and J.R. Struthers (eds), *New Contexts of Canadian Criticism*. Peterborough: Broadview Press, pp. 25–73.

Terkessidis, M. 2015. 'Kultur und Ökonomie – Betriebsprüfung und Ökonomie', in Y. Erol and M. Hill (eds), *Nach der Migration: Postmigrantische Perspektiven jenseits der Parallelgesellschaft*. Bielefeld: transcript Verlag, pp. 89–101.

Tsianos, V., and J. Karakayali. 2014. 'Rassismus und Repräsentationspolitik in der postmigrantischen Gesellschaft', *ApuZ* 13–14: 33–39.

Touré, N. 2011. *Who's Afraid of Post-Blackness?* New York: Free Press.

Yildiz, E. 2013. 'Postmigrantische Verortungspraktiken: Ethnische Mythen irritieren', in P. Mecheril, O. Thomas-Olalde, C. Melter, S. Arens and E. Romaner (eds), *Migrationsforschung als Kritik? Konturen einer Forschungsperspektive*. Wiesbaden: VS Verlag für Sozialwissenschaften, pp. 139–53.

Zick, A., B. Küpper and D. Krause. 2016. *Gespaltene Mitte: Feindselige Zustände. Rechtsextreme Einstellungen in Deutschland 2016*. Bonn: Dietz. Retrieved 17 March 2017 from http://www.fes-gegen-rechtsextremismus.de/pdf_16/Gespaltene%20Mitte_Feindselige%20Zust%C3%A4nde.pdf.

Part III

Refugee Encounters

Chapter 7

New Year's Eve, Sexual Violence and Moral Panics

Ruptures and Continuities in Germany's Integration Regime

Kira Kosnick

The so-called refugee-crisis in 2015 and 2016 – the arrival and reception of people seeking asylum or some status of protection in record numbers in Germany – has arguably had a significant impact on the domestic political climate. The rise of rightwing, anti-immigrant populism, in the form of the Pegida movement and the election successes of the newly established Alternative for Germany (AfD) party, has been fuelled by a perception of this crisis.[1] In the German context, the notion of crisis has been defined less in terms of the desperate, worldwide plight of displaced people than in reference to the supposed overburdening of German public infrastructures, finances and its population's ability to offer hospitality. There is, of course, no direct relationship between the number of arrivals and the limits of German capacities and/or goodwill, even though this is exactly what not only extreme rightwing discourses, but increasingly also members of the responsible government began to articulate. In this chapter, I examine how dominant public perceptions of 'crisis' shifted in the wake of certain highly mediatized events, most significantly the events of the 2015 New Year's Eve celebrations in several major cities, and discuss the particular conjunction and fusion of both anti-refugee and anti-Muslim sentiments with positions usually associated with feminism.

Several events that made media headlines have contributed to shifts in the public perception regarding the plight of refugees. While the televised images of overcrowded boats in the Mediterranean Sea and of dead, mostly Black, bodies washed upon the shores of European holiday destinations seemed to have become almost commonplace and of little consequence considering their emotional impact on a wider German public – with the exception of reinforcing a fear of being 'swamped' among some[2] – the image of a little white boy lying face down on a Turkish beach in September 2015 managed to convey a sense of humanitarian responsibility and compassion. The death of three-year-old Alan Kurdi – the carefully choreographed representation as the iconic photograph that circulated through social media and newspapers around the world – conveyed very emotionally the sense of a crisis suffered by human beings in need of help. Alan Kurdi appeared as the worthy recipient of humanitarian attention. The photograph evoked tragic isolation and the victim's innocence: the boyhood of a young white child deserving of protection and a better life. As an iconic image, it seemed to vindicate Chancellor Angela Merkel's earlier decision to open Germany's borders to refugees stranded on the so-called Balkan route from Greece to Austria, and led even the then U.K. Prime Minister, David Cameron, to promise the actualization of Britain's moral responsibility, following a long period of inaction.[3]

Yet not quite four months later, another event managed to shift the terms of the German debate on the 'crisis' significantly. Already shaken by the terrorist attacks that devastated Paris in November 2015, the violence against women committed during public New Year's Eve celebrations in several German cities, most prominently in Cologne, provoked a public outcry and a different sense of urgency regarding refugees: regarding their containment, deportation and disciplining. The beginning of 2016 marked to some extent the end of what had exuberantly been called *Willkommenskultur*, a welcoming culture of hospitality that had appeared to dominate German reactions to the increasing numbers of refugees arriving in the country. There could hardly have been a starker contrast between the images of people at major German train stations, cheering the arrival of those seeking refuge, and the reports of sexual violence and theft apparently committed by groups of young men of North African origin, targeting women in public spaces on 31 December 2015. In the wake of first reports on sexual violence in Cologne, a media frenzy developed, which both included and prompted vocal reactions from the political establishment, ultimately leading to and legitimizing the passing of federal legislation that limited the rights of asylum seekers and certain groups of refugees significantly.[4]

The New Year's Eve events were simultaneously nontransparent with regard to what had actually unfolded – few of the perpetrators were identified and even fewer received court sentences – and yet highly overdetermined and brutally clear in their indicative meanings regarding the so-called refugee crisis, Muslim masculinity and public sexual violence against women, as Gabriele Dietze has remarked (2016). In the weeks that followed, 'Cologne', as the events came to be called, dominated print newspaper and online coverage, became the focus of all relevant political talk shows, and forced a wide range of social groups and all political parties to position themselves and discuss adequate responses. Representations of the events in Cologne mainly drew upon already existing widespread anxieties concerning the possible and negative consequences of mass immigration, particularly from Muslim countries: coverage and debates entangled fears regarding criminal activity, incompatible cultural norms and values, and religious extremism and terrorism. The events were interpreted as highlighting another familiar point lamented by the critics of Islam in Germany and other Western countries: the supposed oppression of women and the lack of gender equality among Muslims, culminating in the normalization of sexual violence (Amir-Moazami 2011). As Kristina Schröder, the former Minister for Family, Seniors, Women and Youth Affairs, wrote on Twitter, using the hashtag #*Köln* (German for 'Cologne): 'They have long been treated as a taboo, but we have to deal with the norms of masculinity that legitimate violence in Muslim culture.'[5] In 2016, the increasing popularity of the AfD party in the regional elections illustrated that the intensification of a political climate in which the arrival and settlement of refugees is perceived as a crisis of social stability, moral conventions and cultural norms facilitated the establishment of rightwing populism as a major political force in the country. The Dresden-based populist and anti-Muslim Pegida movement, with close ties to the AfD, started to stage public protests against immigration and Muslim minorities in Germany in 2014 (see Bock, Chapter 9 in this volume). For Pegida participants, 'Cologne' seemed to confirm precisely their unheeded warning: Muslims represent a threat to the very fabric of German society, Western cultural values, social order and public decency.

The mass-mediated representation of the New Year's Eve events in Cologne and several other cities bears all the hallmarks of a moral panic. Moral panics, as Stanley Cohen set it out in his classic work of media sociology *Folk Devils and Moral Panics* (2002 [1972]), tie into popular folklore and common-sense assumptions to scandalize the 'deviant' behaviour of particular social groups, and present this as a matter requiring urgent intervention to preserve social stability and morality. What prompted this sudden and intense focus on 'Cologne' across different media platforms and audiences is not so much the events themselves with their relative opaqueness – one year later, hardly any of the attackers had been prosecuted and few convictions have been obtained – but rather the coming together of endemic racialized fears that articulate hegemonic knowledge, affects and sentiments regarding gender, culture, religion and national community, as will be explained in more detail below. 'Cologne' was taken not just to starkly confirm knowledge regarding the sexual danger emanating from men raised in 'Islamic cultures', but also elicited strong emotional responses of outrage, alarm, anger and disgust as foreign men were felt to have violated not just specific women, but the collective boundaries and body of the nation too (Boulila and Carri 2017; Messerschmidt 2016). Their combined articulation as a moral panic can be seen as an orchestration of consent 'through the use of highly emotive and rhetorical language which has the effect of requiring that "something be done about it"' (McRobbie and Thornton 1995: 562). The 'folk devils' as identified in the Cologne Panic share numerous similarities with the young, working-class, violent males who were at the centre of Cohen's early study in Britain. Cohen himself acknowledges in his foreword to the third edition that refugees and asylum seekers have moved to the centre of a 'hostile new agenda' in Europe (Cohen 2002 [1972]: xxii). However, what clearly differentiates them is their relation to the 'folk' as *Volk*,[6] in that the 'devils' of the Cologne Panic are not simply seen as deviant, but also as alien and potentially or factually impossible to integrate into a moral order that is both explicitly and implicitly a national and liberal-secular cultural order (Amir-Moazami 2016). The topic of integration has emerged as a key hegemonic concern ever since the rather late admission of the political establishment, in the early 2000s, that Germany was indeed a country of immigration (see also Foroutan, Chapter 6 in this volume). A particular characteristic in German debates about integration is the pre-eminence of culture, including religion, as a central issue over which different political camps are divided.

The Culturalization of Integration

When the German Chancellor Angela Merkel declared in 2010 that multiculturalism had failed in Germany, long before the steep rise in asylum applications, she knew exactly where to put the blame (see also Kosnick 2014). 'Not enough' had been demanded of immigrants, she said: migrants themselves were responsible for learning German, forced marriages ought not to be tolerated, migrant families could not refuse to let their daughters join school excursions and criminal behaviour must be punished quickly.[7] This approach of 'getting tough' with migrants was much appreciated among the conservative and centre-right electorate, not to mention the extreme rightwing fringe. Her statement demonstrated several assumptions that characterize the political climate in Germany more widely, illuminating why 'Cologne' could trigger such a strong response. First, many people in Germany continue to regard integration as something that immigrants have to perform and deliver, simultaneously demanded and policed by the state. Second, integration is mainly talked about – by political elites as well as in civil society discourses – in cultural terms, framed as a process of adjusting one's ways and adapting to German cultural norms and values, which are implicitly posited and constructed as homogeneous and often as universal (Radtke 2009; Tezcan 2018). Third, the domain in which a particular need for change is identified is that of gender relations, particularly the treatment of women and girls – especially when it comes to Muslims, who are assumed to 'lag behind' and oppose gender equality, implicitly constructed as a reality in the country. Fourth, entangling references to the diversity of culturally shaped attitudes and practices with delinquency reinforces the assumption that Muslim immigrants in particular are incompatible with, and even destructive of, German ways of life. Migrants are thus required to change their ideas, habits and behaviours.

Already in the early 1990s, race-critical theorists pointed to a shift in European racializing logics. The language of race and races, largely discredited not only scientifically but also through its association with the atrocities of the Holocaust in the European context (Goldberg 2009), had given way to arguments based on an alleged incompatibility of ethnonational cultures (Balibar 1991; Hall 1991; Stolcke 1995). This 'culturalizing' of racialization was, of course, nothing entirely new, as many earlier racist logics had also made connections between racial and cultural hierarchies. However, what was specific to the kinds of cultural racisms articulated most prominently by resurfacing rightwing populist parties in many EU countries was the mainly 'defensive' logic by which culture was used to mobilize against immigration and against ethnic minorities, which were posited as culturally foreign and incompatible with supposed singular national cultures or the achievements of European civilization. The exporting of European culture through colonialist projects had been constructed as a legitimate conquest and rule in the name of 'civilizing missions' (Stocking 1968) that would benefit those poor souls lagging behind the God-ordained, natural development of 'mankind'. By contrast, claims about cultural incompatibility have emerged in the wake of European retrenchment, 'empires coming home', and with immigration from the non-Western world more generally. The language of race had been discarded in favour of culture: still very much hierarchical, but tied to the widely accepted notion that nations are fundamentally cultural communities that have roots in a particular homeland.

The Romantic Nation

In order to understand why the incorporation of immigrants is so strongly framed as a cultural challenge in German public discourses, it is necessary to understand its difficult history of nation-state formation. The idea of the nation as a cultural community carries particular resonance in Germany, where its origins go back to Johann Gottfried Herder and his romantic-nationalist conceptions of nations growing in particular territorial climates, each with their own language, traditions and values, and thriving only when nurtured by their natural surroundings (Malkki 1992). As a late nation state in the European context, the idea of nations as already existing cultural units in need, and worthy, of political self-representation was particularly important for the creation of modern Germany (Brubaker 1992). Much has been written about the all-but-natural forging of national cultures out of the cultural, linguistic and religious heterogeneity that marked most European states (Alonso 1994; Anderson 1983; Corrigan and Sayers 1985; Hobsbawm and Ranger 1983). Despite this tradition of critical analyses regarding romantic nation states' claims to social homogeneity and cultural unity, such thinking of bounded national units is still prevalent and relevant among a majority of Germans – even among those who endorse multiculturalist ideas and embrace the idea of immigration as social, economic and cultural enrichment. Part of the 'achievements' of the modern world-system of nation states has been the naturalization of national cultural identities, albeit that this has been less successful among states that owe their existence too evidently to a history of (mostly European) empire, during which the territorial borders of colonies where often drafted on imperial drawing boards.

Even the affirmative theorists of multiculturalism have, with the best intentions, usually relied implicitly or explicitly on the idea that cultural heterogeneity is the result of immigration alone, with immigrants as representatives of their own particular culture for which they aspire and deserve to achieve recognition within the receiving state and its majority culture. As the German cultural sociologist Andreas Reckwitz (2001) has shown, Charles Taylor's and Will Kymlicka's conceptions of culture, both of them eminent theorists of multiculturalism, rely on a notion of culture that understands it as a holistic background knowledge and identity represented by a collective, very close to Herder's romantic vision of nations as cultural communities. However, what has probably left even more of a mark on the hegemonic understanding of ethnonational culture in Germany is the literature and practice of intercultural education and engagement, intercultural management and, more recently, the 'diversity' turn (Kosnick 2014). While multicultural policies have never been officially embraced and institutionalized in Germany, either on the federal level or on the regional level, it is nevertheless the case that 'culture' has become a main arena of concern for integration politics at different levels of politics and civic engagement. There are countless intercultural encounter weeks and centres for intercultural exchange, festivals of cultures (in the plural), intercultural pedagogy courses, intercultural management and cross-cultural initiatives, and intercultural cooking events bringing together urban neighbourhoods – all of them well-intended attempts to develop a better understanding among immigrants and nonimmigrant Germans by learning more about 'each other's culture', as it is usually put.

Though differing entirely in their political goals, proponents of this form of interculturalism or multiculturalism share with their opponents an understanding of culture and religion as fundamental features of social – usually nationally or ethnically bound – groups. These features are seen as central to identity formation, supposedly shaping the behaviour of group members. Furthermore, there is an implicit assumption that these traits are bound by a set of clear traditions, which are historically more or less stable. Cultures in this sense have mutated into actors on a global stage, where they appear to confront each other (as in Huntington's (1996) famous 'clash of civilizations'). In the context of single nation states, cultural actors appear to vie for recognition, exist in 'parallel societies' or try to engage with one another. Much has been written about the problematic concept of culture undergirding this debate. In such critiques, notions of cultural hybridity (Bhabha 1994) or hermeneutically informed plural notions of cultural horizons of understanding (Reckwitz 2001) have appeared. However, the significance of the notion of culture has not been subjected to the same scrutiny, in particular in the context of its politicized use in migration or integration debates, or regarding alternative conceptions (but see also Radtke 2009; Tezcan 2011).

Since the turn of the millennium, it is particularly the cultural difference of Muslims – always understood as immigrants – that has been the primary focus of attention in German public debates about integration and cultural difference. When Merkel publicly announced in 2010 that 'multiculturalism' had failed, she listed a number of phenomena among immigrants that she deemed to have been met with too much lenience by the German state, among them forced marriages and parent prohibitions regarding school excursions for girls, most of them thinly veiled references to 'Muslim' problems that the government-ordained German Islam Council had also already identified as issues requiring intervention (Aguilar 2018; Amir-Moazami 2016; Kosnick 2014; Tezcan 2018). This particular problematization of immigrant culture as Muslim has as much to do with the postmillennial 'war on terror' as with the countries of origin of people currently seeking refuge in Germany. In the early stages of the Federal Republic's guestworker programme – which brought many of those now recognized as ethnic minorities into what was then West Germany in order to staff its plants and factories in the 1950s and 1960s – 'culture' was discussed as a particular trait of *Südländer*, people from the European South, with particular temperaments and habits (Italians, Turks, Greeks and Spaniards). In the late 1990s, attention focused on 'Turkish culture' as a problem, before the 'war on terror' shifted debates on difference and framed religion as the key concern. Levent Tezcan has shown how culturalized religion could become the prime focus of integration debates in Germany, turning certain immigrant groups into a Muslim collective that was supposed to be both understood and addressed as a unified group. Sometimes, this group even became a partner, for example, in the context of the German Islam Conference, which was established by the German government in 2006 in order to initiate a 'dialogue' between state authorities and Muslim associations (Tezcan 2011; see also Shooman 2014). However, most people considered 'Muslim' in Germany are not affiliated with any of the Islamic organizations invited to represent their concerns at the conference.[8] Furthermore, the German government invited even outspokenly critical voices to the meetings; these critics were seen as informed and reliably Muslim because of their ethnonational descent, but did not necessarily self-identify as religious Muslims at all, which only demonstrates the cultural ethnicization of religion in this context.[9] Unemployment, school violence, gender inequalities – these have been the problems identified as major topics to be addressed at the German Islam Conference. Apparently, these issues therefore need to be seen as ethnoreligious concerns attributed to Muslims' cultural and religious difference. These incompatibilities are then framed as obstacles to integration into German culture. However, it is rare that the cultural views or religious ideas held by members of the German majority society are invoked when explanations for unlawful actions or social problems are sought. Sexual violence is a case in point. Male sexual violence against women is quite common in Germany. When this is addressed, however, which is rare enough, it is not discussed as a collective cultural issue.[10] Yet, acts committed by those individuals who are conceptualized first of all as Muslims are always assumed to reflect ideas held by a supposedly homogeneous Muslim group, with religious-cultural specificity. This attribution of collective cultural responsibility explains how the New Year's Eve events could turn into a collective shock moment: the attacks were interpreted as exposing a culturally rooted sexual threat carried by all male Muslim refugees entering the country in large numbers. This perception was reinforced by the circumstance that the Cologne attacks

seemed to have been deliberately organized and exercised by predatory groups – even though such allegations could not be corroborated
by police investigations. Acts of sexual violence committed by groups of
men understood to be members of the majority society (though certainly
not named as such) have rather tended to be interpreted as the result of
individual problems, peer pressure or excessive alcohol consumption, not
as the result of a cultural trait that is specific to their ethnicity or religion.
Culture thus comes into play particularly when the racialized 'Other' is at
issue. It is people deemed foreign due to their visual appearance, religion,
nationality or descent who figure as *species* beings of culture.[11] The deeds
and actions of one such foreign individual are seen to be an expression of
their qualities in general; they always carry the burden of representation
(Schiffauer 2004).[12] This was already true during the times of European
imperialism, when colonial masters justified their oppression of allegedly
inferior 'races' on the basis of biological or genetic/eugenicist arguments.
The culturally based racism of late modernity exhibits strong continuities
in this regard.

Germany's political establishment reacted hastily to the unfolding
news story around 'Cologne'. The government quickly presented new
asylum regulations and promised to overhaul sexual violence legislation –
the latter initiative, however, while heralded as a fast crisis response, had
languished for years in the protracted political process. The legal difficulties faced by women who tried to provide evidence for sexual attacks had
previously ranked very low on the political agenda.

Sexual Politics

The centrality of sexuality and its regulation for racial formations still
remains little understood. When Margarete Jäger warned of an ethnicization of sexism in Germany long before the New Year's Eve events (Jäger
1999), she criticized the generic attribution of sexist attitudes to Muslim
men as a form of racism. What rendered the events in Cologne particularly scandalous was the indisputable evidence of actual sexual violence
perpetrated by men, collectively identified as Muslim asylum seekers,
against women assumed to belong to Germany's majority society. What
caused the New Year's Eve events to be seen as particularly shocking was
perhaps not just revelations regarding sexist attitudes and violent behaviour of Muslim refugees, but rather the spectre of that racialized male
Other forcing himself on white German women. This spectre has certainly
long haunted the sexual phantasies and fears of Western modernity (Said
1978). This vision of the lustful nonwhite male, the colonized man, the

racialized Other as a sexual threat to white women has routinely shaped
the policing of racial difference, as Ann Stoler has shown for French and
Dutch colonialism (Stoler 1989). The history of racial segregation in the
United States has also been conditioned by fears of the sexually predatory
behaviour of the Black man (D'Emilio and Freedman 1988). Lynching was
a frequent form of terror and punishment afflicted by white men on racialized male Others, with allegations of rape offered to legitimize avenging
white womanhood. Miscegenation laws prohibiting 'inter-racial' sexual
relations were presented as measures to protect white women, but never
women of colour from being exploited by white men (Carby 1985; Stoler
1989). In the United States, acts of sexual violence committed by men
considered racially superior against colonized women and women cat-
egorized as nonwhite, even after the formal end of slavery, were over-
whelmingly not recognized as such and were even institutionalized in
brothels or concubine arrangements. Conversely, rape allegations against
men of colour after the end of the Civil War were hardly ever substanti-
ated, yet were used to legitimize murder in the interests of policing racial
divisions.

An understanding of colonial racisms and post-slavery racial formations can help us illuminate the strong emotional reactions to the New
Year's Eve events. While often portrayed as a critique of sexism, such reactions in fact exhibited both racist and sexist dimensions. Gabriele Dietze
has written a poignant analysis of the media reactions that scandalized the
events. The weekly news magazine *Focus*, for example, printed on its cover
the contours of a naked, white, female body. While the head remained
invisible, the figure sought to protect her breasts and genitals against
multiple black hands attacking her (Dietze 2016: 96). In the heated climate
of the post-Cologne media frenzy, some calls for a harsh response even
included immediate punishment and deportation. Dietze herself draws
an analogy between the 'rape-lynching-complex' of the post-slavery climate in the United States and the 'harassment-deportation-complex' that
she identifies as characteristic of the media response. She concludes: 'The
event Cologne [the term she coins for the New Year's Eve violence] demonstrates how a racist production of truth is asserted with the help of
sexual politics' (Dietze 2016: 99).

Wittingly or unwittingly, German feminists have for some time played
their part in turning sexual politics into a weapon for racist, anti-Muslim
and anti-immigration groups (see Kosnick 2014). A hastily assembled
paperback that appeared in German bookstores not long after the media
frenzy scandalized Muslim migrants: an edited collection called *The Shock:
New Year's Eve in Cologne*, or *Der Schock: Die Silvesternacht von Köln* in
German (Schwarzer 2016). The editor, Alice Schwarzer, is notorious in

Germany for her feminist engagement and as the founder and publisher of the feminist magazine *Emma*. She has fought for abortion rights and sexual self-determination since the 1970s, and with much publicity; since the turn of the millennium, however, she has made headlines primarily as a critic of Islam in general and Islamic religious fundamentalism in particular. Schwarzer's book brought together several prominent critics who shared her position, identifying Islam, brought into Western countries by immigrants, as the main threat to women's rights and gender equality. The events in Cologne, she argued, were a stark reminder of those dangers – an assessment shared wholeheartedly by the contributors to her volume. Several chapters had already been published elsewhere; they featured again to corroborate warnings about the spread of Islam, on the one hand, and accusations against the left-liberal political spectrum, whose supposed denial of dangers was criticized for fanning religious fundamentalism and surging rightwing populism, on the other. However, one of the main problems with the criticism of Islam presented by the Schwarzer camp is the assumption that gender inequality and the oppression of women are intrinsically entangled with religion, and that most Muslim men's actions towards women can be explained as a consequence of a shared culture and the enactment of religious principles. The sociologist Necla Kelek – well known for her scathing stance towards Islam and one of the critical participants of the German Islam Conference – claims in her chapter for Schwarzer's book that the Quran legitimates not only male supremacy, but also male violence towards women (Kelek 2016: 67). Kelek argues that religious doctrine is paramount in both private and public affairs for Muslims, and suggests that this is not the case for the Christian Bible: only 'the laws' of the Quran are supposedly non-negotiable and dictate conduct. This short-circuiting of doctrine, belief and individual behaviour not only ignores a long and complex history of Quran exegesis, but also turns Muslim men into mere executors of religious doctrine. Similarly, the French-Algerian writer Kamel Daoud argues that Muslim refugees find themselves in a 'culture trap' (Daoud 2016: 51). His contribution to the volume was originally published in the French newspaper *Le Monde* shortly after Cologne's New Year's Eve and was quickly republished in English-language and German newspapers. 'In Allah's world', he writes in a slightly amended version, 'the relation to women is the second Gordian knot. The woman is repudiated, rejected, killed, veiled, locked-in or taken possession of' (Daoud 2016: 51). In a different context, his argument might have been read as a polemic to instigate internal discussions among Muslims themselves. In the context of wider European debates on the presence of Muslims immigrants, however, his piece turns into universal condemnation of their thinking and conduct.

Alice Schwarzer also continues her critique of the Muslim headscarf as a 'stigmatizing piece of cloth' (Schwarzer 2016: 115). She suggests that 'just like the flag of the Islamists, the headscarf embarked upon its crusade in the 1980s right into the heart of Europe' (Schwarzer 2016: 110). Her metaphors align perfectly with the rightwing rhetoric that condemns refugee migration as a religious and cultural invasion, framed in militaristic terms (Korteweg and Yurdakul 2014). This kind of rhetoric not only casts people in need of protection as hostile invaders, but also constructs the vision of a Western or European world, in which Islam and Muslims do not belong – a place in which they always have to remain alien.

Self-avowed German feminist critics of Islam – such as Necla Kelek and the lawyer and writer Seyran Ateş, both of whom have been invited as 'insider' critics to the German Islam Conference – rarely mobilize the fear of a threat to national cultural tradition. For them, it is rather cultural and political progress that is at stake. In a commentary addressing possible links between the New Year's Eve events, young Muslim men and Islam, Ateş claims that 'we [feminists in the West] are simply much further ahead' with regard to gender norms and feminist struggle (Ateş 2016). The personal experience of political struggle might undergird this understanding of historical progress – a vision that holds that feminist achievement is not preordained, but the contested result of prolonged political engagement. However, it also underwrites a vision of Western societies as the spearhead of global human development, with predominantly Muslim countries lagging behind in a time gap (Aguilar 2018). The paradigms of uneven historical development and European supremacy have been extensively analysed as central features of European modernity and colonialism (Said 1978; Spivak 1994 [1988]; Stocking 1968; Wolf 1982). Various experts, most prominently Daoud (2016), followed this logic in the wake of the Cologne attacks, suggesting that the problem with male Muslim refugees was not so much that they carried incompatible cultural traditions, but that the task of cultural integration, the task of bringing supposedly backward people into the Western present, was an enormous challenge and perhaps impossible to accomplish.

In this context, feminist Islam critics claimed that collective sexual violence is widespread in Muslim societies and that a conservative Islam is ultimately responsible for this, imported by refugees into Europe – but simultaneously still popular among established Muslim minorities. While some critics, such as Kelek, have put the blame squarely on Islam, supposedly an anti-gender-equality religion, others, such as Schwarzer, have attributed such behaviour to the recent rise and spread of particularly conservative forms of Islam. The German Islam Conference, which had also quickly identified issues regarding gender equality and inequality as a primary area of concern and intervention, instead considered traditional patriarchal structures as responsible and was at pains to maintain that such structures are in fact at odds with Islam as an inherently open and tolerant religion.[13] However, the importance of Islam and gender as central topics and areas of intervention in the German Islam Conference showed that gender inequality was instantly considered a pressing problem among German Muslims. While my interest is not in taking sides in this debate of explaining the degrees and causes of gender inequalities and gender norms among Muslims, I certainly do not think that issues such as domestic violence, forced marriages and gender oppression are irrelevant. Nor is it my intention to declare these topics off limits in relation to Muslim or other social groups. Feminist critics of Islam have in different contexts accused other scholars, including myself, of raising accusations of racism as an argument to terminate discussion on gender inequality among Muslims (Schröter 2016). They have even accused these scholars of fuelling racism in Germany by opposing what they see as decisive political action against the oppression of Muslim women, and thereby further fuelling both their oppression and anti-Muslim resentment in the non-Muslim population at large (Schwarzer 2016: 35). Feminist Islam critics argue that accusations of racist undertones ignore the empirical evidence regarding the relative prevalence of gender inequality in Muslim-dominated societies and among Muslim minorities in European countries (the latter measured through a range of surveys, often commissioned by state institutions such as the BAMF,[14] the BMBF[15] and the German Islam Conference). These critics also argue that scholars such as myself and others frustrate the emancipative efforts of women across the world and ignore their plight, ruled over and dominated by Islamic and Islamist ideologies.

Yet, the will to know is never innocent – and in these particular contexts, it cannot be ignored how seemingly progressive feminist agendas become articulated within anti-Muslim and anti-immigrant discourses that declare sexism to be a problem mainly, or even solely, of the non-European, Muslim Other. Seyran Ateş's longstanding legal representation of particularly Muslim women in domestic violence cases in Germany has clearly established her credentials as a feminist advocate for women. Nonetheless, her rise to prominence in German multiculturalism debates owes little to the seriousness with which the German political establishment and mass media treat violence against women – and against migrant women especially. Rather, I would argue that her exposure reveals certain political interests and a hegemonic discursive strand that is obsessed with Muslim immigrants as a problematic social group. At the time of her invitation to the German Islam Conference – an invitation issued by state officials who decided which organizations and individuals were to

represent the Muslim side in the 'dialogue' – Ateş was officially positioned and seemed to understand herself as a secular Muslim (Amir-
Moazami 2011). Her authority to speak on matters of Islam was called into
question by many of the other Muslim participants in the Conference. Yet,
as a woman of Turkish-Muslim descent, her critique of Muslim organizations and Muslim male culture(s) was invaluable to German state representatives, imbuing her positions with an authority akin to a position
of native informant that she also occupies in her frequent mass media
appearances (Aguilar 2018, Amir-Moazami 2011). Since then, Ateş has
shifted her position with the founding of a 'liberal' mosque in Berlin[16]
and taking up training to become an imam, a move that regardless of its
personal motivations certainly lends her even more authority on matters
of Islam. What was never in question was Ateş's first-hand knowledge
of incidents of domestic violence against Muslim women in Germany.
But the way in which she frames such knowledge and mobilizes it in a
myriad of television talks lends itself to a problematic and one-sided scandalization of male Muslim culture as hostile to women, which ties into a
hegemonic demonization of Muslim men as violent and sexist (Aguilar
2018; Amir-Moazami 2016; Ewing 2008; Kerner 2009). The titles of two of
her better-known books give some indication of her particular approach
to understanding violence: *The Multikulti Error* blames a leftist and liberal
German establishment for allowing Muslim immigrant minorities to exist
outside the rule of law, while her more recent polemic *Islam Needs a Sexual
Revolution* operates on a wider, transnational scale, arguing that predominantly Muslim countries, as well as migrant communities elsewhere, have
foregone an important development towards social and cultural progress
by their failure to stage a sexual revolution, as Western countries have
done since the 1960s (Ateş 2007, 2009).

Feminism and Anti-racism beyond the Nation State

The allegations raised by feminist critics of Islam – most prominently
Schwarzer, Kelek and Ateş – pre-date the Cologne events by several years.
In the wake of the public scandal or moral panic they occasioned, however, these figures rose to particular prominence in Germany, assumed
by many to be competent voices whose warnings should have been
heeded. Many younger feminists, however, were critical of what they
saw as a racist instrumentalization of the events. They staged a protest
rally in Cologne and launched a hashtag campaign to highlight that
sexist violence affects German society as a whole and not just its cultural
minorities.[17] This campaign received brief media attention, but quickly

disappeared again from the headlines. Why is it so difficult to counter this hegemonic trend? It can certainly be argued – and many have done so – that racist hegemonic discourses about Muslim men as inherently sexist are responsible for the prevalence of such reactions (Dietze 2016; Ewing 2008; Kulaçatan 2016). In the current political climate, it is difficult to intervene and reframe the New Year's Eve events at the intersection of racialized arguments about a supposed refugee threat with attempts to counter sexual violence in ways that do not turn feminist stances into anti-immigrant and anti-Muslim positions. However, I think that at least part of why it is so difficult for other feminist positions to gain prominence in Germany is the widespread failure, both in the academy and among activists, to think about both feminism and anti-racism beyond the nation state, and to build transnational alliances with feminists based in the Middle East and the Global South.

While arguments concerning intersectionality have spread widely in both domains (Lutz et al. 2010), the need to place both hegemonic gender norms and contemporary racializations in global or transnational contexts is less often acknowledged. This might be because the horrors of the Holocaust and Germany's history of murderous racism rightly loom large in contemporary anti-racist and anti-fascist struggles in the country, and thus suggest a primarily national framing for anti-racist politics. In recent years, postcolonial perspectives on racism have gained increasing attention both inside and outside the German academy, suggesting a need for situating analyses more strongly in histories of European expansion and colonization. The consequences of the engagement with these histories, however, and attempts to 'decolonize' both knowledge production and activism (including feminist activism), have centred mostly on a kind of internal, still very much Western-centric critique of Western (feminist) knowledge production, which this chapter itself has also not transcended.

As far as reaching beyond the nation state is concerned, it has been mostly left to the self-avowed feminist critics of Islam to invoke transnational solidarity with women elsewhere, particularly in the Middle East. Some of them have done so in the context of supporting military interventions (see Hirschkind and Mahmood 2002), re-rehearsing the script of 'saving brown women from brown men' that Gayatri Spivak has demolished so poignantly as a part of a colonial narrative of civilizing the natives (Spivak 1994 [1988]). In the German context, however, feminist critics of Islam have spoken out most noticeably not explicitly in support of military interventions, but in claiming that they are the only ones who practise transnational feminist solidarity by supporting feminists fighting Islamic patriarchies in predominantly Muslim countries. A critique of the orientalizing and racializing mode of much of this invocation of solidarity is important and necessary, and has been performed on these pages as well. It needs to be questioned, however, whether the sensitivity, both in activist and university contexts, for detecting racializing and colonizing modes of knowledge production among Western feminists is coupled with an equal interest and effort in challenging these modes through alternative visions and practices of transnational feminist solidarity (Mohanty 2003). In times when particularly the so-called refugee crisis needs to be understood not simply as a German issue, but as a worldwide crisis linked to global inequalities, such efforts are sorely needed.

Kira Kosnick is Professor of Sociology at Goethe University Frankfurt, Germany. With a background in cultural anthropology, her work focuses on transnational migration and intersectional dynamics of inequality and exclusion in Germany and other European contexts. Her most current research investigates the mobile ageing practices of retirees between Turkey and Germany in the context of gendered care networks and neoliberal transformations of care in both countries.

Notes

1. The Alternative for Germany (AfD) party was founded in 2013 to articulate a rightwing response to the European economic crisis. Its main appeal to voters since 2015 seems to consist of its anti-immigration, anti-Islam agenda. Several of its political representatives have been linked with neofascist and extreme rightwing organizations.
2. To name just one of many possible examples, the German news agency dpa in 2015 subtitled a picture showing a severely overcrowded boat met by rescuers in the Mediterranean Sea 'The increasing flood of refugees forces the EU into action', http://www.t-online.de/nachrichten/ausland/krisen/id_73748814/fluechtlingskrise-eu-plant-wohl-militaeraktionen-gegen-schlepperbanden.html (retrieved 8 July 2018).
3. http://time.com/4477300/alan-kurdi-photo-one-year-later (retrieved 8 July 2018).
4. Historically, this was not the first time that a rise in the number of asylum seekers has been met with warnings regarding fears of *Überfremdung* (foreign infiltration). In the early 1990s, the wave of racist pogroms and arson attacks against immigrants were interpreted by leading politicians as indicators of a tolerance limit in the wider population, prompting legal changes that significantly curtailed the right to asylum (Müller 2010). Two so-called asylum packages were quickly passed to discourage further migration and accelerate the deportation of asylum seekers in late 2015 and early 2016.
5. https://twitter.com/schroeder_k/status/684113837545623552 (retrieved 8 July 2018).
6. The German notion of *Volk* cannot be easily translated into English, as both the concepts of folk and that of the people do not carry the connotations of national cultural homogeneity and organic tradition that the term acquired historically in the period of romantic nationalism and later, with devastating consequences, during National Socialism (Brubaker 1992).

7. These widely reported statements were made by Merkel at a conference of the youth wing of her ruling CDU conservative party, the Junge Union, here quoted after Deutsche Welle: http://www.dw-world.de/dw/article/0,,6118143,00.html (retrieved 8 July 2018).

8. Interestingly, the statistical data for the major study commissioned in the context of the German Islam Conference on 'Muslim Life in Germany' excluded German converts without migration histories and were based on the assumption of certain regions of emigration consisting of Muslim populations, despite their often religiously heterogeneous makeup (Aguilar 2018).

9. Thus, both Seyran Ateş and Necla Kelek were invited, whose positions are discussed below.

10. A relatively comprehensive survey commissioned by the Federal Ministry for Family, Seniors, Women and Youth came to the conclusion that 58 per cent of female respondents had experienced threatening forms of sexual harassment by men, most often in public settings (Müller and Schröttle 2005).

11. In his *History of Sexuality*, Foucault describes the emergence of 'the homosexual' as a species in the context of modern biopolitics, by which he means that homosexual leanings were deemed to pervade the entire person, infusing all actions and thoughts regardless of context. Similarly, modern culturalist racism designates those representing an alien culture to be driven in their thoughts and actions by culture alone.

12. Which some individuals can turn into an advantage: Necla Kelek and others who appear as exceptional 'native informants' on Islam and Muslim cultures derive their authority precisely from their status as marked Muslims, regardless of their specific upbringing, actual religious beliefs or contexts of socialization. However, they are the exceptions who confirm the validity of the general rule (Aguilar 2018).

13. http://www.deutsche-islam-konferenz.de/DIK/DE/DIK/7Rollenbilder/PGRollenbilder/ ErklaerungHaeuslicheGewalt/erklaerung-gewalt-node.html;jsessionid=94152F602008F 27B2F853C94CE1D5F5E.1_cid368 (retrieved 8 July 2018).

14. The Federal Ministry for Education and Research.

15. The Federal Office for Migration and Refugees.

16. The Ibn-Rushd-Goethe mosque in Berlin, https://www.ibn-rushd-goethe-moschee.de (retrieved 8 July 2018).

17. See http://ausnahmslos.org (retrieved 8 July 2018).

References

Aguilar, L. 2018. *Governing Muslims and Islam in Contemporary Germany*. Leiden: Brill.

Alonso, A.-M. 1994. 'The Politics of Space, Time and Substance: State Formation, Nationalism, and Ethnicity', *Annual Review of Anthropology* 23: 379–405.

Amir-Moazami, S. 2011. 'Dialogue as a Governmental Critique: Managing Gendered Islam in Germany', *Feminist Review* 98: 9–27.

_____. 2016. 'Dämonisierung und Einverleibung: Die "muslimische Frage" in Europa', in M. do Mar Castro Varela and P. Mecheril, *Die Dämonisierung der Anderen. Rassismuskritik der Gegenwart*. Bielefeld: transcript, pp. 21–39.

Anderson, B. 1983. *Imagined Communities: Reflections on the Origin and Spread of Nationalism*. London: Verso.

Ateş, S. 2007. *Der Multikulti-Irrtum: Wie wir in Deutschland besser zusammenleben können*. Berlin: Ullstein.

_____. 2009: *Der Islam braucht eine sexuelle Revolution: eine Streitschrift*. Berlin: Ullstein.

_____. 2016. 'Junge Männer und sexuelle Übergriffe: Was hat das mit dem Islam zu tun?', *UniReport* 4. Retrieved 8 July 2018 from http://aktuelles.uni-frankfurt. de/gesellschaft/koeln-was-hat-das-mit-dem-islam-zu-tun.

Balibar, E. 1991. 'Is There a "Neo-racism?"', in E. Balibar and I. Wallerstein, *Race, Nation, Class: Ambiguous Identities*. London: Verso, pp. 17–28.

Bhabha, H. 1994. *The Location of Culture*. London: Routledge.

Boulila, S., and Carri, C. 2017. 'On Cologne: Gender, Migration and Unacknowledged Racisms in Germany', *European Journal of Women's Studies* 24(3): 286–93.

Brubaker, R. 1992. *Citizenship and Nationhood in France and Germany*. Cambridge, MA: Harvard University Press.

Carby, H. 1985. '"On the Threshold of Woman's Era": Lynching, Empire and Sexuality in Black Feminist Theory', *Critical Inquiry* 12(1): 262–77.

Cohen, S. 2002 [1972]. *Folk Devils and Moral Panics: The Creation of the Mods and Rockers*. London: Routledge.

Corrigan, P., and Sayer, D. 1985. *The Great Arch: English State Formation as Cultural Revolution*. Oxford: Blackwell.

Daoud, K. 2016. 'Cologne, Ort der Phantasmen', in A. Schwarzer (ed.), *Der Schock: Die Silvesternacht von Köln*. Cologne: Kiepenheuer und Witsch-Verlag, pp. 49–55.

D'Emilio, J. and Freedman, E.B. 1988. *Intimate Matters: A History of Sexuality in America*. New York: Harper & Row.

Dietze, G. 2016. 'Das "Ereignis Köln"', *FEMINA POLITICA* 25(1): 93–102.

Ewing, K.P. 2008. *Stolen Honor: Stigmatizing Muslim Men in Berlin*. Stanford, CA: Stanford University Press.

Goldberg, D.T. 2009. *The Threat of Race: Reflections on Racial Neoliberalism*. Malden, MA: Wiley-Blackwell.

Hall, S. 1991. 'Old and New Identities, Old and New Ethnicities', in A. King (ed.), *Culture, Globalisation and the World System*. Basingstoke: Macmillan, pp. 41–68.

Hirschkind, C., and Mahmood, S. 2002. 'Feminism, the Taliban, and Politics of Counter-insurgency', *Anthropological Quarterly* 75(2): 339–54.

Hobsbawm, E., and Ranger, T. 1983. *The Invention of Tradition*. Cambridge: Cambridge University Press.

Huntington, S.P. 1996. *The Clash of Civilizations and the Remaking of World Order*. New York: Simon & Schuster.

Jäger, M. 1999. 'Ethnisierung von Sexismus im Einwanderungsdiskurs: Analyse einer Diskursverschränkung', *Duisburger Institut für Sprach- und Sozialforschung, Onlinearchiv*. Retrieved 8 July 2018 from http://www.diss-duisburg.de/Internet bibliothek/Artikel/Ethnisierung_von_Sexismus.htm.

Kelek, N. 2016. 'Islam und Geschlechter-Apartheid', in A. Schwarzer (ed.), *Der Schock: Die Silvesternacht von Köln*. Cologne: Kiepenheuer und Witsch-Verlag, pp. 65–74.

Kerner, I. 2009. 'Alles intersektional? Zum Verhältnis von Rassismus und Sexismus'. *Feministische Studien*, 27(1): 36–50.

Korteweg, A., and Yurdakul, G. 2014. *The Headscarf Debates: Conflicts of National Belonging*. Stanford, CA: Stanford University Press.

Kosnick, K. 2014. 'Nach dem Multikulturalismus: Aspekte des aktuellen Umgangs mit Diversität und Ungleichheit in der Bundesrepublik Deutschland', in H. Drotbohm and B. Nieswand (eds), *Kultur, Gesellschaft, Migration: die reflexive Wende in der Migrationsforschung*. Heidelberg: Springer VS, pp. 297–323.

———. 2016. 'Aus westlicher Sicht: Das "Ereignis Köln" und Perspektiven transnationaler feministischer Solidarität', *FEMINA POLITICA. Zeitschrift für feministische Politikwissenschaft* 25(2): 147–55.

Kulaçatan, M. 2016. 'Die verkannte Angst des Fremden: Rassismus und Sexismus im Kontext medialer Öffentlichkeit', in M. do Mar Castro Varela and P. Mecheril (eds), *Die Dämonisierung der Anderen: Rassismuskritik der Gegenwart*. Bielefeld: transcript, pp. 107–117.

Lutz, H. et al. (eds). 2010. *Fokus Intersektionalität*. Wiesbaden: VS Verlag.

Malkki, L. 1992. 'National Geographic: The Rooting of Peoples and the Territo-rialization of National Identity among Scholars and Refugees', *Cultural Anthropology* 7(1): 24–44.

McRobbie, A., and Thornton, S. L. 1995. 'Rethinking 'Moral Panic' for multi-mediated Social Worlds', *British Journal of Sociology* 64(4): 559–574.

Messerschmidt, A. 2016. '>Nach Köln< - Zusammenhänge von Rassismus und Sexismus thematisieren', in M. do Mar Castro Varela and P. Mecheril (eds), *Die Dämonisierung der Anderen: Rassismuskritik der Gegenwart*. Bielefeld: transcript, pp. 160–71.

Mohanty, C.T. 2003. '"Under Western Eyes" Revisited: Feminist Solidarity through Anticapitalist Struggles', *Signs: Journal of Women in Culture and Society* 28(2): 499–535.

Müller, D. 2010. *Flucht und Asyl in europäischen Migrationsregimen: Metamorphosen einer umkämpften Kategorie am Beispiel der EU, Deutschlands und Polens*. Göttingen: Universitätsverlag Göttingen.

Müller, U., and Schröttle, M. 2005. *Sicherheit und Gesundheit von Frauen in Deutsch-land: Eine repräsentative Untersuchung zu Gewalt gegen Frauen in Deutschland*. Bonn: Bundesministerium für Familie, Senioren, Frauen und Jugend.

Radtke, F.-O. 2009. 'Nationale Multikulturalismen: Bezugsprobleme und Effekte', in S. Hess, J. Binder and J. Moser (eds), *No Integration?! Kulturwissenschaftliche Beiträge zur Integrationsdebatte in Europa*. Bielefeld: transcript Verlag, pp. 37–50.

Reckwitz, A. 2001. 'Multikulturalismustheorien und der Kulturbegriff', *Berliner Journal für Soziologie* 11(2): 179–200.

Said, E. 1978. *Orientalism*. New York: Pantheon.

Schiffauer, W. 2004. 'Vom Exil- zum Diaspora-Islam: Muslimische Identitäten in Europa', *Soziale Welt* 55(4): 347–68.

Schröter, S. 2016: 'Gewaltlegitimierende Gendernormen benennen', *UniReport* 2. Retrieved 8 July 2018 from http://tinygu.de/Gendernormen.

Schwarzer, A. (ed.). 2016. *Der Schock: Die Silvesternacht von Köln*. Cologne: Kie-penheuer und Witsch-Verlag.

Shooman, Y. 2014. '. . . weil ihre Kultur so ist': Narrative des antimuslimischen Rassismus*. Bielefeld: transcript Verlag.

Spivak, G. 1994 [1988]. 'Can the Subaltern Speak?', in P. Williams, and L. Chrisman (eds), *Colonial Discourse and Postcolonial Theory: A Reader*. New York: Columbia University Press, pp. 66–112.

Stocking, G.W. 1968. *Race, Culture and Evolution: Essays in the History of Anthropology*. Chicago: University of Chicago Press.

Stolcke, V. 1995. 'Talking Culture: New Boundaries, New Rhetorics of Exclusion in Europe', *Current Anthropology* 36(1): 1–24.

Stoler, A.-L. 1989. 'Making Empire Respectable: The Politics of Race and Sexual Morality in 20th-Century Colonial Cultures', *American Ethnologist* 16(4): 634–60.

Tezcan, L. 2011. 'Spielarten der Kulturalisierung', *Zeitschrift für Kulturphilosophie* 5(2): 357–77.

_____. 2018. *Das muslimische Subjekt: Verfangen im Dialog der Deutschen Islam Konferenz*. Konstanz: Konstanz University Press.

Wolf, E.R. 1982: *Europe and the People without History*. Berkeley: University of California Press.

Chapter 8

Solidarity with Refugees
Negotiations of Proximity and Memory

Serhat Karakayalı

This chapter explores the emergence of a particularly welcoming societal stance and atmosphere towards asylum seekers and refugees in Germany.[1] In German, this significant cultural shift has been labelled *Willkommenskultur* – or 'a culture of welcome/hospitality' – an attitude that started to emerge noticeably in 2011 and reached its peak in the summer of 2015, when hundreds of thousands of Germans joined voluntary associations and groups to support large numbers of refugees arriving in the country, predominantly from Syria, Iraq and Afghanistan. In fact, around 10 per cent of Germany's adult population joined such initiatives or projects aimed at helping refugees in August and September 2015 alone (Ahrens 2015). In this chapter, I examine some of the political dimensions of this volunteering movement.

The analysis is based on four sets of data. The first two are online surveys – one of them conducted among volunteers and the other with professionals in support organizations. The first survey was conducted in 2014, involving 466 volunteers and seventy-nine representatives from organizations in the field of refugee work; the second survey followed one year later, including 2,293 volunteers. Both were conducted online (EFA 1 and EFA 2).[2] The increase regarding respondents from the first survey to the second survey is due to the significantly higher number of people who were active in 2015 and willing to participate, rather than to a different sampling strategy. The third set of data consists of semi-structured interviews with individuals who coordinate volunteer activities (mostly volunteers themselves) in thirty communities across Germany (I refer to

Notes for this chapter begin on page 209.

the dataset as CO). The semi-structured interviews took place in February and March 2016. By that point, German media coverage on refugees had turned into a stream of negative headlines; the societal culture of welcoming refugees and extending hospitality had begun to subside.

Germany's Long Summer of Migration

The enthusiasm with which large parts of German society joined the welcoming movement was not entirely surprising. Parts of the economic elite have long seen migration as a strategy for labour recruitment and, as such, as an advantage for the economy for three key reasons. Around the mid 2000s, the shortage of skilled workers, the increase in profitability in some sectors as a result of migrant workers and an expected labour shortage caused by demographic recession emerged as important political concerns (Georgi 2016). Dieter Zetsche, the CEO of Daimler-Benz, announced immediately after Angela Merkel's move to accept refugees stranded in Hungary that asylum seekers 'could trigger a new economic miracle' in Germany.[3] It is therefore not surprising that scholars of migration are associating the term *Willkommenskultur* with utilitarian aspects of migration politics (see e.g. Castro Varela 2014). For the majority of political and academic observers, however, the welcoming atmosphere during the first months of the so-called refugee crisis (*Flüchtlingskrise*) came as a surprise. Every major political party, trade unions, companies, public offices and the media joined in celebrating both the arrival of hundreds of thousands of refugees and asylum seekers, and the hospitality and kind reception offered to them by a significant part of Germany's population. The fact that even the populist and usually conservative tabloid *Bild* supported emergent grassroots hospitality with its own campaign (*Wir helfen!* or 'We Help!') remains to be explained. The events reported to the German public – refugees stranded in makeshift camps along the so-called Balkan route from Greece to Austria, trapped and beaten in a Budapest train station, images of suffering families and young children – and positive responses by German authorities and the media helped turn a pre-existent, but small, volunteer movement into a mainstream initiative involving diverse, large parts of German society.

Millions of Germans flocked to the train stations, shelters and other camps at which refugees arrived or were accommodated. Some even drove their cars to Hungary or Croatia to collect those moving across the continent and returned to Germany or Austria with them during this 'long summer of migration' (see Kasparek and Speer 2015; Misik 2015). Nonetheless, however surprising the large scale of projects and involvement was, it did not come out of nowhere. One key result from the first survey in 2014

(Karakayalı and Kleist 2015) was that the number of volunteers had grown between 2011 and 2014 by around 70 per cent, according to employees of organizations active in this field. Almost in parallel to this development, we could observe a steady increase of asylum applications, which had risen significantly since 2008. Nonetheless, this novel development had been preceded by a historical low: in 2007, only 20,000 people had applied for asylum in Germany – the lowest number in decades. With regard to the history of the German asylum system, this is significant in two ways.

Firstly, the German asylum law was established after the Second World War as a consequence of the experience of those Germans who desperately (and often unsuccessfully) tried to find protection in other countries during fascism. As one of the primary articles of the West German constitution, it reflected Germany's particular historical legacy and shaped principles of postwar German identity. The law granted every individual suffering political persecution the right to asylum. As the law was part of the constitution and could therefore not be altered easily, political debates around 'bogus asylum seekers', which started as early as the mid 1970s, resulted in restrictive measures concerning the living conditions of asylum seekers. This pattern changed with the collapse of the Soviet Union, German reunification and as a result of the war in Yugoslavia. Between 1990 and 1992, hundreds of thousands of refugees demanded protection in Germany (many of them had relatives in the country, who had come as so-called guestworkers two decades earlier), causing the first profound refugee crisis in the history of postwar Germany. Although the number of refugees then was much smaller compared with 2015 and although the vast majority of asylum seekers were European, public reaction had been almost entirely the opposite: the media and the government shared a hostile attitude. Given the social climate in 1993, even the main opposition party agreed to support an amendment for the constitution. Asylum seekers could only claim protection if they had not passed through a so-called safe country on their way. This amendment became, due to Germany's authority, one of the primary principles of European asylum policy as well. The reform of the German constitution and the subsequent structural changes in the European migration regime made it increasingly difficult for asylum seekers to reach Germany. However, from the historic low in 2007 onwards, numbers of asylum seekers in Germany began to grow exponentially, which might be one reason why German millennials started to become active in this field. We asked respondents about the time when they had become interested in issues regarding refugees or asylum. More than half of the respondents developed an interest in these topics in 2013 – the year when the civil war in Syria escalated (Karakayalı and Kleist 2016).

Justification and Identity

Based on the empirical data my colleagues[4] and I collected, I address two
central questions. The first concerns how volunteers rationalize their work.
How do they explain and justify their actions? While conventional volunteering in most cases is uncontroversial, the kind of activity that facilitates
the migration of larger numbers of foreigners is not. Migration-related
initiatives are bound up with other issues and public debates concerning
reduced social rights, labour market changes, and questions about belonging and citizenship (Karakayalı 2008). It is therefore not surprising that
migration once more turned into the central topic around which rightwing populist movements organized in Europe and elsewhere (Karakayalı
2016). Because migration is a socio-politically highly contentious issue,
particularly positive attitudes towards immigration are subjected to what
Boltanski and Thévenot call a 'justification imperative' (2007). Those who
advocate immigration and promote diversity are socially expected to provide reasons for their views or engagements. The advantage of a qualitative approach is that attitudes are interpretable not only as aggregates
generated individually as experienced effects of social structures, but that
arguments and justifications are also understood to be located at a 'transin-
dividual' level (Balibar 1998). Although social action is multidimensional
and should not be reduced to individuals and collectives exchanging
rational arguments, justification is a central dimension in democratic societies (Forst 2014). Thus, volunteers supporting migrants or refugees need
to frame and justify engagement in their own social environment. This
constraint to explain and provide reasons for one's involvement is particularly relevant in social spaces in which the majority has negative or hostile
attitudes towards migration, such as many regions of East Germany or
other rural areas across the country – which is why this chapter draws on
interviews with individuals and groups of volunteers across parts of formerly socialist East Germany, conducted in August and September 2016 (I
refer to the dataset as Volunteers in East Germany (VEG)).

   In these cases, volunteers usually outline certain conditions for their
willingness to welcome migrants positively. These include the geographical extension of their solidarity as much as refugees' readiness to adapt
to cultural and social norms in Germany. I suggest that this negotiation
of preconditions is an act of judgement regarding modes of belonging,
or the lack thereof, which affects refugees who settle in German society.
Responding to the need to offer persuasive reasons rather than simply
reflecting on intrinsic motivation, social agents are compelled to engage –
often publicly – with private notions of what is accepted and understood as common sense, as well as with contested and opposing visions

articulated in public. It is assumed here that reason has a constitutively social quality: through reasoning, we make an implicit statement revealing our ideas regarding social relations and the ways in which human beings are connected to one another. Hence, such actors produce different modes of justification, which, in turn, produce different modes of social connectedness.

Frames are generally considered as 'interpretative schemata' (Goffman 1974), which simplify and condense 'the "world out there" by selectively punctuating and encoding objects, situations, events, experiences and sequences of actions within one's present and past environment' (Snow and Benford 1992: 137). However, I argue that frames also include a relational pattern, which predetermines or expresses the scope and the type of social relations implied. For example, a frame of justification that operates with demographic or labour market arguments is based on a utilitarian relationship. The relation is structured by the notion of 'benefit', while the scope of inclusion is not limited by ethnic or cultural markers (in this sense, it is 'open'), but is a function of parameters, such as economic growth, demand for labour, average wage and so forth.

This kind of communication with the social and political environment therefore implies a certain strategic dimension. This is evident insofar as the sociological literature on framing processes conceptualizes frames as functionally equivalent to the concept of ideology, which is criticized for being too static compared to frame theory, which provides, according to its advocates, a stronger mediation between theory and data (Snow 2004; Snow and Byrd 2007; Westby 2002). Social and political agents calculate the possible successes of framing strategies and, as a consequence, estimates about the hegemonic norms, potential connections, interventions or dynamics are incorporated into respective narrative strategies. Frames are thus particularistic in the sense that they favour one perspective over another, but their particularism needs to be expressed in more universal ways – ways that allow others to share this view and thus can find the perspective 'convincing', as formulated in the neo-Gramscian school of political theory (see Overbeek 2000). Usually, these are historically grown orders of justification, with which social agents are confronted, but which also need to be re-enacted, re-actualized and constructed on the micro-level constantly (Boltanski and Thévenot 2007).

One important justification frame in this case is constructed with regard to supposedly similar experiences of flight in the collective memory of the German host society. I suggest that forms of justification that invoke the historical fate of German expellees after the Second World War seek to promote social connections through memories and to create new channels of identification with refugees. Such 'acts of remembrance'

(Bottici 2010: 343) allow, in certain situations, the opening and adjustment of membership and models of belonging. Collective memory, which provides society with a stabilizing and meaningful framework (Misztal 2003: 73), is no longer limited to a nationally defined community of memory. Such acts can be analysed as practices of cross-referencing, which, on the basis of the comparison of different migration experiences, expand the limits of collectives (Rothberg and Yildiz 2011: 34). From this perspective, it is also important to consider correlations between the contents of 'acts of remembrance' and the respective biographies of volunteers. There is a growing body of historiographical work on the politics of integration of refugees through the recognition of flight experiences (cf. Kleist 2013). At the same time, research at the intersection of memory and migration has mostly focused on integrating or excluding the experiences of a particular migrant or racialized group with regard to collective memory (Losego 2012: 100). The downside of these approaches is that respective groups are associated with particular political identities on the basis of supposedly rigid and preformed ethnic, national or religious identities. Acts of cross-referencing, such as those between German political memory of postwar refugees and expellees (*Vertriebene*, or 'those that have been chased away' or 'the expelled') and the arrival of refugees from the Middle East, thereby usually remain out of focus.

The Scope and Scale of Solidarity: East Germany

In this section, I discuss findings predominantly from fieldwork conducted in the eastern part of Germany – the former German Democratic Republic (GDR) – with a focus on volunteers in smaller towns. The population of this region is to some extent still shaped by the experience of GDR socialism. It has undergone rapid and deep transformations of culture and everyday life in a short period of time after reunification in 1990, leading to high levels of unemployment and the mass migration of skilled workers to West German regions. This experience, which has been compared to colonial or other migratory experiences, often serves as an explanation for higher levels of xenophobia among East Germans.[5] The internationalist perspective, which the socialist government embraced in fields such as support for anti-colonial movements or solidarity campaigns, did not impact on its migration policies. The comparatively low number of migrant workers can be explained by the high level of employment in the GDR – in 1989, only 84,000 contract workers from Vietnam and Mozambique lived in the GDR. This has resulted in extremely small migrant populations, usually concentrated in particular areas of large cities.

With the enormous mobilization of volunteers in August and September 2015 – mainly triggered by empathetic and positive media coverage, as well as by the government's initial reaction to suspend EU regulations and offer protection to asylum seekers who had crossed through 'safe countries' on their way to Germany – the composition of the volunteer movement changed almost overnight. This transformation had an impact on the topic of justification: people without previous engagement suddenly became involved in activities and projects. In fact, the volunteering milieu, which used to overlap largely with the radical movement, with its emphasis on universal refugee solidarity, changed. Data from a second survey among volunteers, conducted at the end of 2015 with 2,293 participants, suggest that the composition of volunteer groups changed with regard to age, occupation and local population size. The relative share of younger volunteers, for example, dropped from almost 30 per cent to around 16 per cent, whereas the relative share of people aged over forty increased. In particular, the proportion of active volunteers in country towns (*Landstadt*), i.e. settlements with a population up to 5,000 inhabitants, shifted: it quadrupled from nearly 4 to 16 per cent. The level of volunteering in small towns (*Kleinstadt*, between 5,000 and 20,000 inhabitants) also grew (from 11.1 to 19 per cent). With the exception of very large cities (*Millionenstadt*, with over one million inhabitants), percentage shares in cities as such have decreased. This is an interesting development: the movement seems to normalize, in the sense of reflecting societal reality more representatively, since the majority of Germans lives in mid-size and smaller towns, but also regarding the likelihood of engagement, since the population in nonurban environments usually tends to be less positive about migration.

Given these circumstances, it is not surprising that volunteers have addressed the topic, too. In an interview with a group of volunteers in the East German region of Brandenburg, for example, a number of participants identified themselves as West Germans migrants to East Germany. They explained predominantly hostile attitudes in the village as a result of local experiences in East German society. Referring to a roundtable scheme, which had been established to coordinate volunteering activities around refugees, a volunteer explained that:

> It is usually the newcomers [West German migrants to East Germany], not the locals, who participate in such events. I am also a newcomer; there really are no locals involved. This scares me a little bit. But, okay, people here in Brandenburg always have been quite a special folk.

In another group interview, participants also declared that most of them had come from West Germany and that 'Easterners are really anti' – referring to an attitude of rejection towards migrants and foreigners. In these cases, the term 'newcomer' encapsulates a West German biography; in other scenarios, however, it remained unclear whether the term was used to highlight an East–West divide or the difference between long-established residents and newcomers in general. Such conversations reveal the idea that the attribute *alteingesessen* (long-established) has an implicitly critical dimension: it highlights that residents of small towns 'have not seen a lot', as a volunteer who runs a travel agency explained. She based this assessment on her experience with local customers, describing both the remote countryside location and the GDR past as relevant factors. In another conversation, an interviewee used the term 'really old-fashioned eastern families' (*richtig alte Ostfamilien*) to identify those within the village who had expressed particularly hostile attitudes towards refugees. Although some migration did affect the GDR as well, temporary labour recruitment did not result in settlement, unlike in Western Germany (Herbert 2001). In most cases, migrant workers returned to their home socialist countries after a few years.

As a result, even today, in many regions of the former GDR, the migrant population remains small. In 2016, 23 per cent of West Germans had a migration history in their family, compared with only 4.8 per cent in East Germany (Statistisches Bundesamt 2016: 41). Many volunteers in East Germany described how their relationships with neighbours, customers or patients were affected by their engagement with refugees, resulting in hostile remarks and dismissive behaviour. The spectrum of such reactions was wide: it reached from avoiding contact to confrontation. Our interviews suggested two broad types of interactional patterns: (1) volunteers and refugee supporters tended to isolate themselves in opposition to the local environment, whose 'others' – or local residents – were seen as problematic, backward and hostile; (2) a sort of micro-social engagement with the local environment prevailed, with a significant number of accounts of 'conversions' (from hostile to volunteer). In one particular story, voluntary activities served as a tipping point that were said to prevent the town from becoming an anti-refugee hotspot, in which initially hostile citizens ended up volunteering. During a town hall meeting, at which local authorities informed residents about a planned refugee shelter, a citizen already active in the emerging welcoming movement intervened in a fierce debate:

> Things were getting heated during the assembly, with pretty nasty, racist comments. The audience was split down the middle, fifty-fifty. It seemed that the debate was slipping away, against refugees. But then this guy stood up and said: 'come on guys, listen up. Think about who you are. What are we doing? We are helping people in need'. He spoke with passion and

empathy, he showed true heart; he shifted the audience again and won over the majority. That was the decisive factor that allowed 100 refugees to come and live in our community. And all of a sudden lots of local citizens offered to volunteer.

The story was reported by the national press and served as an example for how the difficulties volunteers faced in East Germany could be overcome. Such stories seem to indicate a greater prevalence of conflict in rural areas or smaller towns, with volunteers facing opposition to their engagement. However, our survey data do not support this assumption. When we asked whether support for refugees was considered important in their social environment, we could not find a correlation between the size of a town and pro-refugee attitudes in respondents' social contexts. There was only a minor indication of this in the survey data collected in 2015, in which residents of smaller towns more often indicated that helping refugees was not something their social environment appreciated. The term 'social environment', however, may have different meanings in the contexts of larger cities, where residents might not consider immediate neighbours part of that group. What the survey data clearly showed was an ideological gap between city people and inhabitants of smaller towns. While almost 40 per cent of volunteers in cities supported open-borders views, only 20 per cent of respondents from smaller towns did. It appears that this difference can be explained by the age variable.

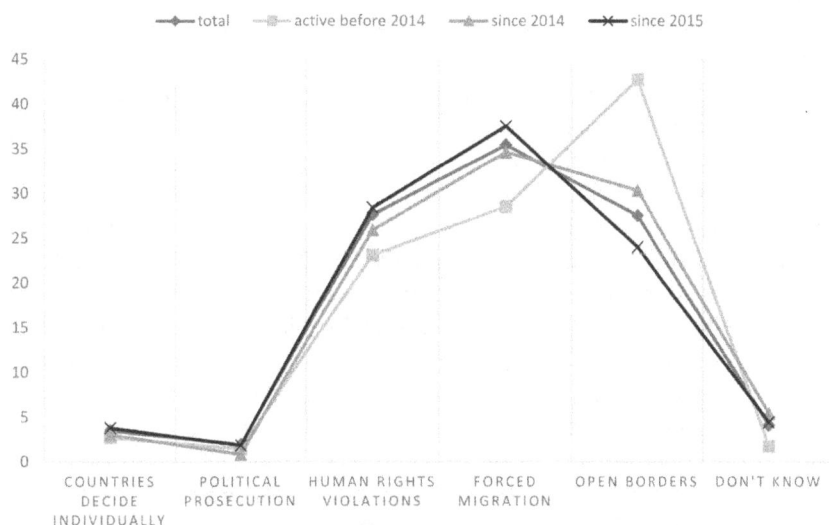

Figure 8.1 What should be the basis for taking in refugees? Figure by the author.

We found that the more radical claim for open borders was less popular with increasing age: 38 per cent of those under thirty supported it
compared with 13 per cent among those over sixty. Age correlates with
urban–rural differences: younger people were more active in larger cities,
whereas volunteers in the countryside were much older. This did not
surprise, since younger people tend to leave rural areas in search of education or jobs.

Political Questions

The two surveys also revealed that older volunteers became mobilized by
the events of 2015, when unprecedented numbers of refugees arrived in
Germany. When we compare the newly mobilized cohort with the people
who had been involved before that watershed year, we can observe a
clear change. The most recent cohort of volunteers did not appear very
different from previous ones in terms of its demographics, but we noted a
change in attitudes. The majority of volunteers had extensive knowledge
regarding the asylum process and they supported generous definitions,
but they also expressed views about conditionality regarding individual
backgrounds, histories and reasons to be granted protection. Our results
suggest that the share of volunteers supporting the unconditional intake
of refugees and the demand for open borders dropped significantly with
rising participation already by 2014. Only 25 per cent of newly involved
activists supported the demands put forward by open-borders movements, compared with 40 per cent of long-term activists. The desire for
open borders is a particular claim that is voiced only by a minority of the
political spectrum.

From these data, the question of whether volunteering ought to be
conceptualized as straightforward political activity cannot be answered
conclusively. With regard to questions over the legitimacy of refugee
migration and their claims for settling in new countries, we found that the
majority of volunteers invoked the generic term 'forced migration' when
expressing a supportive stance. Forced migration, however, is not a legal,
but a moral concept. The notion of 'being forced' resonates with a dominant humanitarian dispositive of migration, in which migrant agency
tends to be conceptualized as economic agency – migrants who make a
choice or 'pick' a country of arrival are suspected of being profit-seeking
economic agents.[6] The broad definition of what should be the criteria for
welcoming refugees is both more open: it does not define particular criteria (they can also include so-called economic reasons, such as poverty,
unemployment or lack of perspectives) and is conditional with regard to
individual motivation.

In conversations, volunteers often associate the term 'political' with political parties, interest groups and organizations, and with national and regional political debates from which they seek to distance themselves. Yet, being distant from politics can mean different things. One respondent told us: 'Politics? We are very far away from that.' She thereby articulated criticism of the political sphere as shaped by power plays and populist strategies before elections. However, there also exists a more fundamental understanding of the concept of being apolitical. In another focus group, a conversation about the term *Willkommenskultur* included the following statement, rejecting an association with political activity or views:

> All those volunteers in Bavaria, the thousands who had spontaneously gone to the train stations, did not know about the concept of *Willkommenskultur* at all. They simply wanted to help for the straightforward reason that we are all human. Nothing else. We are simply helpful Germans, who assist others in emergency situations.

These two versions of 'not being political' might not contradict each other, but they are embedded in very different approaches. The first position reveals distinctive criticism of the political and its mechanisms, deliberately seeking distance to that field. The second position, by contrast, rejects the possibility of any conceptual relationship.

Emotional Involvement

This is the point at which the volunteering phenomenon oscillates between a more generic notion of altruism, on the one hand, and a politically charged engagement with migration and the limits or borders of solidarity, on the other. In our group interviews, we approached this complex issue by discussing possible deportations following negative responses to asylum applications. We were interested in the ways in which responses would be framed: would volunteers question such a decision and resist, or were the relationships that volunteers build with refugees 'conditional' on the formal validation of their status as refugees? In this context, questions about the scope of altruism also emerged: when is it that volunteers felt they needed to act – when migrants were stranded in Macedonia or after they had arrived in German neighbourhoods? During group interviews, we discovered that volunteers employed a number of different approaches when discussing such topics. One of them was to frame responses on the micro-social level. Most of our informants began their involvement at the time when refugees were moved into local shelters or housing facilities, inevitably fusing local lives with the fate of migrants and asylum seekers. Proximity and responsibility were connected, as one respondent underlined:

> We could not deal with the images from Budapest anymore. You cannot watch these scenes, happening 300 kilometres away. It's hard to bear – at least for me and many others I know. That does not mean that everyone in the whole world should come to live in Germany, of course – but there is a concrete problem that requires a concrete and immediate solution.

In the same conversation, another participant said that relationships with refugees would have to remain casual regardless:

> This might sound cruel, but we all have to move on to other places someday. I see it that way. So, if I meet you today, I might find you very nice, but I may well never see you again. Too bad. But I cannot pursue every possible friendship, because I already know enough people. However, if you need help now, or if I see you somewhere on a train and in need of assistance, I support you immediately.

In this sense, proximity and the bonds developed out of contact serve as a regulatory principle to organize decisions about when and to whom voluntary assistance is offered. This principle seems to apply to the emotional realm, too. Volunteers who emphasized that they tried to avoid emotional proximity often employed more utilitarian arguments to justify their involvement. For example, one participant explained that she would never accept dinner invitations from refugees to maintain a certain distance, while strongly emphasizing during her narration that the shrinking village would benefit from refugees, particularly in terms of infrastructure. Such a relationship also became the object of public debate at the height of the so-called refugee crisis, when the head of the Council of the Protestant Church in Germany, Heinrich Bedford-Strohm, advocated what he called an *Abschiedskultur* ('culture of farewell') as opposed to *Willkommenskultur*. The term was soon picked up by other politicians, who argued that it was necessary that Germans prepare themselves for the fact that many asylum seekers would be denied protection due to insufficient reasons or because they had already applied elsewhere. They would have to return. The statement highlighted dimensions of a debate about the role of emotions in decision-making about refugee politics. This topic was addressed in an official document about civil resistance to deportations. The authors of this strategy paper argued that 'for a small, but active part, of the population, as well as in large parts of the media, deportation measures and decisions are being portrayed exclusively from an emotional perspective and not from the perspective of legal frameworks (*ordnungsrechtlich*)' (quoted in Scheer 2016: 3); however, the importance of personal bonds with refugees and the correlation with political claims appear to be more complex.

In their study of deportation protests in Austria, Rosenberger and Winkler (2013) have outlined a typology of arguments used by those seeking to undermine deportation efforts. According to them, three different types of argumentation exist, focusing respectively on concepts of integration, humanity and human rights (Rosenberger and Winkler 2013: 124). While local groups mostly invoke the first principle, translocal groups also refer to the other two principles. Campaigns against deportations are mostly local and centred around an individual, as Ruedin and Merhaut (2016) have shown in a longitudinal comparison of three countries. Proximity seems to allow for stronger kinds of engagement, and often such local campaigns are capable of mobilizing citizens across the political spectrum – under the condition that the initiative be stripped of a noticeable political affiliation. Such personal proximity can also lead to the development of emotional bonds, sometimes expressed in family metaphors, in which German volunteers describe refugees as 'children'. While such involvement can produce strong forms of engagement, it does not necessarily also lead to universalized reasoning about migration, borders and citizenship. There are thus two ways in which one of the most common metaphors for proximity – the family – comes into play: (1) refugees are seen and addressed as family members, and volunteers often describe being enriched socially and culturally by the experience, reflecting a particular possibility towards integration or 'becoming German'; and (2) family terms are not used as a means to describe emerging emotional bonds between volunteers and refugees, but are rather intended to mobilize empathy and evoke the notion of equality – refugees are said to be 'just like us' and their decision to migrate is thus comprehensible, since 'we' would do so too (often also referring to family experience in the wake of the Second World War; see below).

When a desire to help others is based on the experience of proximity and compassion, one might assume that volunteering would contribute to the reproduction of asymmetrical power relations. As Didier Fassin and many others have argued, if caregivers retain the power to decide who will receive what kind of help, this reproduces a 'relation of inequality' (Fassin 2012: 3). According to Fassin, this imbalance lies at the heart of humanitarianism: it does not necessarily result in the claim for fundamental rights. Immanuel Kant made the same argument in his *Perpetual Peace*, insisting that the protection of strangers is not a question of philanthropy, but of right (see Kant 1983 [1795]: Article 3).[7] Philanthropy – a practice based on feelings of compassion, which are in turn conditional, as Boltanski has shown in his work on 'distant suffering' (2004) – can be seen as rather weak ground, leaving the decision of whether or not an individual in need will receive assistance to entirely volatile factors. Most importantly, humanitarianism's tendency to exclude references to the social or political context of suffering plays a decisive role for such critiques (Whitebrook 2002: 530). There are instances in which volunteers seem to feel drawn to the experience of refugees as fellow human beings, leading to an identification of injustices that must be addressed; in other cases, however, volunteers seem to avoid the contextual themes that would bring questions of global inequality to the fore and instead focus on issues of integration. The grievances in such accounts focus on the state authorities' lack of organization to provide resources for integration efforts.

So far, I have outlined observations that might contribute to a better understanding of the relationship between emotions and social bonds of proximity, on the one hand, with conceptual frameworks, abstract political stances and universalizing reason, on the other. While some volunteers seem to have a clear answer as to how these fields connect, others are ambivalent about influences and impacts, and often seem to avoid drawing more far-reaching or universal conclusions. There is clearly no direct path from emotions and affects to political attitudes and standpoints. Empathy and compassion can result in a variety of modes of reasoning. Nonetheless, one particularly important result concerns different levels of coherence in narrative accounts: volunteers reframe the cause of refugees as a local problem, bypassing the social context of flight.

Germans as Refugees

A central discursive frame regarding the civil war in Syria emerged early on in the public debate: the comparison of Syrian refugees with postwar expellees in Germany in 1945. In fact, these German refugees used to be the object of a first integration debate that is often overlooked today (Schwartz 2016). In the 1960s, German *Vertriebene* ('forcibly evicted' or 'expelled'), who resettled in West German cities, towns and villages, were compared with other contemporary refugees – in particular, Palestinians forced out of settlements in the newly established state of Israel. The comparisons and the debate about integration at the time showed to what extent the German public considered those refugees culturally foreign, notwithstanding the fact that the term 'expellee' suggested otherwise. Terms such as *Vertriebene* were rather a result of the political strategy of expellee organizations, which wanted to maintain territorial claims in Silesia and Eastern Prussia. Later on, this migration of Germans became 'invisible' (Smith 2003) because of other migratory experiences, primarily the recruitment agreements and guestworker schemes of the 1950s and 1960s, bringing hundreds of thousands of Italians, Greeks and Turks into West Germany to labour in the country's factories during the economic boom years. For a variety of reasons, the refugee experiences of *Vertriebene* were not addressed as a real migration experience. German refugees formed political organizations, claiming a right to return and contesting postwar European borders, and were thus positioned at the far-right end of the political spectrum. Their revisionist territorial claims in particular contributed to the difficulty of conceptualizing these biographies as a form of migration. Although historians began highlighting similarities in the 1990s (Bade 1990; Ehrhardt 1991), the view that Germany's migration history begins with postwar German expellees has only recently achieved public attention (Amos 2009; Hahn and Hahn 2010; Kossert 2008, 2015).

The 2015 refugee crisis seemed to provide fertile ground for this rearticulation in public discourse. Articles in news magazines linked the experience of postwar displacement with the contemporary Middle East. One prominent example was an article by the historian Andreas Kossert, published in the weekly news magazine *Die Zeit* under the title 'Bohemia, Pomerania, Syria'. Kossert argued that German refugees had experienced more or less the same types of racism and xenophobia to which other migrants to Germany were exposed later. In a previous book, *Kalte Heimat* (2008), Kossert called this 'German racism against Germans'. While Kossert argued from a historian's perspective, comparing the two historical experiences as similar, others suggested that the connection was also cognitive. In the same issue of *Die Zeit*, the novelist Ulrike Draesner speculated whether the ways in which Germans responded to the plight of Syrians and other refugees revealed a collective trauma.[8] While psychological reflections on trauma remained superficial, the comparison became popular and was employed by journalists, politicians and others seeking to mobilize empathy towards Syrian refugees. For example, Sigmar Gabriel, the then head of the German Social Democratic Party (SPD), repeatedly stated that his mother had been an expellee-refugee too, particularly during his initially supportive stance towards refugees. In the East German city of Leipzig, large banners with images of postwar refugees were mounted on the front of the city hall in October 2015. Leipzig's social democratic mayor, Burkhard Jung, explained that almost every family in Germany had flight experience, either because parents and grandparents had lost their home as *Vertriebene* or because they had taken in expellees after the Second World War.

In 2015 and 2016, the German government celebrated the World Refugee Day for the first time, alongside the Commemoration Day for German Refugees on 20 June. In their respective addresses to mark the occasion, the German President, Joachim Gauck, and the Minister for the Interior, Thomas de Maizière, invoked emotional comparisons between the situation of postwar German expellees and current refugees. They highlighted the historical precedent to illustrate German society's capacity to integrate millions of people and pointed out that even German expellees had often been attacked and humiliated as strangers, and accused of failing to belong. This understanding that German expellees had often been characterized as 'foreigners' by the local population seemed to have achieved the status of general knowledge, as it appears in almost identical form in narrations of interviewees (see below) and speeches of politicians. The event therefore demanded more empathy with Syrian refugees, but also sought to raise awareness for the historical suffering of German expellees, whose plight continues to be overshadowed by the larger historical framework of German responsibility for the war, often even depicted as just retribution for the country's belligerence.

Many activists and volunteers to whom we spoke made reference to this particular part of German history, and so we decided to include relevant questions in our surveys. Both in 2014 and 2015, about a third of all volunteers stated that they had family members who had experienced forced resettlement at the end of the Second World War. It is notable, however, that the numbers are altogether higher in East Germany. While between 25 and 35 per cent of volunteers in West Germany say that they have postwar expellees in the family, the same share ranges from 37 to 60 per cent in East Germany, varying across respective regions (*Länder*). Yet, it is not clear how to interpret these numbers. The German government stopped including the category of *Vertriebene* in the micro-census data at the end of the 1970s, where the average was below 20 per cent of the population. At the time, the census included only expellees and their children, not their grandchildren. Nevertheless, forty years later, we have to change the perspective: while the first generation of expellees passes away, their grandchildren seem to perpetuate this particular identity. In a recent survey, 26 per cent of Germans stated to be the descendants of postwar expellees (IfD Allensbach 2015). According to the same study, however, the importance of this refugee experience has become increasingly irrelevant with every generation. More than 70 per cent of respondents below the age of thirty and with an expellee in the family stated that this history does not matter to them. In our survey, the same share of respondents with this kind of family history could be found across age groups. This was surprising, since one might expect someone from the second generation – over forty years old – to have a more significant relationship to that history than someone from the third generation. It is also apparent that German expellees and their descendants do not represent an endogamous, or distinct, group, in the sense that expellees or their children only married and had children with other expellees or their descendants. That is why we can assume that more people in the third or fourth generation today can claim to have, or have had, family members with an expellee background.

The even distribution across age groups can be interpreted in different ways. One such interpretation could be that it is easier to perform acts of cross-referencing for the younger generation than for those who have closer ties to the original history. Almost all respondents were able to identify the particular region from which their parents or grandparents had been expelled (with Silesia, East Prussia and the Sudentenland as the most frequent regions). The various age sets among volunteer groups responded rather homogeneously to questions about links between family history and engagement. A major difference emerged solely when we included the group that had directly experienced the end of the Second World War and displacement. All of these respondents agreed with the following statement: 'I support refugees because I am able to relate to the experience of fleeing from war.' Among other groups, even those including affected relatives, there was far less support for this statement. Almost two-thirds of volunteers with first-hand experience of displacement stated that emotional experience is important for their engagement (the corresponding figure for younger groups is 47 per cent). In the interviews we conducted with volunteers in East Germany, the topic did not feature as frequently. Reference to the history of postwar German expellees was made in four out of fourteen interviews. Two interviewees related their own commitment to the experiences of their parents and grandparents. One participant recounted:

> My grandparents had fled from Silesia via Dresden to Thuringia. They indeed arrived as strangers there. They were not popular. My grandmother said that there used to be the same discussions as we are having in Germany today: the newcomers or foreigners were stealing, were stupid, intellectually incapable and would take away jobs. All of this stuff. Today, we are having exactly the same debate as she witnessed then: they are all criminals. So I thought, well, someone has to disprove it.

Another volunteer made a similar statement. She explained at first that her mother had come from Silesia, before expressing amazement that particularly women of her mother's generation could be so hostile towards refugees, since they had experienced the aftermath of the war. This volunteer also mentioned that she was part of a progressive family – her parents had always wanted a 'better GDR' – which allows the conclusion that her attitude towards refugees might be part of a wider worldview. A young female interviewee mentioned that some of her fellow volunteers had referred to having been Polish refugees themselves, who came to Berlin and West Germany after the breaking up of Solidarność in the 1980s, as a reason for their engagement. Wherever the narrative appears, it is highly interdiscursive: reference is made to earlier statements regarding the political and media public discourse. Social agents in this field regard the notion that German refugees have experienced something similar to refugees today as a valid and acceptable statement, notwithstanding counter-narratives in which such a comparison is rejected on the grounds of supposed cultural difference between the groups. At the time of writing (2018), there is not enough evidence to support the hypothesis of a transgenerational transmission of the historical experience of having been a German expellee to subsequent generations. Instead, it seems that the practice of referencing, or cross-referencing, operates on the level of political memory. Cross-referencing is employed by public intellectuals to evoke empathy, and individual volunteers then occasionally copy this practice in their accounts.

Conclusion

This chapter explored two main dimensions of the phenomenon of volunteering in Germany, particularly in the wake of the so-called refugee crisis. The first aspect regards questions about the extent to which the explosion of voluntary engagement can be considered a political movement (see also Schiffauer, Chapter 12 in this volume). Is helping refugees merely a humanitarian gesture or can we make the argument that volunteers are political agents? The answer remains ambivalent. Neither our survey data nor qualitative interviews provide evidence that volunteers consider themselves political agents in any conventional sense. We found that volunteers were often reluctant to identify the work they do as political, but nevertheless often framed their engagement in political contexts, most importantly in response to rightwing populism. We also found a tendency to avoid drawing coherent conclusions from the volunteering experience and the feelings of solidarity that emerge with it: there seems to be little correlation between the personal experience of social proximity and the construction of fundamental and universal notions of justice. The second aspect regards the practice of cross-referencing the experience of German postwar refugees with the situation of Syrians, Iraqis or other asylum seekers arriving in Europe and Germany in the 2010s. This chapter suggests that politicians, journalists and public intellectuals employ the narrative of similarity to promote empathy and solidarity. While references to this comparison are prominent and visible in public debate, they did not often emerge in the spontaneous accounts we collected from volunteers. Respondents defined their own engagement only rarely as a direct result of supposed similarity; other sources of empathy emerged as more important. It thus remains to be scrutinized whether the collective experience – even trauma – of German flight at the end of the Second World War can have an unconscious transgenerational impact on attitudes and feelings, and thus also on the ways in which Germans think about the experience of cultural difference and belonging.

Serhat Karakayalı is a member of the Berlin Institute for Integration and Migration Research (BIM) at the Humboldt-Universität zu Berlin, Germany. His core academic focus is on the political sociology of migration, practices and media coverage of solidarity in immigration societies, and diversity in civil society organisations.

Notes

1. The concept of 'atmosphere' has been discussed recently by scholars such as Anderson (2009) with a Spinozian framework and by scholars in the realm of aesthetics or with a phenomenological approach (Löffler 2013). An atmosphere can only partly be captured by interviews through surveys; rather, it is bound to spatial and material situations and constellations. These might be architectures and public spaces, as well as other forms of complex cultural environments, in which meaning (as a mere content analysis would be confined to) is combined with 'sentiments', with affective states and emotions. In our case, the atmosphere was established in the physical encounters with arriving refugees at train stations all over Germany and the distribution of images, stories and short videos about these events, mostly through social media. Also, an accelerative dynamic of institutions and organizations, which publicly declared their support for refugees, contributed to this atmospheric change; however, as the meteorological metaphor suggests, atmospheres are not stable but are subject to (sometimes sudden) change.
2. According to representative survey data on volunteering in Germany, the number of volunteers working with migrants or refugees as clients from 2009 was so small (0.72 per cent of the sample in the FSW Study from 2009) that we could not use the existing database on volunteering. From this distribution, we also concluded that random sampling methods would require the collection of rather large gross sample of around 50,000 (Gensicke and Geiss 2010: 23).
3. Deutsche Presse Agentur (DPA), 15 September 2015; see also http://www.spiegel.de/forum/wirtschaft/zuwanderung-das-zweite-deutsche-wirtschaftswunder-thread-399400-19.html (retrieved 8 July 2018). The term 'economic miracle' (*Wirtschaftswunder*) possesses mythical connotations in Germany and is commonly used to refer to a phase of economic expansion and growing prosperity in the 1950s, following defeat and destruction in the Second World War. Contemporary sociologists, such as Helmut Schelsky, suggested in the 1960s that the wave of German postwar refugees, as a flexible and mobile workforce, were partly responsible for this miraculous boom.

4. The surveys were conducted together with Olaf Kleist (University of Osnabrück) and the interviews were conducted in cooperation with Ulrike Hamann (Humboldt-Universität) and our student assistants Mira Wallis, Leif Höfler and Laura Lambert.
5. The political party Die Linke (The Left), heir of the Sozialistische Einheitspartei Deutschlands (Socialist Unity Party), which governed the GDR from 1949 to 1989, is still successful in East Germany. Simultaneously, some East German regions – particularly Saxony and Saxony-Anhalt – are known as far-right territory. While this picture suggests a profound level of polarization, it should be noted here that a large proportion of voters of the rightwing nationalist Alternative für Deutschland (AfD) party derives from previous Die Linke supporters. This suggests that a one-dimensional matrix of the political spectrum (left/right), comprising only the vertical opposition between 'the people' and an economic elite, is not sufficient to understand the particular condition of the East German political arena.
6. In a study of social media data, Vis and Goriunovaet (2015) have analysed the use of the terms 'migrant' and 'refugee' as indicators for empathy. Respondents interpreted tweets using the term 'migrant' as more hostile and critical, while those using the term 'refugee' were understood as sympathetic with the cause of people leaving their countries. The term 'migrant' has the association of leaving not out of necessity, but rather following economic choice.
7. 'Es ist hier, wie in den vorigen Artikeln, nicht von Philanthrophie, sondern vom Recht die Rede, und da bedeutet Hospitalität (Wirthbarkeit) das Recht eines Fremdlings, seiner Ankunft auf dem Boden eines andern wegen, von diesem nicht feindselig behandelt zu warden' (Kant 1983 [1795]: Article 3).
8. In an ongoing project at the Berlin Institute for Integration and Migration Research, conducted with Ulrike Kluge, we are looking into transgenerational transmission of trauma in the context of the German postwar refugee experience.

References

Ahrens, P.A. 2015. *Skepsis oder Zuversicht? Erwartungen der Bevölkerung zur Aufnahme von Flüchtlingen in Deutschland*. Hanover. Retrieved 9 July 2018 from https://www.ekd.de/ekd_de/ds_doc/20151221_si-studie-fluechtlinge.pdf.
Amos, H. 2009. *Die Vertriebenenpolitik der SED 1949 bis 1990*. Munich: Oldenbourg Wissenschaftsverlag.
Anderson, B. 2009. 'Affective Atmospheres', *Emotion, Space and Society* 2: 77–81.
Bade, K.J. 1990. *Neue Heimat im Westen: Vertriebene, Flüchtlinge, Aussiedler*. Münster: Westfälischer Heimatbund.
Balibar, É. 1998. *Spinoza and Politics*. London: Verso.
Boltanski, L. 2004. *Distant Suffering: Morality, Media, and Politics*. Cambridge: Cambridge University Press.
Boltanski, L., and L. Thévenot. 2007. *Über die Rechtfertigung: Eine Soziologie der kritischen Urteilskraft*. Hamburg: Verlag Hamburger Edition.
Bottici, C. 2010. 'European Identity and the Politics of Remembrance', in K. Tilmans, F. Vree and J. Winter (eds), *Performing the Past: Memory, History, and Identity in Modern Europe*. Amsterdam: Amsterdam University Press, pp. 335–58.
Castro Varela, M. d. M. 2014. 'Interview zur aktuellen Debatte um Willkommenskultur', in I. Szuktisch, and A. Merx (eds), *Inklusiv, offen und gerecht?*

Deutschlands langer Weg zu einer Willkommenskultur. Dossier zum Thema. Munich: IQ Fachstelle Diversity Management, pp. 42–45.

Dauvergne, C. 2000. 'The Dilemma of Rights Discourses for Refugees', *University of New South Wales Law Journal* 23: 56–74.

Deleuze, G. 1996. *Abécédaire.* Produced and directed by Pierre-André Boutang (recorded in 1988).

Ehrhardt, A. 1991. *Wie lästige Ausländer . . .: Flüchtlinge und Vertriebene in Salzgitter 1945–1953.* Salzgitter: Arbeitskreis Stadtgeschichte e.V.

Every, D., and M. Augoustinos. 2013. 'Hard Hearts: A Critical Look at Liberal Humanitarianism in Refugee Support Movements', *Refugee Review* 1: 58–66.

Fassin, D. 2005. 'Compassion and Repression: The Moral Economy of Immigration Policies in France', *Cultural Anthropology* 20(3): 362–87.

_____. 2012. *Humanitarian Reason: A Moral History of the Present.* Berkeley: University of California Press.

Forst, R. 2014. *Normativität und Macht.* Frankfurt am Main: Suhrkamp.

Gensicke, T., and S. Geiss. 2010. *Hauptbericht des Freiwilligensurveys 2009: Ergebnisse der repräsentativen Trenderhebung zu Ehrenamt, Freiwilligenarbeit und Bürgerschaftlichem Engagement.* Berlin: Bundesministerium für Familie, Senioren, Frauen und Jugend.

Georgi, F. 2016. 'Widersprüche im langen Sommer der Migration. Ansätze einer materialistischen Grenzregimeanalyse', *Prokla* 183: 183–203.

Goffman, E. 1974. *Frame Analysis: An Essay on the Organization of Experience.* New York: Harper & Row.

Hahn, E., and H.H. Hahn. 2010. *Die Vertreibung im deutschen Erinnern: Legenden, Mythos, Geschichte.* Paderborn: Schöningh.

Herbert, U. 2001. *Geschichte der Ausländerpolitik in Deutschland: Saisonarbeiter, Zwangsarbeiter, Gastarbeiter, Flüchtlinge.* Munich: Beck.

Institut für Demoskopie Allensbach. 2015. *Flucht, Vertreibung, Versöhnung: Zusammenfassung der wichtigsten Ergebnisse einer repräsentativen Bevölkerungsumfrage in Deutschland, Polen und Tschechien.* Berlin: Stiftung Flucht Vertreibung Versöhnung.

Kant, I. 1983 [1795]. *Perpetual Peace, and Other Essays on Politics, History, and Morals.* Indianapolis, IN: Hackett.

Karakayalı, S. 2008. *Gespenster der Migration: Zur Genealogie illegaler Migration in der Bundesrepublik Deutschland.* Bielefeld: transcript.

_____. 2016. 'Für einen neuen Deal der Migration', *Blätter für deutsche und internationale Politik* 9: 13–16.

Karakayalı, S., and O. Kleist. 2015: 'Strukturen und Motive der ehrenamtlichen Flüchtlingsarbeit in Deutschland'. Retrieved 9 July 2018 from https://www.bim.hu-berlin.de/media/2015-05-16_EFA-Forschungsbericht_Endfassung.pdf.

_____. 2016. 'Strukturen und Motive der ehrenamtlichen Flüchtlingsarbeit in Deutschland 2'. Retrieved 9 July 2018 from https://www.bim.hu-berlin.de/media/2015-05-16_EFA-Forschungsbericht_Endfassung.pdf.

Kasparek, B., and M. Speer. 2015. 'Of Hope: Ungarn und der lange Sommer der Migration'. Retrieved 9 July 2018 from http://bordermonitoring.eu/ungarn/2015/09/of-hope.

Kleist, J.O. 2013. 'Remembering for Refugees in Australia: Political Memories and Concepts of Democracy in Refugee Advocacy PostTampa', *Journal of Intercultural Studies* 34(6): 665–83.

Kossert, A. 2008. *Kalte Heimat: Die Geschichte der deutschen Vertriebenen nach 1945*. Munich: Siedler.

_____. 2015. 'Mit der Akzeptanz Fremder gibt es immer Probleme', *Die Zeit*, 28 September.

Losego, S.V. 2012. 'Immigration und kollektives Gedächtnis in Zentraleuropa', *Schweizerisches Archiv für Volkskunde* 108: 97–116.

Löffler, D. 2013. 'Leben im Futur II Konjunktiv: Über das Phänomen Atmosphäre und dessen Bedeutung im Zeitalter der technischen Immersion', in Institut für immersive Medien (eds.), *Jahrbuch immersiver Medien 2013. Atmosphären: Gestimmte Räume und sinnliche Wahrnehmung*. Marburg: Schüren, pp. 23–37.

Misik, R. 2015. 'Der Aufstand der "freiwilligen Helfer": Warum die Flüchtlingshilfe keineswegs nur "karitativ" ist', *Prager Frühling*. Retrieved 9 July 2018 from https://www.prager-fruehling-magazin.de/de/article/1243.der-aufstand-der-freiwilligen-helfer.html.

Misztal, B.A. 2003. *Theories of Social Remembering*. Philadelphia, PA: Open University Press.

Overbeek, H. 2000. 'Transnational Historical Materialism', in R. Palan (ed.), *Global Political Economy: Contemporary Theories*. London: Routledge, pp. 168–183.

Robert, A.C. 2016. 'La stratégie de l'émotion', *Le Monde diplomatique*, February: 3.

Rosenberger, S., and J. Winkler. 2013. 'Anti-Abschiebungsproteste: Mit Empathie gegen die Exklusion', in I Ataç and S. Rosenberge (eds), *Politik der Inklusion und Exklusion*. Göttingen: V&R Unipress, pp. 111–34.

Rothberg, M., and Y. Yildiz. 2011. 'Memory Citizenship: Migrant Archives of Holocaust Remembrance in Contemporary Germany', *Parallax* 17(4): 32–48.

Rozakou, K. 2012. 'The Biopolitics of Hospitality in Greece: Humanitarianism and the Management of Refugees', *American Ethnologist* 39(3): 562–77.

Ruedin, D., and N. Merhaut. 2016. 'Anti-deportation Protest in Austria, Germany, and Switzerland', presented at the 3rd ISA Forum of Sociology, Vienna, 11 July.

Scheer, M. 2012. 'Are Emotions a Kind of Practice (and is That What Makes Them Have a History)? A Bourdieuian Approach to Understanding Emotion', *History and Theory* 51(2): 193–220.

Schwartz, M. 2016. 'Assimilation versus Incorporation: Expellee Integration Policies in East and West Germany after 1945', in M. Borutta and J.C. Jansen (eds), *Vertriebene und Pieds-Noirs in Postwar Germany and France: Comparative Perspectives*. Basingstoke: Palgrave Macmillan, pp. 73–94.

Smith, A.L. 2003. *Europe's Invisible Migrants*. Amsterdam: Amsterdam University Press.

Snow, D.A. 2004. 'Framing Processes, Ideology, and Discursive Fields', in D.A Snow, S.A Soule and H. Kriesi (eds), *The Blackwell Companion to Social Movements*. Oxford: Blackwell, pp. 380–412.

Snow, D.A., and R.D. Benford. 1992. 'Master Frames and Cycles of Protest', in A.D. Morris and C.M. Mueller (eds), *Frontiers in Social Movement Theory*. New Haven, CT: Yale University Press, pp. 133–55.

Snow D.A., and Byrd, W. 2007. 'Ideology, Framing Processes, and Islamic Terrorist Movements', *Mobilization* 12: 119–36.

Statistisches Bundesamt. 2016. *Bevölkerung und Erwerbstätigkeit: Bevölkerung mit Migrationshintergrund – Ergebnisse des Mikrozensus 2015.* Wiesbaden: Statistisches Bundesamt.

Sznaider, N. 2001. *The Compassionate Temperament: Care and Cruelty in Modern Society.* Lanham, MD: Rowman & Littlefield.

Ticktin, M.I. 2002. 'Between Justice and Compassion: "Les Sans Papiers" and the Political Economy of Health, Human Rights and Humanitarianism in France', Ph.D. dissertation. Stanford, CA: Stanford University.

———. 2011. *Casualties of Care: Immigration and the Politics of Humanitarianism in France.* Berkeley: University of California Press.

Vis, F., and O. Goriunova (eds.) 2015. *The Iconic Image on Social Media: A Rapid Research Response to the Death of Aylan Kurdi.* Sheffield: Visual Social Media Lab.

Westby, D.L. 2002. 'Strategic Imperative, Ideology, and Frame', *Mobilization* 7: 287–304.

Whitebrook, M. 2002. 'Compassion as a Political Virtue', *Political Studies* 50(3): 529–44.

Chapter 9

Negotiating Cultural Difference in Dresden's Pegida Movement and Berlin's Refugee Church

Jan-Jonathan Bock

In 2012, Germany received almost 80,000 asylum applications. In 2013, the number rose to 128,000 and in 2014 to over 200,000. In 2015, 890,000 asylum seekers arrived in Germany (Bundesamt für Migration und Flüchtlinge 2016). The increase – in 2015 and early 2016 in particular – was accompanied by alarming crisis rhetoric that cast the arrival of foreigners and the demand on state institutions, which in many cases struggled to register and accommodate newcomers adequately, in the language of chaos, failure and emergency (Bock 2018). The turbulent situation had an impact on public attitudes: in December 2015, over 90 per cent of respondents identified issues regarding 'foreigners/integration/refugees' as Germany's principal problem or challenge; previously, their main concerns had been economic ones, the eurozone crisis and unemployment (Forschungsgruppe Wahlen 2016). The reported chaos in the management of asylum seekers and their applications gave rise to concerns regarding a loss of state control and heightened a sense of insecurity, exacerbated by media coverage of terrorist attacks and acts of sexual violence on New Year's Eve 2015 in Cologne (see Kosnick, Chapter 7 in this volume). Pollsters found that positive attitudes towards the future were declining as rapidly as they had during the 1970s oil crises and in the wake of 9/11 (Losse 2015). The situation had a tangible impact on public discourses, perceptions of public order and private lives.

Between September and December 2015, thousands of asylum seekers entered Germany daily. Dramatic media footage portrayed tired migrants from Middle Eastern and Asian countries crossing the border between Austria and Germany, straining registration centres and emergency reception facilities. The supposed cultural otherness of the newcomers – mainly Muslim men – emerged as a contested dimension in news coverage and debates that surrounded the developments, which were soon discussed as a national refugee crisis, *Flüchtlingskrise*, with a range of implications.

In this chapter, I investigate this claimed nationwide experience of crisis and show that it was neither uniform nor collective. I suggest that no shared manifestation or interpretation of such a crisis existed. In order to illustrate this point, I explore two illuminating local initiatives, both of which channelled growing awareness of issues regarding cultural difference or, rather, the production and perception of difference, with a focus on the newcomers' ascribed cultural, religious and gender identities. This chapter compares how cultural difference was conceptualized and contested in the anti-establishment and anti-Islam Pegida movement – Patriotic Europeans against the Islamization of the West – in Dresden and in Berlin's newly established refugee church (*Flüchtlingskirche*). Pegida appeared to be one of a range of types of rightwing antagonistic activism, with a focus on migration, which emerged across Europe in the mid 2010s. The Protestant Church's initiative in Berlin, on the other hand, represented a more established type of social action: as key civil society institutions, churches promoted tolerance and respect for newcomers to Germany, stressing a Christian view of shared humanity. In order to explore reactions to the arrival of foreigners and examine meanings of cultural difference in debates about the 'refugee crisis', interpreted and negotiated in various ways, I spent time with Pegida protesters in Dresden and followed refugee church staff and volunteers. I found that both initiatives reflected specific local contexts that cannot be extended across Germany, even though they might appear to constitute merely opposite ends of the German public response to the 'refugee crisis', ranging from *Willkommenskultur* to a populist rightwing backlash. However, rather than reducing both positions to points on a national scale or seeing them as parts of a wider trend, I aim to show that they instead illustrate the power of local imaginaries in shaping visions for community life and coexistence in response to the arrival of foreigners and questions about the diversity they introduce. Both responses, I argue, constructed new public spheres in which participants expressed ideas of belonging and identity, rooted in local history and urban culture. Even during times assumed to be violently transformative and challenging, and often described by pundits as a nationwide crisis, local continuities shaped how changes and challenges were perceived by Pegida supporters in Dresden and refugee church volunteers in Berlin.

Among Pegida supporters, the city's difficult history, expressions of regional pride and slow recovery from postwar decline produced an association that linked unwanted social change with the settlement of unknown groups of foreigners. Protesters viewed the embrace of coexistence of Christian and other cultures as the imposition of a Western ideal – multiculturalism – which they considered a social failure and inappropriate for the state of Saxony, of which Dresden is the capital. Pegida supporters dismissed multiculturalism as detrimental to their aspiration of restoring a homogenous and peaceful homeland, ravaged by the Second World War and the socialist regime. At the same time, protest participants articulated an alternative notion of difference: ethnopluralist visions of spatially separate and distinctive nations. Hostility to migrant settlement in Dresden and Saxony expressed discontent with Germany's elites – in politics, the economy and the media – who were accused of despising Saxony's particular, culturally Christian identity. In Berlin's refugee church, the emphasis on social action and tolerance was intended to entice a largely atheist population to volunteer. Initially, church events represented cultural diversity as exciting and exotic, a pleasant addition to local urban life, united by shared humanity. Over time, however, many volunteers also began to notice the difficulty of accommodating different lifestyles and values, and reported misunderstanding, distrust and disappointment. Views on cultural difference and its impact on local realities changed through direct contact in the church. Pegida protesters expressed a desire for cultural separation and distinctive identities, accompanied by the rejection of the possibility of 'German Islam' and multiculturalism. In the refugee church, as a result of encounters between participants, the initially abstract embrace of difference as variations in language, cuisine or creativity turned into more nuanced reflections on the implications of differing worldviews and values for private relationships.

Pegida's Revolutionary Self-Image

Dresden's Theaterplatz is a stunning ensemble framed by the Zwinger Galleries, the Semper Opera House, the Elbe River and the Catholic Court Church (Hofkirche). In a city scarred by the February 1945 bombing raids, this beautifully restored square clashes with the functional, socialist postwar quarters that dominate the city. Because of its historical aesthetics, the Theaterplatz became the preferred site for Pegida's weekly rallies, which started in October 2014, initially expressing fears about the so-called Islamic State and discontent with plans to accommodate Muslim asylum seekers in tent camps in Dresden (Vorländer et al. 2016: 6). Within weeks, the Monday-evening protest marches attracted thousands of participants. Supporters were heterogeneous and voiced anger with globalization, the government, Chancellor Angela Merkel, refugees, Islam, free trade negotiations between the United States and the European Union (EU), warmongering against Russia, American imperialism and the euro. Migration was one theme amongst others in the wide-ranging resentment. The rallies copied elements from the 1989 Monday demonstrations in East Germany. Back then, protesters had demanded free elections and the abolition of the Stasi security service. Their popular chant 'we are the people' (*'Wir sind das Volk'*) also became a leitmotif at Pegida rallies, to the dismay of 1989 civil rights campaigners. In early 2015, participation peaked at around 25,000 people. In addition to migration, protesters attacked what they considered to be the arrogance of political elites, a liberal media bias and discontent with Germany's asylum politics (Vorländer et al. 2016: 67). 'Just look at the name', Frank Richter, then the director of Saxony's State Office for Civic Education (Landeszentrale für Politische Bildung), suggested to me. 'Patriotic. Europeans. Islamization. West. There is something for everyone', he explained.

Despite accommodating such diverse concerns, Pegida was in decline in the summer of 2015. Numbers had dwindled before the refugee situation revitalized the group. With hundreds of thousands of strangers coming to Germany, the Pegida leadership instrumentalized concerns and pushed topics such as Islam, terrorism and security to the top of the group's agenda. An emphasis on the supposedly dangerous cultural particularities of Muslim newcomers and their attitudes to women or ritual slaughter re-energized the movement. After the attacks on women during New Year's Eve in Cologne, Pegida supporters invented a new slogan: 'rapefugees not welcome'. Migrants and refugees were depicted as criminals and predators; 'Islam' was portrayed as a religion whose texts justify violence towards non-Muslim women. Pegida protests attacked multiculturalism as a Western ideal of managing cultural difference that expanded the Muslim presence in Germany, and undermined Christian values and national safety. The movement's supporters accused Chancellor Merkel and other politicians of plotting to replace the German people with foreign immigrants to extinguish German identity. The possibility of peaceful multicultural coexistence was rejected as unrealistic and naïve for Germany, and for East Germany in particular.

It was a biting cold evening as I waited for protesters to fill the Theaterplatz square in January 2016. Besides Germany's black-red-gold stripes, the most common flag was the so-called Wirmer-Flagge, which features a black cross with a gold rim on red ground. The Wirmer flag is associated with resistance to the Nazi dictatorship by Claus von

Stauffenberg, who attempted to assassinate Hitler with a bomb in the
Wolfsschanze bunker in 1944. Pegida supporters portrayed themselves
as a courageous uprising against injustice and oppression, combining
the imagery of anti-Nazi resistance with references to the 1989 demonstrations against Germany's second dictatorship. For them, the current
government was just as much an unwanted regime as the past ones. In
speeches and conversations with me, Pegida leader or supporters called
Merkel a 'tyrant'. I asked a protester waving the Wirmer flag why he
chose this unusual symbol. 'It's the Germany we wanted', he explained,
'a Christian country should have a cross in its flag, like the Scandinavians.
We don't want to be a part of Anglo-American imperial capitalism.' He
told me that he did not consider the German state legitimate, elaborating a
conspiracy theory that the United States was still occupying Germany as a
nonsovereign colony. Placards demanded 'Ami [American] go home' and
accused Merkel of having been a Stasi official ('IM Erika') who wanted to
destroy Germany. 'Merkel go to Siberia, Putin come to Berlin', the crowd
chanted, praising Vladimir Putin, the Russian President, as a strong leader
who resisted the United States and defended Russian (Christian) culture
from multiculturalism. The square filled up quickly. The majority of participants seemed to be over sixty years old and male, but there were also
women and young people. Large signs showed the names of towns and
villages across Dresden's hinterland. The emphasis on Saxony as a shared

Figure 9.1 Pegida, Wirmer flags. Photo by the author.

homeland – or *Heimat* – that had to be defended was common. The role of Christian culture and values, expressed through the Wirmer cross, was central to this defence of local identity.

Many aspects of Pegida deserve closer scrutiny, such as its rejection of political elites and the media, or the desire for closer ties with Eastern European peoples. Here, however, I focus on the desire to preserve *Heimat* – an ideal of Saxony as a culturally united, historically rooted and shared homeland – and how this aspiration coloured views of cultural difference. One group among Pegida supporters were the so-called Identitären, predominantly young people who promote resistance to what they attack as the destructive effects of US-led cultural imperialism, militant Islam, and social and cultural liberalism. The group has been identified as a central force of the New Right across Europe, seeking to shed the toxic anti-Semitic and racist language of the past, and instead focusing on questions of cultural purity and the defence of distinctive Christian identities and values (Glösel et al. 2013). The Identitären put forward an important demand shared by Pegida supporters and the New Right in general: the protection of distinctive cultural identities in an ethnopluralist world (Spektorowski 2010). According to this ideology, different ethnic groups should live in their respective national territories and should not mix with each other in order to stop the further expansion of a homogeneous and American-dominated global culture that cannot provide meaningful identities and a sense of belonging. They promote an alternative version of cultural difference: with nations as spatially segregated containers of distinctive cultural forms that must not intermingle. Ethnopluralists reject the local coexistence of lifestyles, religions, values and customs. In an ethnopluralist world, Saxony, as well as other German regions, would maintain its supposedly distinctive and internally harmonious identity and culture. In the case of Saxony and Dresden, one key factor allowed this rejection of multiculturalist visions of coexistence in one place to become an important mobilizing factor: the city's history.

Dresden's destruction is a source of the hostility to heterogeneity, which Pegida supporters and others understand as a way of preventing the remaking of a past lost in the 1940s. Dresden still lives in the shadow of a history that ended on 13 February 1945, destroyed by Allied bombers. The city's 'reconstruction' during the 1950s and 1960s saw the clearing of ruined baroque quarters and old cobbled streets, which were replaced with oversized avenues and unattractive socialist housing blocks. The city's celebrated landmark, the Church of Our Lady, remained a ruin until the 2000s. The site crystallized a sense of victimhood and Dresdeners' longing for an increasingly nostalgically remembered and romanticized past (Vees-Gulani 2008). Responsibility for the Nazis' rise to power was ignored in postwar commemoration: 'Overnight, Dresden underwent an unexpected metamorphosis from a European *Kulturstadt* [culture city] to the German *Opferstadt* [victim city]' (Joel 2013: 6).

The victim metaphor remained powerful: in their 2015–16 demonstrations, protesters accused the political elites of seeking to turn them into the passive objects of multiculturalist nation building. In response, they claimed to lead a popular resistance. The victim narrative is a legacy of Nazi propaganda, invented and popularized by propaganda minister Joseph Goebbels. The Sozialistische Einheitspartei Deutschlands' (SED; Socialist Unity Party of Germany) socialist dictatorship maintained the narrative during the Cold War. Socialist leaders called the city's destruction the result of 'Anglo-American terror bombing' and failed to historicize Saxony's Nazi past (Margalit 2002). East Germany's government recast Dresden as a city of peace, in contrast to the West's purported warmongering. In February 1985, over 200,000 people crowded into Dresden's Theaterplatz to commemorate the destruction, as GDR leaders combined peace rhetoric with attacks on the capitalist West (Joel 2013: 121). The dictatorship instrumentalized acts of memory and commemoration for political ends (Jerzak 2015). Thirty years later, peace was also a key demand at Pegida's rallies. 'Without violence and united against religious wars on German soil' was a central slogan. Originally, Pegida's organizers had considered calling the movement 'Peaceful Europeans against the

Figure 9.2 Pegida, peace protest. Photo by the author.

Islamization of the West', but the acronym Fegida (the first f representing *friedlich*, or 'peaceful') was not persuasive (Locke 2014). Pegida leaders and followers describe the intermingling of cultural and religious groups as a source of conflict, exemplified by the so-called Islamic State terrorist group, which protesters contrasted with their vision of the peaceful ethnopluralism of nations.

Following the march around Dresden's historic centre in January 2016, protesters returned to the Theaterplatz. Lutz Bachman, one of Pegida's leaders, addressed the crowd. He denounced what he called the 'lying press' – *Lügenpresse*, a loaded term with historical associations used to denounce critical journalists or the foreign press during Germany's two dictatorships (van Raden 2016) – and accused reporters of stirring up hatred against Germans 'and against Saxons in particular'. Bachmann played a message left on Pegida's answerphone:

> I'm a West German who invested money in you shit Easterners (*Ossis*). I want this shit to stop over there. You don't have any foreigners. You don't have any problems. But your disgusting group is pissed off about too many foreigners. What do you shit wankers want? I want to put the Wall back up again. GDR back. End of story. You won't have any TVs anymore. I don't give a shit. You can kiss my arse. For years, we have been paying for you wankers and now you are becoming arrogant. We have enough dirty *Ossi* pigs over here in the West. And what do they do? Nothing. Big talk but no action. Go back home! Saxons back! I don't want to see any more disgusting Saxon faces in Bavaria. You people over there make me sick. (My translation)

As Bachmann played the recording, unsurprisingly, the crowd booed and hurled insults about arrogant West Germans (*Besser-Wessis*) into the air. Bachmann instrumentalized hurt pride and collective victimhood, which strikes a chord across East Germany, but in Saxony in particular. At a rally a few weeks later, he fired up the crowd from the loading space of a small pick-up truck in front of the reconstructed Frauenkirche on Dresden's Neumarkt square. The previous week, an arson attack on a refugee shelter in Bautzen, one hour east of Dresden, and a mob attack on a coach with asylum seekers in the village of Clausnitz, south of Dresden, had shocked Germany. Pundits and politicians were asking: why always Saxony? A West German newspaper had featured a black-and-white map of Germany on its cover: only Saxony had been coloured brown; in Germany, the colour is associated with Nazism. It was entitled *Der Schandfleck*, 'stain of disgrace'. 'For me', Bachmann shouted, 'there is only one disgrace: those assembled under a glass dome in Berlin', or Germany's Parliament. The crowd cheered. Bachmann demanded local resistance as he portrayed Saxony – the homeland recovering from the socialist dictatorship – as under attack from outsiders who did not respect how Saxons wanted to live. He accused the political elites, elected MPs, of ruining the country.

Pegida's leaders mobilized a powerful narrative of Saxons suffering from injustice, previously fostered during the Nazi and socialist dictatorships. Neo-Nazi ideology has long 'appropriated Dresden's symbolism as the quintessential German *Opferstadt* as a political asset to advance its claims that Germans were victims of a "Bomben-Holocaust"' (Joel 2013: 264). Anti-American sentiment marked commemoration events by East German political elites before 1990 and then by neo-Nazi groups after reunification (Taylor 2004: 477). The same hostility to US dominance resurfaced at Pegida rallies. American politicians were attacked for undermining German sovereignty through a puppet government, and Chancellor Merkel was suspected of replacing Germans with a mixed-race *Mischvolk* at the orders of the United States, of which the settlement of Muslim immigrants was a key tactic. In this context of suspicion, victimhood, conspiracy theories and longing for the past, Pegida protesters envisioned and repudiated one approach to managing diversity and difference: multiculturalism. The Wirmer flag symbolized what Pegida supporters considered their Christian resistance to the feared dismantling of identity in an increasingly multicultural country. Pegida combined longing for recovery in the wake of destruction and oppression, a history of victimhood, resistance to elites and anti-Americanism into a movement that rejected the presence of non-Christian culture, instead advocating ethnopluralist separateness. As an emergent social form, Pegida negotiated two visions of cultural difference: it promoted the ethnopluralist view of distinctive national cultures, on the one hand, and dismissed the supposedly dangerous intermingling of multiculturalism with its dilution of meaningful identities, on the other. The fear of losing distinctiveness has remained strong in some parts of Saxony, which is why Pegida could mobilize thousands of participants in Dresden, but not elsewhere in Germany.

A Romanticized Past

Dresden's bookshops are filled with titles such as *Old Dresden* or *Dresden before 1945*. A gigantic panoramic image of prewar Dresden in a former gasholder became a major attraction for residents and tourists after its opening in 2006. The loss of baroque beauty is remembered with pain: authentic reconstructions that evoke prewar Dresden clash with the brutal legacy of socialist urbanism. Reconstruction projects in Dresden cause intense disputes between traditionalists and modernists (Paul 2011). An entire urban quarter around the Church of Our Lady has been rebuilt with historicizing baroque facades (James 2006). Features of lost Dresden are slowly returning as copies of monuments and squares that were gone for decades. Dresdeners support such reconstructions, longing for a return to an unspoilt prewar past and its material manifestation (McFarland and Guthrie). Just as this distinctive culture and heritage – or *Heimat* – is being restored, however, the settlement of foreigners is rejected as a threat to recovery. This is not to argue that all people in Dresden or Saxony support Pegida or its anti-multiculturalist objectives. What I suggest is that Pegida's leaders manipulated nostalgia and fear of change in a culturally conservative environment that constructs identity and belonging out of narrow historical references (James 2009).

Furthermore – and this is particularly important – Pegida supporters associated immigration into West Germany with social decline. 'We don't want Dresden to be like Frankfurt, where you don't see Germans anymore', an angry lady explained to me at one rally, referring to the fact that 50 per cent of inhabitants in the West German city of Frankfurt have at least one parent or a grandparent who was not born in Germany. I was repeatedly told that Christmas celebrations were no longer permitted in areas with significant Muslim populations in Berlin – including Neukölln, the area in which I lived, and Kreuzberg, the seat of the refugee church. Such accusations were unfounded and revealed a lack of experience with immigration and ethnoreligious diversity. Unlike West Germany, the

Figure 9.3 Reconstructed baroque facades in central Dresden. Photo by the author.

isolated socialist eastern part did not experience immigration and settlement until the 1990s. The few foreign contract workers in the GDR were isolated, segregated and discouraged from interacting with the native German population, and so the experience of cultural difference was one of the most important, and for many disturbing, dimensions of everyday life in post-reunification Germany (Bade and Oltmer 2005; Geyer 2001; Wolle 2015; Zwengel 2011).

Still, even in the mid 2010s, just 4 per cent of people in Saxony had a migration history (*Migrationshintergrund*), many of them from the former Soviet Union, a share significantly below the national German average of almost 20 per cent (Der Sächsische Ausländerbeauftragte 2015: 85). By contrast, West German cities have been visibly shaped by decades of immigration and settlement, including from Islamic countries (Schönwälder et al. 2016). In Pegida, rejecting multiculturalism was not based on direct experience, but rather on abstract fears of religious conflict and cultural incompatibility, to which media hysteria and 'fake news' about violence, sexual harassment and other crimes committed, or allegedly committed, by asylum seekers contributed. Even though Chancellor Merkel herself had been raised in East Germany, her stance on asylum seekers and immigration was attacked as typically West German madness. Pegida supporters rejected this as an imposition that they feared would undermine distinctive local identity, something that Saxons were just recovering following the homogenizing 'democratic centralism' imposed by the socialist regime (Palmowski 2006).

The attempt to recover a sense of order, created by a manageable and homogeneous world, led to support for Pegida in a part of Germany that romanticizes its past more than others. The particularly negative view on multiculturalism emerged in response to unwanted change, fear of globalization and scepticism towards West German values. In that association, multicultural difference was rejected. 'The GDR world was quite small', Frank Richter, the then director of Saxony's State Office for Civic Education, put it in a conversation with me. 'With reunification, it became suddenly bigger and then relentlessly huge. People started to realize what it means to live in an open society, in an open world: all conflicts can reach you in your living room.' Islam became a prominent aspect of this expansion. With the expansion of so-called Islamic State and Islamist terrorism, fears spread that Muslims would bring violence to East Germany. Pegida localized global developments in a peculiar way. Understanding Pegida solely as a variant of Europe-wide rightwing populism in response to migration can lead to an oversight of the important mobilization of particular political and cultural sentiments, and local history, paired with the absence of direct contact with foreigners and Muslims in particular. That is why Pegida struggled to establish branches elsewhere, and particularly in West Germany.

A very different response to the so-called refugee crisis emerged in Berlin at the same time and also mirrored the urban sociocultural environment – the refugee church.

Berlin's *Flüchtlingskirche*

In the autumn of 2014, Berlin's Protestant church (EKBO) announced the establishment of a dedicated refugee church (*Flüchtlingskirche*). When it was inaugurated in October 2015, the refugee situation was discussed as a *Flüchtlingskrise* and dominated German public debate. Berlin is a difficult terrain for organized religion. The city's population has a reputation for being sceptical towards faith. Berlin has even been described as 'the atheist capital of Europe' (Connolly 2009). Andreas Götze is a pastor responsible for interfaith dialogue in Berlin's Protestant church. Born and raised in Frankfurt (West Germany), he found Berlin a challenging environment:

> When the Wall was still in place, people used to flee from their devoutly conservative families in towns and villages in southern Germany and came to West Berlin. They didn't want to have anything to do with a church they had experienced as oppressive at home. The result was a leftwing, environmentalist and anti-religious counterculture. After 1990, this West Berlin environment joined East Berlin, where atheism had been political state ideology.

Protestant and Catholic churches in Berlin still struggle with the legacy of West Berlin's alternative counterculture – while not averse to spirituality, certainly suspicious of organized religion – as well as of East Berlin's state-managed atheism, which turned the German Democratic Republic into one of the most anti-religious lands on the planet (Müller et al. 2013). Attendance of Catholic mass or Protestant services is lower than anywhere else in Germany, even though church buildings remain a prominent feature of Berlin's cityscape, with high steeples and imposing domes. One of them is St Simeon, a towering red brick structure from the late nineteenth century, topped by a green spire. The building stands surrounded by functional postwar condominiums in one of Berlin's most ethnically diverse neighbourhoods, Kreuzberg, which has a reputation as the city's hotspot of left-wing counterculture and radical activism. During the Second World War, Allied bombers razed the area surrounding the church. The neighbourhood was subsequently rebuilt with modernist housing blocks. In the 1960s and 1970s, the neighbourhood attracted so-called foreign guestworkers (*Gastarbeiter*), many of them from Turkey.

Families later joined these first immigrants. This part of Berlin enjoys an ambivalent reputation for its ethnic communities, May Day riots and multiculturalism. Kreuzberg is either hailed as an example of creative coexistence and powerful minority engagement (Lang 1998; Yurdakul 2009) or lambasted as an underdeveloped ghetto, suffering from school failure and crime (Buschkowsky 2012: 59, 81; Sarrazin 2010: 325, 404).

As the Turkish community expanded, the Christian population dwindled. St Simeon became awkwardly large for its small congregation of Lutherans. In the 2000s, Ghanaian Evangelicals started using the church for their own services and quickly outnumbered white German Protestants. Their peaceful sharing of the church was one of the reasons why St Simeon was chosen to promote intercultural exchange between Berliners and asylum seekers. Situated in multicultural Kreuzberg and used to different religious practices, St Simeon was considered an ideal site to reposition Berlin's Protestant church as a key actor in the management of a social challenge, accompanying transformations and facilitating encounters between newcomers and residents. The refugee church project combined theology with social and political activism to attract believers as well as atheists and secularists.

In October 2015, the church was inaugurated with a multilingual service. The nave's pews were packed with hundreds of people despite the cold weather; a storm battered against the high glass windows. The church's pastor, Beate Dirschauer, and two colleagues celebrated the inaugural service. 'Greet those sitting next to you with the *Friedensgruß* (kiss of peace). *Salaam, schalom,* may peace be with you, *la paix soit avex vous, Friede sei mit dir',* the pastors encouraged the congregation to shake hands. The service combined traditional elements of northern Germany's progressive Protestant theology with Tuarek music from North Africa and readings in French, English and Arabic, and involved participants who had recently arrived as asylum seekers or immigrants. Berlin's Protestant bishop, Markus Dröge, delivered the sermon. He recalled a recent visit to the borderland between Greece and Macedonia. 'Migrant routes may change, but the suffering remains the same, and it screams at us', he said. The bishop was moved by his experience. His sermon combined personal recollections with Christian theology:

> God loves everyone. He supports those who suffer persecution and thus become refugees. All of us need his protection and care, not just refugees. Hence, this church isn't simply a church for refugees: it is a church for everyone.

Dröge's sermon questioned the concept of the refugee as a person in need of special care and protection. Instead, he underlined, all humans need

God's love to be saved: 'the figure of the refugee is the figure of the human', he elaborated. While Dröge acknowledged that the political tasks were enormous and many challenges lay ahead, he downplayed distinctions between those who might appear rooted, at home and safe, on the one hand, and homeless people fleeing and in need of care, on the other. He emphasized shared humanity and the universal desire for love: the refugee church was a space for encounters among equals. The Protestant bishop joined theology with social advocacy and urged that the refugee church become a vocal civil society actor, going beyond spirituality to unite people and produce solidarity. In a social context in which liturgy might cause scepticism, his account of visits to sites of political failure and his embrace of open-border views positioned the Protestant Church initiative strategically. Cultural difference was approached in two particular ways during the service: first, even though challenges were acknowledged, the significance of difference in terms of values and ways of life was downplayed through an emphasis on shared humanity and solidarity uniting bearers of different cultural identities; and, second, music, dance and prayers in foreign languages created an innocent experience of diversity as folk culture.

Political Churches

One week after the inaugural service, I met with Beate Dirschauer, the church's new pastor. Dirschauer had been raised in a small village in West Germany. As a student, she said, she finally escaped from what she described as 'rural narrow-mindedness'. In Berlin, she moved to Kreuzberg intentionally, where she relished the area's anonymity and sociocultural diversity. Dirschauer was explicit about the political aspirations of the refugee church, which she saw as an opportunity to improve the standing of organized religion in Berlin:

> I'm not from a particularly devout family. I studied theology for political reasons. The peace movement had an impact on me when I realized that one can bring about political change as a pastor. The gospel and Jesus are political. If I had been brought up in a different part of the world, I would have picked up a different religion. I see the refugee church as a space in which we can come together and learn from one another, without having to surrender our respective beliefs. I don't want some kind of esoteric mishmash. I want to be able to argue with others, too, to exchange views as equals.

> It is important for me that the idea of the refugee church attracts Berliners who haven't been interested in the church or religious matters before. This church is a chance for missionary work – but a mission into our non-religious society. I don't want to convert refugees. I hope that practical charity can bring sceptics closer to the church. They are watching the two big churches [Protestantism

and Roman Catholicism] and how they respond to the refugee challenge.
I have friends who are atheists and they tell me that this project is important.
The church cannot just preach and then fail to respond to such a crisis.

In a city in which suspicion towards religion is common, Dirschauer
conceptualized the initiative as a political project to remake trust in the
church as a bipartisan and reliable civil society actor. 'Many want to help',
she told me in October 2015, at the height of the *Willkommenskultur* enthusiasm, 'and they see the state struggling. So they call their church and ask
what they can do. It's a chance for us to show that we still matter.' The
first few months were exciting and chaotic. Besides full-time staff, volunteers offered German classes, counselling sessions for women and legal
advice. Public readings or theatre shows were held. The refugee church
became an important node in an expanding network of organizations

Figure 9.4 The
Flüchtlingskirche
(refugee church) in
Berlin-Kreuzberg.
Photo by the author.

and voluntary activity for asylum seekers. Nonreligious initiatives also used the church for their work. Dirschauer set up an International Café, which took place every fortnight in the large common room. Volunteers prepared tea and coffee, food and snacks, and newcomers joined local residents to learn more about each other.

Producing encounters (*Begegnungen*) was a shared theme across activities. Following bishop Dröge, organizers spoke about the transformative potential of direct contact, without much reflection on the challenges that such contact could entail. Encounter was seen as generally good or positive. The refugee church was designed as a venue for the experience of human dimensions of what was discussed as a national crisis, learning about each other and emphasizing shared humanity. The project connected Christian theology with left-wing activism. It produced an emergent community rooted in shared values, challenging assumptions of ethnicity as the overriding identity. The aspiration was that differences could be overcome through contact. In this vision, there was little consideration for the difficult aspects of diverging values, routines or worldviews, which can strain social relations. Instead, Pastor Dirschauer described how encounters were mediated by a 'third space':

> This is how our churches can become more relevant again. They provide a third space: beyond the terrible conditions in the refugee shelters or in public, on the one hand, and volunteers' private homes, on the other. We live in a time of epochal change. People in Germany are understandably concerned. They also need a private, protected space in their house, because everything around them is changing. It isn't easy to invite strangers into your home. The refugee church can be this important third space.

The refugee church was designed to provide a semi-public platform for engagements between Berliners and newcomers. The city's atheist environment shaped how this initiative was designed, attaching less importance to theology in favour of social action. The initial emphasis on shared humanity and uncomplicated dimensions of difference – music, dance, creativity and nonlocal food at the International Café – positioned the refugee church as a promoter of multicultural tolerance, situated in an area of Berlin with experience in coexistence. However, with time and greater involvement in each others' lives, volunteers and staff at the refugee church encountered more intimate dimensions of difference. Frustrating experiences and disappointed expectations induced more nuanced reflections on how much variety people could accept. Volunteers and staff struggled to maintain their focus on shared humanity when value clashes challenged the assumption that contact alone could overcome scepticism and produce new friendships and deeper solidarity.

Shifting Ideas of Difference

Two regular refugee church volunteers were Arnold and Sophia. They were originally from southern Germany, which they had found stuffy and narrow-minded. Following retirement, they moved into a small flat in Berlin. They described themselves as tolerant, cosmopolitan and in favour of multiculturalism, and contrasted their views with the conservatism they had fled in Bavaria. At one International Café session, they met Rashad, a Syrian refugee, who struggled with Germany's bureaucratic management of asylum applications. Arnold and Sophia began to look after him. Their experience with the authorities shocked them. They reported a sense of guilt that their rich country was treating the newcomers with little dignity and respect. Rashad's account of spending ten hours queuing – only to be turned away eventually – with women who collapsed while waiting and beatings by security personnel confirmed media coverage of administrative chaos. Arnold and Sophia were enthusiastic about becoming Rashad's guardians and were able to demonstrate to him the kind support that the state did not muster. They invited him for lunches and shared activities.

Over time, however, their relationship became fraught. A few months after their first encounter, Arnold and Sophia revealed their frustration with Rashad, who had, once again, not joined them at the International Café. Sophia elaborated:

> He is always like this, so unreliable. He has also changed his shelter many times and we always helped him, but he only complains: the food isn't good enough, the beds are uncomfortable, there are too many people, everything is too slow. He hasn't bothered learning German either. We have got an app on our phone to translate Arabic. But Rashad often doesn't reply to messages. We told him about the International Café today, but he didn't respond, even though we know he's seen our message. He only contacts us when he needs something. We have also given him money before.

> A few weeks ago, we invited him for lunch, but he turned up two hours late! Arnold was very annoyed, because he had cooked especially for him. We told Rashad that this is not how we do things in Germany. You can't just be that late. The next time we invited him, I called to make sure he would be punctual, but he said that we hadn't fixed a time. But we had. So he cancelled again. We haven't invited him since.

Sophia emphasized that she was hurt and did not know how to interpret Rashad's behaviour. When I asked her whether she wanted to cut contact, she was torn. 'But he cares about us', she was nonetheless sure, 'he calls us his German mother and father.' Arnold became sick in early 2016. 'When we told Rashad that Arnold was not well, he insisted on coming to see him. But we just wanted to be left alone so Arnold could recover. Rashad was so pushy. We didn't know whether he just wanted to be nice, but it was very uncomfortable.' Arnold and Sophia continued to help at the International Café, where they talked about their experience and sought advice. They self-identified as open-minded and tolerant, but the mismatch between their expectations and Rashad's behaviour brought disappointment. They struggled to make sense of Rashad, who did not seem to reciprocate generosity as they assumed he ought to: by being punctual, reliable and respectful of their privacy. Their insistence on explaining 'how we do things in Germany' shows that they attributed what they saw as Rashad's lack of conscientiousness to his cultural background. They found southern Germany too parochial, but, in Berlin, they struggled with intercultural communication when it impacted on their expectations and routines. For them, Rashad failed to act respectfully and appreciate gestures of support. Nonetheless, they continued to seek ways of supporting other asylum seekers, even though Sophia admitted that she was sleeping badly and struggled emotionally with the failure of establishing a meaningful relationship with Rashad.

Over time, pastor Dirschauer also reported that initial enthusiasm was tempered by the strain on volunteers. Civil society actors demanded more state resources to lift the burden on their private lives. 'I've realized that

Figure 9.5 Encounters at the international café in the refugee church. Photo by the author.

you need more professionalism for this challenge or you'll struggle to get things done. Idealism is necessary, but you need professionals alongside "refugees-welcome" idealists like myself to manage the situation', she explained six months after the refugee church had been inaugurated. She confessed to me that she had lost much sleep over a conflict involving a Nigerian cook and an Egyptian refugee. In the end, the cook had to be dismissed because of his aggression towards the refugee. 'We also have a problem with homophobia', the pastor admitted. 'We have had a number of cases in which asylum seekers showed strong disapproval of homosexuality. At least one volunteer stopped helping out because he was insulted repeatedly.' She sighed and looked out of the window. When I asked Dirschauer a few days later whether her experience had changed how she viewed cultural difference, she nodded slowly:

> Different ethnic groups don't just get on as we – positive church idealists – might have hoped. I'm more sceptical or realistic now. There hasn't always been peace and harmony here. I do worry a bit more about the future and integration in our country, also because of what goes on among newcomers, which we didn't always think about. It is a big task for Germany, but I still believe that we will manage. Nonetheless, people like Arnold and Sophia also have to learn that new relations have to be two-way. Living with difference isn't easy when you stick to certain expectations and want others to become just like you.

> At the beginning, members of the local Christian community in St Simeon were sceptical. They thought we were going to take their church away. They feared this might become as chaotic as the city's registration office and that people would camp in the street. But some community members came to the International Café, brought friends along and painted with the refugees. They overcame their scepticism: this was still their community's space, but simultaneously a new one. The third space. So this kind of engagement has also happened here. People confronted their fears in this familiar space. I look at cultural difference in a more nuanced way now. I have a more profound sense of what it can mean for different people, and how much of a challenge coexistence can be for all parties involved.

In the 'third space' of the refugee church, between the intimacy of the home and an intimidating public, encounters challenged how the church had initially presented cultural difference in the inauguration service: as simple variations in cultural practice, easily bridged by shared humanity. Challenges became more apparent. The emphasis on shared humanity, which reflected local activist histories as well as theology, and reduced cultural difference to folk customs and culture, did not sufficiently consider how the experience of different habits and values could strain social relations – and led to an emphasis on what divides people rather than on what unites them. Rashad's behaviour, difficult relations among refugees

and discrimination against homosexual volunteers made staff and supporters reflect differently on the implications of 'cultural difference' for
social harmony and friendships. A pastor from another Protestant community, also situated in an ethnically diverse part of Berlin, revealed similar experiences when we spoke about homophobia in the refugee church:

> When you encounter *real* difference – people with really different views of life
> and values – then that is not easy. It can actually be very painful. Many people
> are realizing this now. Muslims are my neighbours here. They live next to me. I
> share my life and living space with them, and this is what motivates me to learn
> more about them. But there is also this personal struggle to overcome a sense of
> frustration when appointments are missed or agreements are not kept. How do
> you trust people when you feel they don't respect your way of life or your rou-
> tines or your views on gay rights, for example? I want to remain open-minded,
> and so I consciously want to be involved in these encounters, even when they
> produce disappointment. But I need to force myself to do it sometimes.

This pastor contrasted 'real' difference in worldviews and values with
the more sanitized versions that were initially characteristic of how the
refugee church staged performances of diversity. In the third space of
the refugee church, views of cultural difference could change with personal experience. Another regular volunteer was Franka, a veterinarian.
'I don't have much free time, because of my job and teenage children',
she introduced herself during an International Café session, 'but I want
to be involved. It's great that people are coming to Germany, but I want
to know who they are.' She admitted scepticism regarding the arrival of
strangers and wanted to shape the local future:

> When I was younger, I was a strong supporter of female emancipation. I want
> to make sure that we don't go back on what we have achieved. When I look
> at younger friends or my kids, they don't pay much attention to these issues
> anymore, to feminism or equality. They take everything for granted. And you
> hear that at least some refugees have very conservative ideas about women and
> gender roles. I don't want to have mono-cultural ghettos (*Parallelgesellschaften*)
> in Germany, in which female emancipation is rolled back.

Franka articulated fears about conservative gender roles returning
to Germany and warned that gender equality could not be taken for
granted. However, unlike Pegida demonstrators with similar scepticism, she became involved to protect what she considered to be achievements for women. She taught a regular German class in the refugee
church. While she found a certain lack of commitment frustrating, when
a number of participants dropped out or failed to attend regularly, she
nonetheless secured a core group of enthusiastic students. Months later,

she was still involved and reported many positive experiences. In her case, initial pragmatism – helping to secure women's achievements and keeping an eye on developments – transformed into a sense of purpose that continued for a long time and produced new social relations even outside the classroom.

Thus, the experimental 'third space' of the refugee church enabled transformations in views and social relations, albeit not always in the straightforward sense of expanding respect and tolerance – shared humanity – envisioned by its organizers. The refugee church produced both purposeful and long-term engagement, as in Franka's case, and more ambivalent views, such as the disappointment reported by Arnold and Sophia. With hindsight, pastor Dirschauer considered her view of difference – a lack of mutual knowledge that could be overcome through contact – as too idealistic. The church was a social laboratory, in which transformations in the understanding of cultural difference, which accompanied asylum seekers' arrival, took many forms.

Conclusion

Anti-migration movements emerged across Europe in the 2010s. However, rather than viewing Pegida simply as one of superficially similar groups, I have shown that its success depended on a context that localized global developments in a particular way. While shared factors certainly existed – fears about foreigners and Muslims in particular led to alliances among Pegida and similar groups across Europe – there are crucial local aspects that deserve acknowledgement and analysis to explain the group's traction in Saxony. A desire for recovering the prewar past was powerful in an area in which a sense of victimhood and resistance to intrusion remained widespread, exacerbated by the everyday urban experience of a city belatedly recovering from destruction and socialist urban planning. Multiculturalism was interpreted as a project of the West German elites, invented to undermine the remaking of Saxony. Pegida viewed the multiculturalist vision of difference as the imposition of unwanted change at the hands of globalization and West German politics. This view was also enabled by abstract fears of religious conflict after the rise of the so-called Islamic State. Pegida supporters promoted an alternative vision of difference: ethnopluralism, with demarcated nations as containers of distinctive cultural identities. The urban reality of West German cities, such as Frankfurt, was dismissed as inappropriate for Saxony, a region in the process of rebuilding its distinctive identity following forced socialist homogeneity. Pegida's leaders manipulated local history and fused conspiracy theories about a replacement of 'real Germans' with concerns about the impact of global changes on trajectories of recovery inspired by a romantically enhanced past.

In the third space of the refugee church, by contrast, multiculturalism was initially embraced as positive. There was enthusiasm for customs from Africa and the Middle East. The emphasis on shared humanity also attracted atheists and secularists, and downplayed the challenges of living with different ways of life and worldviews, which emerged over time and through personal contact. The third space of the church was flexible enough to accommodate a range of motivations and experiences: volunteers could sense what an increasingly multicultural Germany might be like and reflect on values and goals for new friendships. Interpretations shifted from abstract and idealistic concepts – bridged by the Christian emphasis on shared humanity – to more nuanced considerations in the face of misunderstanding and conflict, which highlighted the impact of the kinds of difference that challenge one's own view of the world and strain social relations. Whereas in Pegida, multiculturalism was rejected as an inappropriate model for local society, coexistence in Berlin underwent changes: from living side by side in the sought-after Kreuzberg area to more serious involvement in each other's lives and routines through encounters in the refugee church.

The term 'refugee crisis' does not capture how Germans and newcomers negotiated new types of cultural and ethnoreligious diversity in encounters and emergent social forms. The chapter has challenged the rhetoric of a shared national emergency, caused solely by the arrival of foreigners, and highlighted instead the relevance of locality in responses and interpretations, regarding both the importance of *Heimat* and victimhood discourses for Pegida in Dresden, on the one hand, and the positioning of the church as an explicitly political actor that promotes tolerance and respect in atheist Berlin, on the other. I have discussed two important social developments that illuminate how 'cultural difference' and its appropriateness for German society became contested dimensions of the migration phenomena that marked German society in 2015–16. Both Pegida and the refugee church responded to newly pressing questions regarding coexistence, identity and belonging. As such, specific though they are, both phenomena also illustrate the complicated fractures and divisions regarding interpretations of difference, and experiences with diversity, that shape a changing Germany.

Jan-Jonathan Bock is Programme Director at Cumberland Lodge, Windsor, United Kingdom. He received his Ph.D. in Social Anthropology from the University of Cambridge in 2015. His publications include *Austerity, Community Action and the Future of Citizenship in Europe*, coedited with Shana Cohen and Christina Fuhr.

References

Bade, K. J., and J. Oltmer. 2005. 'Migration, Ausländerbeschäftigung und Asyl-politik in der DDR', *Bundeszentrale für politische Bildung*. Retrieved 9 July 2018 from http://www.bpb.de/gesellschaft/migration/dossier-migration/56368/migrationspolitik-in-der-ddr?p=all.

Bock, J. 2018. 'State Failure, Polarisation, and Minority Engagement in Germany's Refugee Crisis', *International Journal of Politics, Culture, and Society*. Preview retrieved 23 August 2018 from https://link.springer.com/article/10.1007/s10767-018-9288-8.

Buschkowsky, H. 2012. *Neukölln ist überall*. Berlin: Ullstein Verlag.

Bundesamt für Migration und Flüchtlinge. 2016. 'Aktuelle Zahlen zu Asyl'. Retrieved 9 July 2018 from https://www.bamf.de/SharedDocs/Anlagen/DE/Downloads/Infothek/Statistik/Asyl/statistik-anlage-teil-4-aktuelle-zahlen-zu-asyl.pdf?__blob=publicationFile.

Connolly, K. 2009. 'Atheist Berlin to Decide on Religion's Place in its Schools', *The Guardian*, 26 April. Retrieved 9 July 2018 from http://www.theguardian.com/world/2009/apr/26/berlin-germany-religious-education-ethics.

Der Sächsische Ausländerbeauftragte. 2015. *Jahresbericht 2014*. Bautzen: Landtag Sachsen.

Forschungsgruppe Wahlen. 2016. 'Wichtige Probleme in Deutschland seit 01/2000'. Retrieved 9 July 2018 from http://www.forschungsgruppe.de/Umfragen/Politbarometer/Langzeitentwicklung_-_Themen_im_Ueberblick/Politik_II/9_Probleme_1_1.pdf.

Geyer, S. 2001. 'Die ersten Opfer der Wende', *Der Spiegel*, 23 May. Retrieved 9 July 2018 from http://www.spiegel.de/politik/deutschland/auslaender-in-der-ddr-teil-zwei-die-ersten-opfer-der-wende-a-135601.html.

Glösel, B., J. Bruns and N. Strobl. 2013. *Die Identitären: Handbuch zur Jugendbewegung der neuen Rechten in Europa*. Münster: Unrat.

James, J. 2006. 'Undoing Trauma: Reconstructing the Church of Our Lady in Dresden', *Ethos* 34: 244–72.

———. 2009. 'Retrieving a Redemptive Past: Protecting Heritage and Heimat in East German Cities', *German Politics and Society* 27(3): 1–27.

Jerzak, C. 2015. 'Memory Politics: The Bombing of Hamburg and Dresden', in K. Gerstenberger and T. Nusser (eds), *Catastrophe and Catharsis: Perspectives on Disaster and Redemption in German Culture and Beyond*. Rochester: Camden House, pp. 53–72.

Joel, T. 2013. *The Dresden Firebombing: Memory and the Politics of Commemorating Destruction*. London: I B Tauris.

Lang, B. 1998. *Mythos Kreuzberg: Ethnographie eines Stadtteils (1961–1995)*. Frankfurt: Campus Verlag.

Locke, S. 2014. 'Die neue Wut aus dem Osten', *Frankfurter Allgemeine Zeitung*. Retrieved 9 July 2018 from http://www.faz.net/aktuell/politik/inland/pegida-bewegung-gegen-islamisierung-des-abendlandes-13306852.html.

Losse, B. 2015. 'Die Deutschen sorgen sich um ihre Sicherheit', *Wirtschaftswoche*. Retrieved 9 July 2018 from http://www.wiwo.de/politik/deutschland/allensbach-umfrage-die-deutschen-sorgen-sich-um-ihre-sicherheit/12737298.html.

Margalit, G. 2002. 'Der Luftangriff auf Dresden: Seine Bedeutung für die Erinnerungspolitik der DDR und für die Herauskristallisierung einer historischen Kriegserinnerung im Westen', in S. Düwell and M. Schmidt (eds), *Narrative der Shoah: Repräsentationen der Vergangenheit in Historiographie, Kunst und Politik*. Paderborn: Ferdinand Schöningh Verlag, pp. 189–207.

McFarland, R., and E.R. Guthrie. 2015. 'The Bauwerk in the Age of its Technical Reproducibility: Historical Reconstruction, Pious Modernism, and Dresden's "süße Krankheit"', in G. Cliver and C. Smith-Prei (eds), *Bloom and Bust: Urban Landscapes in the East since German Reunification*. Oxford: Berghahn Books, pp 225–247.

Müller, O., D. Pollack and G. Pickel. 2013. 'Religiös-konfessionelle Kultur und individuelle Religiosität: Ein Vergleich zwischen West- und Ostdeutschland', *Kölner Zeitschrift für Soziologie und Sozialpsychologie* 65: 123–48.

Palmowski, J. 2006. 'Regional Identities and the Limits of Democratic Centralism in the GDR', *Journal of Contemporary History* 41: 503–26.

Paul, J. 2011. 'The Rebirth of Historic Dresden', in A. Fuchs, K. James-Chakraborty and L. Shortt (eds), *Debating German Cultural Identity since 1989*. Rochester: Camden House, pp. 117–29.

Sarrazin, T. 2010. *Deutschland schafft sich ab: Wie wir unser Land aufs Spiel setzen*. Munich: Random House.

Schönwälder, K., S. Petermann, J. Hüttermann, S. Vertovec, M. Hewstone, D. Stolle, K. Schmid and T. Schmitt. 2016. *Diversity and Contact: Immigration and Social Interaction in German Cities*. Basingstoke: Palgrave Macmillan.

Spektorowski, A. 2010. The New Right: Ethno-regionalism, Ethno-pluralism and the Emergence of a Neo-fascist "Third Way"', *Journal of Political Ideologies* 8: 111–30.

Taylor, F. 2004. *Dresden, Tuesday February 13, 1945*. London: Bloomsbury.

Van Raden, R. 2016. 'Pegida-Feindbild *"Lügenpresse"*: Über ein massenwirksames verschwörungstheoretisches Konzept', in H. Kellershohn and W. Kastrup (eds), *Kulturkampf von rechts: AfD, Pegida und die Neue Rechte*. Münster: Unrast, pp. 201–12.

Vees-Gulani, S. 2008. 'The Politics of New Beginnings: The Continued Exclusion of the Nazi Past in Dresden's Cityscape', in G. Rosenfeld and P. Jaskot (eds), *Beyond Berlin: Twelve German Cities Confront the Nazi Past*. Ann Arbor: University of Michigan Press, pp. 25–47.

Vorländer, H., M. Herold and S. Schäller. 2016. *Pegida: Entwicklung, Zusammensetzung und Deutung einer Empörungsbewegung*. Wiesbaden: Springer Fachmedien.

Wolle, S. 2015. Geschlossene Gesellschaft. *Die Zeit*, 18 December. Retrieved 9 July 2018 from http://www.zeit.de/zeit-geschichte/2015/04/ddr-propaganda-auslaender-einwanderer/komplettansicht.

Yurdakul, G. 2009. *From Guest Workers into Muslims: The Transformation of Turkish Immigrant Associations in Germany.* Newcastle upon Tyne: Cambridge Scholars Publishing.

Zwengel, A. (ed.). 2011. *Die 'Gastarbeiter' der DDR: Politischer Kontext und Lebenswelt.* Berlin: LIT Verlag.

Part IV

New Initiatives and Directions

Chapter 10

Interstitial Agents
Negotiating Migration and Diversity in Theatre

Jonas Tinius

The movement of refugees to Germany from 2014 onwards and its impact on society have already been described as Germany's *zweite Wende*, or 'second turning point', since the 1990s (Vertovec 2015). The term *Wende* typically refers to the dismantling of the Socialist German Democratic Republic (GDR) and German reunification, thus evoking a momentous historical connotation in modern German history. As the arguable driver of a major social transformation, this recent phenomenon of migration into Germany also prompted a wide-ranging re-emphasis of the political role of artistic institutions. At the time of writing (early 2018), a large number of public theatres and fringe performance groups have explicitly addressed migration in their employment policies and programmes.[1] Many started refugee theatre initiatives, founded new ensembles with migrant actors, and new regional and federal schemes were introduced to fund projects involving refugees. These artistic initiatives rely on existing civil society alliances, such as churches and voluntary organizations, which cut across distinctions of left and right, but they also forge new moral expectations, reciprocities of compassion, and eventually new policies and theoretical concepts.

This chapter discusses insights and analyses from ethnographic fieldwork with two public theatre groups that engaged with these shifts in German society. In particular, I focus on the ways in which their artistic work is embedded in, but also critically reflects and repositions, civil society organizations and public policies aimed at migrants and refugees in inner-city contexts. Rather than relying on existing and often generous arguments about local or community art and theatre projects as performative facilitators of new forms of citizenship (see Crehan 2011; Ingram 2011; McNevin 2010), I have analysed the reflexive and relational agency of such projects (Tinius 2015a). What kinds of ideas about migration and diversity do they offer to residents, public authorities and refugees themselves? How do they mobilize or enact them? And what can these initiatives tell us about the concepts we, as academics and scholars, use to explain diversity and difference in the context of refugee migration to Germany?

The case studies explored in this chapter – the Theater an der Ruhr (hereinafter TaR) and the Ruhrorter refugee theatre project in the Ruhr Valley city of Mülheim in Western Germany – are artistic organizations that operate in-between various kinds of local social actors in the city, such as churches, municipal government or social workers, and yet relate to federal and even national levels of government through the funding they receive. These theatres, I argue, are thus situated in the 'interstices' of civil society in ways that allow them to reconstitute social relations on multiple scales, from public authorities to local and voluntary work with refugees. They are at once engaged by municipal authorities to help refine diversity and migration policies concerning refugees, for instance, but also operate autonomously with volunteers and artists to challenge these policies. Located in a city of about 170,000 inhabitants, which between 2014 and 2017 struggled to respond to the refugee influx by reverting, for example, from its pioneering policy of distributed housing to previous refugee housing campsites, these local theatre projects acted as refractors and mediators, speaking to and across multiple institutions. Their interstitial function, multiple locations and diversified funding from the city, the federal state and their host theatre made them both more resilient, i.e. less dependent on a single organization, and more effective, since a lot of work regarding refugees and migrants relies on networks of expertise and voluntary work. Rather than merely illustrating or commenting, the artistic projects and institutions I discuss here have the capacity to respond to municipal policies about migrant populations by refashioning and enacting alternative and interstitial propositions for sociality and diversity.

Since most theatres in Germany are run as municipal institutions, it is not unexpected that they are linked to other civil society actors and institutions, such as schools, migrant initiatives or municipal authorities. As the two case studies discussed in this chapter show, however, public authorities trying to respond to the influx of refugees from 2014 onwards drew on artistic initiatives for advice on networking across civil society initiatives and other forms of assistance in pre-empting possible xenophobic backlashes and creating sustainable projects for integrating refugees. While the swift response of public theatres in creating refugee initiatives that address the plight of migrants coming to Germany from 2014 onwards is commendable, the sustainability and the impact of these projects on precarious social relations is undocumented and not yet analysed (Warstat et al. 2017). The impact in terms of the conceptual challenges that come from within these often highly reflexive institutions and projects has also only received scant attention (Tinius 2016b). Exceptions are the projects and discourses around so-called 'post-migrant theatre' (Langhoff 2011), initiated at the Ballhaus Naunynstraße in Berlin and later consolidated at the Maxim Gorki Theater, also in the German capital. At the latter, projects such as the 'Exile Ensemble' propose the notion 'exile' instead of 'refugee' to highlight and appreciate previous experiences of often forced migration suffered by intellectuals and artists. Yet, these projects often act with artistic modes of performance that rely on reified notions of cultural difference with exaggerated biographical narratives and political polemics. The two artistic institutions in this chapter, however, challenged such depictions of diversity and migration, seeking instead to work both more practically on the ground to facilitate social integration and with different, nonbiographical or documentary aesthetic forms of theatre. Furthermore, they did so through artistic collaborations and efforts to communicate with artists from other countries both in Germany and abroad, refugees and otherwise, as well as through aesthetic practices that do not rely on migratory narratives, but rather seek shared tropes and concerns, such as the family, dreams, labour and language, which can be used to think through experiences of refuge and migration without mentioning them. It is for this reason that I choose to use 'diversity' as an analytical term meaning 'modes of differentiation', that is, the ways in which 'people, from context to context, situation to situation, mark themselves and each other as different' (Vertovec 2009: 9). The term as I use it, then, encompasses a variety of forms of differentiation that occur within the fields I describe and the ways in which different agents position themselves in-between and against existing institutions or aesthetic and theoretical discourses. It is thus an analytical term to encompass scholarly definitions and municipal integration policies that deploy the concept of 'diversity', as well as practices of artistic differentiation used by those actually affected by state migration policies.

My interlocutors' artistic focus on experiences of social exclusion and migrant itineraries in Europe and beyond does not therefore merely provide a detached artistic commentary on, or seek to 'portray', the social and psychological realities of refugees and settled migrants. The Ruhrorter project, for instance, temporarily opened up otherwise abandoned inner-city businesses, former refugee accommodation and even a disused prison as ateliers, performance spaces and salons, in which city-residents listened to, or met to enter into dialogue with, refugee participants and their peers. In addition to the plays themselves, the exchanges and encounters that the group facilitated were principally based around archives that explored the histories of these sites that were located in different parts of town (e.g. the industrial harbour and a former women's prison, both of which had also served as refugee accommodation) and often only peripherally known to those who came to visit, site-specific installations that allowed visitors to walk through otherwise closed parts of these sites, and discursive formats that facilitated discussion with the largely city-resident publics. These processes were noticed by the municipal Integration Department (*Koordinationsstelle Integration*), which invited members of the group to its own meetings and started collaborating with the theatre project to draft the Department's new policy papers on integration. These mediated relations raise the question, among others, to what extent we can think of the two theatre initiatives I discuss as prefigurative political agents that operate in-between civil society and public administration, and propose alternative political spaces and concepts. This chapter thus describes what actually happened 'close to the ground' in the often intimate and interstitial encounters between artists, whose parents had themselves migrated to the Ruhr region as guestworkers since the 1950s, and refugees arriving since 2014. These artists and theatre projects worked with, conjured up and practically encouraged ways of dealing with difference and diversity that facilitated new forms of cooperation, but also critique between state authorities and cultural institutions, thus acting as interstitial problematizers of both public policies and concepts about diversity and immigration.

Establishing Cosmopolitan Theatre

German theatre and the free performing arts scene have been engaging with migration in Germany in a number of aesthetically and theoretically significant ways for decades, offering sustained social critique and institutional spaces for critical reflections on the ways in which migration is conceived within policy frameworks on diversity and integration, and how images and experiences of migration are mediated to the various publics, such as schools and universities, associated with these artistic institutions. Between 2012 and 2016, I accompanied the TaR, which paired artistic critique with public engagement by creating a hitherto uncommon interstitial institutional structure. Founded in 1980 by the Milan-born émigré director Roberto Ciulli, his dramatic advisor Helmut Schäfer and the stage designer Gralf-Edzard Habben, the TaR operated as a public–private partnership, which granted the directors greater freedom regarding employment, length of contracts and artistic directorship.[2]

The primary reason for setting up an institution that could employ a small but close-knit ensemble was to work towards the founders' vision for a cosmopolitan theatre, by which they understood a theatre that speaks beyond national canons and languages. To do so, the TaR initiated its own series of transnational exchanges and collaborations with artists from regions of the world that were witnessing difficult political times. They thus made diversity relevant by inviting foreign actors to become part of the local ensemble, providing a site of creative integration, by which I am referring, for instance, to co-productions across national and linguistic differences, and sometimes even in spite of international boycotts, which challenged both the lack of municipal initiatives and policies regarding integration as well as a lack of diversity within the theatre system in Germany. Already in the mid 1980s, Ciulli and the theatre travelled to, and gave refuge to, politically persecuted groups, such as the Roma Pralipe theatre group, which fled Yugoslavia during the Yugoslav wars and was later integrated into the TaR not as a guest troupe, but as an integral part of the institution.[3] The TaR also co-produced plays and conducted exchanges with politically progressive Turkish theatres under President Erdoğan's restrictive cultural policies, with dramaturges and actors from Iran – despite a lack of official German diplomatic support – or with artists from the Maghreb region, whose work was suppressed in their home countries. These co-productions directly involved artists that perceive themselves as stateless or transnational strangers in the production of dozens of theatre plays and intellectual soirées, book discussions and public debates. As the former director of the Ballhaus Naunynstrasse and the subsequent head of the Maxim Gorki Theater in Berlin, Shermin Langhoff (2016), points out, theatres such as the TaR, or the projects conducted by Ariane Mnouchkine at the Théâtre du Soleil, a Parisian avant-garde theatre collective known for its international travels and collaborations, stand in a tradition of being 'places of exile' (*Exilorte*) that host those who have fled their countries in search of an intellectual or artistic environment elsewhere.

From the beginning, Ciulli and his ensemble saw theatre as a way of thinking beyond linguistic, national and cultural borders, about the creative integration I mentioned above, by facilitating artistic encounters with those who felt estranged from their own countries for political, cultural or other reasons, and those who wanted to reach beyond national, and often nationalist, cultural canons. Their innumerable co-productions of plays organized under the heading of their International Theatre Landscapes Project have been supported by local, regional, national and international organizations, such as the Goethe Institutes, German embassies and regional governments. These have led to longstanding partnerships between theatres and exchanges of actors and directors, technicians and journalists, many of which have led to employment in the TaR or other German cultural institutions. The TaR has thus established itself as a type of artistic nongovernmental organization (NGO), which has worked internationally both with and in spite of foreign policy, by which I am referring, for instance, to creating diplomatic ties and financial support for cases in which the German government refused to do so or for which there existed no agreed foreign cultural exchanges. This role as a diplomatic mediator through art – as an interstitial agent – has been appreciated by various international theatre directors and actors whom the TaR supported, because it promoted these exchanges through the medium of artistic rather than primarily pedagogic or political exchanges. As the actor and former ensemble member of the TaR, David Hevia, told me during an interview: 'At the Theater an der Ruhr, I was taken seriously as an artist and not a folkloristic import from an exotic country', before going on to explain that as a foreign actor with Mexican citizenship in various German theatres, his different accent, style of moving and nationality had not previously been judged on artistic terms, but reduced to cultural difference. Prior to joining the Theater an der Ruhr ensemble, he explained, 'I was the *foreign* actor, not an actor', noticeably stressing the word 'foreign' and thereby showing how an understanding of 'diversity' in theatre can also serve to reify difference rather than breaking it down through a focus on aesthetic experience and acting.

The TaR's approach, however, led to a greater emphasis on finding the right structural means by which transnational artistic work takes place, underlining, for instance, long-term institutional partnerships or apprenticeship exchanges rather than short-term festivals and productions. The conjunction of artistic expertise and intellectual reflection relatively unique to German public theatres, where directors and dramaturges function as critical intellectuals rather than mere 'producers', has allowed for a sustained conceptual reflexivity about the figure of the stranger, the migrant and the refugee. It may also have been a reason why public theatres became such useful partners for public authorities when the refugee situation and its reception in the city became urgent and critical. Indeed, right from its inception, the TaR promoted a notion of theatre dedicated both to a critical discussion of categories such as home, nation or belonging, and to being an actual refuge in ways that mattered to the people concerned: artists exiled, voluntarily or involuntarily, from their home countries. All of its members with whom I became closely acquainted during my fieldwork, many of whom found their own exile in the theatre from other countries or otherwise alienating working conditions, articulated this in one way or another: for some, the theatre enabled the articulation of their own experience of 'otherness' and 'estrangement' regarding the countries from which they came (Iran, Turkey, Macedonia, Serbia, Croatia); for others, born and raised in Germany, it allowed engagement with their own estrangement from German nationalism or national culture. Here, the diversity of different forms of otherness and estrangement was not a case of other, foreign artists allowed inclusion in a German public theatre – rather, the experience of alterity was deliberately facilitated to provide a means of confronting and troubling German nationalism. As Ciulli put it, 'even when it doesn't travel, this theatre is the theatre for the stranger (*für den Fremden*)' (cited in Bartula and Schroer 2001: 87–90). He uses this term in his writings and public appearances with the TaR to create an idea of the strangeness that encompasses distinctions between German and non-German, suggesting that even a German can feel 'estranged' from his or her own country and can thus be a stranger at home.

Thirty years after the founding of the TaR, another label – post-migrant – became well established within German political theatre. Coined by the German theatre director Shermin Langhoff (2011), who has been at the forefront of discussions of diversity and difference in the arts through her role as director of the Maxim Gorki Theater and previously Berlin's Ballhaus Naunynstraße, post-migrant theatre is an art form that recognizes 'urban life as a globalized encounter of diversity without constant reference to a person's country of origin and migration background'.[4] It assumes difference and diversity as starting points, rather than trying to categorize and consolidate cultural and national differences (see Ndikung and Römhild 2013; Römhild and Bojadžijev 2014). This relation between depictions of diversity, critical self-reflection and the responsibility of theatres in Germany's engagement with the so-called refugee crisis sparked the idea for a project whose initiation and development I witnessed during my fieldwork at the TaR: the Ruhrorter refugee theatre collective. It became an interstitial agent not just because of the way in which it negotiated and produced encounters and representations of diversity in the city and with municipal authorities; rather, it did so through artistic projects involving otherwise ostracized migrant populations.

Interstitial Agency: A Refugee Theatre Collective

Founded in 2012, Ruhrorter has since been led by a young businessman and former lay-actor at the TaR, Adem Köstereli, who receives professional and personal as well as artistic and administrative support from

Ciulli and his ensemble. His previous initiatives (small-scale theatre projects with immigrant youths from low-income and low-level education households) had already led to a number of productions with schools and vocational colleges. His dissatisfaction with the overly mediatized role of artistic projects for marginalized communities, which he voiced to me when I first met him, struck me as being at odds with his own work on the subject. He had previously tried to avoid media attention, he told me, arguing that larger projects trying to affect and change audiences were bound to be exploited by political parties and would have little effect. In his view, many projects were short-lived and did not challenge some of the ways in which they reproduced what he regarded as 'anachronistic ideas about diversity', which neatly categorize people into foreigners, or *Ausländer*, on the one hand, and Germans, on the other. 'We all have migration backgrounds (*Migrationshintergründe*), but the term is often used in a thoughtless way by artistic projects. I find that very problematic', he said, adding that he wanted to find ways of relating to people without framing them as 'other' initially. Therefore, he focused on working with a small group of migrants and participants. Long-term rehearsal processes, he said, would allow strong social bonds to emerge and trust to build up among participants. For him, this social dimension remains more important than the eventual public reception of a play, since it is during these rehearsals that social and psychological transformations can take place, whereas a focus on public presentations only creates pressure through expectation. However, following several meetings and conversations in the city and at the theatre, it became clear to me that Köstereli was concerned with the discrepancy between the tasks, as he put it, 'heaved onto' artistic projects, which 'range from psychotherapy to legal advice and social work', and the capacities and resources of such projects. 'They are simply incompatible and overburdening', he said, 'leading to a situation where artists are more concerned with the visible social effects of their work, but without the proper social, legal or psychological training', while existing social workers are further marginalized because they are harder to market as 'soft cultural capital' by funders, parties and cities. Our conversations gradually involved more people from the theatre, as a tragic boat wreck with more than 300 deaths off the coast of Lampedusa in October 2013 brought the plight of refugees, in this case Sub-Saharan migrants crossing through Libya, closer to the attention of the German public, and theatres began addressing possible reactions more seriously. For the TaR, it was obvious that an initiative directly speaking to, and involving refugees in, the Ruhr Valley was needed. The TaR directors particularly welcomed Köstereli's focus on people in the process of applying for asylum and thus actively engaged in seeking refuge, and he was willing to work with the TaR and the city council that funded the project on expanding his previous work and networks in the city.

In late 2013, Sven Schlötcke, one of the artistic directors of the TaR, and Köstereli conceived of a more specific funding proposal for work with refugees in Mülheim and the neighbouring cities of Duisburg and Oberhausen. Since I had begun documenting Köstereli's relation to the TaR's work with migrants, it occurred to them that it might be productive to include me as an ethnographer as well as part of the project.[5] The application for such project-based productions (as opposed to the publicly funded institutional labour at the Theater an der Ruhr, for instance) required an elaborate methodological and theoretical framework with a detailed budget and production plan for which they also drew on our discussions concerning the work of Giorgio Agamben, Hannah Arendt and Michel Foucault regarding a more theoretical framing of the question of encampment, governmentality and migration.

In early 2014, once the funding had been granted, Köstereli, a friend of his from the freelance performing arts scene and I set out to contact the Buildings Department (*Baudezernat*) of the city of Mülheim to inquire about available spaces for the project. Köstereli favoured an almost entirely abandoned disused shelter not far from the theatre, which had once housed asylum seekers from the former Yugoslavia and now was partially used as a rehearsal space by the TaR. This site was made available to the group, but it required cleaning efforts to gain access to what was to become a stage on the fifth floor of the building and a site-specific installation on its second floor. Both floors had been living quarters for asylum seekers and still bore the marks of this use. This process itself became a form of research and documentation, since we came across numerous traces from former inhabitants, including inscriptions on the walls, newspaper articles and stories told by facility managers or those who had lived in the building and whom we encountered as the project was underway.

While the 'venue' began to take shape and we negotiated with an increasing number of departments in the city administration that became interested in the project, Köstereli had begun to draw on his network of school teachers, voluntary workers and former participants in other projects to contact refugee camps, families and high schools in order to find people interested in the new venture. Based on information from former participants, word-of-mouth and help from voluntary workers, Köstereli knew of several refugee shelters. Since Ruhr Valley cities employ varying accommodation strategies, these locations differed vastly. Twenty years ago, Mülheim, for instance, used abandoned centralized shelters to avoid social tensions. In collaboration with the social housing corporation, the city rented out individual apartments. Frequently, more than one family shared run-down flats in low-income areas, but the situation in Oberhausen, one of the financially most unsuccessful cities in Germany, which has housed asylum seekers in campsites, was revealed to be far worse when Köstereli and I visited. Water and mud sat on the concrete courtyard, often running into ground-floor apartments; toilets were broken and shared by dozens of people; there was no support for trauma victims. One of our project participants, an Iranian industrial designer and former lecturer at the University of Tehran, who had escaped political persecution, repeatedly told us how hard it was for him to work in a small room he shared with four Afghan men who drank heavily, were seriously traumatized and often screamed at night.[6] What added to his discomfort was anxiety over xenophobic attacks. A one-floor, two-room nursery with fenced windows formed the 'centre' of the *Heim* – German for 'shelter' and 'home' simultaneously. Some families had been living on this site for nearly a decade, we learned, kept in limbo by the legal status of repeated *Duldung* ('temporary suspension of deportation'). It was from this *Heim* that most participants for the initial 2014 Ruhrorter project joined Köstereli and the group.

During a discussion of a rehearsal with the inconsistent group (a core of about seven participants stayed throughout the entire year, but many came irregularly, others were deported, some fled, others disappeared or were married into families in other parts of Germany to escape deportation), the name for the entire project and, later, the collective came about: Ruhrorter. The name means 'pertaining to the places/people along the Ruhr river' and it was also the name of the long street on which the industrial rehearsal space for the group was located, but it served primarily as a reference for the diverse and diffuse itineraries of migrants and asylum seekers in the Ruhr Valley. For the group, the building and the name became a sort of symbol of the movement of the people participating in the project and for the migration history of the region.

Rehearsing Alternative Imaginations of Difference: Estrangement as Method

The first major output of the Ruhrorter collective was a trilogy of plays and installations, which focused on long-term rehearsal processes and on the investigation of a specific building in the city of Mülheim that were related to migration, refugees or asylum. In the first project, consisting of a theatre play entitled *Zwei Himmel* (*Two Skies*) and an installation entitled *Palimpsest*, rehearsals lasted for nine months and brought together about fifteen asylum seekers from the former Yugoslavia, Syria, Afghanistan, Iran, Egypt and other countries. The play was going to be performed on the top floor of the abandoned building in the industrial harbour of Mülheim on the Ruhrorter street. In addition, an installation and archive were created in the former living quarters of the lower floors. As soon as the group had permission to use the Ruhrorter building, they would meet two (later three or four) evenings each week to improvise scenes and narratives about belonging and experiences of settling in Germany. These were thematic entry points that Köstereli chose to initiate scenic improvisations and to gather themes. These rehearsal processes were aimed at physically, emotionally and intellectually training participants so that they could abstract from existing markers of their identity (refugee, Syrian, child) and find new categories for self-ascription and imagination beyond these categories. These created unusual aesthetic outcomes with ambivalent figures and scenes on stage where no clear identities were prescribed, and while they required a kind of discipline that not everyone was used to, participants described these processes as liberating, and some even as a welcome output for their creative energies or simply as an important social occasion.

Every rehearsal was structured around certain training routines, lessons for bodily comportment and improvised attempts to link collected stories. Crucially, however, the group approached theatrical improvisation not as a means to an end, a playful kind of therapy or social work, but as a technique that could be learned, as a specific form of relation to the self (see Tinius 2015a). Köstereli's method of eliciting stories over months during the Ruhrorter rehearsals was not so as to create a pool of 'authentic autobiographical narratives' (Köstereli, personal comment) that participants in the group would simply enact, but they were merely the starting point for performance-based inquiries. One participant's intimate revelation of her insomnia, for example, was depersonalized so as to detach the phenomenon from the individual ('a way to protect actors from over-identification and emotional dependency', Köstereli said) and joined up with other stories about sleepless nights to create a range of figures, scenes and stories about dreaming, nightmares and voices that could be heard in the dark of the building. Accompanying the months-long rehearsal processes, I noted how participants, such as the then nineteen-year-old Egyptian refugee whose insomnia had preoccupied her during many rehearsals, trained to detach themselves from their often traumatized identities by creating fragments of characters and scenes that were different from the experiences they retold during the rehearsals. This process of first looking at oneself and treating oneself as a fictional 'other' in order, subsequently, to reappropriate a playfully amended version of oneself is part of their complex theatrical method, which I have referred to elsewhere as 'dialectical fiction' and 'rehearsed detachment' (Tinius 2016a).

This rehearsal method, which focuses on the inward-oriented training of actors, also offered a significant aesthetic challenge to verbatim or documentary representations of diversity (see e.g. Schipper 2012 and Wilmer 2018). For Köstereli, it was problematic and even 'dangerous' to have actors merely play themselves on stage. 'Any art, but especially arts that are as immediately about corporeal and emotional experiences, such as theatre, can bring to the fore or trigger difficult affects and social memories that one needs to handle with great care', he explained one evening after a participant had broken down in tears during a rehearsal. 'Theatre is not the same as social work, and I am not trained as a psychotherapist. We should therefore not claim to be one or the other, especially when working with people who are struggling with trauma', he continued, explaining to me that these experiences show how difficult and complex the questions and problems are that a theatre engaging with migrants and refugees needs to face. 'This is a different kind of theatre, and yet we manage to have audience members speak about the artistic imagery, the content of the performance, rather than reduce everything to the individuals performing in it', he commented. Therefore, Ruhrorter also gave critical feedback on colleagues' calls for participants that the group deemed inappropriate or unrealistic, and they positioned themselves openly against what they perceived to be a 'voyeuristic revelling in tragic self-authenticating narratives' (personal comment) prevalent among documentary theatre practices.

Unlike in a plethora of contemporary 'minority theatre plays' or artistic practices with diverse actors, which emphasize the authenticity of refugee actors 'enacting themselves',[7] the Ruhrorter group refused to associate characters on stage with the persons enacting them and their personal stories. This required sustained physical and conceptual labour to understand how and why this method and direction was adopted. Needless to say, the language used by Köstereli is not merely descriptive, but also propositional, trying to establish new concepts and methods to speak about migration in the arts. I witnessed their frustration in interviews with journalists and public administrators, but also fellow directors in community projects, who sought to rely on biographical narratives to establish the relevance of theatre projects with migrants and refugees. This translated into a variety of methods in the more intimate working situations of rehearsals. All scenes on stage, for instance, were deliberately estranged from personal experiences, in a gesture that a then twenty-year-old Syrian project participant rather poetically described to me as 'a way of dancing through many facets of me'. In a way, these processes could be seen as playing with the definition of diversity I mobilized earlier, that is, as 'modes of differentiation'. Participants even went beyond differentiation to some degree, trying to move past their status as refugee or Syrian or Arabic-speaker, by playing with languages they might not know, impersonating other roles or reading scripts they had written for each other. The process prodded them to disconnect, temporarily, from these identities, but not in a way that might become disorienting for the participants. Rather, they were invited to try and create different imaginations of how and who they could be, thus bringing in elements of other identities as a playful repertoire of characters to recompose themselves through fiction. This was not always a smooth process, causing confusion and exhaustion with those not used to training physically and mentally on such intense reflections on self and identity. Yet what I had not anticipated was that Köstereli and the participants took precisely such instances of disorientation as productive instances in which one could draw on the experience to understand and control self-alienation and re-adjustment. The long-term rehearsal processes were thus at once corporeal and psychological training for participants to contemplate and relate to the categories by which they had been marked out as different from German citizens, or how some asylum seekers were deemed by authorities as legitimate and others not.

One of the many scenes that emerged from such discussions ended up making it into the final few minutes of the play *Zwei Himmel* (*Two Skies*): it showed a participant emerging at the top of a set of stairs leading up to a podium, from which she threw a stack of yellow letters (identifiable as deportation notices) into the vast space of the stage, pointing to an act of seemingly random decision-making. The letters had appeared in different ways throughout the play and resurfaced in the archive and installation that visitors saw after the performance. Many elements of the play's aesthetics were inspired by this specific experience of being a 'tolerated' refugee 'temporarily suspended from deportation', as the technical translation for many participants' legal status reads in English, and constantly threatened with expulsion from their temporary homes in Germany.

Such and other symbolic gestures were initially only intended to be shown in one of the six intimate theatre performances, each of which had space for only about thirty audience members. The principal work done in and through the theatre project, Köstereli repeatedly discussed with the participants, was meant for the participants themselves: an interrogation and reflection on their identity as migrants, for instance, or their status as refugees and their desires to realize personal or professional activities, such as artistic production or further education. But as Köstereli and the other project participants entered into discussions with voluntary groups, the artistic director of the TaR suggested that they engage the city public differently. The Ruhrorter group staged rehearsed scenes in the Oberhausen shelter or conducted orchestrated performance interventions in the desolate high streets of Mülheim, seeking to attract residents for discussions on the situation of migrants through art.

From the Stage to the City: Political Commentary and Artistic Mediation

The project also became locally known due to its extensive inter-city net-works with voluntary associations, church groups and artistic organiza-tions. Eventually, the city councillor in charge of cultural affairs and other local politicians recognized the public platform that Ruhrorter had cre-ated for discussions of diversity in the city. As one person in the municipal administration told us in a meeting, 'your networks and actions exceed what we could and have achieved merely through top-down policy work', thus appreciating the interstitial networking competence of the collective. By the end of its trilogy in 2016, which took place in an aban-doned business premise in the high street of Mülheim, the initiative was well known among journalists, local politicians, voluntary workers, art-ists and residents, and its funding from the federal government had been increased as the projects grew in size and scope. Through local newspaper reports, social media publicity by the group itself and the advertisement of the TaR, Ruhrorter's projects had drawn attention to neglected and abandoned sites in the city once associated with the administration of refugees, and their involvement with refugee camps was recognized as a sustainable alternative to address otherwise ostracized migrant popu-lations in the city. A combination of all of these factors meant that the Ruhrorter group had become an interstitial agent in the city. It did so in dialogue with municipal councils responsible for integration policies, in a city whose non-German population had doubled since the 1990s to nearly 15 per cent of the population in 2011, while neighbouring cities in the Ruhr Valley witnessed similar demographic changes.[8]

Following Köstereli's frank comments during conversations with local politicians regarding the failure of municipal initiatives to reach out to families of asylum seekers in the city, as well as his project's increasing presence in the city's voluntary initiatives, civil engagement and volun-tary groups, he was invited to join an advisory board for the city's first ever official policy paper on integration (*Integrationskonzept*). The munici-pal Department for Integration and the regional government Council for Education, Health, Sports and Culture developed this paper to outline housing strategies and funding plans. Furthermore, it gathered a network of various civil cultural actors and organizations that the municipal government could access to extend their reach, including Ruhrorter. Köstereli participated in working groups, feeding back into the city council his experience with local NGOs, refugee initiatives, church groups and other voluntary organizations with whom he had been in touch for years through his theatre work. He also criticized and altered sections with the group. For instance, in one of several passages to which he alerted me, the policy paper claimed that 'from the point of view of the residents of Mülheim, no foreigner problems (*Ausländerprobleme*) have ever been encountered'. The group discussed these and other examples of what they regarded as unclear phrasings, problematic claims about the city's and region's demographic constitution and past, and problematic positions regarding migration and diversity with the Ruhrorter participants and his team ('What are *Ausländerprobleme*? Who is classified here as "resident" and who as "foreigner"?'), suggesting in-depth edits for the paper. These were included in the final draft and various members of the Department for Integration acknowledged Köstereli's work.

Throughout the peak of the refugee arrival in Germany in late 2015 to early 2016 and beyond, the municipal authorities of Mülheim continued to support the activities of the Ruhrorter collective, meeting with Köstereli and his production team to initiate further and sustainable collaborations among other cultural initiatives in the city. It had become apparent to the city councillor in charge of cultural affairs that Ruhrorter 'had established important links between our [the public authorities'] efforts to reach migrant and refugee populations in the city and voluntary initiatives' (personal comment). He proposed further collaboration and promised to find additional ways of bringing in Ruhrorter as a mediator between the city government and its inhabitants. Köstereli concurred, responding that 'work on migration in Ruhr Valley cities cannot just end once a single project is over; migration constitutes our cities, so we need to keep working'.

In November 2016, Köstereli and the Ruhrorter group invited me to join them for an end-of-year working meeting to discuss the future of the initiative and their possible role in the city of Mülheim and beyond. One of the reasons for this meeting was to reflect on the development of the project since 2012 and to evaluate how its projects tackled specific issues that, in one participant's view, 'should have been the responsibility of the city authorities'. He voiced concern over the outsourcing and delegation of vital municipal responsibilities (mediating between civil society initiatives, revitalizing inner-city environments and abandoned properties, and initiating archival research activities on the history of migration) that had been an undercurrent of discussions in the group throughout their involvement with the city authorities. The Ruhrorter group spent a large part of this evening contemplating how to use their interstitial position more successfully, since they had 'better links to voluntary workers and migrants than the municipal authorities', as one participant remarked. This prompted the group to discuss and reassert the importance of its approach: not to replace the social and therapeutic work done in applied theatre initiatives, but to underline an aesthetic approach to negotiating diversity with migrant populations and to complement activities. One of the artists in the group, Wanja van Suntum, regularly conducted workshops with theatre pedagogues and began teaching applied approaches to theatre with migrants at a local university to bring his practical expertise back into other spaces of learning. 'We want to begin with the idea that what we do is art, and not political activism or social work, because we believe in the experimental value of aesthetic experience', another participant in the meeting summarized. 'But this doesn't mean that we end there', he added. As an example of how they went 'beyond art', the group also reflected on its own vocabulary, noting that it successfully proposed within the theatre and city's integration councils to rethink the council's usage of categories of diversity, employing the neutral term *Geflüchtete* instead of *Flüchtlinge*, for instance, to avoid the infantilizing associations of the German diminutive suffix '-ling'.

Artistic Imaginaries of Diversity

German public theatres, such as the TaR, are tasked by municipal departments for cultural affairs (*Kulturdezernate*) with certain guiding educational mandates (*Bildungsauftrag*) that include addressing cultural and social diversity through outreach activities, language programmes or cultural activities for migrants and refugees. These mandates, often loosely defined by federal educational boards in reference to the pedagogical traditions associated with German public theatres and *Bildung* (Bruford 1975), are designed to foster closer ties between schools and theatres, for instance, through the inclusion of canonical plays in educational curricula and repertories that can then be watched in theatres and prepared in schools. However, the regular appearance of certain playwrights (e.g. Büchner, Shakespeare and Goethe) raises questions about the ways in which such ties between schools and theatres homogenize repertoires and curricula. In a region like the Ruhr and in cities like Mülheim, labour migration as a consequence of industrialization (coal and steel mining in particular) has marked demographics, social and cultural life for decades, even more than a century. And yet most cities' major public theatres and cultural institutions in the region reproduce a German mainstream cultural curriculum through their repertoires and ensembles. Few institutions position themselves firmly against national inflections in curricula or try institutionally to create alternatives; the Theater an der Ruhr has been an outspoken example of such a critical stance against the role of homogeneous cultural representation in curricula and repertoires.

Tensions about such curricular canonization contained within these official mandates for cultural education came to the fore, for instance, at a public discussion at the TaR in June 2016, during which a federal parliamentarian from Düsseldorf, the dramaturge of the TaR, a Green Member of Parliament and I were discussing these mandates. The exchange was initiated by a retired local high school teacher, who commented on the restrictiveness of German literary canons set in curricula. He argued that the national canons presented in schools by federal educational boards were at odds with the social realities of cities in the Ruhr Valley, where migration had shaped cities for decades. He used the word *Leitkultur* (dominant or mainstream culture) to critique the idea that curricula and public cultural institutions such as operas and theatres are meant to reflect on centuries-old German mainstream values identified 'presumably by white Christian middle-class politicians' rather than take in influences from the people who have migrated to Germany over the last fifty years. For him, the encounters facilitated by forums, plays and projects like the Ruhrorter refugee theatre group at the TaR – representatives of which were present that evening – had opened alternative and subtle possibilities for thinking about diversity: not to create representations of other cultures though German plays, but to invite actors and artists from other countries, refugees and migrants, and also Germans with a migration background, to co-produce plays with German colleagues. The dramaturge of the TaR then spoke about the ways in which even something we might identify as today's 'German mainstream culture [*Leitkultur*]' has been assembled over centuries from diverse and varying, even conflicting, fragmented traditions of small sovereign nations within Germany, shaped by movement to and from German countries. The moderator of the panel, Oliver Keymis, Vice President of the Regional Parliament, then asked the dramaturge to explore how and why a theatre like the TaR started to produce theatre with people who had either migrated to Germany themselves or whose parents or grandparents did so. He added that 'besides particular political aims, art needs to be funded irrespective of its direction – that is a result of Social-Democratic democratization of institutions'. The dramaturge nodded, before responding with great care and intensity: 'When we founded this theatre', he said, 'we already recognized that even the idea of *national* cultures was nonsense. No culture has ever been national, they have always been mixed and mediated.'

The dramaturge traced some of his ideas back to what he described as the 'long restoration phase following the French Revolution' and the Second World War, suggesting that ideas about 'mainstream' or 'guiding' national cultural canons were problematically mistaken and would seriously reduce the 'plurality of communicative competence' that we could learn through artistic practices. 'Art facilitates a form of understanding', he continued, 'that is not just logical or reasoned, but associative and aesthetic. We wanted to create conversations with these forms of understanding that are embedded within other, non-German or non-European, cultural art forms and to bring them here. Nationalisms are ordering mechanisms that restrict the learning potential in aesthetic understanding.' Schäfer then referred to some of the ways in which the Theater an der Ruhr had been striving to welcome actors and actresses into their ensemble, such as those who did not speak German fluently or at all, recognizing linguistic differences and accents as an enrichment rather than as a deficiency that ought to be overcome through training. They also, in turn, often did not supertitle their German-language plays when performing abroad – which they did frequently over their thirty-five-year history – mostly providing instead a brief personal introduction to the play in the local language beforehand or discussing some of its themes with local intellectuals and artists afterwards (see Tinius 2015c).

The exchange that evening came to a conciliatory conclusion when the city councillor in charge of cultural affairs (*Kulturdezernent*), Ulrich Ernst, and the director of the Ruhrorter refugee theatre initiative, Adem Köstereli, spoke about the way in which the artistic projects instigated by the TaR assisted municipal government in rethinking the ways in which it met the challenges of migration to this Ruhr Valley city. In a previous private meeting I held with Ulrich Ernst and Sven Schlötcke, one of the artistic directors of the TaR, Ernst had explained that some of the principal concerns of the city were the possible reactions by concerned citizens and the backlash from far-right groups. These concerns articulated by the city councillor and the theatre's artistic director were not just abstract anxieties; one day, the refugee theatre group received an invitation from Ernst to join him and his office staff in a counter-demonstration against an anti-Muslim protest group that marched through Mülheim, trying to gather support for a Cologne-based initiative against the construction of mosques in Germany (*Pro NRW*). Protesters clashed in a central square in the city, barely kept apart by police, and racist slogans against Muslims and refugees were chanted. 'I wonder how we can anticipate these reactions, show differently how migrants enrich the city, how they can integrate', he said, adding that the TaR and the Ruhrorter initiative were exemplary in this regard. He singled out a series of newspaper portraits of participants from a Ruhrorter project, which creatively worked with their aspirations for theatre and had left a lasting impression on him, since 'they reached many citizens, some of whom called us to say how moved they were by the personal portraits'.[9] Following our conversation, the Integration Department of the municipal Department for Cultural Affairs had invited the Ruhrorter collective to comment on and help draft a novel local integration policy paper for the city of Mülheim and to sit on the council for urban development plans linked to asylum policies, such as new housing or campsites, and they frequently contacted the group to plan joint projects in many of the desolate inner-city shops, offering reduced rents or even sponsorship for future projects.

As I outlined in the introduction, the Ruhrorter collective and its patron institution, the TaR, therefore did not just create artistic representations of migration; they actively and jointly with the city administration engaged in preparing strategies, policies and actions against xenophobia. These artistic projects also acted as reflexive sites and dialogue partners for the public authorities, the local newspaper, citizens and local parties such as the socialist *Die Linke* and the Green Party. Representatives and party leaders of these parties had contacted the Ruhrorter initiative to join local panel discussions on migration and transregional working groups, for example, on language training, political education and legal advice for the federal political foundation of the Green Party, the *Heinrich Böll Stiftung*.[10] As Ernst stated in conversation with me, the Ruhrorter project and the TaR could make tangible the complex experiences of multiple identities and processes of creative reshaping of themselves that refugees underwent when arriving in Mülheim. This was important, he noted, since it would allow people to move from an abstract fear of the other, the migrant, to a different kind of relation to this experience; not through sensationalist reporting in the newspapers or political party slogans, but 'human beings and their creative imagination'. Ruhrorter had a public presence, through its social media outreach and links to newspapers, but its ways of creating aesthetic experiences about the complexity of relocation added an important dimension that the city council could not convey. Not unlike other public cultural institutions, such as museums, theatres can impact on our social imagination by creating, as the Ruhrorter project director Adem Köstereli expressed in the panel discussion I cited earlier, 'multiple and subjective pictures of migrants as human beings with constructive aspirations rather than just fear and needs'.

Conclusion

This chapter analysed the interstitial agency of artistic institutions, specifically theatres, which are situated in-between, and sometimes act as part of municipal, federal and national politics. I argued that these institutions actively position and reposition themselves and other civil society institutions and networks in response to public policies on migration, thus complicating the ways in which migration and diversity are publicly framed and addressed. As interstitial social spaces, such artistic institutions are variously engaged and called upon by municipal authorities and operate in-between various kinds of social actors. Institutions and projects, such as Ruhrorter and the TaR, which have established long-term programmes and strategies for addressing refugees in regions shaped by migration for many decades, are not passive or recent illustrations of a short-term German 'culture of welcome' (*Willkommenskultur*). Rather, they constitute interstitial agents between other civil initiatives or voluntary organizations and public authorities, which create experimental spaces for alternative artistic representations and encounters with diversity, and whose long-term concerns for the value and role of migration in society have shaped these encounters. These practices are also not secondary to the political economy of integration, belonging or solidarity, but anticipatory of political formations and policy-making. As 'pragmatic utopias' (Bock 2016) that have an impact on municipal and other political configurations of diversity, these interstitial organizations harness a kind of expertise that should be mobilized and studied rather than patronized and 'defused' as merely aesthetic, that is, as epiphenomena to more significant social formations, such as political or religious movements. The aesthetic realm of political engagement and representation of diversity I described in this chapter is therefore not a mere decoration, but functions as a flexible and prefigurative political space that develops visions for, and practices of, difference, diversity, citizenship and belonging.[11]

As my case studies have shown, cultural institutions themselves act as critical public theorizers, which develop discourses and concepts that may be of interest to public policy makers and local politics, as well as to academic reflections on experiences of difference and diversity in Germany. These include the potentially problematic reification of migration categories in representations of diversity. Reflecting on their own usage of concepts in application forms, Ruhrorter began employing and successfully changed the usage in policy papers used by the city's integration council. As sites that offer an aesthetic experience and engagement with the lived experience of migrants and refugees, both for audiences and participants, theatre projects like the TaR and Ruhrorter share another responsibility that comes with such negotiations of categories that represent diversity: the encounter with people affected by such notions and the policies associated with these people. Public cultural institutions concerned with the creation of encounters and representations of diversity shed light on the development of political categories and strategies for dealing with diversity in the context of migration. The two artistic organizations on which I focused seek to work interstitially to create networks of support for, and reflection on policies about migrants, and refugees in the inner-city context of post-industrial Ruhr Valley cities. Crucially, these collaborations work within existing municipal frameworks and are concerned with the temporary rejuvenation of abandoned institutions with previous, albeit forgotten links to migration and asylum. This has allowed the TaR and Ruhrorter to establish sustainable ties and collaborations with political foundations and public authorities, on the one hand, and civil society initiatives and private organizations with an interest in urban development and migration, on the other. These networks range in scale across different social milieus and settings, from the local bar run by children of former Turkish guestworkers or restaurants owned by refugees from the Yugoslav Wars to established Iranian businessmen who seek to rejuvenate an abandoned building in the city. Working with both these local entrepreneurs as well as funders, such as political foundations and municipal authorities, these interstitial artistic organizations are situated to witness the reception of migration and its relation to urban and social transformation from multiple vantage points. This position enables them to institute artistic organizations as active mediators and interstitial agents to guide and accompany, rather than just to witness and comment on, these significant transformations in German society today.

Jonas Tinius is a postdoctoral research fellow at the Centre for Anthropological Research on Museums and Heritage (CARMAH) in the Department of European Ethnology, Humboldt-Universität zu Berlin, Germany. He studied British and American Studies as well as Social and Cultural Anthropology at the Universities of Münster (Germany) and Cambridge (United Kingdom), where he also completed a doctorate on German public theatre and political self-cultivation (2016). His current research explores how Berlin-based curators of art institutions engage with notions of alterity to reflect on European and non-European heritage. He is convener of the Anthropology and the Arts EASA-Network (with Roger Sansi).

Notes

1. The well-known professional theatre platform 'nachtkritik' (2016) issued a call entitled *#refugeeswelcome*, inviting public theatres and projects engaging with migrants and refugees to submit information about their initiatives. Between late September 2015 and late January 2016 alone, during which time 'new announcements were submitted almost on a daily basis', over entries were collected. Following the closure of the collection in late January 2016, more comments added further examples. With over 140 public German stages, it is likely that the majority has engaged in one way or another with projects addressing migration and refugees. This list also mentions the Ruhrorter initiative at the Theater an der Ruhr, which is discussed in this chapter.
2. This setup, connoted in other fields with a greater privatization of public sector work, was itself a form of institutional critique against the then dominant models of working in the arts, especially directed at short-term contracts and project-based working conditions on the one hand and public bureaucracy on the other (see Tinius 2015b).
3. This was highly controversial at the time, since Mülheim had thitherto been unable to cope with the growing numbers of migrants (Cornelsen 1986; Raddatz 2006: 54).
4. The German original reads: 'Darüber hinaus steht "postmigrantisch" in unserem globalisierten, vor allem urbanen Leben für den gesamten gemeinsamen Raum der Diversität jenseits von Herkunft' (Langhoff 2011). Insightful discussions of this topic can, for example, be found on the online forum *nachtkritik.de* – see e.g. Diesselhorst 2015 and nachtkritik n.d.
5. This seemed a productive form of what Dwight Conquergood called 'coperformative witnessing' (Donkor 2007: 822), that is, a collaborative act of critical but generative observation.
6. In agreement with the persons concerned, I am anonymizing some interlocutors from the project.
7. See Heinicke et al. (2015), Long (2015) Nikitin et al. (2014) and Stegemann (2015) for discussions of such forms of documentary and realist theatre.
8. Information from http://www.metropoleruhr.de/regionalverband-ruhr/statistik-analysen/statistik-portal.html (retrieved 1 November 2016).
9. See the Ruhrorter project website press archive for the year 2014 (http://www.ruhrorter.com/presse.html).
10 Ruhrorter participated in a series of workshops on the integration of refugees in companies and possibilities of political participation, such as the following one held in Essen and organized by the Heinrich Böll Foundation on 25 January 2018 (https://www.unternehmen-integrieren-fluechtlinge.de/event/angekommen-und-dann-politische-partizipation-von-gefluechteten-und-was-politische-bildung-leisten-kann).
11. By using the word 'prefigurative', I am invoking an argument I developed elsewhere with Alex Flynn that performance and artistic encounters not only provide social transformations by *doing* things, but also by reflecting on possible future political and social arrangements (see Blanes et al. 2016; Juris 2015).

References

Bartula, M., and S. Schroer. 2001. *Über Improvisation: Neun Gespräche mit Roberto Ciulli*. Duisburg: Trikont.

Blanes, R., A. Flynn, M. Maskens and J. Tinius. 2016. 'Micro-utopias: Anthropological Perspectives on Art, Creativity, and Relationality', *Journal of Art and Anthropology/Cadernos de Arte e Antropologia* 5(1): 5–20.

Bock, J. 2016. 'Approaching Utopia Pragmatically: Artistic Spaces and Community-Making in Post-earthquake L'Aquila', *Cadernos de Arte e Antropologia* 5(1): 97–115.

Bruford, W. 1975. *The German Tradition of Self-Cultivation: 'Bildung' from Humboldt to Thomas Mann*. Cambridge: Cambridge University Press.

Cornelsen, D. 1986. 'Für Sinti und Roma nichts: Romani Rose im Gespräch', *Frankfurter Rundschau*, 15 January.

Crehan, K. 2011. *Community Art: An Anthropological Perspective*. Oxford: Berg.

Diesselhorst, S. 2015. 'Die Demut des Theaters: Werden die Theater in der "Flüchtlingskrise" wieder wichtig?', *nachtkritik.de*, 5 October 2016. Retrieved 30 March 2016 from https://nachtkritik.de/index.php?option=com_content&view=article&id=11590:die-theater-reagieren-auf-die-fluechtlingsdebatte&catid=53:portraet-a-profil&Itemid=83.

Donkor, D. 2007. 'Performance, Ethnography and the Radical Intervention of Dwight Conquergood', *Cultural Studies* 21(6): 821–25.

Heinicke, J. et al. (eds). 2015. *Theater als Intervention: Politiken ästhetischer Praxis*. Berlin: Theater der Zeit.

Ingram, M. 2011. *Rites of the Republic: Citizens' Theatre and the Politics of Culture in Southern France*. Toronto: University of Toronto Press.

Juris, J. 2015. 'Embodying Protest: Culture and Performance within Social Movements', in A. Flynn and J. Tinius (eds), *Anthropology, Theatre, and Development: The Transformative Potential of Performance*. Basingstoke: Palgrave Macmillan, pp. 82–104.

Langhoff, S. 2011. 'Die Herkunft spielt keine Rolle: "Postmigrantisches Theater" im Ballhaus Naunynstraße', interview with Shermin Langhoff, *Bundeszentrale für politische Bildung*, 10 March. Retrieved 20 March 2016 from http://www.bpb.de/gesellschaft/bildung/kulturelle-bildung/60135/interview-mit-shermin-langhoff?p=all.

——. 2016. 'Nur kein Voyeurismus: Shermin Langhoff, die Chefin des Berliner Gorki-Theaters, gründet ein "Exil Ensemble" mit Geflüchteten', *Süddeutsche Zeitung*, 20 July. Retrieved 14 October 2016 from http://www.sueddeutsche.de/kultur/exil-ensemble-nur-kein-voyeurismus-1.3085203?reduced=true.

Long, N. 2015. 'For a Verbatim Ethnography', in A. Flynn and J. Tinius (eds), *Anthropology, Theatre, and Development: The Transformative Potential of Performance*. Basingstoke: Palgrave Macmillan, pp. 305–33.

McNevin, A. 2010. 'Becoming Political: Asylum Seeker Activism through Community Theatre', *Local-Global: Identity, Security, Community* 8: 142–59.

nachtkritik. n.d. 'Die Türen sind offen: #refugeeswelcome – wie die Theater in der Flüchtlingskrise aktiv werden'. Retrieved 30 March 2016 from https://nachtkritik.de/index.php?option=com_content&view=article&id=11497:immer-mehr-theater-engagieren-sich-fuer-fluechtlinge&catid=1513:portraet-profil-die-neuen-deutschen&Itemid=85.

nachtkritik. 2016. '#refugeeswelcome: Wie die Theater in der Flüchtlingshilfe aktiv werden'. Retrieved 10 April 2018. https://www.nachtkritik.de/index.php?option=com_content&view=article&id=11497:immer-mehr-theater-engagieren-sich-fuer-fluechtlinge&catid=1513:portraet-profil-die-neuen-deutschen&Itemid=85.

Ndikung, B.S.B., and R. Römhild. 2013. 'The Post-Other as Avant-Garde', in
D. Baker and M.Hlavajova. (eds), *We Roma: A Critical Reader in Contemporary Art*. Amsterdam: Valiz, pp. 206–25.

Nikitin, B., C. Schlewitt and T. Brenk (eds). 2014. *Dokument, Fälschung, Wirklichkeit: Materialband zum zeitgenössischen Dokumentartheater*. Bielefeld: transcript.

Raddatz, F.M. 2006. *Botschafter der Sphinx. Zum Verhältnis von Ästhetik und Politik am Theater an der Ruhr/Ambassadors of the Sphinx: On the Relationship between Aesthetics and Politics at the Theater an der Ruhr*. Berlin: Theater der Zeit.

Römhild, R., and M. Bojadžijev. 2014. 'Was kommt nach dem "transnational turn"? Perspektiven für eine kritische Migrationsforschung', *Berliner Blätter. Ethnographische und Ethnologische Beiträge* 65: 10–24.

Schipper, I. 2012. *Ästhetik versus Authentizität: Reflexionen über die Darstellung von und mit Behinderung*. Berlin: Theater der Zeit.

Stegemann, B. 2015. *Lob des Realismus*. Berlin: Theater der Zeit.

Tinius, J. 2015a. 'Aesthetic, Ethics, and Engagement: Self-Cultivation as the Politics of Refugee Theatre', in A. Flynn and J. Tinius (eds), *Anthropology, Theatre, and Development: The Transformative Potential of Performance*. Basingstoke: Palgrave Macmillan, pp. 171–202.

———. 2015b. 'Institutional Formation and Artistic Critique in German Ensemble Theatre', *Performance Research* 20(4): 71–77.

———. 2015c. 'Bilder, Reisen und Theaterlandschaften: Roberto Ciullis Theater an der Ruhr', in L. Schirmer (ed.), *Das Deutsche Theater im 20. Jahrhundert*. Berlin: Gesellschaft für Theatergeschichte, pp. 127–51.

———. 2016a. 'Rehearsing Detachment: Refugee Theatre and Dialectical Fiction', *Journal of Art and Anthropology/Cadernos de Arte e Anthropologia* 5(1): 3–20.

———. 2016b. 'Authenticity and Otherness: Reflecting State(lessness) in German Post-migrant Theatre', *Critical Stages/Scènes Critiques* 14/2016.

Vertovec, S. 2009. 'Conceiving and Researching Diversity', *MMG Working Paper* 09-01.

———. 2015. 'Germany's Second Turning-Point: Long-Term Effects of the Refugee Crisis'. *openDemocracy*, 30 September. Retrieved 20 March 2016 from https://www.opendemocracy.net/can-europe-make-it/steven-vertovec/germany's-second-turning-point-long-term-effects-of-refugee-crisi.

Warstat, M. et al. (eds). 2017. *Applied Theatre: Frames and Positions*. Berlin: Theater der Zeit.

Wilmer, S.E. 2018. 'The Institutional Response of the German Theatre', in *Performing Statelessness in Europe*. London: Palgrave Macmillan, pp. 189–208.

Chapter 11

Articulating a Noncitizen Politics
Nation-State Pity vs. Democratic Inclusion

Damani J. Partridge

Germany received a great deal of global credit for accepting so many refugees in the late summer and autumn of 2015. In 2016, continuing into 2017, as the world seemed to be turning towards nationalist populism as a solution to fears of globalization and global migration, and at a time when many fewer migrants actually made it to Germany, its Chancellor, Angela Merkel, was being celebrated across the world as the one who stood up against the otherwise exclusionary sentiment. The results of that extended moment of welcome should not be forgotten. Real people benefited from the possibility of living and staying in Germany. Still, one needs to ask: 'Under what conditions?' When one looks more closely at the forms of incorporation that took place during this time marked by 'refugees welcome' initiatives, one should consider both the extent to which these forms of incorporation were also exclusionary (see Partridge 2012) and, further, who got left out of the so-called *Willkommenskultur* (culture of welcome).

It is also critical to think through the ways in which forms of incorporation in that summer and autumn might have established the conditions for future partial (if not total) exclusion, making it subsequently much more difficult to immigrate as a refugee (or migrant 'of colour'). Of course, unwelcoming people 'of colour' is not explicitly stated as part of German or European policy, but countries from which 'people of colour' come are much more stringently regulated in terms of the possibilities for their citizens to migrate into Europe. This is true even for citizens of those

---

countries that continue to face realities of constant war, including those who were initially welcomed.

For some time, and particularly after the fall of the Berlin Wall, it has been clear that Germany, and Berlin in particular, are important destinations for those wanting to flee seeming impossibility elsewhere, from more conservative environments in southern Germany (moving to Berlin) to war in Syria. In the summer of 2015, the consequences of war were heating up as people sought refuge throughout Europe. While they were not initially welcomed with open arms, as the autumn approached, due, in part, to what one might call a politics of 'pity', 'Refugees Welcome' signs began to appear across the country. One important contributing factor was the much-publicized death of a boy found on the shores of Turkey on (what had been) his journey to Greece as part of a path that typically led to Germany, and by the German Chancellor's subsequent willingness to accept responsibility for those fleeing war, with a policy more open than any of Germany's European neighbours.[1]

This chapter thinks through the relationships between this 'pity' and how it works vis-à-vis the possibility for a participatory politics (in their new 'host' country) for the noncitizens themselves. It examines further the extent to which 'pity' is necessary for the initial welcome, but also how 'pity' differentiates the citizen from the noncitizen 'guest'. Hospitality, as I will show, sustains the hierarchical position of the citizen in this relationship. Even while he, she, or they welcome(s), he, she, or they also sustain a morally superior position in a relationship in which reciprocity seems impossible. The memory of the lost child is quickly overwhelmed by the good of the subsequent policy shift and the many refugees who do, in fact, come. (For those who arrive, there is not a chance to return the gift of the postsacrifice welcome. Even if it could be returned, the enormity of the offer of refuge cannot be matched.) The 'refugee' is then left with the position of needing to be eternally grateful. Moreover, the logic of hospitality dictates, as one of my German host fathers once told me, that 'the fish starts to stink after three days'. While the guest is initially welcome, the duration of stay could easily change the relationship – one that is not built on equality, but on a host/guest dynamic.

In the last part of the chapter, it will become clear that while 'solidarity' might initially seem capable of saving the day, in the sense that solidarity implies a mutuality that does not exist in the host/guest relationship, the *actual practice of solidarity* makes mutual understanding difficult. The host/guest relationship persists. Europeans do not generally imagine themselves as having a responsibility for the crisis beyond pity and compassion. The historical and contemporary links between European culpability and war or economic disaster in Syria or Sub-Saharan Africa are constantly cut, largely escaping notice in the popular imaginary.

Filming the Future from Berlin: Towards a 'Refugee'/Noncitizen Politics

In that summer of intense migration that ultimately led to the (temporary) culture of welcome, I was conducting research on noncitizen perspectives on 'The Future from Berlin' for a film project bearing this name. Most of the participants were refugees from Syria, including one Palestinian refugee who had previously lived in Syria. He had to carry papers to show that he was from Syria but not Syrian and thus was without a passport.

In the project 'Filming the Future from Berlin: Noncitizen Perspectives', which took place over one month in July 2015, in addition to the people from Syria – among them were also three Kurdish participants – the project included three students from Canada/Spain, the United States and the United Kingdom. Furthermore, there were three participants from Berlin who might also be identified as noncitizens, in the sense that they were descendants of people from Pakistan, Turkey and India, in addition (in two of these cases) to having one German parent. In one of the films that emerged out of the 2015 project, the non-German artistic director and activist who had also helped accompany and guide the films concludes:

> Give us our rights. Hannah Arendt talks about the right to have rights . . . It's a wide thing. It's not just a question of refugees. It's a question of fighting, of collectivity, of helping each other. Sometimes you're weak. Sometimes you're strong. Together . . . We have to do it together.

Here, he gestures towards solidarity, a concept that I will address later in this chapter. The other point, however, is the one about politics. To what extent can 'refugees' or 'noncitizens' articulate a politics amid a context in which they are seen as guests? What right does the 'refugee'/noncitizen have to make demands on the state that offers him or her refuge? Amid pity and crisis, the extent to which refugees can become political actors in the places in which they arrive to claim asylum leads one to ask to what extent these politics require solidarity and, on the other hand, the degree to which that solidarity is always already caught up in asymmetrical relations of power.

In the spring of 2016, Chancellor Merkel stood behind relaxing agreements that had allowed open borders within Europe, but that had also restricted noncitizen movement. The agreements had declared that refugees must claim their need for asylum at their first European point of entry. This politics, a reflection of the Helmut Kohl era – i.e. the era of German ('re')unification that was also linked to the subsequent national fervour – insulated Germany, particularly in the wake of the enlargement of the EU in 2004, leaving the responsibility for refugees coming to Europe to Mediterranean countries, such as Italy, Greece and Spain, while simultaneously making possible the 'freedom of movement' for those recognized as (implicitly 'White') Europeans. In the pre- and post-Cold War moment of the 'Iron Curtain', freedom of movement was an important achievement, a demonstration of the Enlightenment *freedom* ideal,[2] then also caught up in the anti-communist push towards the capitalist appropriation of the Enlightenment term. As I have noted elsewhere:

> Reference to foreign (and particularly African) migration in contemporary Germany is often a reference to an asylum law that the national legislature changed in accordance with EU norms in 1993. These changes occurred amid increasing discussion about the social and economic costs of unification, in which the financial and social support for East Germans and for ethnic German migrants from other parts of Eastern Europe was leveraged against the state's ability to support those thought of as unnatural, economic refugees. The legislation created many more restrictions for the latter, requiring, for example, that refugees leave Germany if the state deems that the situation from which they fled is again safe. Refugees who first land in neighbouring countries deemed to be 'safe third countries are excluded from the right to political asylum' in Germany (Donle and Kather 1993). These include all countries on Germany's borders. The possibilities for asylum within Germany thus have become much more limited. "By 1993, about eighty per cent of all applications for political asylum within the EC [European Community] had been filed in Germany. More than ninety per cent of these applications were finally rejected as unfounded" (Donle and Kather 1993: n.p.). At the beginning of the twenty-first century, the number of successful applicants has dropped even further. According to a UN High Commissioner for Refugees report from April 2001, asylum seekers have seen a steady decline in the number of cases the German government officially recognizes or that are filed at all. The numbers went from 23,470 out of 127,940 applicants in 1995 to 10,260 out of 95,110 applicants in 1999 (Hovy 2001: 11–12). (Partridge 2012: 78)

More recently, with her turn towards the welcoming of refugees, Chancellor Merkel signalled a new era, which re-invoked Enlightenment values as tied also to their Christian roots. Germany could lead through moral authority, showing that it had learned from its past and, as a result, could take on the moral responsibility that seemed to be absent almost everywhere else, with the exception of those countries that were Syria's immediate neighbours, where the most refugees from the Syrian war were still residing.

Amidst what seemed to be a magnanimous approach, an additional problem emerged: pity. With pity and what had come to be called a 'refugee crisis' – a crisis that seemed to be more about a crisis of the claims of Enlightenment universality versus the reality of differentiation between

Europeans and its others – Merkel seemed to be claiming, in her magnanimous act, an air of moral legitimacy against the backdrop of remembering the claims of 'freedom' after the fall of the Berlin Wall, while also remembering the Third Reich politics of refuge denial and its consequences. Moral legitimacy, here, is linked to a politics of moral superiority, in the sense that, as I have noted above, the one hosting the refugee is able, on the surface, to offer more than the refugee will ever be able to give back. Reading the situation in this way is, of course, also dependent on the host never fully grasping what the refugee does have to offer. This is not to say that Merkel did not believe in what she was doing or that she was instrumentalizing refugees in order to gain a morally superior position. But the discourse (including the practice) of pity allows one to see how the differentiation among Europeans, refugees and other noncitizens took place. This is demonstrated, in part, through the emergent impossibility of a noncitizen politics (with an emphasis on local political participation) that could be articulated by the newly arrived refugees themselves, even if their own crisis in (and flight from) Syria (and other global contexts) had emerged as a result of their initial political assertions in the first place (i.e. via the 'Arab Spring').

In thinking about a politics of moral superiority, intent is not nearly as important as an analysis of the effect of the host/guest dynamic. Even if one does not intend to establish one's position as morally superior, this is the kind of relationship that has emerged. While solidarity (i.e. solidarity with the newly arrived refugees in Europe) may appear as the morally legitimate counter to pity, even solidarity seems to differentiate. But before showing how, I would first like to think through the (well-intentioned) articulations of pity and their counter.

Against 'Pity': Filming the Future from Berlin

Based on a related initiative that I had started in 2014 in Detroit in the summer of 2015, I began the film project in Berlin with the help of two Berlin-based artists. The point was to produce short films about the future from the perspectives of noncitizens in the cultural and political capital of one of the world's favourite countries.[3]

We initially left the term 'noncitizen' open, and 'the future' as the stakes for a politics that had yet to emerge. The future would be filmed *from* (as opposed to 'of' or 'about') Berlin, because noncitizenship was the subject, and many noncitizens do not intend to stay in this city forever. But Berlin, as a post-industrial city with major public financing for the arts and a history of unaccounted for (not yet reprivatized) property, offered distinct possibilities for living, creating and imagining futures. So we – refugees, 'post-migrants', a youth theatre artistic director, a filmmaker and an anthropologist – met every weekday at 2.30 pm for one month. Our project was to make a collection of short films for a broader public. It was also an opportunity to see how noncitizens imagined their futures from the vantage point of Berlin and how they would contribute to a politics of reshaping them.

Pity No More

In the ensuing discussions, one young participant decided to make his film a pronouncement against pity. He had been in Berlin for two years and the authorities had recently recognized his asylum case. From the Kurdish region of Syria, he wore thick black-rimmed glasses, had a sarcastic smile and constantly referred to himself playfully as a *scheiß Flüchtling* (shit refugee). He hated pity and was making fun of the way people saw him, turning that image into a flattened caricature so blatantly ridiculous that it could not be believed. Through the persistent performance of the caricature, he was also showing that he was not a 'desperate refugee', but a reflective artist. The attention to the caricature as a caricature ultimately created the possibility for him to emerge as a new self.

In response to his argument against pity, another participant from southern Germany (whose mother is German and whose father is South Asian) said that he also wanted to make a film about pity, but from the other side. He wanted to extol pity as a laudable Christian value. The artistic director intervened, telling him that pity was hierarchical, that it put the pitied person beneath he or she who was pitying. 'But', the young man retorted, 'pity can be good.' He went further to say that 'White' men also deserve pity. However, in the final screening at a packed cinema in the district of Berlin-Kreuzberg, the audience refused this move. Through its laughter, in response to the seemingly normative young 'White' German male's call for the possibility to be pitied, the audience was demonstrating that it could only read the 'White' German male's call to pity him as ironic. In spite of the filmmaker's intent, the audience read his film as a meta-commentary against pity. The 'White' German male characters were too robust, too confident, too self-assured. The audience's laughter suggested that the claim that 'White' men do not receive enough pity, if any at all, was being rejected. The film spent a great deal of time going to the sites where the filmmaker assumed that he could find an understanding of Christian pity. He went to 'White' German priests, to 'White' German male social welfare activists and to the artistic director from the theatre from which many of the participatory filmmakers came:

Artistic director: I say not 'thank you very much, that you're giving us a little place on the edge of existence, outside your city'. Don't recognize us. Naked humans. We are the invisible people not allowed to work in all of these things. We have to say: 'Thank you'? And then get pity? Do you think . . . someone is pitiful? It's also *Ekel*. It's also disgust.

Filmmaker (narrating the film offscreen): Pity seems to reaffirm hierarchies and inequalities between citizens and noncitizens on an emotional level, all while being very friendly helpful and polite. Citizens underline their superior position questioning pity to noncitizens, by helping through pity. Is pity different from the German word *Mitleid* (literally, 'to suffer with someone')? Do Christians have a different perspective on pity?

In response to a question about whether or not he as a 'White' German man has been the recipient of pity, responding to the filmmaker's query, the man notes that at some point in his life that he likely has, but he cannot recall any recent experiences. He goes on to argue that the society is not oriented towards pity, and especially not for White men. 'Pity is reserved for small cute animals, small children, Blacks and women. Men are, in principle, excluded.' It is at this point that the audience in the Kreuzberg-Berlin theatre, in association with his call to potentially be pitied, which is simultaneously tied to a projection of arrogance, breaks out into laughter. From here, the filmmaker goes on to talk to religious thinkers and authorities:

Religious character in the film: one identifies Jesus's association with suffering (one part of the German word, *Leid*) and argues that, in the suffering, he is encountering God.

In the film, though, he does not say how one should address this suffering in contemporary life, but he does say that Jesus, in identifying himself with suffering people, said: 'I was hungry and you gave me something to eat. I was a stranger and you gave me a place to sleep.'

The Filmmaker goes to a religious institution, apparently also in Berlin, and asks 'what role does pity play in your everyday life? What role does it play for you as a priest?':

Priest: I would say that pity is not a relevant category for me. Maybe it's because this is a university community. There is a privileged target group. It's actually my responsibility to show people how much wealth they have in their lives. My praxis is marked by the fact that the people have the problem that they have too many possibilities as opposed to too few.

In the same room, another participant in the conversation says that he does encounter pity and refers immediately to refugees. He says that he sees his role as trying to reduce the suffering (again, referencing part of the German word *Mitleid*):

> Recently, I had contact with a refugee who said that he needed urgent legal advice. Then I felt pity (*Mitleid*) for a person who has come from a foreign country, who doesn't properly speak the German language, who is overwhelmed by his engagements with the German authorities. I could understand that this was a situation of suffering. I tried to help a bit. I am a lawyer . . . I didn't just stay with the question of pity. I also tried to reduce the suffering a little bit. Maybe that is a positive meaning of pity, not just to look from above at the pitied, but to stand on the side of the suffering, and to try to bring him out of his suffering.

> Filmmaker (offscreen): In the end, the question is the same for citizens and noncitizens. How can we get beyond pity?[4]

The question does not seem to be one of 'identifying with the poor', as another religious figure in the film suggests, but to live as a poor person oneself: 'with faith as the background, pity would probably fall away', the priest (who does not encounter pity) says. 'Then I would most likely turn to the category of rights.' The film concludes with this category. 'Give us our rights', the artistic director of the youth theatre demands. In another instant, in real life outside of the film, the artistic director argues that one should not give up on making demands on the state and one should not turn to private funding or private resources, even as a noncitizen: 'It's our money.'

Chancellor Merkel Expresses Pity

Over the same summer, in a televised conversation with Chancellor Merkel, a Palestinian teenager, Reem Sahwil, speaking perfect, fluent, native German, tells the Chancellor her story: 'we had a hard time recently, because we were close to being deported' (the girl speaks in a shaky voice, hesitantly, seemingly on the verge of tears, as if she would rather not tell the story. But it is also clear that she wants to use this opportunity to plead her case, not just for herself, but for her entire family). Merkel interrupts: '[You were told] you should go back to Lebanon?' Sahwil: 'Yes, exactly' (the footage that shaped how this event was perceived by the public then cuts to another moment in the conversation):

> Merkel: I understand this. Umm . . . However, umm . . . [she hesitates slightly]. I must now also . . . umm – and sometimes politics is hard so, when you're standing in front of me, and you're a very pleasant (*sympatisch*) girl, but you know, in the Palestinian refugee camps in Lebanon there are thousands and thousands. And if we now say, 'you can all come, you can all come from Africa, you could all come' – we just can't achieve this.[5] And we are in the situation, and the only

answer we have is: don't let it take too long until these things are decided. But some people will have to go back.

[The video clip then cuts to an awkward pause, before Merkel walks over to the young girl, who has started crying.]

Merkel: Ach komm.' [In English, one might say, 'oh, don't worry'].

[The camera goes to a wider shot that shows the host and the audience of schoolchildren, including the girl, as Merkel approaches her.]

Merkel: But you did that really well [as if to congratulate a child on a recital performance, even though it was not successful].

[The host jumps in:] I don't think that this has anything to do with 'doing it well'. It's a distressing situation.

Merkel [retorting]: I know it's a distressing situation.

[Merkel tells the girl:] I still want to stroke you once. Because I – because we don't want to bring you all in such a situation. Also, because it's difficult for you. And because you have depicted the situation many, many others can get into. Yes? [6]

At the moment when Chancellor Merkel walks over and awkwardly strokes the girl's arm, as if to say, 'don't worry', she does not offer a legal remedy. However, perhaps as a result of her tears, the girl has the potential benefit of the exception. In addition to the tears, 'medical care for Reem Sahwil, who has cerebral palsy and a shortened Achilles tendon, is among the reasons her family wants to stay in Germany' (Coburn 2015). After this incident, her family received a temporary residence permit until 2017. Is it the Chancellor's awkward pity that led to this temporary relief?

While potential 'pity' rules one day, the threat of 'terror' rules another. Even as Germany agreed to take in hundreds of thousands of Syrian refugees, it was speeding up the legal frameworks for the deportation of others. Just after the three-year-old dead Syrian child's body washed up on the shore of Turkey, his boat having capsized on the way to entering the EU shores in Greece (see Parkinson and George-Cosh 2015), the mainstream German public, again, displayed an outpouring of German pity, guilt and compassion (on compassion, see also Ticktin 2006, 2011; and Fassin 2012). Both compassion and guilt, while suggesting at least temporary social hierarchies through feeling, are nevertheless of a different order than pity. Pity immediately signals the social alienation of the pitied person.

Many young people from Syria participated in our film project, all of whom were well educated and mostly middle class. One had originally applied for political asylum, but did not get his case recognized until he switched from *political* to an application for *humanitarian* asylum. Pity worked for the specific (Syrian) case, but not as a general rule (for Afghanis, Pakistanis, Palestinians, Bosnians or 'Africans'). Neither pity nor compassion nor guilt work for those who are seen as conscious or calculating, as demonstrated by the response to those seen as 'economic migrants'. On the other hand, in taking in so many refugees, Germany seemed to be showing that it had learned from the past and that it could claim moral superiority, a term that points simultaneously to the virtues and the problematic hierarchy associated with this morality as articulated most prominently through pity (Partridge 2015). Germany's asylum policy is a direct result of its working to find a new national (and global) direction after its Nazi-led Holocaust. As a financial and political leader within the European Union, it is at a point at which it can teach the world (including the United States) about how it should be acting. But what would constitute solidarity in this context? Is solidarity even enough?

Sexual Violence: A Turning Point?

Before turning to solidarity, I will continue to theorize the relationship between pity, hospitality and noncitizenship, where noncitizenship is defined in terms of social, legal, political and/or economic nonbelonging. 'You live in the country, but it doesn't belong to you', as one of the refugee participants in the Future Cities (see filmingfuturecities.org) project put it. Others in the project linked it to being homesick, not being able to go home or not having rights. 'You hold the citizenship, but you still feel homesick' or 'you can't have your values valued'.

Amidst pity and noncitizenship, it is important to think about sexual violence and how it served as a turning point. The 'refugee crisis', some have argued, was caused less by the number of people coming to Germany and more by the question of how to respond. It was, in this sense, a crisis of rich, predominantly 'White' Christian, state-sponsored morality, a crisis that Chancellor Merkel initially seemed to overcome with her 'welcome culture'. It was a crisis, because European practices of Christian morality dictated against refusing people who clearly needed refuge, but then some members of the Bavarian regional sister party of Merkel's own Christian Democratic Union (CDU) began to revolt, as did new members and voters of the Alternative for Germany (AfD) party, a more nationalistic group who argued that refugees were getting too many of the state's resources and the national government's compassion. Here, one might recall the film that initially wanted to make a case for pity and the 'White' German man's claim that 'White' men generally are not the recipients.

As part of what emerged next, sexual assault ruptured the possibility even for pity, as a discussion about it became part of a generalized discussion about refugees, even if it was not refugees who were primarily involved in the assaults at the 2015 New Year's Eve celebration in Cologne (see Kosnick, Chapter 7 in this volume). Mainstream journalists and suspicious politicians read these attacks as the result of the culture of hospitality – *Willkommenskultur* – and the other side of compassion, with refugees and North Africans attacking German women. Conservative activists claimed the mantle of feminism and condemned 'their' culture of sexual violence, simultaneously sparking fear in large segments of the population, even leading, for example, to a temporary ban on male refugees at a public swimming pool in Bornheim, a small town not far from Cologne in North Rhine-Westphalia. The other side of pity is the turn that happens after sexual violence in which the refugee and 'his culture' are seen as the culprit. Pity requires a kind of helplessness that is undermined by the perpetration of violence that then gets generalized in this case as being perpetrated by 'North Africans', but also with a persistent suspicion about refugees.

Inevitably, Merkel shifted in order to maintain her own political future and the differentiation between refugees, 'good' vs. 'bad', Syrian vs. other, humanitarian vs. economic, intensified. Amidst this shift, activists and others known for their anti-racist positions in the past suddenly began writing and giving interviews in the popular press that they were now also afraid. Refugees are guilty before they arrive. Compassion is undermined by fear, and while the formal political discussion focuses on German interests, the noncitizen wonders in which kind of politics she or he needs to participate. Who will be accountable to him or her and his or her interests beyond voluntary compassion or sudden condemnation?

Pity and Hospitality

Regarding hospitality, one of the refugee filmmakers from Syria spoke about staying in a friend's house. At some point, he also stayed in our apartment. He spoke about being asked to sleep on a mattress on the floor of that other German friend's apartment as if that friend were doing him a favour by asking him to sleep on the floor. He felt insulted and spoke about all of the property his family owned in Syria. In speaking about hospitality, he noted that if a family friend came to his house and refused the initial offer of tea and he didn't offer again or even if he only offered two more times, that family friend would leave and tell people that he came to his house and he did not even give him anything to drink. On the one hand, a good host treats the guest with honour. On the other hand, when that guest is pitied, sleeping on the floor seems good enough. Even after being asked to sleep on the floor, the host who pities expects gratitude. Eventually, even this gratitude might not be enough. As Merkel said, 'some will have to go back'.

The Christian examples of the 'Good Samaritan' and St. Martin are illustrative. Here, the Christian form of incorporation offers a distinct form that reaches out to strangers as those to be pitied. One should not, however, ignore the speech of the stranger in response to this 'pity'. It is important to listen beyond the imagination of the thoughts of the person who pities in the Good Samaritan or the St. Martin stories.

Making Demands in Spite of Pity: Speaking through Film

In one scene in the 'Filming the Future from Berlin: Noncitizen Perspectives' film against pity, the noncitizen filmmaker is confronted with trying to find housing for his friend. 'What are you doing?', the artistic director who is helping him with the project asks him off screen. 'I'm trying to help a refugee.' The artistic director goes further: 'you know we're trying to make a film, right?' The filmmaker: 'I know, but I won't leave him like I did yesterday.' (One night, when we were editing the films, his friend slept on the floor in the next room.) 'He has no place to sleep.' In the meantime, the asylum hostel worker searches for housing online. 'Sold out', she reads from the website. The friend has vouchers from the welfare office for €50 to get housing. Since all of the shelters are already full, he has to look to the private housing market.

The filmmaker: 'for me, I don't help. I do it all the time. And I don't have to say that, "I am helping" and all this shit.' (He says the, 'I am helping', part in a mocking tone, imitating the 'ideal helper', pointing to the fact that he is not doing it to get moral credit. His motivation, he suggests, goes beyond pity.) He goes on: 'but I must do [it], for me.' (It is an obligation, not a charity act. His reasoning suggests the opposite of the contemporary reading of pity.) 'For me, I was also in this situation. I can feel him, I can understand what the refugees suffer, because I'm also a refugee. But in the beginning, it's difficult and different, not like now.' (His search for housing for the newly arrived refugee is an obligation that is distinct from the regular contemporary reading of the Good Samaritan (biblical) form of compassion. The newly arrived refugee looking for housing is a version of himself.)

The fact that they would have to rely on pity to get housing, even though they had a voucher, revealed the dehumanizing effect. Even money was not enough to secure housing. In this case, the refugee was not even entitled to (paid for) hospitality. The hospitality/pity link is a mode of incorporation. Without it, one might not find a place to live at all. On the other hand, needing to resort to mercy is not an empowering position. The William Blake poem (as cited in the film) follows:

PITY would be no more

If we did not make somebody poor; And Mercy no more could be

If all were as happy as we.

(1908)

Pity (in this form) de-historicizes. It hides the relationship between Europe and those to be pitied. It does not demand accountability. At the very least, though, solidarity takes the relationship out of the realm of a voluntary emotion and puts it into the arena of political practice. In practice, though, solidarity acts like (this articulation of) pity. It does not necessarily eviscerate hierarchy. Institutions to support the accountability of those who claim to be in solidarity are now largely absent. On the other hand, when the filmmaker says that he wants to help his friend, that he must, there seems to be a moral imperative that is based not on hierarchy, but on the experience of having been in the same situation (of retrospectively suffering with), and knowing what that is like. The knowing (in German, *Betroffenheit* – i.e. having been affected by the same situation) is critical. In my analysis of holocaust memory (see Partridge 2010), I use the work of Leslie Adelson (2005) to think about what she calls touching tales, that is the ways in which historical experiences of racism and genocide provide links (see also Rothberg 2009), which is not to say that experiences are the same but they can (and do) produce connections (what one might think of the possibility of suffering with). Perhaps, these sorts of connections are what one should require for a more efficacious articulation of political connection and potential collaboration.

Solidarity

Amidst these shifting politics, solidarity works as a constant for those opposed to the dehumanization of refugees, but what does solidarity mean in practice? Is it, as a University of Michigan graduate student (Sam Shuman) viewer of the *Pity No More* film suggested at a public screening, similar to pity in the sense that it differentiates between the one who offers solidarity and the one who receives it? To what extent can 'the refugee' be in solidarity with the normative 'White' German citizen, who decides whether or not to accept his or her claim to asylum, who is never accused of being, by nature, a sexual predator? In the *Pity No More* film, the main protagonist expresses solidarity with a new acquaintance who has recently arrived from Syria and who also seeks to claim asylum, but it is hard to see what he would mean if he said that he was in solidarity with the border agent. (Here I do not mean the border agent as a specific individual who might also struggle through the contradictions of contemporary life, including the symbolic violence represented in his or her position vis-à-vis refugees; rather, I refer to the border agent as a legal category/subject position, under Schengen Law and the Dublin Regulation, intended to control the movement of refugees.) Less obvious than the symbolic distance between the refugee and the border agent is that between the pro-asylum activist and the refugee.

Writing about the dynamics between her role as an anthropologist, her role as a shelter director and her connection to the young women who lived in the shelter in her ethnography *Shapeshifters: Black Girls and the Choreography of Citizenship*, Aimee Cox notes:

> The social spaces that we created together were rife with power differentials. There were many things I was not. I was not homeless, not a girl, not born and raised in Detroit, not an hourly staff member, and not a parent. There were other things that I was. I was a PhD student, a program director with the power to hire and fire, and a middle-class Black woman. The things that I was and was not, the labels that preceded me, and the ways in which these labels were attached to privilege mattered in every context for how I was both seen and able to see. It also mattered that I was often able to witness and write about struggles that did not necessarily affect me outside of my own political investments and commitments to these girls and women. (2015: 33)

In a different context, Fiona Wright refers to 'a kind of solidarity that enacts its own violence' (2016: 132). Alexander Koensler writes about 'the difficulty of enacting solidarity in practice without new boundaries or misunderstandings resurfacing in unexpected ways' (Koensler 2016: 352). While 'solidarity' appears to suggest equality, in fact it inevitably means hierarchy. One advocates a politics of solidarity, and yet the conditions of the German pro-asylum/anti-border activist and the recently arrived refugee are not the same. The means for enacting social change are not equal. If the refugee and the German activist disagree about the best political strategy, sometimes without realizing it, the German activist has an advantage and may unwittingly enforce his, her, or their own will over the refugee's own desire. The pro-asylum activist might be willing to take certain steps, but not others.

In the summer of 2014, some 'African' refugees occupying a Berlin-Kreuzberg school threatened suicide. Here, 'African' operates as a broad category that differentiates too little among 'Africans', but nevertheless reflects the European differentiation between 'legitimate' and 'illegitimate' migrants, often via the category of 'economic' versus 'humanitarian' or 'politically persecuted' refugees. Furthermore, in the German context, it is well known amongst activists and asylum camp workers that 'Africans' whose asylum cases have yet to be decided are unlikely to get the right to stay in Berlin. One asylum hostel worker in Berlin told me that I would not find any 'Africans' in the hostel she managed as a result of this national placement policy. In the protest at the square in Kreuzberg, the 'African' refugees (who notably were not from one single country in 'Africa') used occupation as a means of achieving their ends, protesting against the German asylum policy and the legal regime that refused to allow them to live in the parts of Germany or in the parts of Europe they chose. In this instance, solidarity only seemed to go so far. The existential questions and the potentially necessary political means were not the same for everyone. This suggests the need to think more rigorously about possibility of a noncitizen politics.

Noncitizen Politics: Possibilities and Limits

In his account of politics, philosopher Giorgio Agamben (1998) refers back to the literature of the ancient Greeks to differentiate between what Aristotle called bare life and political life. Bare life is, according to Agamben's reading, life that can be killed but not sacrificed. For him, this distinction leads all the way to Auschwitz, the death camp and the lives of those who would be murdered as a matter of state policy. In *Casualties of Care*, Miriam Ticktin refers to bare life as the 'universal suffering body best exemplified by the sick body, or by the racialized, sexually violated body' (2011: 4). Under French humanitarianism, the incorporation of bare life is the exception to the rule of 'deportability' (see de Genova and Peutz 2010), in the sense that French law incorporates bare life only to the extent that these bodies will likely die if deported. They have no right to stay in France other than the fact that the French are compassionate and have developed a humanitarian exception. They are differentiated from 'political life' in the sense that political bodies have rights, like the right to work, the right to get an education and the right to stay forever in France. Ticktin calls the form of care that incorporates bodies through the humanitarian exception a 'politics of care that is a form of antipolitics' (2011; see also Ferguson 1990). It is not the result of noncitizen activism, but a humanitarian exception that allows the almost dead (or suffering body) to stay until or because they do not have access to appropriate care in their 'home' countries. They can stay because they are suffering and might die if they leave. In an earlier piece, Ticktin argues:

> Although both human rights and humanitarianism are complexly constituted transnational institutions, practices, and discursive regimes, in a broad sense, human-rights institutions are largely grounded in law, constructed to further legal claims, responsibility, and accountability, whereas humanitarianism is more about the ethical and moral imperative to bring relief to those suffering and to save lives. (2006: 35)

In Agamben's discussion, bare life, which connects the ancient Greek concept both to the death camp and to the refugee camp, where the refugee does not yet have full rights (while his, her, or their case is being decided). Agamben's analysis, though, tells us little about the political practices and imaginations of those imprisoned in the camp. Even Ticktin's hope for human rights as more grounded in law is obscured by the lack of accountability that state institutions have vis-à-vis the unrecognized refugee as he or she waits for asylum. The nation state is too imperfect an institution to enforce 'universal rights'. As Agamben points out, even in states in which it claims universal rights, the rights of the citizen are distinct from 'the rights of man'.[7] The state enforces the citizen's rights, not 'man's' rights. Solidarity is too unstable as a universal legal or social category, as can be seen in the case of actually existing socialism (see Partridge 2012). The socialist brothers and sisters who came as contract workers or students to the German Democratic Republic in East Germany were nonetheless distinct from the national members of the republic.

Noncitizenship is the juncture at which we need to be theorizing the political because it immediately points to the problematic distinction between the 'universal human' and the citizen. Human rights suggest that no human life is truly bare. There is always the potential to invoke claims to 'human rights'. The gap between citizenship and 'human rights' is reflected in the position of the noncitizen for whom no sovereign entity necessarily claims responsibility.

One of the short 'Filming the Future from Berlin' films depicts, through fictionalized re-enactment, after months of waiting, a refugee (playing a version of himself) who ultimately switches his case from political to humanitarian asylum. He recalls the period before he made the switch. His fictionalized character travels by train from the town he has been assigned while his case is to be decided. Even though he has made frequent inquiries by telephone and in person with local authorities, he ultimately decides to travel by train to the initial centre where his original claim is processed in order to find out about the status of his case. He had received ambivalent messages; he has even heard that some of his documentation might be missing. The scene begins at the asylum officer's office. He knocks politely and she barely opens the door. Even before she opens it, we can see him primping. She opens the door slightly, just to take his ID before closing it again. He is forced to wait. The officer comes back (after spending some time on Facebook) with no additional information other than that he will have to wait. He then starts talking about brandy and asking what kind she likes most. While initially engaging him in this discussion, and even smiling slightly, the conversation quickly turns, and she closes the door abruptly in his face. 'I know what you are trying to do!' The title of the film is *Please Take My Money*. At one point in the film, he speaks to the audience as if they were her: 'You're getting paid to do this job, so why can't I just give you a little more to get you to do your job a little faster?'

What is striking about this scene, and also about the film *Pity No More*, is the extent to which 'the refugee' is not simply a vehicle through which a politics of morality, crisis and fear gets expressed. There are intervening discussions that one does not normally hear if one is not already involved in the daily lives of noncitizens or is not already a noncitizen himself/ herself/themself. Gratitude, expressed by those who might get asylum, is not the end of the story. In the summer's discussions, many noncitizens expressed discomfort with the fact that they were constantly expected to say 'thank you', even when the help that they were receiving was the result of pity, not a mutual recognition. A more equal relationship would have recognized the refugee's expression of political demands, e.g.: 'I want to stay, but under these specific conditions. . .' Those offering the help imagined themselves as being in solidarity with the more recently migrated, but important aspects of mutual respect went missing. It is this discrepancy that suggests the necessity for a noncitizen politics. In this sense, we need to expand the theorization of the politics of the noncitizen. We need to think further about the degree to which the noncitizen's disrespect for national borders itself is an expression of a kind of politics, even if it at first appears merely as desperation. In our conversations during the film project, many spoke of their experiences and strategies for crossing borders. They spoke of the Turkish border as the most difficult crossing point.

In other discussions about the border and the recent migrations from Syria and elsewhere in the world, colleagues, activists and the experience of refugees suggest that Europe cannot actually enforce its borders. If people are determined to come, they will get in (see also de Léon 2015 for a US example). Depending on European policy, though, more or fewer will die trying.

Deportation is expressed, at times, as a legal desire, but it will prove impossible on a mass scale, not least because of the memory of

Nazi-inspired European genocide. This is the case even if, as has become part of the German discussion, the threat of imminent deportation is no longer announced. People's lives will, of course, become more precarious, as de Genova and Peutz, the authors of *Deportation Regime* (2010), point out, but they will not all, ultimately, leave. In addition to the insistence on coming in, that refusal to leave Europe is also an expression of a noncitizen politics, in which one does not necessarily appeal to a political representative (like the German Chancellor) because one does not belong to institutional networks in which one's participation is recognized as a right. Even human rights fail him or her, because these are only minimum standards with no guarantees, with no sovereign who is institutionally committed to appeal to or protect him, her, or them. On the other hand, if one looks carefully at how Chancellor Merkel and German voters responded to the 'refugee crisis' between the summer of 2015 and the spring of 2016, the movement politics of refugees, who chose to come to Germany via Turkey and Greece or from North Africa via the Mediterranean, suggests that this is, in fact, politics – that these movements do have effects on national elections and geopolitical relations.

By 'welcoming refugees' in the summer of 2015, Germany seemed to be taking a moral high ground that would shame even its former (post-Second World War, democracy-teaching) occupiers, who were, in spite of war and their participation in it, unwilling to take in many refugees – even those living with civil war. But in the late winter of 2015 and spring of 2016, in part because of internal pressure from a more anti-immigrant wing of her own party and the voter support of the more stubbornly racist right, the German Chancellor was forced (pursuing political survival) to change her position. On the other hand, even though she was not representing refugees, their presence in Germany forced her to find a political solution at the beginning of the summer of 2015. At first, she adjusted, via a politics/anti-politics of pity, in favour of welcoming. Then, through a politics of political representation that painted 'refugees' as sexually violent Muslim men (the other side of a pity politics that relies on voluntary compassion, which then turns to disgust), she adjusted again. But to what extent can one openly organize around noncitizenship and a politics that refuses border regimes, but nevertheless appeals to nation state-based welfare?

Conclusion

In the late winter of 2016, at a weekly meeting organized by refugees at an important Berlin-based cultural institution, someone in the audience, a 'Black' man, speaking in French, commented on the upcoming Global Day against Racism: 'Many people fear that if they join the demonstration, they will face deportation.' A friend did not know about the demonstration. He was in Potsdam. 'Many people are isolated in refugee camps.' He also asked about the security of the refugees at the demonstration. The main organizer responded: 'We also have the problem that some refugee camps don't allow our posters. This is the problem with my refugee camp. I have tried three times.' In a show of solidarity, a 'White' German organizer added: 'There will be a legal team with legal support.' Pointing to the strategy, apparently against explicit politicization, another organizer noted: 'The name of the event is Carnival.' A West African man, active in organizing undocumented migrants, added: 'You don't hear the voice of the refugees. Most of the refugees are traumatized and they stay in the camps.' Once again, the possibilities for noncitizen politics become significantly reduced through the forms of 'care' to which they seem most likely to gain access.

If moral superiority was the initial story, then Germany was losing it in the spring of 2016, as the European Union (under Merkel's leadership, many in the German and international press were arguing) formed an agreement with Turkey to return migrants from Greece, and Germany made family reunification more difficult for those who had already arrived in the country. With so many new restrictions and oppositions to their entry, it seemed that many more people would die in the Mediterranean or elsewhere en route. Money (at least money to travel to Germany) seemed to be less of a problem than the fact that European and American governments fail to facilitate flights for Syrians, Iraqis, Kurds or Palestinians from countries torn apart by war.

A class analysis cannot attend to some of the racial tensions that are the result of global trends in migrations, war and the associated geopolitics. German Social Democratic politicians have written some of the most racist political interventionist texts in recent memory (see Sarrazin 2010; and Buschkowsky 2012), and the Red-Green coalition, led by Gerhard Schröder between 1998 and 2005, seemed to be more about compromising the rights of migrants/noncitizens than reformulating the discussion. In refusing to speak more often and more explicitly about racialized exclusion in everyday life, even Cem Özdemir, the former Turkish-German co-head of the Green Party differentiated between everyday racialized exclusion and a the more explicit racism of the populist right.

Merkel put her own political future at stake by opening things up. She shifted on issues of immigration and asylum in ways that one would not have anticipated if one had assumed that right versus left was an ideal guide for understanding contemporary life. On the other hand, her Christian commitments (to compassion) and her experience of growing up on the more restricted side of the Berlin Wall (at least in terms of the potential for travel west and the consumption of Western goods) led her to see contradictions in the rigidity of fortress Europe (see van Ackeren 2016). Then again, the other side of pity and compassion is the quick turn towards hatred and resentment, because compassion is not a right. It is a voluntary sentiment, and who deserves compassion is a matter of interpretation. Furthermore, the pitied person might lose all of the compassion if he, she, or they do(es) not seem grateful enough, and especially if he is suspected of being a rapist. The humanitarian beginnings of more open borders – even if refugees had to spend and risk a lot more to walk as opposed to fly to Europe – are making the politics more difficult. But maybe there will be a social movement in Europe organized by the refugees themselves. This has happened before, so why not again? Even if things begin with compassion, a more robust politics can still emerge. A politics against pity, in its contemporary hierarchical articulation, might be a good start, that is unless pity, solidarity, and compassion start again to mean 'suffering with'.

In this volume, when thinking about my contribution in relation to questions of 'difference' and 'diversity', I am struck by the fact that both difference and diversity are produced in the relationships and terms of 'crisis'. Scholars such as Scott Page (2007) have argued that 'diversity' is valuable to business and social science in the sense that a 'diverse' group comes up with better, more sophisticated answers more efficiently. Institutions, such as universities and corporations, should strive for diversity if they want to be the best. On the other hand, in thinking about 'refugees' and their incorporation through 'pity'/compassion, I am struck by the fact that 'diversity' has not been a central part of this public discussion. Labour markets and declining birth rates persist as notable realities. As some German politicians have noted, it seems clear that Germany will benefit from immigration and well-educated contributors.

In my analysis, though, I am more concerned with the possibility of participation than with the politics of 'diversity' or analyses that assume 'difference', although it is clear that nationalist populism is emerging in response to the fear of perceived 'difference' and the seeming decline of the social welfare state. In thinking about the society that might emerge, taking refugees and other immigrants seriously as political participants will actually produce better outcomes. This is the case even if one goes beyond the language of 'diversity', which, even in the best instances, is still caught up in the related logic of 'how much is too much?' or 'how much is already enough?' (See also Partridge and Chin (forthcoming).)

Damani J. Partridge is Associate Professor of Anthropology and Afroamerican and African Studies at the University of Michigan in Ann Arbor, Michigan, United States. He has published on questions of citizenship, sexuality, post-Cold War 'freedom', Holocaust memorialization, African-American military occupation, 'Blackness' and embodiment, the production of noncitizens, the culture and politics of 'fair trade', and the Obama moment in Berlin. In 2012, the Indiana University Press published his book *Hypersexuality and Headscarves: Race, Sex, and Citizenship in the New Germany* as Part of their New Anthropologies of Europe series edited by Matti Bunzl and Michael Herzfeld. Among other bodies, his research has been supported by the Alexander von Humboldt Foundation, the Fulbright Foundation, the German Research Foundation (DFG), the National Science Foundation, the School for Advanced Research and the Wenner-Gren Foundation.

Notes

Parts of this chapter have been published in Damani Partridge, 'Refugees, Pity, and Moral Superiority: The German Case', *Cultural Anthropology* website, 28 June 2016.

1. Here, his death is ultimately read retrospectively as a sacrifice, even if initially unintentional. Unlike Agamben's noncitizen *Homo Sacer*, who can be killed without being sacrificed, the European contribution to the boy's death, which an analyst might otherwise read as the result of a murderous European immigration/refugee politics, is redeemed through the shift in Merkel's position. His death is now given new meaning. He was retrospectively killed so that others might come. However, this resignification does not undo the horror of his loss. It also cannot completely remove the stains of blood from the hands of those who retroactively sacrificed and now pity.

2. See, for example, Susan Buck-Morss's account of Hegel's thinking about the Haitian revolution in relation to his theorization of the master/slave dialectic. For European Enlightenment philosophers including Locke, Hegel and Rousseau, theorizing the possibilities for 'freedom' was a central concern. According to Buck-Morss: '[By] the eighteenth century, slavery had become the root metaphor of Western political philosophy, connoting everything that was evil about power relations. Freedom, its conceptual antithesis, was considered by Enlightenment thinkers as the highest and universal political value' (2000: 821).

3. See http://www.filmingfuturecities.org. In various polls over the years through which I conducted this research, Germany was ranked as either the best (see Chew 2016) or the most popular (see http://www.bbc.com/news/world-europe-22624104) country in the world. I would argue that the fact that so many refugees came to Germany during the 'crisis' suggests that refugees also saw it as one of their most highly desired destinations.

4. One should note that speaking as if pitied people and citizens are actually equals in the eyes of the economy or the law glosses over the power dynamics.

5. The translation in the *New York Times* uses the word 'imagine'.

6. The translation here is a mixture of the translation in the *New York Times* and my own. I occasionally changed the words when I thought that alternative words were more

important. I also added descriptions in parentheses to give a sense of the scene. Finally, as noted in the text, I added the 'umms' heard in the original video to convey the awkwardness of the exchange. Merkel is usually regarded as a well-spoken leader, but, in this moment, she struggled to find the right words. See https://www.nytimes.com/2015/07/21/world/europe/legislation-gives-hope-to-girl-who-shared-plight-with-merkel.html?_r=0 (retrieved 11 July 2018).

7. While supposedly universal, the terminology is problematically gendered.

References

Adelson, Leslie. 2005. *The Turkish Turn in Contemporary German Literature: Towards a New Critical Grammar of Migration*. New York: Palgrave Macmillan.

Agamben, G. 1998. *Homo Sacer: Sovereign Power and Bare Life*. Stanford, CA: Stanford University Press.

Blake, William. 1908 [1794]. 'Songs of Experience: The Human Abstract', in J. Sampson (ed.), *The Political Works of William Blake*. London: Oxford University Press. Retrieved 11 July 2018 from http://www.bartleby.com/235/87.html.

Buck-Morss, Susan. 2000. 'Hegel and Haiti', *Critical Inquiry* 26(4): 821–65.

Buschkowsky, Heiz. 2012. *Neukölln ist überall*. Berlin: Ullstein Buchverlage GmbH.

Chew, Jonathan. 2016. 'Germany: This Country was Named the Best in the World', *Fortune*, 20 January. Retrieved 11 July 2018 from http://fortune.com/2016/01/20/germany-best-country-usnews/.

Coburn, Jesse. 2015. 'Tearful Moment with Merkel Turns Migrant Girl into a Potent Symbol', *New York Times*, 30 July. Retrieved 11 July 2018 from http://www.nytimes.com/2015/07/21/world/europe/legislation-gives-hope-to-girl-who-shared-plight-with-merkel.html?_r=0.

Cox, Aimee. *Shapeshifters: Black Girls and the Choreography of Citizenship*. Durham, NC: Duke University Press, 2015.

De Genova, N., and N. Peutz. 2010. *The Deportation Regime: Sovereignty, Space, and the Freedom of Movement*. Durham, NC: Duke University Press.

De Léon, J. 2015. *The Land of Open Graves: Living and Dying on the Migrant Trail*. Oakland: University of California Press.

Donle, Christian, and Peter Kather. 1993. 'Germany', in Dennis Campbell (ed.), *International Immigration and Nationality Law*, vol. 2. The Hague: Kluwer Law International.

Fassin, D. 2012. *Humanitarian Reason: A Moral History of the Present*. Berkeley: University of California Press.

Ferguson, James. 1990. *The Anti-politics Machine: 'Development', Depoliticization, and Bureaucratic Power in Lesotho*. Cambridge: Cambridge University Press.

Hovy, Bela. 2001. 'Statistically Correct Asylum Data: Prospects and Limitations'. Retrieved 11 July 2018 from http://www.unhcr.ch/cgi-bin/texis/vtx/home?page=search.

Koensler, Alexander. 2016. 'Acts of Solidarity: Crossing and Reiterating Israeli–Palestinian Frontiers', *International Journal of Urban and Regional Research* 40(2): 340–56.

Page, Scott. 2007. *The Difference: How the Power of Diversity Creates Better Groups, Firms Schools, and Societies*. Princeton, NJ: Princeton University Press.

Parkinson and George-Cosh. 2015. 'Image of Drowned Syrian Boy Echoes around the World'. *The Wall Street Journal*. Retrieved 21 August 2018 from https://www.wsj.com/articles/image-of-syrian-boy-washed-up-on-beach-hits-hard-1441282847.

Partridge, D. 2012. *Hypersexuality and Headscarves: Race, Sex, and Citizenship in the New Germany*. Bloomington: Indiana University Press.

_____. 2010. 'Holocaust Mahnmal (Memorial): Monumental Memory amidst Contemporary Race', *Comparative Studies in Society and History* 52(4): 820–850.

_____. 2015. 'Monumental Memory, Moral Superiority, and Contemporary Disconnects: Racisms and Noncitizens in Europe, Then and Now', in H. Merrill and L. Hoffman (eds), *Spaces of Danger: Culture and Power in the Everyday*. Athens: University of Georgia Press, pp. 101–31.

Partridge, D. and Matthew Chin. Forthcoming. 'Interrogating the Histories and Futures of Diversity: Transnational Perspectives'. *Public Culture*.

Sarrazin, Thilo. 2010. *Deutschland schaft sich ab: Wie wir unser Land aufs Spiel setzen*. Munich: Deutsche Verlags-Anstalt.

Shryock, Andrew. 2012. 'Breaking Hospitality Apart: Bad Hosts, Bad Guests, and the Problem of Sovereignty', *Journal of the Royal Anthropological Institute* 18(S1): S20–S33.

Ticktin, M. 2006. 'Where Ethics and Politics Meet', *American Ethnologist* 33(1): 33–49.

_____. 2011. *Casualties of Care: Immigration and the Politics of Humanitarianism in France*. Berkeley: University of California Press.

Van Ackeren, Margarete. 2016. 'Muss sie gehen?', *Focus*, 30 January, 20. Retrieved 21 August 2018 from https://www.focus.de/magazin/archiv/titel-muss-sie-gehen_id_5246926.html.

Wright, Fiona. 2016. 'Palestine, My Love: The Ethico-politics of Love and Mourning in Jewish Israeli Solidarity Activism', *American Ethnologist* 43(1): 130–43.

Chapter 12

The Refugees-Welcome Movement
A New Form of Political Action

Werner Schiffauer

In 2015, almost one million refugees arrived in Germany, creating an enormous task for the authorities, which struggled to register, process and accommodate them. In addressing the challenges posed by the large number, Germany witnessed a significant process of reinvention and reinvigoration of civil society groups. Hundreds of thousands of volunteers welcomed asylum seekers at train stations and makeshift shelters, waving placards with Arabic-language greetings, flowers and toys for children. Countless initiatives, grassroots groups, support projects, language courses and much more were established across the country within weeks. In this chapter, I suggest that the enormous expansion of civil society activity and dedication amounted to a social movement.

The social and cultural relevance of this emergent civil society activism to welcome refugees can only be conceptualized adequately against the background of other analyses of social life in Germany, which, before 2015, had emphasized a different trend for the country: radical individualization, widespread withdrawal from social responsibility and the general atomization of neoliberal society.[1] These negative analyses were at least seriously questioned by the dynamics of social activism that emerged in the summer of 2015 and the subsequent months. During the so-called refugee crisis, observers witnessed an energetic and dynamic civil society emerge, seeking original answers to challenging problems and pursuing the development of new structures of solidarity. Grassroots responses to the challenges posed by flight and dislocation also carried the potential

Notes for this chapter begin on page 307.

to develop a fundamentally different societal approach to immigration in general. In short, emergent civil society initiatives provided an alternative to hysteria and panic, which were expressed in calls for tougher border controls and deterrence to prevent further migration.

Grassroots projects and activism illustrated alternatives to anxiety-ridden paralysis, which dominated civil society reaction to migration to Germany in the 1990s. In the long term, refugees-welcome initiatives appear capable of enhancing the public culture of what is called an 'immigration society' in German (*Einwanderungsgesellschaft*), referring to a society in which the reality of immigration is accepted and embraced as one of many constituents facts of social life and its diversity. In the wake of the refugees-welcome movement, a new space for the development of new attitudes to heterogeneity and difference opened up. This is particularly relevant with regard to German Muslims and Islam in the wake of 9/11, when they became the prime object of unease with regard to immigration, affecting different parts of society, including the better educated and the middle classes. The refugees-welcome movement enabled the development of new relationships and engagements across religious or cultural identities. Many of the refugees who settled in Germany were Muslims, and German citizens, Muslims and non-Muslims, came together to cooperate in addressing the so-called refugees crisis collectively, pooling knowledge and resources.

In this chapter, I analyse the results of a research project by the Council of Migration (Rat für Migration), of which I have been a part, funded by the Federal Government Delegate for Migration, Refugees and Integration (Beauftragte der Bundesregierung für Migration, Flüchtlinge und Integration). As one part of this study, conducted in the autumn of 2015, we identified 1,000 relevant projects that supported refugees and developed new forms of creative engagement. In a first overview, we found that the following fields of activity were pursued most widely: housing, health, trauma therapy, internet access, employment, education (school), education (university), legal advice, leisure (sports, music, theatre), public relations (counter-publics), networking, supervision of volunteers, support with bureaucracy, self-organization and support in refugee camps or shelters. For the study, we selected ninety pioneering projects and analysed them with ethnographic methods (Schiffauer et al. 2017). It became apparent that the initiatives constitute a rich social experiment, in which new ways of approaching diversity and rethinking citizenship beyond the ethnonational community can be explored and tested. These experiments put into practice Hannah Arendt's conceptualization of the political as the realm in which initial strangers build a political community through acts in which they can recognize each other as bearers of rights (Arendt 1993). This allows for completely new ways of experiencing difference and of negotiating belonging and civic participation.

The Specific Character of the Movement

The size of the refugees-welcome movement is difficult to establish. A conservative estimate would hold that at least 15,000 projects were founded after June 2015, involving between 800,000 and one million active volunteers, helpers and organizers.[2] The size of the movement is remarkable. More remarkable, however, is the new type of political approach that unites diverse initiatives. We claim that the refugees-welcome movement is misunderstood if it is conceived primarily as a humanitarian movement motivated by compassion. Its political character can be overlooked when the political is too narrowly conceived as the realm relating to issues of power, i.e. either as a struggle for domination (as in established political theory) or as a struggle for empowerment (as in the theory of social movements). Its political character becomes apparent, however, when we apply a more foundational concept of the political found in Arendt's (1993) reflections on fragments of a philosophy of the political. According to Arendt, the core of the political is the constitution of the political community. Different from a community based on kinship or affinity, a political community, such as the Greek *polis*, is essentially a community of strangers who establish bonds by mutually recognizing each other as political subjects, i.e. as the bearers of rights.

Issues of power, which are at the centre of classical political theory, do play a role, but only secondarily: *after* the foundational political act has taken place. Among others, Rancière (2002) has taken inspiration from this definition, considering the political as the act by which the border between those who count and those who do not count is shifted. It is the act by which the orders of the visible and audible on which the political community rests are transformed. Arendt's understanding of the political also underlies Engin Isin's conceptualization of a performative theory of citizenship (2008). Isin argues that the classical conceptualization of citizens' rights, deriving them from formal citizenship-membership of a nation state, is too static. Citizenship constitutes itself in active acts of citizenship, for example, in the struggle for or taking of rights. One becomes a citizen by engaging oneself in acts of citizenship. Following Rancière (2002), it could be argued that demands for political rights have to be heard. If this is the case, the political space reorganizes itself. The right to have rights is then granted to those who had remained invisible before or whose claims were considered to be nonsensical noise, but not meaningful voice. This often takes the form of expressing rights to the city rather than rights to the nation (Lanz 2016).

If one takes such a concept of the political as a point of departure, the political character of the refugees-welcome movement becomes apparent.

It focuses less on the question of power (whether in the form of empowerment or resistance) or on political agenda setting, but rather on political community building and the formation of political culture. It aims at inventing new and more inclusive local institutions, or at appropriating and opening existing ones, thus laying the foundations for a new understanding of a collective political identity – a new 'we'. Rather than label these initiatives a 'refugees-welcome movement' we should speak of a 'citizens' movement'. This is a political movement, even though its character differs from that of classical social movements (which fight for the rights of specific groups), from that of new social movements (which fight for solutions of specific problems) or from that of practice movements (which share the same pragmatic approach, but respond only to the demands of particular groups). The citizens' movement, on the other hand, focuses on the community at large and its political culture as a whole. It may be mentioned that its political relevance can be measured by the fierce reactions it provokes among rightwing populists. These political opponents are quite aware of the far-reaching political implication the citizens' movement has.

Based on our qualitative analysis of ninety projects, I have identified eight features that are characteristic for the citizens' movement: strong localism; community building; experimental character; new cross-cutting alliances; personal character; critique of humanitarianism; glocal identities; and the inclusion of self-organized groups.

The Importance of Locality

Many movements came into existence when the arrival of busloads of refugees posed a logistical challenge for the local authorities in towns, cities and villages across Germany. In most cases, public administration depended on the support of volunteers to handle tasks such as initial registration, distribution of food and clothing, and the preparation of emergency shelters. While compassion and the desire to do good motivated many volunteers, local identity also played an important role in relevant activities. We found that many volunteers and community organizers were explicit in their desire to prevent inhumane and degrading situations for the newcomers, which would conflict with the view that local residents had of themselves, their values and the ways of life that characterized open, tolerant and liberal communities – their self-image. In cases in which the administration showed flexibility and openness to this kind of cooperation between the authorities and civil society engagement, results were particularly positive.[3] An example of such cooperation was the Bavarian city of Nuremberg, where a dedicated administrative

department, staffed with two full-time employees, has a history of coordinating the activities of such voluntary initiatives.[4] In the autumn of
2015, they managed to establish well-functioning support structures for
refugees and organized volunteer work in a very short space of time.
The inclusion of local citizens with migration backgrounds was particularly important. A synergy between citizens' efforts and urban institutions
emerged, which made citizens' engagement particularly efficient. The
joint effort of municipal authorities and citizens produced strong feelings
of communal identity and local pride. A second motivating factor was the
wish to prevent negative or even hostile anti-refugee groups from domi-
nating news coverage about a response of a particular place to the arrival
of newcomers. Volunteers were often clear in their conviction to stand
up to xenophobic and anti-immigration sentiment, determined to produce a clear statement against neo-Nazis. 'There were quarters were the
political Right tried to mobilize against refugees. This led to an increased
engagement of pro-refugee groups', a female volunteer from Nuremberg
explained. According to research conducted by Serhat Karakayalı (see his
chapter in this volume), these statements were quite common: this type
of motivation successfully mobilized local resources. This is a remarkable
development. It illustrates the existence of strong concerns about local
political culture. Such desires reflect a shared objective to demonstrate to
outsiders, as well as to hostile local groups, that a large part of a particular
population aspires to live in an open and tolerant community that enacts
solidarity with refugees and other vulnerable people.

The ties to locality thus play an important role in processes of incentiv-
izing citizens to accept more responsibility for their community. Local
pride shapes how challenges can turn into chances. Instead of leaning
back and calling for the state to solve the crisis, citizens took over state
responsibilities across the country, when the authorities' struggle to cope
with the situation could not be ignored. This can be interpreted as a
reappropriation of tasks that used to be managed more autonomously
by citizens and were delegated to the state only in the second half of the
twentieth century. This goes hand in hand with the reinvigoration of a
collective, public spirit.

Community Building

Our research found that many emergent initiatives have had a significant community-building effect. The collective effort to cope with a great
challenge, which was often portrayed as a global crisis with enormous
ramifications, created new social ties and reinforced existing ones. The
result of a shared aspiration to confront challenges and provide solutions

led to mutual recognition: 'we realized how important the contribution of Germany's long-term immigrants is. We have about eighty activists with a migration background in our group; they translate or accompany refugees to the city administration, to GPs and hospitals, or to school meeting, as cultural mediators', the same volunteer in Nuremberg explained. In this context, local Muslim communities and their voluntary activity in particular came to be seen as a valuable resource for urban society, allowing novel forms of participation and the sharing of common objectives that had long been foreclosed to Germany's minority groups. Other projects focused on community building and actively included refugees in these efforts. In Erkrath, a town of 45,000 people near Düsseldorf, an initiative called Planetvalue organized a series of events described as *Aktionstage* (action days). The idea was to bring citizens from across society together to realize projects of shared social value, such as constructing a playground, building benches or cleaning parks. Local companies were asked to concede employees interested in volunteering the possibility to do so during work time and without loss of salary. Migrants and refugees were actively approached to participate in these activities. The three annual *Aktionstage* were a success: in 2013, 2014 and 2015, 164 projects were realized. Sixty-three companies and forty-two nonprofit organizations took part. One important side-effect was the intensification of local networks: nonprofit organizations came into contact with companies (68 per cent of them established new ties), potential employees with employers, and migrants and refugees with the non-migrant population. Many of the new connections would not have been established without the *Aktionstage* and they led to further cooperation and projects. The initiatives in Erkrath were explicitly not advertised as projects to support only migrants and refugees in order to avoid othering processes and resentment among other vulnerable social groups, such as the long-term unemployed and pensioners. Instead, the projects aimed at creating a shared space in which established residents and newcomers could work together on projects that had a shared benefit not just for refugees, but also for the entire local community. The idea was to establish a new sense of community.

Other projects were initially developed to serve the needs of refugees, but then expanded to include other members of the community at large. The *Mehrgenerationenhaus* (multigeneration house) in Ludwigsburg was designed as a point of contact not only for asylum seekers, but also for all families in the quarter. A similar initiative, predominantly funded by the Protestant Church, was launched in Berlin's multicultural Neukölln district, Sharehaus Refugio: twenty refugees could share a large apartment building with twenty Germans (some of them with their own migration histories), with comfortable individual rooms and communal spaces. The initiative also established a coaching programme with a focus on German-language teaching and facilitating access to the job market. Workshops and neighbourhood markets were set up as regular events connecting Sharehaus residents with the surrounding quarter. These projects aimed at creating win-win situations, benefiting newcomers and the needs of the local neighbourhood in equal measure. The guiding principle that emerged across such initiatives was that integration can only succeed when established residents do not feel left behind. Instead, they need to realize that they too benefit from resources, activism and novel projects. Such realizations among the established local community often helped overcome initially hostile or at least sceptical attitudes.

The village of Golzow, in a remote part of the mainly rural and structurally disadvantaged region of Brandenburg, may serve as an example. When local residents first heard that a large shelter for asylum seekers was to be established in the village, they formed an anti-refugee initiative, which led the authorities to drop the plan. The mood changed, however, when the village mayor explained that more young children were necessary to prevent the local school from being closed by the regional authorities. Demographic decline has affected many areas in Brandenburg since the 1990s. The mayor thus contacted a crowded refugee shelter in a nearby city, Eisenhüttenstadt, and invited refugee families with young children to move to Golzow instead, where property was available and cheap, and housing would be much more comfortable than in large camps or shared facilities. There was initial hesitation among asylum seekers, since they feared hostility and attacks, but eventually two families with schoolchildren followed the invitation. They found a warm welcome in Golzow, where a support group was set up. The school remained open.

The political relevance of these examples lies in the experimentation with new ways of establishing solidarity. Instead of basing solidarity on feelings of cultural proximity, conscious efforts are made to base it on visions of a common good and thus to overcome tensions between residents and newcomers. Instead of zero-sum scenarios, in which gains for some entail losses for others, win-win situations are made possible: the added value works for the benefit of all. Participation was made possible for every member of a local community, averting feelings of exclusion or being disadvantaged. In a practical way, active kinds of involved citizenship were developed locally.

Social Laboratory

Our research found that many new projects combined inventiveness, creativity and originality. One might go as far as suggesting that the new challenges posed by the arrival of hundreds of thousands of refugees and asylum seekers unleashed social potential and rigorous engagement that would otherwise have remained undiscovered or unrealized. The spectrum of innovative ideas reaches from making use of communal gardening for trauma therapy (Brunswick [Braunschweig]), through attempts to tap media skills for refugee radio projects (Berlin), to re-inventing higher education through online access and certificates for refugees who are unable to access proper university courses because of bureaucratic hurdles (Kiron University). New avenues opened up, while, in other cases, innovative ideas developed in the past received increased attention and often also additional funding. Among the projects we examined, there were a high number of professional or semi-professional start-ups, but also other initiatives that remained explicitly nonprofessional and social movement-oriented. Not all initiatives will be sustainable, but the important observation is that the arrival of refugees and the increased attention paid to issues of diversity and difference, and to the management of multiculturalism in large cities and smaller towns and villages, led to a busy atmosphere of creative enthusiasm, unleashing entrepreneurial spirit and youthful optimism.

The political relevance of this activism lies in creating new possibilities that allow the departure from traditional and well-trodden paths. By extending the realm of what can be thought and realized by civil society actors in the face of state inactivity, new forms of social and political critique also become possible – and these forms are more substantial and successful that theory-based ones. The pursuit of projects demonstrated that German society 'could do better' than many official schemes had done in the past, particularly with regard to the management of difference and the practice of solidarity. The citizens' movement, through its diverse initiatives, thus permitted a powerful critique of ineffective or punitive political and administrative practice, namely by realizing concrete projects and novel ways of responding to a changing society and its demands.

New Cross-cutting Alliances

Another remarkable aspect is the heterogeneity of the citizens' movement. The varied initiatives almost suggest that volunteering has been re-invented. Volunteering in Germany was traditionally organized in countless associations or clubs, called *Vereine*, which were characteristic for Germany's particular kind of civil society. The 'traditional volunteers' active in the fire brigade, football and other sports teams, or in church-based associations were now joined by groups that had previously shown little interest in that kind of volunteering, such as school and university students. Particularly during the early phases of the citizens' movement, the share of students or post-migrant youth increased significantly. Over time, the social composition of the movement increasingly resembled society as a whole (Karakayalı and Kleist 2016: 3). The wide-ranging inclusion of volunteers is also reflected in the heterogeneity of what motivates engagement. Anne Eilert (2014) studied the motivation of new volunteers in Berlin and found three distinctive motivational factors. One group was motivated by humanitarian individualism: volunteers contributed their particular skills, for example, in language courses or legal advice. In a second group, humanitarian motivation was connected to political motivation. The latter gained importance when volunteers experienced bureaucratic mismanagement in immigration offices or shelters. The third group was neighbourhood-based and church-based.

This diverse social composition demanded new forms of cooperation among people who had not been in regular contact previously, even bridging different political affiliations. Seemingly well-established political divides became less important and new coalitions emerged as a result, connecting Christians, Jews and Muslims, political activists and entrepreneurs, conservatives and left-wingers. Most important, perhaps, was the cooperation with Muslim communities. After many years of scant attention by mainstream society, the considerable engagement of Muslim communities and their contribution to civil society was both recognized and appreciated. New forms of collaboration between political activists and state agencies, such as public schools and administrations, also emerged. This cooperation induced a process of opening: groups that had never considered participating in public protests suddenly reconsidered their stance and took to the streets to confront far-right extremisms and neo-Nazis. Political groups with a focus on theoretical engagements also discovered the relevance of more pragmatic politics in solving concrete problems. However, such novel forms of cooperation are rarely without tension, in particular with regard to strong-willed activists, on the one hand, and schools and public administrations, on the other. At the same time, municipal volunteer agencies have often played an important role in resolving misunderstandings or conflicts.

Personal Character

From its inception, the movement established personal, face-to-face contacts between local residents and refugees. Many initiatives organized services such as mentoring, support with public administration, accompanying asylum seekers to state offices or teaching language classes. In developing new relationships or friendships out of challenging situations, the sharing of biographies is of particular importance: it leads to empathy and confronts processes of distancing or even othering, which might otherwise highlight the difference between life experiences rather than foregrounding similarities as the basis for solidarity. Individual contacts and biography-sharing were particularly important, since, in many cases, activists came into contact with people from Muslim backgrounds for the first time at such initiatives. The strength of personal ties and positive individual experience was of central importance to the continuity of projects in the wake of the events during New Year's Eve 2015 in Cologne, when dozens of people with nontraditional German backgrounds attacked women, which resulted in a media frenzy and moral panic that painted Muslim refugees as incompatible with German culture (see Kosnick, Chapter 7 in this volume). In many cases, however, individual volunteers could draw on different personal experiences with the people they had supported over many months, countering the effects of hysteria and an anti-asylum backlash across media outlets and political camps. This finding also helps to make sense of the fascinating results of a study by Eisnecker and Schupp (2016): defying widespread expectations, they showed that the level of engagement remained stable in January and February 2016 – the two months following New Year's Eve, which were dominated by critical, even hostile, media coverage regarding Muslim masculinity and the supposed exposure of vulnerable German women (including volunteers) to what was increasingly depicted as Arab sexual depravity.

The strong interpersonal character of the movement also acted against official and bureaucratic classifications of refugees, which divided asylum applicants right away into those with a so-called 'perspective to remain' (*Bleibeperspektive*) – with a strong likelihood to be granted asylum – and others who were assumed would be eventually deported, predominantly because of their supposedly safe country of origin. Through personal interaction, the complexities of personal situations are communicated more successfully and the shortcomings of bureaucratic classifications dividing refugees into different categories become apparent. It is noteworthy, however, that such personal relations and the resulting resilience to negative media coverage or hostile comments did not necessarily translate into universal political attitudes. The aspiration to create a world without borders did not unite new groups of volunteers, but remained a shared objective only for a minority of activists, albeit a large and very vocal one (Karakayalı and Kleist 2016).

This personal orientation also opened up a further space for the development of political awareness. Many activists with initially humanitarian motives were disappointed and frustrated by the ways in which various levels of statehood – from federal to local – managed the crisis. In his chapter for this volume, Serhat Karakayalı shows that their involvement brought many middle-class Germans for the first time and on a daily basis into contact with the structural violence inflicted by a harsh and restrictive welfare system on non-German migrants, often with low education levels. The same German state, which seemed to be effective, fair and well organized from a middle-class perspective, suddenly appeared simultaneously as arbitrary and repressive in its interaction with the weakest members of society. Supporting refugees by accompanying them to appointments with German bureaucratic procedures emerged as a wake-up call in political education.[5]

A further step in creating political awareness was taken when a Bavarian refugee initiative called for a strike of activists across Bavaria for 1 October 2016. The Bavarian regional government had consciously cultivated a reputation for its hardline approach to refugee politics. Horst Seehofer, then the region's governor, emerged as one of the most outspoken critics of Chancellor Merkel's humanitarian response. He gained a reputation for his strongly worded – routinely even populist – statements about supposed states of emergency, a loss of control, and the decline of order and the rule of law in Germany. The strike was intended to send a strong message to Seehofer and others advocating tougher responses and measures, such as more restrictive asylum legislation, which was passed in October 2015 and February 2016; the so-called Integration Law then passed in July 2016. Experts familiar with Germany's asylum legislation, such as the Council for Migration (Rat für Migration), criticized all three pieces of legislation strongly.[6] Official statements, released to explain the pan-Bavarian strike day of volunteers and activists in the refugee sector, were equally scathing of the haste and harshness of new asylum legislation intended, first of all, to deter more people from seeking refuge in Germany:

> The aim of this warning strike is to send a strong message to politicians that this has to come to an end. The legislative initiatives and the continuing tightening of laws put severe strain on refugees as well as on activists. The seemingly haphazard implementation of the Integration Law, in particular with regard to restrictions concerning the choice of residency, confronts us with a situation that compels us to act. (Doris Schlüter; Integrationshilfe LLäuft)

This initiative, based in the Bavarian city of Landsberg, mobilized activists, as well as public sentiment, by highlighting that the new legislation had profound practical consequences that would render the work of volunteers more difficult and was prohibiting, or at least decelerating, processes of integration. The message of the strike was: we are managing the situation if you just let us do our work and abstain from creating an atmosphere of distrust (Sonnenschein 2016). The one-day strike action made it clear that integration is not a straightforward one-way process, for which only newcomers are responsible, being required to reorient their cultural and other behaviours. On the contrary, the state – through legislation and the work of institutions – is chiefly responsible for successful integration. This strike day was an important event: for the first time, initiatives from the refugees-welcome movement used one of the classical tools of social action to mobilize on nonlocal levels.

Sensitivity Regarding Diverse Dimensions of Humanitarianism

It was noticeable that many volunteers and activists displayed high sensitivity with regard to what I want to call the traps of humanitarian assistance. These traps are often a product of the dichotomy between helpers and the helped: this division can create a situation in which the latter find themselves forced into passive and even degrading positions, from which an obligation to be grateful and compliant seems to derive. Many projects were very aware of the risks regarding relationships and the development of solidarity that could stem from perceived hierarchy, and sought solutions to address unwelcome feelings of dependence and forced passivity. Internet-based projects in particular emphasized the necessity of empowerment on the part of refugees. By giving everyone equal and uncomplicated access to information, such initiatives sought to render asylum seekers autonomous and thus able to reject more hierarchical forms of aid or assistance. Theatre projects emphatically provided public spaces and forums that would allow refugees to have a voice of their own, telling their stories without being restricted or expected to be grateful.

We found a shared concern among activists and volunteers in their aspiration to show commitment not simply to the refugee cause, although this certainly played a decisive role in the early phase, but rather to work towards a more generic and universal 'better society'. Naturally, we did also find a number of projects and initiatives that continued to depict and treat refugees first of all as passive victims in need of outside support – but they were a small minority. Overall, our study found a remarkable process of learning since the mid 1990s regarding this issue. Stefan Dünnwald's (2006) excellent ethnography of a neighbourhood initiative that took care of refugees in the 1990s illustrates the prevalence of a very different set of attitudes and objectives among volunteers: the dominant view was shaped by pedagogical and charitable concerns, combined with an unquestioned othering of asylum seekers as people in need of support and attention. In the wake of the new millennium, however, new forms of cooperation between left-wing activists, who emphasized the political implications of charitable and hierarchical assistance, and neighbourhood initiatives seems to have led to heightened sensitivity. Novel approaches to cooperation uniting activists from more traditionally German and non-German backgrounds may have contributed to this process.

In such changes, we see a tendency that could be characterized as a transformation of humanitarianism. Didier Fassin (2012) has arguably been the most prominent critic of humanitarianism. He has argued that the focus on assistance and support only serves to depoliticize inequality and domination, because humanitarian measures would replace political struggle. Simultaneously, Fassin has shown that charity merely entrenches hierarchies between recipients and donors, thereby reinforcing dependencies. Knowingly or unknowingly referencing Fassin's arguments, many of the activists with whom we spoke were keen to illustrate their awareness of the problematic dimensions of charitable assistance. By developing alternative models of support, often in cooperation with the people concerned, they put Fassin's critique into practice. Refugees-welcome initiatives thus critiqued one of the most powerful ideas of our time and designed better alternatives.

Opening up to the World

Another common feature of initiatives was that they were opening up the local arena to the world: through the encounter with refugees and their biographies, local populations were confronted in a drastic way with the real consequences of global politics, creating new understandings of connectedness and the production of local worlds. The initiatives we examined were 'glocal' – combining global and local realities – and thus transcended the parochialism that can often characterize local projects. Refugees-welcome projects provide unique civic education through insights into global entanglements.

Karakayalı and Kleist (2016) have shown that many refugees-welcome activists were conscious of the problematic dimensions of culturalism. Instead, curiosity and openness with regard to the newcomers and their own cultural behaviours were predominant. Many initiatives also showed particular interest in the possibility of intercultural training. The authors highlighted that the much-expressed desire to understand difference challenges a way of thinking that interprets differences primarily as deficits. The new forms of local identity that emerge in such contexts have been described as 'progressive localism' (MacKinnon et al. 2010). The concept takes up Doreen Massey's (1994) relational approach to the local and gives it a political twist: Massey had argued that 'what gives place its specificity is not some long internalised history but the fact that it is constructed out of a particular constellation of social relations, meeting and weaving together at a particular locus . . . this . . . allows a sense of place which is extroverted, which includes a consciousness of its links with the wider world, which integrates in a positive way the global and the local' (Massey 1994: 154f). According to this theory, local identity refers less to homogeneous and clearly bounded places than to the process of localizing global phenomena. Local uniqueness thus emerges as the result of interactions involving places and social relations. This is evident for multicultural and creative neighbourhoods, such as Berlin-Kreuzberg or Berlin-Neukölln, which derive their identities from being places where the world meets; it is also evident with regard to economic actors – for example, in the case of a certain location that prides itself on hosting the headquarters of a globally operating company. Now, local communities pride themselves on their success in integrating refugees, thereby contributing in a very specific way to managing a global crisis. In these places, a glocal identity emerges. The local collective is not defined by boundaries with the outside, but rather by the specific ways in which it incorporates the global outside into a local sense of 'we'. This is a particularly significant development since it provides an alternative localist imagination to emergent populist localisms.

Voicing

A central element of the citizens' movement concerns self-organized projects by refugees, called *Flüchtlingsproteste* (refugee protest) in German: a movement of noncitizens or a refugee movement. These initiatives are a particularly important part of the citizens' movement, since the vulnerable position of refugees makes them extremely sensitive with regard to power structures related to, or derived from, social positions. Departing from their own precarious position, new practices are developed, or existing practices are appropriated, in order to make oneself heard and promote a change in perspective. The contributions of these self-organized groups lie in their questioning of hardenings that affect all movements. They name and criticize the global dependencies that forced them to flee and they put their hopes in the formation of a civil society that makes itself heard and questions political or economic. Like the citizens' movement as a whole, the refugee movement is pluralistic, global and diverse, and speaks with many voices. It is obvious that the critique coming from members of this group often hurts, for example, by questioning feminist approaches from the angle of a wider human rights perspective. At the same time, it is crucial that self-organized projects cooperate with others in the citizens' movement: this creates the critical mass that expresses the right to have rights collectively and thus amplifies that demand for a wider public. This is the precondition for a speech act that does not simply happen, but also creates a new reality (Austin 1979 [1962]).

One can argue that the self-organized projects turn the citizens' movement into a *citizens' movement* in the proper sense of the term, i.e. a movement of *citoyens* who fight for the right to have rights, for equality and freedom of all.

A New Type of Political Movement?

Reviewing these shared aspects of the refugees-welcome movement, a shift in political orientation becomes apparent. The eight core characteristics are clearly political, since they refer to issues regarding the political community as a whole: the vision of an open society; new forms of solidarity; social laboratories in which new ways of addressing societal challenges can be tested; new political alliances overcoming established divides; a personal and concrete approach (implying critique of the alienating categories on which politics is often assumed to be founded); new sensitivities to hierarchies; worlding; and a new sense of social responsibility. All of these aspects shape new forms of political community building. However, the refugees-welcome movement is particular in its approach to politics: its actors do not focus on the transformation of power relations (emancipation, resistance), but rather on practices of solidarity. Through this emphasis on the nature of political community, refugees-welcome initiatives echo the fragments of a philosophy of the political formulated by Hannah Arendt during the late phase of her life. In her writings, Arendt highlighted the task – and challenge – of politics as the establishment and organization of communities of diversity, rather than the reorganization of power relations between the dominant and the dominated (Arendt 1993: 14). 'Politics deals with the coexistence of the different' (Arendt 1993: 9, my translation). In a way, the eight characteristics described above seem to spell out Arendt's vision in a practical way. The refugees-welcome movement therefore ought to be characterized as a citizens' movement.

In order to grasp the specificity of such a citizens' movement, it is helpful to emphasize the contrast with other types. Social movement theory distinguishes classical social movements, which seek to advance the social rights of discriminated groups, from new social movements, which focus on concrete solutions to particular societal problems (Roth and Rucht 2008; Rucht 1997). Both classical and new social movements are characterized by: (1) the formulation of political demands that (2) address political stakeholders at a (3) national or international level in order to influence (4) political agenda setting or the framing of problems. In these movements, (5) charismatic leadership usually plays an important role in giving a prominent 'face'. The central strategy to reach certain goals is (6) mass mobilization through political rallies or demonstrations, which usually go hand in hand with (7) processes of identity formation. The key difference between classical and new social movements lies in the fact that the former tend to create strong identities (workers, women, LGBTQ), whereas the latter are characterized by 'one issue' approaches, which permit different combinations and alliances (rainbow coalitions) and create space for multiple, or hybrid, political identities.

In the 2000s, some authors suggested adding a third category – practice movements (Bayat 2000; Eckert 2015; Lanz 2016). Their political characters would be found less in the formulation of explicit demands than in concrete practices advanced by multitudes to appropriate certain rights. Examples would include the occupation of public territory (Bayat 2000), squatter settlements (Holston 2007) or the insistence on freedom of movement (de Genova 2009; Mezzadra 2006). These practice-oriented activities put an emphasis less on critique than on appropriation. In her overview, Eckert demanded broadening the concept of the political in order to do justice to practice movements:

> The attention to social movements once overcame the narrow focus on formal political institutions to come to an understanding of political processes. For an adequate understanding of the realm of politics, however, we need to expand our perspective even further and look beyond organized collective action to include the transformative aspects of the practices of practice movements on normative and institutional structures. (Eckert 2015: 571)

By adding the citizens' movement to the classification of social movements, I draw on this creative approach to the political. With the practice movements, the citizens' movement shares its local and pragmatic objectives. The citizens' movement is not characterized by mass demonstrations or rallies to voice demands, but by concrete acts through which local institutions are created or appropriated and transformed. Similar to practice movements, refugees-welcome initiatives address problems locally, even though their origins lie at the national and international levels. Neither practice nor citizens' movements, however, seek to transform these root causes. There are hardly any attempts to influence political agenda setting, although critique is outspoken and explicit. In contrast to practice movements, the carrier of a citizens' movement is not a particular group (which articulates a general problem through practical engagement), but a broad coalition of citizens from different backgrounds. In this respect, a

Table 12.1 Typology of social movements.

Phase	Aim: improvement of situation of own group	Aim: improvement of society at large
Focus: practical solutions	*Practice movements*	*Citizens' movements*
Focus: political demands	*Classical social movements*	*New social movements*

citizens' movement resembles the rainbow coalitions of new social movements (in particular, the third world movements, ecology movements or children's rights movements). Citizens' movements also share their concern to improve society as a whole rather than simply advance the position of one's group, with new social movements.[7]

If we take this into account, we might add the citizens' movement to the other types of movements.

The strengths, but also the weaknesses, of the refugees-welcome movement are its local character and down-to-earth approach. On the one hand, focus on such issues renders the movement resilient: even events such as those of New Year's Eve in Cologne or terrorist attacks in two Bavarian towns in 2016 did not undermine motivation to remain involved.[8] On the other hand, the refugees-welcome movement never managed to speak with one voice or to concentrate its efforts through a single prominent persona. In order to achieve long-term success, however, it is important that such a movement develops a national understanding of itself, as well as a distinguishable profile. A movement has to politicize in order to be able to exert political pressure. Critique resulting from first-hand experiences with political and administrative mismanagement ought to be generalized and brought into the public. Again, this would require the intensification of translocal connections. Our research project has also been an attempt to achieve such a network: it documents different approaches by diverse initiatives to make the citizens' movement visible as a whole and lay the basis for political self-understanding.

In early 2017, the movement's enormous strength in numbers had not translated into sustained and directed political pressure. If the volunteers and activists involved had coordinated efforts to stage mass rallies and formulate clear political demands, as classical or new social movements do, their impact could have been enormous. But the chance was missed.

The focus on community building ought to be complemented by a focus on empowerment, even though the task is difficult, since migration emerged as a divisive and highly contentious issue as the so-called refugee crisis developed. As a result, Germany's political camps divided along the question of how to deal with – define, police, protect, defend – national borders. Neither political position of an increasingly dichotomized debate could find acceptance among a centre-ground majority: on the one hand, we had demands for a closed border and nationally exclusivist positions, favouring national protectionism and demanding national solidarity. Such calls also managed, at least partly, to engage social questions, demanding national solidarity and alleging that refugees would threaten the welfare system. On the other hand, there emerged a radical open border and internationalist position, which, in a way, is also closely allied to neoliberal ideas; after all, global companies are much in favour of open-border policies, too. Hence, the debate produced a situation in which the meaningful alternatives were rigid and exclusive nationalism, on the one hand, or open border and free-movement neoliberalism, on the other. Positions that emphasize the social *and* the international – in other words, that develop a convincing leftist internationalist position – became a challenge.

Is the Movement Dead?

From its inception, the refugees-welcome movement was assumed to be on its last legs. The question of 'when will the mood turn?' accompanied emergent involvement since the autumn of 2015. In the wake of the New Year's Eve events in Cologne, 'the mood has turned' became a truism across media and public discourses, even though all empirical studies showed that attitudes were remaining remarkably stable. The Social Science Institute of the Protestant Church of Germany (SI EKD) examined attitudes towards refugees through four surveys (one in 2015 and three more in 2016). The researchers found slight fluctuation, but views favouring either acceptance or rejection did not change significantly. To the question 'will Germany be able to cope with the challenges posed by the acceptance of refugees?', 38.3 per cent of respondents expressed a negative assessment in November 2015 and 34.4 per cent answered negatively in August 2016. A total of 34.1 per cent expressed a positive view in November 2015, and 34.6 per cent answered 'yes' in August 2016. The number of people who could report a positive personal experience with refugees rose from 26.2 per cent in November 2015 to 37.2 per cent in August 2016 (Ahrens 2016). Similar results were obtained by the SOEP (Stimmungsbarometer zu Geflüchteten in Deutschland) survey, which measured attitudes to, and engagement in response to, refugee migration between January and August 2016 (Eisnecker and Schupp 2016). A final study by the Berlin Institute for Integration and Migration Research (BIM) confirmed previous results (Karakayalı and Kleist 2016). The claim that 'the mood has changed' was thus without scientific or other empirical evidence.

Why did the media follow this new narrative in the wake of the Cologne attacks? One reason seems to be a widespread fear among journalists of being accused of naiveté. In fact, Thomas de Maiziére, Germany's conservative Interior Minister, had already criticized journalists in August 2015 for their positive reporting on refugees-welcome initiatives, demanding a greater critical distance to replace collective enthusiasm. Among critics of Merkel's humanitarian stance, the claim that the mood would have to change sooner or later was uncontested. This finally seemed to find confirmation after New Year's Eve 2015. The moral panic triggered by events appeared to be shaped by such assumptions that a long-expected change in the public mood was now inevitable. A second reason was polarization. Surveys showed that while positive attitudes towards refugees remained stable, this was also true of negative views. In between outspoken pro-refugee and anti-refugee groups, a large section of the undecided remained (Eisnecker and Schupp 2016). The political right had been silenced temporarily by the euphoria of September 2015. Silenced discontent, however, found expression in support for the populist Alternative for Germany (AfD) party in several regional elections in 2016, in particular in East Germany. There was no growth in numbers, as surveys showed, but the discontented achieved more visibility. In the wake of the Cologne attacks, rightwingers managed to build up political pressure. A third reason is the political establishment's ambivalent reaction to the refugees-welcome movement. There was recognition and financial support for engagement by state agencies, since it compensated for state failure and helped overcome logistical challenges. On the other hand, many politicians – among them prominent conservatives, such as Horst Seehofer, then the Governor of Bavaria, and Thomas de Maizière, at the time Germany's Interior Minister – sought to suppress the AfD party by copying some of their demands: they supported tighter border controls and deterrence. Whereas Merkel had encouragingly, and repeatedly, stated that Germany would manage the challenge, many other conservative politicians expressed contrary views, fearing that any positive comment would only encourage further refugees to seek to come to the country. A political ambivalence of this kind is compatible with the claim that 'the mood has changed', since it portrays both attitudes in short succession, if not simultaneously.

Even more significant, however, was the problematic attempt by Seehofer and de Maizière to focus on numbers. The success of a politics of deterrence and tighter border controls will be judged by the number of arriving and deported refugees. The two conservative politicians were highly successful in establishing the rhetoric of numbers: even those politicians with a more favourable outlook on migration felt increasingly under pressure to consider reduction targets and even caps. In September 2016, new figures were released that showed that Germany had taken in just short of 900,000 refugees in 2015 – below the previous estimate of 1.1 million asylum seekers – and conservative politicians received the news with relief. Turning the rhetoric of numbers into the key benchmark of political success, however, is highly problematic: the implicit message is that each refugee is a problem and the more that arrive, the greater the problem will be. Furthermore, this is also a highly risky strategy, since the future is by definition uncertain, and the numbers reached in 2015 could well be surpassed again. Given the political conditions in the second half of the 2010s, as well as the uncertainties resulting from global warming and displacement, an increase in numbers is even likely. When this happens, the success of politics could be measured according to the benchmarks established by a rhetoric of numbers and would be doomed a failure. Such a development would only benefit rightwing extremists and populists, such as the AfD party or the Pegida movement. An alternative evaluation of success, of course, would have been to define successful integration on the local, regional and federal level as the benchmark to judge political performance. The future success of the refugees-welcome movement will depend on its ability to regain control over this central symbolic struggle.

Werner Schiffauer is Senior Scholar at the chair for Comparative Social and Cultural Anthropology Europa-Universität Viadrina Frankfurt/Oder, Germany. He has worked on the transformation of rural and urban Turkey, labour migration, the organization of diversity in European societies and Islam in Europe. Currently, he is studying how Germany's Ministry of the Interior develops its political approaches towards Islam. His last books were *Schule, Moschee, Elternhaus. Eine ethnologische Intervention* and *So schaffen wir das: Eine Zivilgesellschaft im Aufbruch* (coedited with Anne Eilert and Marlene Rudloff).

Notes

1. A telling example was the famous speech that the President of the Federal Republic gave on 26 April 1997, in which he called for a collective effort to overcome egocentrism and selfishness in society.
2. Other estimates are much higher. According to a survey of the Sozialwissenschaftliches Institut der Evangelischen Kirche, 8.7 per cent of the German population above the age of fourteen were actively engaged in such initiatives in May 2016, which would amount to a figure of well above five million activists (Ahrens 2016).

3. However, this was not always the case. There were also many instances in which local authorities responded critically to activist engagement, feeling threatened by the pressure of heightened and critical examination on the part of local citizens.
4. Other examples we included in our volume were in Halle, Schwäbisch-Gmünd and Norderstedt (Schiffauer et al. 2017)
5. The potential of such acts of support is not acknowledged by authors like Graf (2016) or Dyk and Misbach (2016), who argue that voluntary engagement promotes the neoliberal privatization of public services. The authors argue that voluntary expansion could lead to deprofessionalization and the disenfranchisement of refugees, who, instead of being treated as legal subjects with legitimate legal claims, would become dependent on the goodwill of ordinary citizens. By contrast, I argue that citizens' engagement can be interpreted as a reappropriation of fields of action, which had previously been monopolized by state agencies. Such acts therefore partially reverse the colonization of the life-world identified by Habermas. Graf, and Dyk and Misbach underestimate the systemic constraints characteristic of professional work, which effectively prevent relevant critique – partly because of professional blindness and partly because of the risks for job security.
6. The Asylverfahrensbeschleunigungsgesetz was criticized by experts of the Rat für Migration at the Bundespressekonferenz (Federal Press Conference) on 29 September 2015. With regard to the Asylpaket 2 legislation, see https://www.bundestag.de/doku mente/textarchiv/2016/kw08-pa-innen/408800 (retrieved 11 July 2018). With regard to the integration law, see Rat für Migration (2016).
7. Serhat Karakayalı has made a similar argument, but, taking a more historical approach, argues that the welcome-refugees movement underwent a transformation from a 'conventional social movement', in which 'help' was connected to different forms of political protest, to a civil society movement around the developments of 2015. In order to describe the focus of the latter phase, he coined the term 'civil society infra politics'. This transformation went hand in hand with a change in the composition of activists. Leftist activists had dominated the early phase; subsequently, a broad alliance of citizens representing the 'middle of society' became dominant.
8. On 22 July 2016, a young Afghan refugee injured a family of four on a local train near Würzburg. Two days later, a mentally unstable refugee turned into a suicide bomber and injured fifteen people in the city of Ansbach. In both cases, the attackers had pledged allegiance to the so-called Islamic State (ISIS or ISIL).

References

Ahrens, P.A. 2016. *Skepsis oder Zuversicht? Erwartungen der Bevölkerung zur Aufnahme von Flüchtlingen zwischen November 2015 und August 2016*. Sozialwissenschaftliches Institut der Evangelischen Kirche Deutschlands Retrieved 11 July 2018 from https://www.ekd.de/si/download/ fluechtlingsstudie-2016.pdf.
Arendt, H. 1993. *Was ist Politik? Fragmente aus dem Nachlass*. Zürich: Piper.
Austin, J.L.1979 [1962]. *Zur Theorie der Sprechakte*. Stuttgart: Reclam.
Bayat, A. 2000. 'From Dangerous Classes to Quite Rebels: Politics of the Urban Subaltern in the Global South', *International Sociology* 15: 533–57.
_____. 2010. *Life as Politics: How Ordinary People Change the Middle East*. Stanford, CA: Stanford University Press.
De Genova, N. 2009. 'Conflicts of Mobility and the Mobility of Conflict: Rightlessness, Presence, Subjectivity, Freedom', *Subjectivity* 29(1): 445–66.

Dünnwald, S. 2006. *Der pädagogische Griff nach dem Fremden*. Frankfurt: IKO – Verlag für Interkulturelle Kommunikation.

Dyk, S., and E. Misbach. 2016. 'Zur politischen Ökonomie des Helfens: Flüchtlingspolitik und Engagement im flexiblen Kapitalismus', *Prokla* 183: 205–22.

Eckert, J. 2015. 'Practice Movements. The Politics of Non-sovereign Power', in D. Della Porta and M. Diani (eds), *The Oxford Handbook of Social Movements*. Oxford: Oxford University Press, pp. 567–577.

Eilert, A. 2014. 'Bürgerschaftliches Engagement im sozialen Feld Berliner Flüchtlingsheime – Motive und Methoden von Beteiligten'. Masterarbeit. Fakultät für Kulturwissenschaften. Europa-Universität Viadrina.

Eisnecker, P., and J. Schupp. 2016. 'Flüchtlingszuwanderung: Mehrheit der Deutschen befürchtet negative Auswirkung auf Wirtschaft und Gesellschaft', *SOEP – The German Socio-Economic Panel Study at DIW*, Berlin. Retrieved 11 July 2018 from https://www.diw.de/documents/publikationen/73/diw_01.c.527676.de/16-8-4.pdf.

Fassin, D. 2012. *Humanitarian Reason. A Moral History of the Present*. Berkeley: University of California Press.

Graf, L. 2016. 'Freiwillig im Ausnahmezustand: Die ambivalente Rolle ehrenamtlichen Engagements in der Transformation des Asylregimes', *Widersprüche* 141: 87–96.

Holston, J. 2007. *Insurgent Citizenship: Disjunctions of Democracy and Modernity in Brazil*. Princeton, NJ: Princeton University Press.

Isin, E. 2008. 'Theorizing Acts of Citizenship', in E. Isin und G.M. Nielsen (eds), *Acts of Citizenship*. London: Zed Books, pp. 15–43.

Karakayalı, S. 2017 '"InfraPolitik" der Willkommensgesellschaft', *Forschungs journal Soziale Bewegungen* 3: 16–24.

Karakayalı, S., and J.O. Kleist. 2016. *EFA-Studie 2: Strukturen und Motive der ehrenamtlichen Flüchtlingsarbeit in Deutschland, Forschungsbericht: Ergebnisse einer explorativen Umfrage vom November/Dezember 2015*. Berlin: Berliner Institut für empirische Integrations- und Migrationsforschung (BIM), Humboldt-Universität zu Berlin.

Lanz, S. 2016. *Die ganze Welt der Stadt im Blick: Versuche einer pluralisierten kritischen Stadtforschung*. Frankfurt an der Oder: Europa-Universität Viadrina.

MacKinnon, D. et al. 2010. 'Rethinking Local-Central Relations: Progressive Localism, Decentralisation and Place'. *Inaugural Conference of the Sheffield Political Economy Research Institute*. Sheffield: University of Sheffield.

Massey, D. 1994. *Space, Place and Gender*. Minneapolis: University of Minnesota Press.

Mezzadra, S. 2006. *Diritto di fuga: Migrazioni, cittadinanza, globalizzazione*. Verona: ombre corte.

Rancière, J. 2002. *Das Unvernehmen: Politik und Philosophie*. Frankfurt am Main: Suhrkamp.

Rat für Migration, Pro Asyl, Paritätischer Wohlfahrtsverband, Diakonie. 2016. 'Brief an Innenminister de Maiziére', 19 May. Retrieved 11 July 2018 from http://www.rat-fuer-migration.de/pdfs/GemeinsamerBriefIntegrationsge setz.pdf.

Roth R., and D. Rucht (eds). 2008. *Neue soziale Bewegungen in der Bundesrepublik Deutschland.* Frankfurt am Main: Campus.

Rucht, D. 1997. *Modernisierung und neue soziale Bewegungen: Deutschland, Frankreich und USA im Vergleich.* Frankfurt am Main: Campus.

Schiffauer, W., A. Eilert and M. Rudloff (eds). 2017. *So schaffen wir das – eine Zivilgesellschaft im Aufbruch: 90 wegweisende Projekte mit Flüchtlingen.* Bielefeld: transcript.

Sonnenschein, Raphael. 2016. 'Interview mit Radio Dreyeckland', 30 September. Retrieved 11 July 2018 from https://rdl.de/sites/default/files/audio/2016/09/20160930-streikderehr-w6073.mp3.

Zeit Magazin. 2016. 'Was geschah wirklich', 28 June. Retrieved 11 July 2018 from http://www.zeit.de/zeit-magazin/2016/27/silvesternacht-koeln-fluechtlings debatte-aufklaerung.

Conclusion
Refugee Futures and the Politics of Difference

Sharon Macdonald

In this final chapter I offer a reflection from 2018. By now, the refugee crisis is talked about in the past tense. However, the debates that it prompted and its wider implications for German society, and beyond, continue. People seeking refuge still arrive, albeit at a lower rate. Migration remains highly contested and is never far from the top of the political agenda, with positions within Germany and elsewhere in Europe often sharply divided. Moreover, the work and experience of settlement, integration and accommodation, arising directly from the events of 2015 and 2016, as well as from earlier and subsequent movements of people, are ongoing. So too are those of displacement, differentiation and rejection. Although activities once widely reported as part of the culture of welcome are now rarely newsworthy, policies and initiatives directed at – and working with – refugees flourish.

Below, I first provide a brief update on the situation by mid 2018, three years since the beginning of the refugee crisis that is the focus of this book. Partly because my coverage is brief, it must be accompanied by a caution that it is necessarily sketchy and awaiting fuller documentation and analysis. Nevertheless, it is worth thinking about where things are at by this point, not least because this helps to provide further context for the chapters in this volume, especially for the directions that they have indicated. As part of this contextualizing reflection, I couple information from secondary sources with some of my own observations and personal experience. This includes discussion of museums and heritage – a significant

Notes for this chapter begin on page 329.

area, I argue, for the work of making differences and diversities as well as of signalling and enacting belonging. I then turn back to the volume's chapters in order to reconsider them in retrospect, including in light of the original questions posed. In particular, I revisit the question of what the events of 2015 and 2016 show about German society with respect to diversity and difference, especially whether there is change underway. As we will see, considering the collective outcome of the book also suggests other questions that might productively be asked. As such, *Refugees Welcome?* presents not only a landmark set of answers to the question of what has been going on in the run-up to, and during, the events of 2015 and 2016, but also opens up further considerations for a new research agenda.

The Long Summer of Migration and since: Figures of Interpretation

Numbers figure frequently in discussions of the refugee crisis – indeed, they are a prime mode through which it is constituted – as in those of migration more widely, and they appear frequently in this book too. There is, however, always a risk as well as a politics to presenting numbers, perhaps especially with regard to migration, as Werner Schiffauer points out in his chapter: greater numbers are easily read as producing greater difficulties, thus constituting each individual refugee or migrant as a problem or unit of difficulty. While we should not ignore quantitative effects – especially in the face of scarce resources (such as a lack of decent accommodation) – we should also be mindful of how figures are deployed, especially when they supposedly 'speak for themselves'. In practice, as so many chapters in this volume show, directly encountered numbers are not what constitute apprehensions of what is going on and perceptions of where problems lie so much as conceptual categories, actions and forms of representation. That in places such as Dresden (discussed by Jan-Jonathan Bock) with relatively low numbers of migrants, there are higher rates of perception of being overrun is just one indication of how 'geographies of fear' – to use Arjun Appadurai's term from his *Fear of Small Numbers* (2006) – produce, and are produced within, specific numerical imaginaries. This fear is shown too in relation to the assaults carried out on New Year's Eve 2015 in Cologne, which were small in number by comparison with overall national rates of violence against women, but that were given extensive media coverage (as Kira Kosnick's chapter here discusses). The point here is not to argue that smaller numbers of assaults are less disturbing, but it is in order to highlight that numbers alone have little explanatory traction. To take a different kind of example: when young people in

Berlin's Neukölln district, which is often described as having high levels of visible diversity, talk about their discomfort in going to less diverse areas, they indeed speak partly about numbers – that there are not so many 'black-heads', to use the term that they use to describe themselves, around (Tize and Reis chapter 5). But even in this case, the issue is not simply one of overall numbers and is indeed only partly about relative numbers. Rather, it entails a phenomenology of difference and familiarity in which they perceive themselves as being, or are made to feel, out of place.

With these cautions in mind, I want to introduce some post-2015 figures about arrivals of those seeking asylum – and some of their interpretations. As pointed out in the Introduction, we need to be mindful here too of terms and their connotations. Attempts to distinguish between kinds of migrants – often with ideas of a relativity of deservingness at their core – are integrally tied into acts of counting and, again, numbers help to substantiate the categories themselves (e.g. Sigona 2018). Here I mostly follow the terms that were deployed to produce the particular figures; in other words, I treat these as ethnographic objects of the field itself. Formed through such fields and processes, numbers nevertheless tell us something, especially when they change – not least about their affordance for various interpretations.

As this book's Introduction and various other chapters have already noted, the numbers officially recorded as arriving and being registered as seeking asylum or protection as war refugees (both usually referred to as 'refugees') in Germany in 2016 – 280,000 – were considerably lower than those of 2015 (890,000) and far fewer than had been predicted or feared. The year 2017 showed a further reduction of almost 100,000, to 186,000. Although presented in this way the figures seem to indicate a clear line of reduction – and that is how they have been widely proclaimed, especially by those in political power – a closer examination of the figures suggests that following higher levels during the first quarter of 2016, numbers stabilized that year and during 2017 to around 15,000 new entries per month.[1] It has also been pointed out that these figures do not include those arriving as part of resettlement programmes or family members joining those whose asylum has been granted, and that they do not take into account possible reductions in numbers of those leaving (which seem especially difficult to track). They are also distinct from arrivals by other kinds of migrants who did not seek asylum. However, the reduction in the figures of those arriving as refugees was reported widely in Germany and indeed internationally. It was hailed by those in political power, for example, Thomas de Maizière, the CDU's Interior Minister, in October 2016 as evidence that the migration process was being successfully organized and steered by the government – and that, in effect, the crisis was over.[2] This argument was often repeated, being especially expedient during the run-up to elections in 2017. By contrast, the AfD (Alternative für Deutschland) party, the far-right opponents of the government, were keen to emphasize that the overall numbers were still high and they also claimed that there were many illegal entrants who were not recorded, as well as arguing that there were many more who would be likely to come in the future.[3] For them, the crisis remained, if not so visibly, and was, moreover, part of a potentially even greater crisis to come.

Insofar as it was agreed that there was a reduction in arrivals, there were also disagreements about what this showed. Measures such as severely curtailing the Balkan and Mediterranean routes to entry were generally agreed to have made the most significant difference. But whether this was a stop-gap – a partial but probably temporary stemming of a flow – or even driving of entries underground, as the far-right claimed, or a returning to a more stable continuing situation, as, for example, the government agency dealing with migration and refugees (BAMF) suggested, or whether it was even a turnaround, as was implied by politicians such as de Maizière, was disputed. At stake, in effect, were different assessments not only of the existing situation but also of competing visions of likely future trajectories.

Presence and Absence in Public Space

Despite arguments about the figures, the reduction of numbers of arrivals that they show since early 2016 has been matched by considerably reduced media coverage of 'the refugee issue'. During the long summer of migration in Germany, often harrowing stories of those making their way to Europe and images of makeshift accommodation were the main news items almost every day. In Berlin – I speak here from my own observations and discussions with others – almost every opening speech at public and academic events, whatever the topic, contained some statement about refugees – usually to the importance of welcoming them, and numerous talks and events were specifically dedicated to considering their plight. Theatres – in which the idea of the category 'post-migrant' (discussed in this volume for society in general by Naika Foroutan and specifically for theatre by Jonas Tinius) had already been strongly articulated – staged works not only about the refugee situation but also involving refugees, as Jonas Tinius describes.

Dramatic works could also escape institutional walls, becoming part of a larger set of artistic interventions in public space – making the plight of refugees impossible to overlook. In February 2016, the Chinese dissident artist Ai Weiwei wrapped Berlin's Concert House – located in the centrally located and upmarket Gendarmenmarkt – in orange lifejackets, salvaged from beaches in Southern Europe and worn by those who had crossed the dangerous waters to reach them (e.g. Dasser 2016). Also in Berlin's centre, the art collective Center for Political Beauty staged a particularly chilling work in mid 2016 called 'Eating Refugees – Distress and Circuses' (*Flüchtlinge Fressen – Not und Spiele*).[4] This was organized in collaboration with the Maxim Gorki Theater, whose director had set a highly political agenda, including influentially deploying an idea of the postmigrant. The first that my colleagues and I knew about the work, however, was when we walked one warm evening up to the Main Building of the Humboldt-Universität, next to the Maxim Gorki Theater, and were puzzled by some strange guttural and anxiety-inducing sounds. These came, we were astounded to discover, from live tigers, contained in large cages near the Theater, which paced under the eye of a keeper dressed as a Roman centurion. A lit-up countdown showed the number of days until when a refugee – who had volunteered to be eaten – would be fed to the tigers unless a plane of Syrian refugees stranded in Turkey due to a legal clause that had played a part in lowering numbers of asylum-seeker arrivals (by making travel from Turkey to the European Union without a visa illegal for them) was allowed to take off. The previous year, the Center for Political Beauty had already performed another dramatic work to bring the refugee crisis to public and political attention. In *The Dead are Coming*, they staged funerals in Berlin for refugees who had died on their way to Germany, whose bodies they exhumed in Southern Europe. One part of this work consisted of a planned *Memorial for the Unknown Refugee*, to be constructed in front of the Reichstag, the seat of the German parliament. Inspired by the call, about 5,000 people turned up to begin digging – before police interventions and arrests stopped them. While these political art works were staged in central Berlin, they received widespread media coverage far beyond. Moreover, there were many further works elsewhere. These included thousands of graves for unknown refugees that were dug all over Europe, inspired by the Center's *Memorial for the Unknown Refugee*.

Since 2016, there have been other art works that have acted as reminders of refugees' existence and situation, even while the widespread news coverage has largely subsided. These include, notably, the work 'Monument' by the Syrian-German artist Manaf Halbouni, consisting of three up-ended buses that had been used as a barricade against sniper-fire in Aleppo.[5] First unveiled in Dresden in February 2017, these entered into precisely the distinctive and fraught memory culture described by Jan-Jonathan Bock in his chapter in this volume. Positioned near the

Figure 13.1 *The Dead are Coming; Memorial for the Unknown Refugee.* Photo by Nick Jaussi. Reproduced courtesy of the Center for Political Beauty.

Figure 13.2 *Monument* by Manaf Halbouni. Photo by Sharon Macdonald.

Frauenkirche (the Church of Our Lady) – reconstructed only decades after its destruction by the Allies in the Second World War – it was condemned by conservative Dresdeners, as well as AfD and Pegida members, as an affront to the city's own memory of suffering, even while others saw in it a potential for solidarity across times and spaces of distress (e.g. Oltermann 2017). Later that year, with little opposition, it was shown in Berlin, next to the Brandenburg Gate – where tourists stopped to pose for photographs against it. Alongside these high-profile and often hotly contested works are many other artistic and creative projects and initiatives that receive less coverage, but that nevertheless act not just as reminders of refugee presence, but also as modalities through which refugees themselves may potentially define their own subject positions within German society, as the chapters here by Damani J. Partridge and Jonas Tinius show in different ways. Some such projects were already underway in 2015, as these two chapters show, sometimes as part of longstanding work with migrants. Such projects have continued, perhaps shifting their focus from issues of arrival and immediate settling in to ones of more long-term negotiation of belonging and difference. In this, these kinds of initiatives are like many others in wider public space that continue, but without so much fanfare – yet with important consequences for the lives of those directly involved, as for German society more widely.

From Welcome to Integration

By now, most of those seeking asylum are no longer housed in emergency accommodation, such as school sports halls and airport hangars, as they were until well into 2016, and the calls for clothing and bedding are no longer being made with frequency or urgency. Nevertheless, while the frontline volunteer work described by Serhat Karakayalı and Werner Schiffauer has been scaled back, as they both note, considerable numbers of initiatives – as with artistic initiatives – remain or have even been begun since then. In Berlin, for example, the refugee church described by Jan-Jonathan Bock continues its work. Its emphasis is still on shared activities in which refugees and volunteers participate across differences between them, coupled with the provision of practical assistance.[6] Its main webpage lists sessions on giving advice about how to apply for asylum, alongside events in which there are opportunities to cook 'international dinners' together. More widely too, services offering help with accommodation and language learning abound.[7] Although little reported, such activities – and many people giving their time to help – continue. This suggests that the changes triggered by the refugee crisis – and perhaps especially an accommodation of difference – may be continuing in slower, less obviously perceptible ways.

In addition, there is the more long-term settling into everyday life for those who have been granted leave to stay.[8] While many of those given such leave are no longer housed in emergency accommodation, they are likely to still be in substandard housing, such as 'container villages', namely accommodation made of shipping containers.[9] As one inhabitant was reported as saying about the latter: 'if the baby cried at night, everybody woke up' (*Der Spiegel* 2017). Accomodating refugees together puts them with others with whom they will share a situation, but it ignores differences of culture, religion, nationality and class between them – differences that have sometimes led to tensions within refugee camps. Furthermore, it simultaneously separates them from other parts of German society. The system of distribution of refugees to different parts of the country can lead to families, as well as those from the same places, being split up. Moreover, being housed away from others from the same country certainly does not ensure acceptance or integration, as the occasional coverage of such cases by journalists reveals (*Der Spiegel* 2017).

Gaining work is widely recognized as an important step in enabling refugees and former refugees to participate as citizens. However, the 2018 figures from the BAMF show that only 10 per cent of 2015 arrivals and 6 per cent of 2016 arrivals had gained employment. Nevertheless, the text accompanying these figures is relatively upbeat, pointing out that 31 per cent of 2013 arrivals had done so (see also *Der Spiegel* 2017). An analysis by the *Financial Times*, however, shows that the majority who came in 2015 and 2016 have been moved to parts of the country where rates of unemployment are relatively high, so even though there are many initiatives that are supposed to prepare those recently arrived for work, the locational odds stack against them too (Romei et al. 2017). Even where work is available, as the BAMF surveys show, employers regard insufficient German language skills as the main obstacle to employing those who came to Germany as refugees (BAMF 2017) – supporting Uli Linke's observations in this volume that language often provides the key fault line in maintaining boundaries between Germans and those who Damani Partridge, in his chapter in this volume, calls 'noncitizens'.

Both Linke and Partridge, in different ways, make the point that citizenship is not just a matter of legal definition, but of recognition and of effective participation in society. Rather than seeing it as an absolute state – one is a citizen or not – it is more helpful analytically to regard it as a matter of degree, as has been argued, for example, by Nick Stevenson (2003). Integration – which is how debates are often framed in Germany – may be usefully considered as a matter of citizenship in this sense (though see Bojadžijev and Karakayalı 2007). Below, I look further at what contributors to *Refugees Welcome?* variously argue about integration and possible transformations underway in German society before and during the refugee crisis. Before doing so, however, I offer a brief interlude on the subject of heritage and museums, which operate as significant institutions of citizenly recognition and whose roles in relation to refugees, asylum seekers and migrants more generally are therefore deserving of attention.

Heritage, Museums and Recognition

In introducing this section, I should explain that I myself moved in the summer of 2015 from the United Kingdom to Berlin to take up a Professorship at the Humboldt-Universität (it insists that its German name should be used) and to establish the Centre for Anthropological Research on Museums and Heritage (CARMAH).[10] As part of this, I also launched a research project called 'Making Differences: Transforming Museums and Heritage in the 21st Century'. Drawn up considerably earlier, my project outline was concerned with the ways in which museums and heritage were changing, especially in relation to trying to recognize greater cultural diversity, particularly that produced by migration, and postcolonial challenge. How ideas, practices and experiences of difference and belonging might be changing in Germany was therefore a central concern. What was unanticipated, however, was the scale of the events in 2015, which made it feel imperative to consider these concerns through the prism of the refugee crisis and the long summer of migration. At the point at which Jan-Jonathan Bock and I began organizing the workshop, however, I had not appointed any researchers to the project and we were not aware of anybody already conducting work on the refugee crisis in relation to museums and heritage in Germany. This is perhaps not surprising in view of the more pressing immediate needs faced by refugees, as well as the often longer timescales of museum and heritage developments than those of theatre and art works. Nevertheless, I regarded the workshop and this subsequent book as an important part of that research project – setting out wider contexts and questions that would be of major relevance for examining museum and heritage transformations in Germany.

This should be seen as supplementing the now sizeable literature looking at questions of cultural diversity, migration and citizenship in relation to museums and heritage (see, for example, Gouriévidis 2014; MELA 2015; Whitehead et al. 2015). A central focus in this literature is on how already established museum- and heritage-scapes – which were generally produced to uphold ideas of distinct, stable and relatively homogeneous cultural (and especially national) identities – can respond to the cultural diversity of their national or local populations. This is also a very practical and indeed pressing question for many museums and heritage sites themselves. At issue is how they can or should today fulfil their societal roles of shaping and encouraging citizenship in recognition of cultural and other forms of difference. By looking at how museums and heritage organizations understand their remits and how they seek to meet them, as well as by examining the challenges that they face in doing so, it is possible to gain a deeper understanding of how difference and diversity are being tackled – and indeed produced – in practice.

Here I should note that while the terms 'difference' and 'diversity' are used in various ways, including by the contributors to this book – we did not seek to impose uniformity – I have found it useful in the Making Differences project to distinguish them as follows. 'Difference' I take to indicate the various kinds of distinctions between people that are made in practice and that are often but not always expressed via naming – so differences might be made, for example, between Germans and non-Germans, to use the title of one of the parts of this book. 'Diversity', however, is a particular model of society and/or culture that understands it as being made up of many various kinds – many differences. Analytically, as I see it and as is the case in many chapters in this volume, it is important to attend to both of these. That is, we need to look both at the kinds of differences that are invoked – for example, in policy-making, media representation or everyday encounters, and also at the models of difference, i.e. diversity, that they articulate. How diversity itself is imagined also needs attention. It might, for example, be regarded as consisting of distinct communities, each being accorded their own cultural expression – a multicultural model of diversity – or as entailing the creation of new and hybrid forms that do not solidify into such community distinctions. It might be seen as possible to accommodate with unity and solidarity – or as running against it. In this volume, we see, in effect, different such models being played out in practice. As Jonas Tinius argues for the case of theatre, museums and heritage are important to consider because of their capacity to offer up and reflect upon such models – to act, in effect, as 'theorizers' of difference and diversity within society (see also Macdonald 1996, 2016). Because museums and heritage representations may be around for a long time and because they are usually imbued with a particular kind of authority, their role here is likely to be especially significant.

Let me here briefly note some of the initiatives of museums in Berlin during the refugee crisis. As yet, these have been relatively short-term – that is, activities such as guided tours or temporary exhibitions rather than permanent galleries – though some collecting, in order to document the events of 2015 and 2016 for posterity, has begun. Nevertheless, they are significant as indications of attempts to take on socially active roles and to include those who have not been accorded full citizenship.

Given considerable press coverage was an initiative called *Multaka as Meeting Point* (in German: *Multaka: Treffpunkt Museum*), the Arabic word Multaka meaning 'meeting point'.[11] Begun in December 2015, it sought to train refugees or migrants, especially from Syria and Iraq, to act as guides for tours by newly arrived refugees in four of the major museums in the centre of Berlin: the Bode Museum, the German Historical Museum, the Museum of Ancient Near-Eastern Cultures and the Museum of Islamic Art. The idea behind this, as explained by Stefan Weber, Director of the Museum of Islamic Art and a main instigator of the project, was that:

Through experiencing the appreciation which the museum shows towards cultural artifacts from their [i.e. refugees' and migrants'] homelands, we hope to strengthen the self-esteem of refugees and allow for confident and constructive connection with our cultural institutions. (Weber n.d.: 1)

Moreover, in a clear articulation of the idea of how the initiative could facilitate integration, he explained:

Cultural self-affirmation is in the debate on immigration always designated as an obstacle to integration. We believe the opposite is the case: if one feels appreciated – feels included and not excluded – one can get into society much easier. Refugees conquer the Museum Island and make this country with its cultural institutions their own. The step in the museums and the active(!) discussion of our common historical heritage is the first step to wave new threads of belonging into one's own cultural garb. Democracy is based on responsible citizen participation. *Multaka* facilitate cultural participation and encourage this participation on the way to be an active member of our society. (Weber n.d.: 5)

From an in-depth ethnographic study conducted by Rikke Gram (2018) in connection with the Making Differences project, it is clear that this attempt to position refugees and migrants more fully as citizens was appreciated by some of those who participated and that it helped in other areas of their identity-affirmation, as well as in practical networking. At the same time, however, some of its potential was reduced by, for example, the idea that refugees and migrants would give tours specifically for other refugees, thus limiting their participation to that with other not-full-citizens and marking it off as distinct from regular museum activity.

Nevertheless, this remains an important development and it still continues. It exists alongside other, less high-profile but nevertheless significant initiatives. This includes work done by the Neukölln Museum – in the

Figure 13.3 Participants in a guided tour of the project *Multaka as Meeting Point* in the German Historical Museum. Photo copyright Milena Schlösser, the National Museums in Berlin and the Museum of Islamic Art. Used with permission.

Figure 13.4 KUNSTASYL's rehearsal in their exhibition *daHEIM: Glances into Fugitive Lives* at the Museum of European Cultures. Photo by Katarzyna Puzon. Reproduced courtesy of Barbara Caveng, KUNSTASYL, and the National Museums in Berlin and the Museum of European Cultures.

highly diverse district of Berlin studied by Tize and Reis in this volume. Under the directorship of Udo Gößwald, including objects and stories from migrants and refugees has long been business as usual for this museum and is also part of its everyday work with a highly diverse secondary school next door.[12] That is one reason why it was well placed to become a destination for visits from 'welcome classes' (*Willkommensklassen*) of refugees as part of integration initiatives, providing information about German culture as well as the opportunity to practise the German language. As Jan-Jonathan Bock and I witnessed in December 2015, a peach stone carved with a dove from a refugee from Syria in the 1990s was capable of evoking considerable interest from a class of unaccompanied minors, all boys, and meeting for a lunch hosted by teenagers at the local school was clearly a very welcome opportunity for conviviality (see also Bock 2015).

There have also been instances of refugees being substantially involved in the making of exhibitions – a still more extensive form of participation. One example here is a temporary exhibition called *daHEIM: Einsichten in flüchtige Leben* (*daHEIM: Glances into Fugitive Lives*), which was held at the Museum of European Cultures in Berlin for a year from July 2016.[13] It involved residents from a hostel for asylum seekers who worked with artist Barbara Caveng, in a project called *Kunstasyl* (meaning *Art Asylum*), to produce the exhibition, and also accompanying events such as a series of performances at the Museum. Although the exhibition was temporary, some of the objects from it have become part of the permanent collection.

Refugees Welcome? A Changing Germany?

In these initiatives we see, then, attempts to welcome refugees and not simply make them the object of representation, but to also involve them, to put them in the position of participants and creators, albeit to varying degrees. Even though refugees are not formally citizens, such initiatives afford them at least some possibility of active participation, as well as opportunities to imagine themselves into future belonging within Germany. The latter is, I suggest, one of the most crucial dimensions of a welcome capable of extending beyond arrival moments. It is needed in order to transcend the refugee status itself – without being required to forget that personal and political history.

This is not exclusive to the museum and heritage context. It can be seen too in some of the initiatives and longer-term developments discussed in the chapters in this book, and it is consonant with the 'postmigrant paradigm' set out by Naika Foroutan. It entails a humanistic

awareness of possibilities of connection – potentials for solidarities that
are not confined to ethnic or other identity categories, and especially
not to the divide between migrants and non-migrants. Chapters here
show many examples of initiatives and developments that offer up this
potential. These include the collective activities organized for volunteers
and refugees at the refugee church in Berlin (Bock). They also include
the work of the refugee theatre in Mülheim, in which participants are
not supposed to act themselves, but must adopt the subject positions
that are not their own in order – so it is claimed – to better enable them
to forge new connections with others (Tinius). Also holding promise
for transcending the immediacies of the refugee crisis and new migration arrival is the vernacular creativity witnessed by Petra Kuppinger in
her long-term research with Muslim communities in Stuttgart. Her work
shows well how it is possible for there to be distinctiveness of religious
and cultural practice – and senses of identification as Muslim in this
case – but without this being either only about the maintenance of tradition or acting as a boundary with the rest of society. Rather, it is the very
distinctive practices themselves that become the source for new creativity
through which their practitioners actively participate in urban civic life.
This is a crucially important possibility – one that holds much potential
for hope for the future. It is worth noting here too that this kind of activity is relatively 'quiet' and easily goes unnoticed. Research such as that
undertaken by Kuppinger is vital for bringing it to wider attention. Other
types of in-depth research and analysis reveal continuing forms of exclusion and inhibitions to participation that may operate in practice – even
in contexts in which one might have expected them to have been transcended. Young people whose parents came to Germany as refugees or
other kinds of migrants who themselves were born and/or brought up
here might, for example, be expected to feel senses of belonging to the
country. But as the ethnographic research of Tize and Reis in Berlin's
Neukölln district shows, they do not, and, moreover, they use the
term 'Germans' (who they sometimes specify as 'real' or 'blue-eyed')
as different from themselves (who they self-refer to as 'black-heads').
They do, however, have a strong sense of belonging with Neukölln
itself – something that on the one hand means that they do imagine
their futures within Germany, but on the other limits this to the more
localized area.

   The ways in which exclusion may continue is also emphatically illustrated by Gökce Yurdukul's identification of continuing modes of stigmatization of Jews and Muslims – produced, for example, through the ways
in which positions in debate over circumcision are articulated. Likewise,
Uli Linke's argument about how ideas of German language purity can

be mobilized as boundaries to inclusion shows this at work even in relation to apparent moves towards diversification. Neither discusses the term *biodeutsch* – 'biologically German' – that came into use in the 2000s, but its spread in some ways illustrates their claims of the pervasiveness of attempts to identify 'real Germans' against 'others' (see Müller 2011). Although it has often been used ironically or by those who would not identify as *biodeutsch*, it easily slips, even in relatively self-aware and politically progressive contexts, into a handy use for those who are assumed to lack a 'migratory background', as I have witnessed directly in academic and cultural political discussions.

These kinds of divisions – and especially a strong bounding of 'German society' against Muslims – were frequently revived and intensified during the refugee crisis. The anti-Islam group Pegida, discussed by Bock, also drew new energy and membership in the face of the crisis. Indeed, the very characterization of the arrival of larger numbers of migrants as a 'crisis' supported their wider calls for the need for special measures and added urgency to their claims about the inadequacy of the existing political establishment. It also fed into a crystallization of conceptual boundaries between Germans – or Europeans – and 'others', especially Muslims, as part of an imagined protection of the former in the face of physical and geographical boundaries that were perceived as being breached. This was further entrenched through its mapping onto the breach of bodily boundaries, as in the New Year's Eve rape accusations in Cologne, as Kira Kosnick shows. Like other moral panics, as she argues, the refugee crisis brought certain 'endemic fears' and lines of social fission to the surface. This has continued since, sometimes relatively in the background, but periodically this is brought forcefully to the fore again, especially in relation to terrorist attacks, such as that on a Berlin Christmas market in December 2016. Such shocking but also unusual events readily become a lens through which refugees or migrants or Muslims *tout court* are viewed and thus implicitly, and sometimes explicitly, cast as suspected rapists or terrorists. However, it was not only in relation to such episodes or stark divisions, or even only in hostile or sensationalist contexts, that the refugee crisis revived or produced divisions and exclusions between Germans and others. Bock's sensitive analysis of the refugee church volunteers' disappointment and puzzlement at the behaviour of those they were seeking to help shows well how this can operate in the detail of everyday practice, as well as in the most well-meaning of circumstances. Partridge's insightful dissection of the very ideas of hospitality – and the mobilization of 'pity' that these often entailed – likewise shows how acts of 'trying to help' can bring not only exclusions but also implicit hierarchies and senses of superiority with them.

Both Serhat Karakayalı and Werner Schiffauer draw on extensive quantitative and qualitative studies of participation in the culture of welcome, in part in order to try to grasp whether it does indeed indicate a significant change underway in German society. Karakayalı, providing in-depth analysis of motivations given for participation in welcoming activities, asks whether the participation amounts to a political action. The answer, he suggests, is ambivalent. While many express opposition to rightwing populism, most do not go further in articulating their positions politically, and while the idea of solidarity with refugees as part of a historical memory of Germans as expellees during and after the Second World War (i.e. that of the *Vertriebene*) is made in the public sphere, this rarely seemed to be articulated by research respondents. Schiffauer, by contrast, argues more strongly that the actions did add up to a new social movement and, as such, a significant political action that runs counter to so many other social trends, such as increasing individualization and atomization, and the widespread xenophobia and racism that have been characteristic of the growth of new far-right nationalism across Europe, exemplified by Pegida and the AfD in Germany. More specifically, he argues that features including the culture of welcome's setting out of a new vision for society, its forging of alliances across political divides and its fostering of new forms of social responsibility amount to a specific kind of social movement, namely a citizens' movement. While this allows for and even embraces diversity, it does not seek to bring about more far-reaching political change. In this reservation, Schiffauer's conclusion is not, perhaps, so far from that of Karakayalı. At the time of writing in 2018, this translation of the citizens' movement into something more political seems no further advanced. Nevertheless, those hopes and actions towards solidarity across difference remain an important indication of at least one direction of change that is underway – even if it is not the only one or the only possible one for the future.

Directions

We were aware in editing this book that we could have put the chapters in various orders – and indeed we did so several times – and that the order might suggest some directions of social change over others. Ending with Schiffauer's chapter does not exactly provide a happy ending, though it is relatively hopeful and that seems a good place to end. But the volume certainly does not add up to presenting a single developmental trajectory. Rather, it highlights different coexisting currents; some relatively longstanding and others newer. It shows some evidence for a greater embracing of diversity and perhaps even glimmers of a more ramifying political change that would allow for even greater solidarity and civic participation. But it also reveals persistent and even additional barriers towards achieving these – barriers not only erected by rightwing populists but also, unexpectedly, sometimes in welcome initiatives themselves. Highlighting and understanding this complexity – and in its intricacies of practice – is a major contribution of this book. We need to understand the detail of actual engagements in order to more accurately identify the ways of thinking and acting that can reinforce problematic positions and outcomes. Doing so is vital for more successful future integration efforts and initiatives.

We need to ask, then, not just whether there is change underway, but also what kinds of change. What are its diverse currents and its limitations? Important too is the question of where change for the better may lie, even if we have not yet seen its full potential realized. This book has, we believe, provided original research towards all of these. It has done so by bringing together a range of disciplinary expertise, methodologies and research focuses. These include some studies over relatively long periods of time, thus helping to get a handle on more durable continuities as well as possible ruptures, and also recent studies directly of the events of 2015 and 2016. Attempts to identify existing and also possible models for thinking and doing integration and diversity are included alongside empirically rich studies of what is going on. These latter include wider survey work and analyses of media representations, as well as more specifically focused ethnographic studies. The scope of who is studied ranges from rightwing populists to volunteers in welcome movements, from policy-makers to cultural workers, from longstanding migrant communities to more recent refugees and asylum seekers. This is a considerable coverage of a recent and as yet only very partially addressed set of developments. It constitutes, we hope, a significant intervention into ongoing debate.

The debate is not restricted to Germany. Questions of refugees and migration, and of changing configurations of difference and diversity, are of global significance. Finding ways of living optimally together while recognizing the experience and self-definition of difference is a major challenge worldwide. Within Europe at present this challenge is especially pressing – not least in the face of the rise of rightwing nationalisms and populist movements, whose 'solutions' to difference are generally to eliminate or contain it. Other approaches – capable of addressing fears rather than simply dismissing them – are desperately needed. Pointing to cases of peaceful cultural co-existence, conviviality and creative enrichment through diversity, reminding of 'successful' earlier migration experiences, understanding and openly addressing anxieties, and developing practices to allow these to happen, can all contribute here. As this book has shown, the situation even in one country is complex and cannot be settled with one fix; but as it has also shown, there are specific approaches and initiatives that can help.

How European countries respond to the needs of those escaping harsh regimes has major consequences for the lives of many, including, obviously, those of refugees and other migrants but extending far beyond them. Within border areas, 'hot spots' and in areas where many refugees have arrived, life is changed not only by the presence of 'others' but also by the specific forms of securitization and humanitarian apparatuses set up to receive – and sometimes reject – them.[14] More widely, as refugees settle, the ways in which they may change the places in which they reside often becomes a focus. As we have seen for the case of Germany in this volume (see especially the Introduction), however, this is often discussed in general terms, with a focus on a feared 'importation' of cultural difference, especially in the form of Islam. This is not only so in Germany but also in other European countries. In some European-level discourse too what thus happens in effect is that Europeanness is defined in opposition to Islam. The relentless questioning of how Islam might problematically change European society itself operates as a form of asserting what it 'really is' to be European.

As Dace Dzenovska (2016) suggests, 'every crisis produces Europeanness anew'. Even countries that have not taken in many migrants are nevertheless caught up in the ramifications of the refugee debates. In the case of the 'refugee crisis', East European countries – which have mostly taken in few refugees and which have often expressed considerable reluctance to do so – find themselves being viewed as exhibiting a 'failed Europeanness'. As she points out, Germany plays a major role in exemplifying and setting the agenda for what counts as morally worthy Europeanness (2016). She sees this as problematic for those European countries that find themselves cast as lacking in necessary Europeanness, an assessment that is often applied *en bloc* to East-European countries, ignoring the variations in their histories and positions as well as the reasons for their stances. Like Partridge in this volume, she questions the way in which 'compassion' operates and how it may serve to establish hierarchical relationships – in this case, not between German and refugee, but between European and 'not quite European'.

More research is needed, however, within Germany and across Europe. This is not just in order to add more studies to increase the range of cases and try to assess which directions seem to have more weight. That is part of it. But we also still need to understand better some of the difficulties of practice, the affects and subtle means through which difference is produced and felt. We also need to be able to further recognize the multiplicity of positions and their inherent tensions, and to be better able to identify where transcending the latter is possible and where other hopeful possibilities may lie. It is the hope of this book's editors and authors that this volume contributes to such a future research agenda.

Acknowledgements

I offer many thanks to the contributors to this volume for the chapters on which this one is based. Jan-Jonathan Bock deserves particular thanks not only for his comments on this chapter and role as coeditor but also for persuading me to undertake some fieldwork – including the visit to the event at the Neukölln Museum mentioned here – at a time when I felt buried in the paperwork of being a new arrival in Germany. I am also grateful to my colleagues in CARMAH, the Institute of European Ethnology and the Department of Sociology at the University of York for many conversations that have helped shape my thinking on these matters. Any infelicities or errors remain my own. The Alexander von Humboldt Foundation has my considerable thanks for financially supporting this research.

Sharon Macdonald is Alexander von Humboldt Professor of Social Anthropology in the Institute of European Ethnology, Humboldt-Universität zu Berlin, Germany. She founded and directs the Centre for Anthropological Research on Museums and Heritage (CARMAH), and its major project *Making Differences – Transforming Museums and Heritage in the 21st Century*.

Notes

1. The main source of official figures is the Bundesamt für Migration und Flüchtlinge (BAMF), whose webpages include a wealth of information: http://www.bamf.de/DE/Infothek/Statistiken/Asylzahlen/asylzahlen-node.html. Reimann (2017) also contains a useful discussion of some of the arguments about the figures. The following discussion is also based on these sources.
2. See, for example, Bundesregierung (2016). This was also widely reported in the press.
3. See reports on the announcements of the figures, e.g. http://www.spiegel.de/politik/deutschland/fluechtlinge-280-000-menschen-suchten-2016-asyl-in-deutschland-a-1129516.html.
4. This was the official title in English. See the Center's website: http://politicalbeauty.com/eatingrefugees.html. The following work is also profiled on the site http://politicalbeauty.com/dead.html and is discussed by Lewicki (2017).

5. See his website at: https://www.manaf-halbouni.com/work/monument.
6. See its website at: https://www.neukoelln-evangelisch.de/gefluechtete-willkommen.
7. See, for example, this list of activities from one Berlin area: https://www.berlin.de/ba-charlottenburg-wilmersdorf/aktuelles/artikel.357643.php.
8. The numbers of applications rejected is recorded by BAMF (2018) as 32 per cent in 2015, 25 per cent in 2016 and 38.5 per cent in 2017.
9. See, for example, *Zeit Online* (2017).
10. The Centre's website also contains information about the Making Differences project: http://www.carmah.berlin. Macdonald (2016) sets out some relevant background ideas.
11. Retrieved 11 July 2018 from http://multaka.de/en/startsite-en. The information given below is also from Weber (n.d.) and is available on the Multaka website.
12. See its website at: http://museum-neukoelln.de.
13. See https://www.smb.museum/museen-und-einrichtungen/museum-europaeischer-kul turen/ausstellungen/detail/daheim-einsichten-in-fluechtige-leben.html for information about the exhibition. See also Tietmeyer (2016). This is currently being researched by Katarzyna Puzon as part of the Making Differences project.
14. For relevant ethnographic accounts see Albahari 2016 and Cabot 2014.

References

Albahari, M. 2016. *Crimes of Peace: Mediterranean Migration and the World's Deadliest Border*. Pittsburgh: University of Pennsylvania Press.

Appadurai, A. 2006. *Fear of Small Numbers: An Essay on the Geography of Anger*. Durham, NC: Duke University Press.

BAMF 2018. 'Aktuelle Zahlen zu Asyl'. Retrieved 11 July 2018 from http://www. bamf.de/DE/Infothek/Statistiken/Asylzahlen/AktuelleZahlen/aktuelle-zahlen-asyl-node.html

Bock, J.-J. 2015. 'An Experimental Approach to Integration', *Neuköllner.net*, 21 December. Retrieved 11 July 2018 from http://www.neukoellner.net/ alltag-anarchie/an-experimental-approach-to-integration.

Bojadžijev, M., and S. Karakayalı 2007. 'Autonomie der Migration: 10 Thesen zu einer Methode', in TRANSIT MIGRATION Forschungsgruppe (ed.), *Turbulente Ränder: Neue Perspektiven auf Migration an den Grenzen Europas*. Bielefeld: transcript, pp. 203–9.

Bundesregierung. 2016. 'Zahl der Flüchtlinge erheblich gesunken', 12 October. Retrieved 11 July 2018 from https://www.bundesregierung.de/Content/DE/ Artikel/2016/10/2016-10-12-asylzahlen-drittes-quartal.html.

Cabot, H. 2014. *On the Doorstep of Europe: Asylum and Citizenship in Greece*. Pittsburgh: University of Pennsylvania Press.

Dasser, S. 2016. 'Ai Weiwei enthüllt Konzerthaus in Rettungswesten', *Tagesspiegel*, 14 February.

Dzenovska, D. 2016. 'Eastern Europe, the Moral Subject of the Migration/ Refugee Crisis, and Political Futures'. *Near Futures Online 1: 'Europe at a Crossroads'*. Retrieved 10 May 2018 from http://nearfuturesonline.org/ eastern-europe-the-moral-subject-of-the-migrationrefugee-crisis-and-political-futures/.

Gouriévidis, L. (ed.). 2014. *Museums and Migration: History, Memory and Politics.* Abingdon: Routledge.

Gram, R. 2018. 'Multaka. Treffpunkt Museum: An Ethnography on Museums and Migration in Berlin', MA Dissertation. Berlin: Institut für Europäische Ethnologie, Humboldt-Universität zu Berlin.

Lewicki, A. 2017. '"The Dead are Coming": Acts of Citizenship at Europe's Borders', *Citizenship Studies* 21(3): 275–90.

Macdonald, S. 1996. 'Introduction: Theorizing Museums', in S. Macdonald and G. Fyfe (eds), *Theorizing Museums: Identity and Diversity in a Changing World.* Oxford: Blackwell, pp. 1–18.

———. 2016. 'New Constellations of Difference in Europe's 21st Century Museumscape', *Museum Anthropology* 39(1): 4–19.

MELA 2015. 'European Museums in an Age of Migration'. Retrieved 11 July 2018 from http://www.mela-project.polimi.it.

Müller, U. 2011. 'Ethnographie und Lokalpolitik: Ein Ausländerrat in Süddeutschland', in Arbeitskreis Ethnologie und Migration (ed.), *Migration – Bürokratie – Alltag: Ethnographische studien im Kontext von Institutionen und Einwanderung.* Berlin: LIT, pp. 19–36.

Oltermann, P. 2017. 'The Bitter Divide over Aleppo-Inspired Bus Barricade Sculpture', *The Guardian.* 7 February.

Reimann, A. 2017. 'Im ganz normalen Krisenmodus', *Spiegel Online*, 28 December. Retrieved 11 July 2018 from http://www.spiegel.de/politik/deutschland/fluechtlinge-so-war-2017-und-so-wird-2018-a-1184058.html.

Romei, V., B. Ehrenburg-Shannon, H. Maier-Borst and G. Chazan 2017. 'How Well Have Germany's Refugees Integrated?', *Financial Times*, 19 September.

Sigona, N. 2018. 'The Contested Politics of Naming in Europe's Refugee Crisis', *Journal of Ethnic and Racial Studies* 41(3): 456–60.

Der Spiegel 2017. 'Integration by Numbers: Germany's Ongoing Project to Welcome its Refugees', 12 May. Retrieved 11 July 2018 from http://www.spiegel.de/international/germany/integrating-refugees-in-germany-an-update-a-1147053.html).

Stevenson, N. 2003. *Cultural Citizenship: Cosmopolitan Questions.* Maidenhead: Open University Press.

Tietmeyer, E. (ed.). 2016. *Glances into Fugitive Lives.* Heidelberg: arthistoricum.

Weber, S. n.d. *Multaka: Museum as Meeting Point. Refugees as Guides in Berlin Museums – Concept and Content.* Retrieved 11 July 2018 from http://multaka.de/en/concept.

Whitehead, C., K. Lloyd, S. Eckersley and R. Mason (eds). 2015. *Museums, Migration and Identity in Europe: Peoples, Places and Identities.* Farnham: Ashgate.

Zeit Online. 2017. 'Flüchtlinge: Unterbringen von Fluuchtlinge in Deutschland bemängelt', 6 December. Retrieved 11 July 2018 from https://www.zeit.de/gesellschaft/zeitgeschehen/2017-12/fluechtlinge-unterkunft-deutsches-institut-menschenrechte-verstoss.

Index

www.ingramcontent.com/pod-product-compliance
Lightning Source LLC
Chambersburg PA
CBHW070902030426
42336CB00014BA/2298